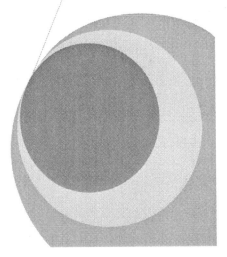

Including
SAP R/3 Enterprise 4.70
SAP ERP ECC 6.0

SAP® FI/CO

Questions and Answers

SAP® FI/CO
Questions and Answers

V. NARAYANAN

INFINITY SCIENCE PRESS LLC

Hingham, Massachusetts
New Delhi, India

INFINITY SCIENCE PRESS LLC

11 Leavitt Street
Hingham, MA 02043
Tel. 877-266-5796 (toll free)
Fax 781-740-1677
info@infinitysciencepress.com
www.infinitysciencepress.com

This book is printed on acid-free paper.

SAP® FI/CO *Questions and Answers*
ISBN: 978-1-934015-22-3

Library of Congress Cataloging-in-Publication Data

Narayanan, V.
  SAP FI/CO questions and answers / V. Narayanan.
      p. cm.
   ISBN 978-1-934015-22-3 (hardcover with cd-rom: alk. paper)
  1. SAP R/3. 2. Accounting--Computer programs. I. Title.
  HF5548.4.R2N367 2007
  657.0285'53--dc22
                                2007050968
8 9 4 3 2 1

Our titles are available for adoption, license or bulk purchase by institutions, corporations, etc. For additional information, please contact the Customer Service Dept. at 877-266-5796 (toll free in US).

Requests for replacement of a defective CD-ROM must be accompanied by the original disc, your mailing address, telephone number, date of purchase and purchase price. Please state the nature of the problem, and send the information to INFINITY SCIENCE PRESS, 11 Leavitt Street, Hingham, MA 02043.

The sole obligation of INFINITY SCIENCE PRESS to the purchaser is to replace the disc, based on defective materials or faulty workmanship, but not based on the operation or functionality of the product.

TRADEMARK ACKNOWLEDGMENT

DISCLAIMER

The contents of this book are the views of the author, together with input from his experiences in consulting in SAP. The views expressed in this book should not be construed as that of SAP AG. Omissions and factual inaccuracies, if any, to correctly depict SAP in the book, are purely incidental without any maleficent intention.

To my dear wife: Meena

ABOUT THE AUTHOR

A post graduate in sciences, a Chartered Financial Analyst (CFA) and a Project Management Professional (PMP), V. Narayanan has more than two decades of work experience in accounting, banking, finance and Information Technology. Trained in SAP FICO, he is a practicing SAP FI/CO Consultant-cum-Project Manager. He has been instrumental in managing SAP implementations (new, roll-outs, upgrades, etc.) for a number of international clients. Experienced in various versions of R/3 as well as mySAP ERP and New Dimension Products of SAP, he currently works in 'SAP Consulting', in one of the Multinational IT Consulting Companies in India. Trained by Thames Valley University in the UK, he is also a professional trainer and a visiting faculty in the areas of ERP, SAP, Banking, etc. He has also authored a best-selling book on *SAP FI Transactions*.

ACKNOWLEDGMENT

A book like this requires input from experts so that the end-product is authentic. I have been fortunate enough to have a number of SAP experts, cutting across various functional and technical modules, who were more than willing to provide me with helpful tips, clarification and reviews in shaping the several questions presented in this book. I consciously avoided listing them here for the simple reason that it may be possible that inadvertently I omit one or more names, and that might look inappropriate in spite of them helping me. Instead, I extend a loud 'thanks' to all of them.

As you will see the book, very uncommon in a book like this, I have peppered the entire volume with a large number of screen-shots taken from SAP applications for easy understanding. Thanks to Mr. Hariharan of Maagnus Infotech, Chennai, India for allowing me to make use of their SAP system for generating these screen-shots .

PREFACE

Like my earlier book (*SAP R/3 FI: Transactions*), this book is also different from the rest of the lot in the market: this one aims at providing an *all-round enrichment* of knowledge in SAP, though the title mentions only FI/CO of SAP. The reason: unless you know the related components in SAP, it will be very difficult to comprehend SAP FI/CO. Yes, the focus is on FI/CO; but there are numerous other areas covered here to provide you with a bird's eye view of the related modules, sub-modules, and components.

The book unravels the complexity of the SAP FI/CO application and some of the related modules, through numerous 'Questions and Answers' in each of the crucial areas. The questions are collected, grouped, and explained in a logical way so that you progress seamlessly from the basic to the advanced topics. Still, should you find it difficult to visualize what is dealt in a particular question/answer: there is help by way of numerous illustrations in the form of screen-shots, diagrams, flow charts, etc. throughout the book. The screen-shots (taken out of SAP R/3 Enterprise 4.70 and SAP ERP ECC6), in particular, will help you to comprehend the material as if you are in-front of a computer running the application!

The contents of the book are arranged in 10 sections:

1. SAP Basics
2. ABAP and Basis
3. Project Implementation
4. Financial Accounting
5. Controlling
6. Logistics
7. Miscellaneous
8. SAP Tables
9. SAP Transaction Codes
10. SAP Terminology

The section, '*SAP Basics*', focuses on the evolution of SAP from a small accounting software to its current stature as the most preferred enterprise computing and management application. All you need to know about the current offerings from SAP are outlined here.

The 2nd section, '*ABAP and Basis*', is on the technical side of the application. It is true that a functional consultant *may* not need to know the technical side of the application in detail. But, it is necessary and often helpful that you have some idea on this area to appreciate how the application works and to comprehend some of the technical jargon you encounter.

Why is there a section on '*Project Implementation*' in a book like this? SAP implementation is a complex piece of work and you need to know every 'tip' and 'trick' to contribute to the successful completion of a project. You will find answers, in this section, for many of the questions which were unanswered earlier.

The 4th section, *'Financial Accounting'*, has the most number of questions (213 to be exact), compared to other sections of this book. This section is sub-divided into:

- General
- Global and Enterprise Settings
- General Ledger Accounting
- Accounts Receivable
- Accounts Payable
- Asset Accounting

Though it is very difficult to cover all of *'Controlling'* in a book like this, an attempt has been made to provide as much information as possible in this section. The following areas within CO are covered here:

- General Controlling
- Cost Element Accounting
- Cost Center Accounting
- Internal Orders

It would really be difficult to understand FI/CO, without understating how other modules are *integrated* with this. Hence, a section titled, *'Logistics'* is also included to provide an overview of the most important components e.g., *Sales and Distribution (SD), Materials Management (MM) and Production Planning (PP)*, their organization and integration with SAP FI/CO.

There is a *'Miscellaneous'* section covering some of the interesting questions which may not strictly fall into any one of the other sections. You will find some very useful information here.

Besides the questions, you will also see two sections dedicated for *'SAP Tables'* and *'SAP Transaction Codes'* and in the system, grouped by application, component-wise/ functionality-wise, which will certainly act as a reference. Unlike an alphabetical listing of Transaction Codes/Tables which is the convention, this book attempts something functional and useful: this information is arranged the way you need it, as most of the time you may not know the transaction code or table to look at, but you know the functionality or task for which you are trying to find the table or transaction code.

Another useful add-on is the last section, *'SAP Terminology'*, which comes at the end of the book, just before the index. An alphabetical list of concepts, terminology, and usage specific, mostly to, SAP, this nearly-100 page section will prove to be your 'ready-reckoner' and 'one-point-reference' should you need some clarification. Yes, it may not be the *complete* listing, but you will appreciate that it covers the most important ones within the scope of this book.

So, how do you use this book?

The answer is simple: Read in any way you want. Pick-up a section and read it, or simply pick-up a question, go to the relevant page and see the answer. Use the book as a reference or a study-guide or a just reading material, but make sure you understand a particular question or concept before moving on to the next.

The answers to all of the 472 questions enumerated in this book will certainly improve your understanding of the subject; whether it is for job interviews in SAP, especially in FI/CO, or just to use the application in a better manner in your current job.

All the best!

V. Narayanan
February, 2008

TABLE OF CONTENTS

Project Implementation   **37**

Financial Accounting (FI) **51**

General **53**

Global and Enterprise Settings **55**

SAP BASICS

SAP Basics

1.   What is 'SAP'?

'SAP' is an acronym for 'Systeme, Anwendungen, Produkte der Dataenverar-beitung,' in German, meaning **'Systems, Applications, and Products in Data Processing**.' Founded in 1972, SAP – with its headquarters in Walldorf, Germany – is the global market leader in collaborative, inter-enterprise business solutions (i.e., business software). SAP employs close to 40,000 employees worldwide, with more than 100,000 installations in about 40,000 companies in 120 countries. More than 12 million people use SAP on a daily basis. There are more than 20 industry-specific 'Industry Solutions,' known commonly as 'IS' (IS-Oil, IS-Retail, IS-Bank, etc.).

2.   Tell me more about (the history of) SAP.

- SAP was founded by five former IBM employees, in **1972**, to develop a standard business application software, with the goal of processing business information in real-time. The company, SAP GmbH, was started in Mannheim, Germany.
- During **1973**, the company released its first financial accounting software, **'R1'** (the letter 'R' stands for 'Real-Time Processing).'
- In the late 1970s, SAP **'R/2'** was released with IBM's database and a dialogue-oriented business application.
- R/2 was further stabilized during the early 1980s and the company came out with a version capable of processing business transactions in several languages and currencies to meet the needs of its international clientele.

- SAP GmbH became **SAP AG** in 1988. Later on, the company established subsidiaries in countries such as the United States, Sweden, Denmark, and Italy.
- The 1990s saw the introduction of SAP '**R/3**,' with client-server architecture and GUI, which ran on almost any database, and on most operating systems. SAP R/3 heralded a new era in enterprise computing, moving from a 'main frame' to a 3-tier architecture (Database-> Application -> User interface), which became the new industry standard.
- By **1996**, the company had more than 9,000 installations worldwide. By the end of the 1990s, SAP had introduced the e-commerce enabled **mySAP** suite of products for leveraging ever-expanding web technology.
- SAP began the twenty-first century with the **Enterprise Portal** and role-based access to business information.
- SAP continues to evolve and innovate, bringing cutting-edge technologies to business-information processing. SAP has already introduced SAP **NetWeaver**, which is based on Enterprise Services Architecture (ESS) with application integration across diverse platforms for providing one-stop end-to-end business processing. With NetWeaver, companies can now integrate people, information, and processes.

3.   What are the 'Solutions' currently available from SAP?

Currently, **SAP Solutions** include the following:
- SAP ERP
- SAP
- SAP Business Suite
- SAP R/3 and R/3 Enterprise
- SAP for Industries
- SAP xApps
- SAP Solution Manager

4.   What are the components of the 'SAP ERP' solution?

- SAP ERP Central Component (ECC 6.0)
- SAP SEM (Strategic Enterprise Management) (SEM 6.0)
- SAP cProject Suite (Project and Portfolio Management 4.0)
- SAP SRM for ERP (SRM 5.0)
- SAP Catalog Content Management (CCM 2.0 for ERP 2004)
- SAP Internet Sales for ERP

5. **What is the significance of the 'SAP NetWeaver' platform?**

The SAP '**NetWeaver**' platform allows organizations to build new business solutions rapidly while realizing more business value from existing IT investments. SAP NetWeaver supports new cross-functional business processes and helps to lower the **Total Cost of Ownership (TCO)** by reducing the need for custom integration. It offers complete life cycle management for all of your applications. It is also the foundation for **Enterprise Services Architecture (EAS)** and helps align people, information, and business processes across organizational and technological boundaries.

6. **What are the components of 'NetWeaver'?**

By providing an open integration and application platform and permitting the integration of the Enterprise Services Architecture, **SAP NetWeaver** helps unify business processes across technological boundaries, integrating applications for employees as needed, and accessing/editing simple information easily in a structured manner.

Components include:

- **Security**
- **People Integration**
  - Multi-channel Access
  - Portal
  - Collaboration
- **Information Integration**
  - Business Intelligence
- **BI (Business Intelligence) Content**
  - Knowledge Management
  - Master Data Management
- **Process Integration**
  - Integration Broker
  - Business Process Management
- **Application Platform**
  - Java
  - ABAP
  - Business Services
  - Connectivity
  - DB and OS Abstraction
  - SAP Knowledge Warehouse

- **Life Cycle Management**
  - Customizing
  - Software Change Management
  - System Management

7. What are the components of the 'SAP Business Suite'?

- SAP Customer Relationship Management (CRM 5.0)
- SAP Supply Chain Management (SCM 5.0)
- SAP Supplier Relationship Management (SRM)
  - SAP SRM 2007
  - SAP Catalog Content Management (SRM-MDM 1.0)
- SAP Product Life Cycle Management
  - SAP Product Life Cycle Management 4.00
  - SAP Environment, Health, and Safety 2.7B
  - SAP PLM Recipe Management 2.1
  - Audit Management
- SAP Compliance Management for SOA
  - Management of Internal controls 1.0
- SAP Learning Solution 2.00
- SAP Strategic Enterprise Management (SEM)

8. What are the most recent releases of the 'SAP R/3' solution?

- SAP R/3 Enterprise Release 4.70
- SAP R/3 Release 4.6C/4.6B/4.5B/4.0B

9. What 'Industry Solutions' (IS) are available from SAP?

There are 22 Industry Solutions available from SAP. They are:
- SAP for Aerospace and Defense
- SAP for Automotive
- SAP for Banking
- SAP for Consumer Products
- SAP Contract Accounts Receivable and Payable
- SAP for Defense and Security

- SAP for Engineering, Construction and Operations
- SAP for Financial Service Providers
- SAP for Healthcare
- SAP for Higher Education and Research
- SAP for High Tech
- SAP for Insurance
- SAP for Media
- SAP for Mill Products
- SAP for Mining
- SAP for Oil and Gas
- SAP for Professional Services
- SAP for Public Sectors
- SAP for Retail
- SAP for Telecommunications
- SAP for Utilities
- SAP for Wholesale Distribution

10. What is 'SAP xApps'?

The '**SAP xApps**' family of composite applications enables continuous business innovation – and provides the flexibility necessary to respond quickly and profitably to business changes. They extend the value of core business investments and maximize the return on strategic assets: employees, knowledge, products, business relationships, and IT.

SAP and SAP certified partners deliver these composite applications that drive specialized business processes, provide comprehensive business insights, and focus on the needs of a variety of industries.

All these applications combine Web services and data from multiple systems in an application design made possible by the SAP Composite Application Framework within the SAP NetWeaver technology platform. This framework includes the methodology, tools, and run-time environment to develop composite applications. It provides a consistent object model and a rich user experience, and gives developers a productive way to create composite applications on top of a set of heterogeneous applications.

11. What are all the components of 'SAP xApps'?

- Duet
- SAP Document Builder

- SAP Global Trade Services
- SAP xApp Manufacturing Integration and Intelligence
- SAP xApp Resource and Portfolio Management
- SAP xApp Product Definition
- SAP xApp Cost and Quotation Management
- SAP xApp Integrated Exploration and Production
- SAP xApp Sales and Operations Planning

12.   What is known as 'Duet'?

A component under SAP xApps, 'Duet' is a first-of-its-kind software solution from SAP and Microsoft that enables users to easily and quickly interact with SAP business processes and data via their familiar Microsoft Office environment. The result of a groundbreaking collaboration between SAP and Microsoft, it is the first joint product created by these two industry leaders and is designed to revolutionize how IT workers interact with enterprise applications.

Duet enables:

- **Budget Monitoring:** Schedule time-critical alerts and notifications to monitor cost centers or internal orders, which are delivered directly to Microsoft Outlook.
- **Demand Planning:** Create and use planning sheets, as well as analyze and manage demand planning data from the SAP System using Microsoft Excel.
- **Duet Reporting:** Schedule reports to be delivered regularly to Microsoft Outlook, receive individual reports on an as-needed basis, and view reports in Microsoft Excel.
- **Leave Management:** Add leave requests as Microsoft Outlook calendar items that integrate approval guidelines in the SAP System and enterprise-defined processes.
- **Sales Management:** Manage CRM accounts and contacts, create business activities, and access sales analytics information using Microsoft Outlook.
- **Team Management:** Access up-to-date information about yourself and employees, open positions, and organizational structures that are integrated from the SAP System into the Microsoft Outlook contacts area.
- **Time Management:** Record time in the Microsoft Outlook calendar, streamlining time entry while ensuring time-reporting compliance in the SAP System.
- **Travel Management:** Create a travel request and a travel expense report in the SAP System using Microsoft Outlook.

13. Explain the 'SAP Document Builder.'

'**SAP Document Builder**' (CA-GTF-DOB) is a content-driven and cross-application solution for building and authoring complex documents. As a generic tool, it can be deployed within international organizations and large corporations to generate contract and bid invitation documents, banking-related documents, auto insurance policies, real estate contracts, and corporate employment policies.

You can deploy SAP Document Builder as a standalone application or integrate it with other SAP or non-SAP components. For example, you can generate business documents required in a procurement system and store them in an electronic data storage system.

The **SAP Document Builder** supports you by:

- Automating and streamlining the document-creation process.
- Enforcing best practices.
- Building documents that reflect company-specific styles and formats from one or more regulation sets.
- Determining inclusion or exclusion of clauses based on legal regulations by means of rules.

14. Explain the 'SAP Solution Manager.'

Providing central access to Tools, Methods, and Pre-Configured Content, the **SAP Solution Manager** provides support throughout the life cycle of solutions -- from Business Blueprint to Configuration to Support.

The features include:

- **Implementation/Upgrade of SAP Solutions**
  - Central access to Project Tools (Project Administration, Business Blueprint, Configuration, Test Workbench, Group Rollout Templates)
  - Central management of Project Information (Roadmap, System Landscape, Documentation, etc.)
  - Enables comparing/synchronizing customizing in several SAP components
- **Solution Monitoring**
  - Central System Administration
  - System Landscape Analysis with System Level Reporting
  - Real-time System Monitoring
  - Business Process Monitoring
- **Services and Support**
  - Access to programs/services for monitoring and optimizing system performance and availability to minimize risks.

■ **Service Desk**

- Solution Support through Work Flow to create and manage Process/ Problem Messages.

■ **Change Management**

- Trace and audit system changes and transports through Change Request Management.

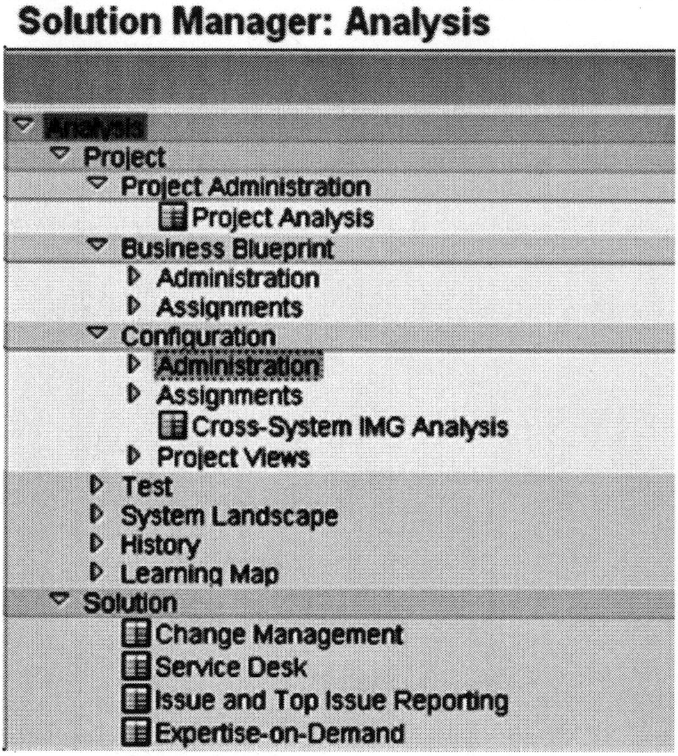

Figure 1: SAP Solution Manager

15.   Explain how 'mySAP ERP Financials' is better/different than 'R/3 Financial Accounting.'

'**mySAP ERP Financials**' is built on the **NetWeaver** platform, which is the foundation for service-oriented business solutions, for deploying financial processes at a faster pace. Irrespective of the business type, mySAP ERP Financials is designed to support financial accounting requirements to provide a single complete platform to achieve excellence in accounting, performance management, financial supply chain, and corporate governance. The features include:

- **Industry-Specific Financial Management**

  mySAP ERP Financials provides a comprehensive and robust analytical framework to consolidate and/or dissect business information generated in industry solutions or core enterprise processes: all managers in all operations have an improved visibility with a single integrated solution.

- **Performance Management**

  mySAP ERP Financials provides a single solution for the entire life cycle of Corporate Performance Management by delivering real-time, personalized measurements and metrics to improve business insight and productivity of non-technical users. Executives, managers, and business workers will now have access to information such as business statistics and **Key Performance Indicators** (KPI) presented in the context of business tasks for better insight and faster decision making. mySAP ERP Financials encompasses:

  - Consolidated financial and statutory reporting
  - Planning, budgeting, and forecasting
  - Strategy management and scorecards
  - Risk management
  - Financial analytics

- **Financial and Management Accounting**

  mySAP ERP Financials helps companies comply with global accounting standards (such as the United States' **Generally Accepted Accounting Principles (GAAP)** and the **International Financial Reporting Standards (IFRS)**. With the '**New FI-GL**' functionality (Refer to Q.181 for more details) you will now have the ability to generate financial statements of any dimension of the business (unit, profit center, geographical location, etc.). This offers greater flexibility to extend a chart of accounts and allows an easier method of reporting by individual management units and segments. This feature helps companies reduce the complexity and costs associated with parallel accounting or managing a set of books by region, industry, or regulatory reporting statute.

- **Corporate Governance**

  With a set of applications and tools, mySAP ERP Financials assists in meeting the specific requirements of today's financial regulations such as the **Sarbanes-Oxley Act**. You now have an intuitive mechanism to collect, document, assess, remediate, and attest to internal control processes and safeguards to ensure transparent business activity. By configuring controls and defining rules and tolerances for your business, you can easily customize internal processes for security, reporting, and error prevention. In addition, you can now document all your internal control processes and make them visible to corporate executives, auditors, and regulators.

■ **Financial Supply Chain Management**

Provides the tools to help you manage your financial supply chain and cash-flow cycle more effectively, through end-to-end process support of:

- Credit Management
- Electronic Bill Presentment and Payment
- Collections Management
- Dispute Management
- In-house Cash Management
- Cash and Liquidity Management
- Bank Relationship
- Treasury and Risk Management Processes

16. What is an 'SAP Solution Map'?

mySAP ERP, besides supporting your most important business processes, also provides tools to help you understand how these processes work. One such tool is the 'SAP Solution Map,' a multi-level blueprint of processes, which helps you visualize, plan, and implement a coherent, integrated, and comprehensive IT solution. SAP Solution Maps also show how various processes are covered, including the processes that SAP and its partners support. With solution maps, you quickly understand business solutions and the business value they can bring.

17. What is 'SAP Business One'?

'SAP Business One' is the low-cost, easy-to-implement business management solution from SAP for Small and Medium Enterprises (SME). Unlike regular ERP software from SAP, this solution gives managers on-demand access to critical real-time information through 'one single system' containing financial, customer relationship management, manufacturing, and management control capabilities. As a result, the solution enables rapid employee productivity, while empowering managers to make better business decisions to stay ahead of the competition. Equipped with a user-friendly interface, SAP Business One serves as your central ERP hub with standard interfaces to internal and external data sources, handheld computers, CRM applications, and other leading analysis tools.

SAP Business One is based on the Microsoft Windows platform making it easier to comprehend and use. The application comes with a 'demo company,' which can be used by the implementing company to become familiar with functionalities.

The modules of SAP Business One include:

- Administration
- Financials

- Sales Opportunities
- Sales – A/R
- Purchasing – A/P
- Business Partners
- Banking
- Inventory
- Production
- MRP
- Service
- Human Resources
- Reporting

ABAP AND BASIS

ABAP AND BASIS

18.   What is 'Basis'?

'**Basis**' is a collection of R/3 programs, which provide the run-time environment for ABAP/4. Imagine Basis as something that is 'sitting' in between the ABAP/4 program code and the computer's operating system. Basis reads ABAP/4 program code and interprets the same into operating system instructions; without Basis you cannot execute any of your ABAP/4 programs.

SAP provides a plethora of tools to administer Basis, which ultimately helps to monitor system configuration, system performance, and system maintenance. The Basis administrator is usually called the 'Basis Consultant.'

19.   Explain the SAP R/3 'System Architecture.'

SAP R/3 is based on a 3-tier **Client-Server** model, represented by the:
- Database Layer
- Application Layer
- Presentation Layer

In a 3-tier Client server model, all the above three layers run on three different machines.

The **Database Layer** consists of an RDBMS (Relational Database Management System), which accepts the database requests from the Application Layer, and sends the data back to the Application Layer, which in turn passes it on to the Presentation Layer.

The **Application Layer** or the server interprets the ABAP/4 programs, receiving the inputs from them and providing the processed output to them.

The **Presentation Server** or 'Presentation Layer' is what is installed on the typical workstation of a user. This is nothing but the SAPGUI, which when started provides the user with the interface of SAP R/3 menus. This interface accepts the inputs from the user, passes them on to the Application Server, processes the inputs and sends back the output. If database processing is required, the Application Server sends the details to the Database Layer, receives the data, and then processes it at the Application Layer level and sends back the output to the Presentation Layer where the SAPGUI may format the data before displaying it on the screen.

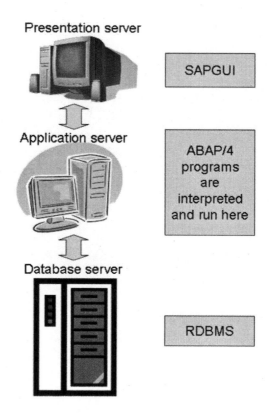

Figure 2: SAP R/3 System Architecture

20.   What is an 'Instance'?

An '**Instance**' is an administrative unit that groups together components of an SAP R/3 system or simply an Application Server, which has its own set of work processes. A Client can contain many instances. Loosely defined, an instance refers to a server.

Sometimes the database is also referred to as an 'instance.' In this case it is called the '**Central Instance**.'

21.   What do you mean by the 'SAP R/3 System Landscape'?

The '**System Landscape**,' in SAP, refers to a number of systems and their deployment within an SAP installation. The various systems may be designated as Development, Test, and Production Clients.

22.   What is an 'R/3 Data Dictionary'?

The '**Data Dictionary**' is a collection of logical structures of various objects (Tables, Views, or Structures) used in application development in SAP, which shows how they are mapped to the underlying RDBMS in Tables/Views.

23.   What is an 'SAP Business Object'?

An '**SAP Business Object**' is similar to real-world business objects such as Sales Order, Invoice, Employee, etc., which consist of various tables/programs that are related to each other in a business context. All the business objects are maintained in the '**BOR (Business Object Repository).**'

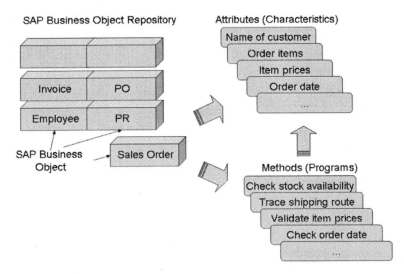

Figure 3: SAP Business Object

The various characteristics of an object are called '**Attributes**.' For example, the business object Sales Order is characterized by the following attributes:

- Date of the order
- Items of the order
- Prices of various items of the order
- Name of the customer to whom the order belongs to

The application program or programs used by the system to change or manipulate a business object are known as Method(s). For example, a program could be used to (*a*) check the availability of stock to deliver, (*b*) trace the shipment route, (*c*) check the item prices, (*d*) validate the order date, etc.

So, attributes and methods collectively represent business objects in SAP.

24. Explain 'Client-Dependent' and 'Client-Independent' tables.

There are certain tables, in SAP, which when changed will not affect similar tables in other Clients. These are known as 'Client-Dependent' tables. All Client-dependent tables have Mandt as their first field.

On the other hand, if a change made in one Client is reflected in another table across various Clients, then such a table is called 'Client-Independent.' In this case, the first field of the table will not be 'Mandt.' You need to be extra careful when changing the settings or content of these tables as this will affect all the Clients.

25. What are the different 'Types' of 'ABAP/4 Programs'?

There are nine types of ABAP/4 programs in SAP:

- 1   Executable Programs (ABAP Reports)
- I   INCLUDE Program
- M   Module Pool/Dialogue programs
- S   Sub-Routine Pool
- J   Interface Pool
- K   Class Pool
- T   Type Pool
- F   Function Group
- X   XSLT Program

26.   What are 'Internal Tables'?

'**Internal Tables**' are standard data type objects which exist only during the Run-time of an ABAP/4 program. They are used to perform table calculations on subsets of database tables and for re-organizing the contents of database tables according to a user's need. Internal tables fulfil the need for arrays in ABAP/4.

There are three types of internal tables:

- **Standard Tables** with a 'linear' index. The key is always 'non-unique.'
- **Sorted Tables** with either a 'unique' or 'non-unique' key.
- **Hashed Tables** (they do not have a linear index) with the key defined always as 'unique.'

27.   What is a 'Logical Database'?

A '**Logical Database**' is a special data-retrieval program delivered by SAP, with its own dynamic Selection Screens. You need to code only the processing logic (GET, CHECK, etc., statements). The logical database consists of a 'read' program in which the structure of the local database is reproduced with a selection screen.

Advantages:

- Check functions to validate that user input is complete and correct.
- Meaningful data selection.
- Central authorization checks for database accesses.
- Excellent read access performance while retaining the hierarchical data view determined by the application logic.

28.   What are the two methods for modifying SAP 'Standard Tables'?

You can modify **SAP 'Standard Tables'** using:

- Append Structures
- Customizing INCLUDES

29.   What is 'BDC' Programming in SAP?

'**BDC (Batch Data Conversion)**' is an automated procedure for transferring large volumes of external or legacy data into the SAP system using batch input programming. There are three ways to do this:

- Call Transaction Method
- Session Method

■ Direct Input Method

Irrespective of the method, the techniques use the following steps:

■ Identify the screens of the transaction that the program will process.

■ Write a program to build the BDC table that will be used to submit the data (i.e., text file) to SAP.

■ Submit the BDC table to the system in the 'batch mode' or as a 'single transaction' by the CALL TRANSACTION command.

The 'Call Transaction' method cannot be used when you want to process multiple transactions. Instead, use the 'BDC-insert function' to achieve this.

30.   What is the 'BAPI'?

The '**BAPI (Business Application Programming Interface)**' is SAP's standardized application interface for integrating third party applications with SAP's business processes and data thereby providing an entry into the R/3 system. A BAPI may be used to create a 'business object' or to change the attributes of a business object. Note that the assignment of a BAPI to a business object is always 1-to-1.

A BAPI Explorer helps you to move around the collection of BAPIs in the system, which is grouped both hierarchically and alphabetically. For each BAPI in the explorer, you are provided with several tabs for details, documentation, tools, and projects (to create new BAPIs).

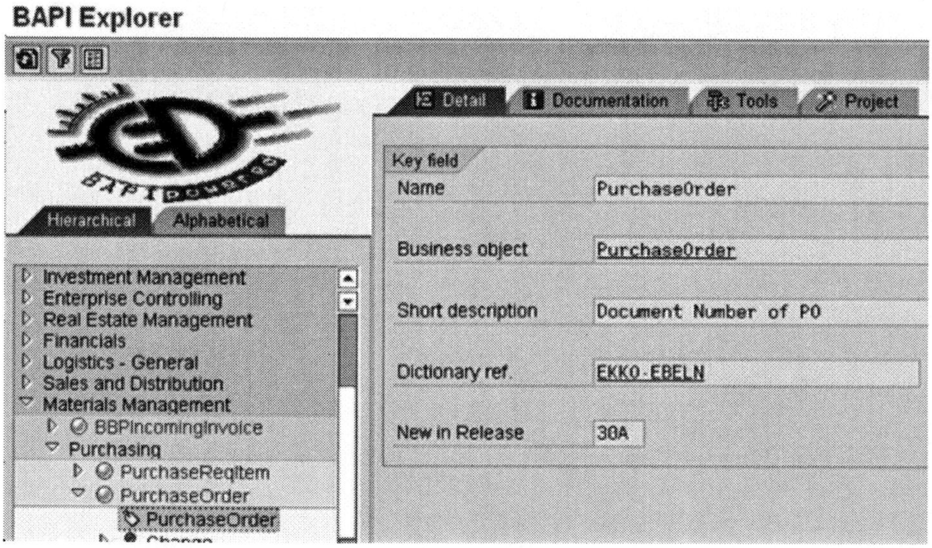

BAPI Explorer

Figure 4: BAPI Explorer

A BAPI can:

- Create a Purchase Order
- Change a Purchase Requisition
- Create a Customer
- Display an Invoice

Transaction Code
BAPI

31.   What is 'ALE'?

'**ALE (Application Link Enabling)**' is used to support the construction and operation of distributed applications, through the exchange of data messages ensuring data consistency across loosely coupled SAP applications, using both 'synchronous' and 'asynchronous' communications without the need for a central database.

ALE is comprised of three layers:

- Application services
- Distribution services
- Communication services

ALE helps to:

- Distribute applications across several SAP systems, such that centralized/ decentralized functions can operate in the same company area.
- Maintain and distribute master data elements from a central system.
- Maintain and distribute control data objects from a central system with the synchronized configuration data (important to decentralize functions yet keep them integrated).
- Link R/2 and R/3 systems.
- Link SAP and external systems, via **IDocs** (Intermediate Documents).

32.   Is 'SAP XI' intended to replace 'ALE'?

Most ALE solutions are custom built with very little re-usability and scalability. The introduction of **SAP XI** along with the NetWeaver technology replaces ALE with out-of-box functionality available in SAP XI.

33. What is an 'RFC'?

A '**Remote Function Call (RFC)**' is a call to a 'function module' running in a system different from the 'calling-system.' The remote function can also be called from within the same system (as a 'remote call'), but usually the 'calling-system' and the 'called-system' will be in different systems.

An RFC helps to take care of the following communication:

- Communications between two independent SAP systems.
- Client-server communications between an external Client and an SAP system acting as the server.
- Client-server communications between an SAP System acting as the Client and an external server.

34. What is 'OLE'?

For the Windows front-end, SAP provides interfaces based on Microsoft's '**Object Linking and Embedding**' Technology (**OLE Automation**) for embedding objects such as Microsoft Excel files.

35. What is a 'Match Code' in SAP?

'**Match Codes**' (now known as **Search Help** with release 4.6) help to search and retrieve data when the key of a record is not known. The technique involves (*a*) creating a '**Match Code Object**' (now known as a '**Search Help Object**') and (*b*) specifying a '**Match Code ID**.' The system helps you to access the match codes (search help) in the following ways:

- Keeping the cursor in the field, and then pressing '**F4**.'
- Keeping the cursor in the field, clicking the 'right' button on the mouse, and then selecting 'possible entries.'
- Keeping the cursor in the field, and then clicking on the 'magnifying glass.'

36. What is a 'Drill-down' Report?

A '**Drill-Down Report**,' also called an **Interactive Report**, is a report with more detail. Imagine that you are looking at a Balance Sheet, presented as a 'drill-down' report.

The topmost list, also known as the '**Basic List**,' contains the top-level information such as current assets, fixed assets, etc., under the grouping 'assets' on one side of the Balance Sheet. The 'drill-down' functionality helps you select a line item from the Basic List (e.g., fixed assets) and 'drill–down' further to a detailed list ('**secondary list**') which displays various components of the fixed assets such as land, buildings, machinery, etc. You may 'drill-down' even further by double-clicking the 'building' line, which will bring up the next detailed list and so on.

You will be able to create a 'drill-down' report with a maximum 'drill' level of 20; that is, including the Basic List you will have a total of 21 levels in a single 'drill-down' report.

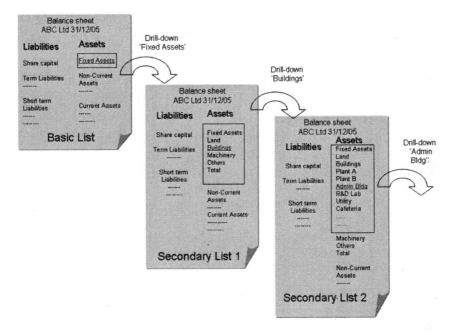

Figure 5: Drill-down report

37.   What is 'ALV' programming in ABAP?

SAP provides a set of '**ABAP List viewer (ALV)**' function modules, which can be used to enhance the readability and functionality of any report output. This is particularly useful in a situation where the output of a report contains columns extending 255 characters in length. In such cases, this set of ALV functions can help the user to choose and arrange columns from a report output and also save different variants for report display. This is very efficient for dynamically sorting and arranging the columns and provides a wide array of display options.

38.   What is 'DynPro'?

'**DynPro**' in SAP refers to Dynamic Programming relating to the screens and 'flow logic,' which controls the processing and display of these screens. On a broader scale, a screen is also referred to as a 'DynPro.'

39.   What is an 'ABAP/4 Query'?

'**ABAP/4 Query**' (also known as an **SAP Query** or **Query**) is a powerful tool used to generate simple reports without any coding. Typically, an ABAP/4 query is created first by defining a **User Group** and a **Functional Group**. The functional group can either be created with reference to a 'logical' table or a database table. Once the functional group is defined, the user group is assigned to the functional group. The last step is to create the query on the functional group that is generated.

An ABAP/4 Query can be used to create the following three types of reports:

- **Basic Lists:** Reports with basic formatting without any calculated fields.
- **Statistics:** Reports with statistical functions such as average, percentages, etc.
- **Ranked Lists:** Ranked lists are used for analytical purposes.

40.   What are the components of 'SAPscript'?

'**SAPscript**' is the SAP System's own text-processing system. SAPscript is tightly integrated and used for many text-processing tasks. SAP Standard Styles and Layout Sets are always held in Client 000.

Layout Sets are used for the Page Layout of SAPscript documents. A 'layout set' has the following elements:

- **Header Data:** Data related to development (created by, development class, etc.) and the layout set information (which elements are used) are both stored in the header data. A start page must be entered here.
- **Paragraph Formats:** Paragraph formats are required in layout sets. However, they are also used for word processing in layout sets, for example, to format text elements.
- **Character Formats:** You can also use character formats to format texts or paragraphs. Unlike paragraph formats, however, they are used to format text within a paragraph.
- **Windows:** Windows are names and window types, which are not physically

positioned until they are allocated to pages and units of measurement are specified.

- **Pages:** Pages are defined to provide the system with a start and end point in text formatting.
- **Page Windows:** Page windows are the combination of windows and pages, where the dimensions of a window and its position on a page are specified.

41. Why do we need 'Enhancements'?

The standard R/3 application may not offer some of the functionality you need for a particular customer or for a particular situation. The R/3 **'Enhancement'** functionality allows you to add your own functionality to SAP's standard business applications or modify the standard one to suit the particular need.

The enhancement may be done through:

- **Customer exits**

    Customers' potential requirements, which do not form a part of the standard software, are incorporated in the standard R/3 as empty modification 'shells.' Customers can then fill these with their own coding. SAP guarantees that all such exits will remain valid across all future releases. The customer exits include:

    - Menu Exits
    - Screen Exits
    - Function Module Exits
    - Keyword Exits

- **ABAP/4 Dictionary Elements**

    These are ABAP/4 Dictionary Enhancements (creation of table appends), Text Enhancements (customer-specific keywords and documentation for data elements), and Field Exits (creation of additional coding for data elements).

42. Differentiate 'Screen Painter' from 'Menu Painter.'

'Screen Painter' is an ABAP Workbench tool used to create or modify the screens for your transactions. The screen painter allows you to make modifications to screen attributes, the flow control logic, or the layout.

Screen Painter: Initial Screen

| Program | | | Create |
| Screen number | 0000 | | |

Subobjects
- ◉ Flow logic
- ○ Element list
- ○ Attributes
- ○ Layout Editor

| Display | Change |

Figure 6: Screen Painter

Transaction Code
SE51

'**Menu Painter**' is a tool used to design the interface components. Status, Menu Bars, Menu Lists, F-key settings, Functions, and Titles are the components of Menu Painter.

Menu Painter: Initial Screen

User Interface Status User Interface Statu:

Program

Subobjects
- ◉ Status | | Test |
- ○ Interface Objects
- ○ Status List
- ○ Menu bars
- ○ Menu list
- ○ F-Key Settings
- ○ Function list
- ○ Title List

| Display | Change | Create |

Figure 7: Menu Painter

Both the screen painter and menu painter are graphical interfaces of ABAP/4 applications.

43.   What is a 'Modification Assistant'?

The '**Modification Assistant**' is the tool that offers you support when making modifications to the standard, by branching to a 'special modification mode' whenever you are modifying objects from the standard in an ABAP workbench editor. Originals are initially protected in this mode and can only be changed with the help of the additional 'pushbuttons' that are placed at your disposal.

All changes that you make to the system are logged with the help of the Modification Assistant. This provides you with a detailed overview of modifications that is easy to read and that dramatically reduces the amount of effort needed to upgrade your system.

The Modification Assistant offers support in the following areas:

- ABAP Editor
- Class Builder
- Screen Painter
- Menu Painter
- Text Element maintenance
- Function Builder
- ABAP Dictionary

If an object can be edited using the Modification Assistant, a dialogue box appears the first time that you attempt to edit that object informing you that editing functions are limited in modification mode. This dialogue box appears exactly once per user for each of the various kinds of transport objects.

44.   What is a 'Spool Request'?

'**Spool Requests**' are generated during 'dialogue' or 'background' processing and placed in the spool database with information about the printer and print format. The actual data is placed in the Tem Se (Temporary Sequential objects).

45. What is the 'CTS'?

The '**Change and Transport System (CTS)**' is a tool that helps to organize development projects (in the ABAP workbench) and customize data (in customizing), and then move/transport these changes between the SAP Systems/ Clients in your system landscape. An example is moving the configuration settings from 'development' to 'test' and finally to the 'production' Client. The changes (such as the creation of a new Company Code, changing a document type, etc.) are assigned to a 'transport request' and transported by the Basis or System Administrator.

46. What is a 'Transport'?

A '**Transport**' in SAP is nothing but the transfer of R/3 System components from one system to another. The components to be transported are specified in the object list of a transport request.

Each 'transport' consists of an 'export process' and an 'import process':

- The **export process** reads objects from the source system and stores them in a data file at the operating system level.
- The **import process** reads objects from the data file and writes them to the database of the target system.

The system maintains a 'transport log 'of all actions during export and import. The '**transport organizer**' helps to manage the transports in SAP.

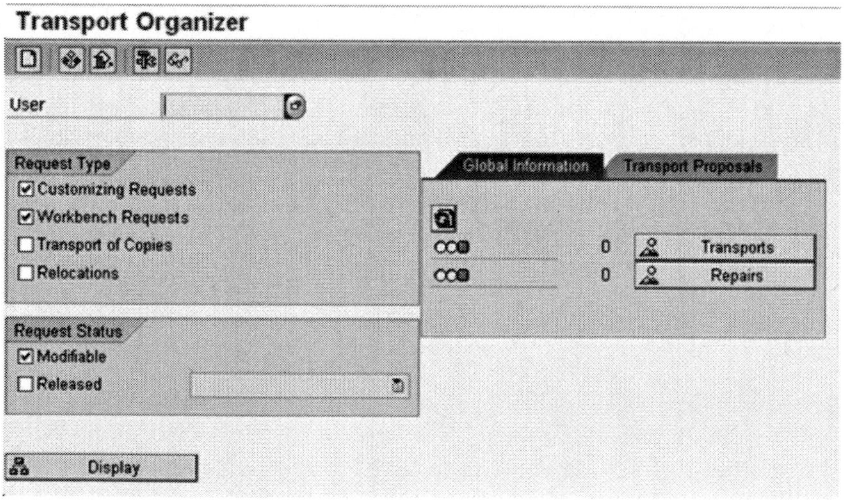

Figure 8: Transport Organizer

Transaction
Code
SE10

47.   How do you find out who has 'Transported' a 'Transport Request'?

Look at Table **TPLOG** (go there using the Transaction Code **SE16**) and input the transport name in the CMDSTRING field with '*.' **Example: *PZDK980001***

48.   What is an 'Authorization' in SAP?

An '**Authorization**' is the process of giving someone permission to do or have something. In multi-user SAP systems, a SAP Basis Administrator defines for the system which users are allowed access to the system and what privileges of use each user gets (such as access to transactions, etc.).

49.   Explain the 'Client' concept of SAP.

A '**Client**' is the top-most organizational structure, which has its own set of master records. A Client is denoted by a 3-character alphanumeric code in SAP, and is a mandatory element. The settings made at the Client level, data maintained, etc., are available across all the Company Codes. A Client should have at least one Company Code defined.

SAP comes delivered with Clients 001 and 002, which contain all the default settings. Usually, copying from the default Clients creates additional and new Clients.

Typically, in SAP, you will have different 'types' of Clients; namely:

1. Development Client
2. Test Client
3. Production Client

In any implementation, you must have at least three types of Clients as mentioned above. There are some companies where you will have more than three. These include:

- Development Client
- Test Client
- Quality Assurance Client

■ Training Client

■ Production Client

A '**Development Client**' is also called a 'sand box' Client and is sometimes known as a 'play' Client. This is the logical place in the SAP system where you try out new configurations, write new programs, etc. This is the place, as the name suggests, where you can 'play' around before finalizing a scenario for customization.

Once you are okay with the configuration or a new program, you will then move it manually (transport) to the '**Test Client**' where you will carry out all the tests (both modular and integration). The end-users are provided with the training using the 'training' Client. Sometimes both the 'test' and 'training' Client are in a single 'instance.' The 'quality assurance' Client helps with necessary quality checks before something is ready to be passed on to the 'production' Client.

After satisfactory results, it will be transported (automatically) to the '**Production Client**' (also called the '**Golden Client**'). You will not be able to make any modifications, manually, to the 'production' Client and the authorization is very limited because this Client is responsible for day-to-day business transactions and any issues here will jeopardize all business operations, which is why this is also called the '**live**' Client.

Do not confuse this term with the 'Client' that denotes a customer in normal business parlance.

50.   How can you find the field/data underlying a 'Transaction'?

A common way to find the technical data underlying a transaction is to place your cursor in the field, press the key '**F1**,' and then click on the button '**Technical Data**' to see the details. This works as long as you are looking at the 'transparent' Table. If the information is populated from a 'structure,' then this will not help you because the 'structure' may be populated from a number of sources including some 'includes,' and may also contain some calculated fields. If the 'include' is in fact a table, then chances are your data comes from that table. Check to see if there is a 'logical' database in the business area you are looking at. Looking at the 'structure' of the 'logical' database often reveals the tables used to drive that business area. Also check to see if the field name you are looking for is in any of the tables. Logical databases can also be useful in determining how tables are linked together.

You may also use other methods (listed below) to zero-in on the field. You can perform any of these, in isolation or in combination, until you find what you are looking for:

■ Debugging

■ SQL Trace

■ Run-time Analysis

Start the 'transaction' in **Debug** mode. Set a 'watch-point' for the structure-field you are interested in. When the debugger 'breaks,' look at the lines just above the 'break-point.' This will show where the field was populated. This may be a 'structure,' in which case you will restart the process using that 'structure' as a 'watch-point.'

Turn **SQL Trace** on, and run your transaction. Switch the 'trace' off, and examine the log. This will detail the tables hit, and the order in which they were hit. Not all tables hit will be displayed; for example, configuration tables tend not to show up, as they are buffered.

The **Runtime Analysis** will show all tables accessed by the transaction.

ABAP Runtime Analysis: Initial Screen

🔳 Tips & Tricks

Measurement

🔘⚪⚪ Reliability of Time Values

Short Descriptn [   ]

In Dialog	In Parallel Session
🔘 Transaction [ ]	⊕ Switch On/Off
⚪ Program [ ]	
⚪ Function module [ ]	**Schedule**
⊕ Execute	⊕ For User/Service

Measurement Restrictions

Variant 🔲 🔳 DEFAULT	From user [ ]

🔲 🔩 ✏️ 🗑 🔳

Figure 9: ABAP Runtime Analysis

Transaction Code
SE30

---

51.   Explain 'LSMW.'

The '**LSMW (Legacy System Migration Workbench)**' is a free SAP-based tool that supports the one-time or periodic transfers of data from non-SAP systems to SAP. The LSMW can be used in conjunction with the **Data Transfer Workbench**. The

LSMW assists in organizing your data migration project and guides you through the process by using a clear sequence of steps. The most common conversion rules are predefined. Reusable conversion rules assure consistent data conversion for different data objects.

The LSMW performs the following steps:

- Reads the legacy data from one or several files (such as spreadsheets or sequential files)
- Converts the data from source format to target format
- Imports the data using standard interfaces **(Batch Input, Direct Input, BAPI, IDoc, etc.)**

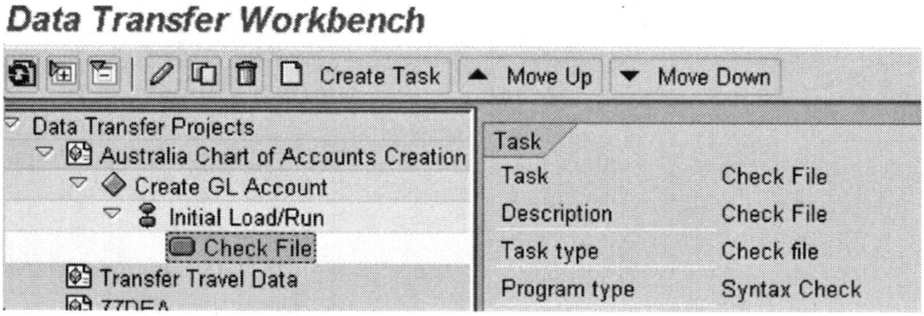

Data Transfer Workbench

Figure 10: Data Transfer Workbench

52.   How do you transport 'LSMW' data from one system to another?

There are two ways to do this:

1. **Export/Import method.** With this method, you have the flexibility of subprojects or objects that need to be transported. Use the Menu Path 'LSMW > Extras > Export project.'

2. **Transport request.** With this method, you will not be able to select the objects, and the project as a whole is transported. Use the Menu Path 'LSMW > Extras >Create change request.'

53.   Can you transport 'Variants' of multiple programs in one step?

Yes. Use program **RSTRANSP** using Transaction Code: SE38.

54. What is 'SAPNet'?

The '**SAPNet**' R/3 Front-end provides a remote connection to SAP's service and support group to provide assistance in the event of an implementation project system or production system problem. Additionally, the SAPNet R/3 Front-end provides information on the latest high-priority SAP system information, including error alarm messages that help you prevent problems before they occur. You can also find release, installation, upgrade, and migration information. This functionality is included in the standard SAP R/3 Basis System. Connection is made using ISDN or a leased line through the project's telecommunications service provider.

PROJECT
IMPLEMENTATION

PROJECT IMPLEMENTATION

55.   What is 'ASAP'?

'**ASAP (Accelerated SAP)**' is a methodology used in SAP for faster and cost-effective implementation of SAP R/3 projects. ASAP helps to (*a*) reduce the implementation time, (*b*) achieve quality implementations, and (*c*) make effective and efficient use of project resources.

ASAP integrates the following three components:

1. ASAP Roadmap
2. Tools (Questionnaires, templates, etc.)
3. R/3 services and training (Hotline, Early Watch, Remote Upgrade, Archiving, etc.)

ASAP Roadmap is aimed at providing step-by-step direction and guidance throughout the project implementation by providing a process-oriented, clear and concise project plan. The roadmap meanders through the following milestones or phases in the project implementation lifecycle:

1. Project preparation
2. Business blueprint
3. Realization
4. Final preparation
5. Go-live, support, and continuous improvement

56.   Explain 'ASAP Roadmap' phases.

Project preparation is the *first* and initial phase of the ASAP roadmap where you are just starting the project. You will perform activities such as preparation of the initial scope, high-level timelines and plans, project charters, identification of project team members, project kick-off, etc.

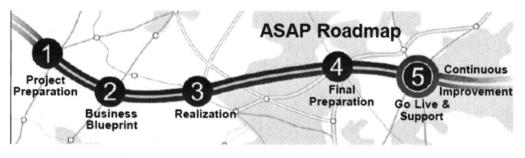

Figure 11: ASAP Roadmap

Business blueprint is the *second* phase in the implementation where you will try, identify, and document business requirements and goals to prepare the foundation for future stages of the project. Ideally, you will organize 'business requirement gathering' workshops with the various business/functional users of the company, lead them through the discussion with structured business functionality questionnaires, understand their existing business processes, and identify and document their requirements in the wake of this new implementation. A 'sign-off' at the end of the phase ensures an agreement to move forward outlining the scope of the project. It is understood that whatever is explicitly stated in the business blueprint document is the only scope; no implied scope will be considered for system configuration in the next phase.

Realization is the *third* phase where the implementing team breaks down the business processes identified in the second phase and configures the SAP settings. Initially, you will do a **Baseline Configuration**, test the system functionality and if necessary make changes to the baseline configuration, and close the phase with **Final Configuration**, signalling that all the business processes have been captured and configured in the system.

Final Preparation is the *penultimate* phase in the project. This phase also serves to resolve all crucial open issues. A 'go-live check' is also conducted to analyze whether the system has been properly configured. This phase is marked by the following activities:

- End-to-testing of the configured system (User Acceptance Test - UAT)
- Training of the end users (Usually follows the concept 'Train-the-Trainer')

- System management activities (creation of users, user profiles, allocation of roles to profiles, etc.)
- Cut-over (data migration activities)

An 'internal help desk' should be staffed and supported mainly by employees of the enterprise. Setting up a help desk involves, among other things, installing office and technical equipment and defining OSS users. Problems that cannot be solved by this internal help desk are forwarded to SAP via the **SAPNet/OSS** system.

On successful completion of this phase, you are ready to run your business in your production system.

Go-Live and Support is the final and *fifth* phase of the project where the configured system is declared 'live' for day-to-day business use. Users make productive (live) business transactions in the system and all the issues cropping up in the wake of going live are supported and resolved by a support team immediately.

57.   List the tools for the 'Project Preparation Phase' of 'ASAP.'

- ASAP Roadmap
- Knowledge Corner
- ASAP MS-Project Plan
- C-Maps (Collaborative Business Maps)
- Quicksizer
- Pre-Configured Solutions (Connect-and-Go, Smart Implementations, etc.)
- SAP Service Market Place

58.   List the tools for 'Business Case Development' in 'ASAP.'

- E-Business Case Builder
- C-Maps

59.   List the tools for 'Project Management and Methodology' in 'ASAP.'

- Solution Manager
- SAP Service Market Place
- ASAP MS- Project Plan
- ASAP Roadmap
- ASAP Question and Answer Database

- ASAP Business Blueprint
- ASAP BPP (Business Process and Procedures Document)
- ASAP BPML (Business Process Master List)
- ASAP Issue Database
- ASAP Implementation Assistant/Knowledge Corner

60.   When do you use the 'ASAP BPML' tool?

The ASAP '**Business Process Master List (BPML)**' is used during the Realization (third phase) of the ASAP Roadmap.

61.   Explain 'Hardware' sizing for a SAP implementation.

ASAP provides a tool called **Quicksizer**, which is used to analyze the hardware requirements (of mySAP.com) and to arrive at the hardware sizing for the project based on your inputs to a list of questions. The tool is Web-based to make mySAP. com faster and easier. The Quicksizer has been developed by SAP in close cooperation with all platform partners and is free. The Quicksizer calculates CPU, disk, and memory resources based on throughput numbers and the number of users working with the different SAP components. The tool gives customers (and prospects) an idea of the system size requirements for running the proposed workload, and is also useful for initial budget planning. Initially used during the Project Preparation and Blueprinting Phases, and anytime after these phases when there is a change in system requirements, the tool helps in arriving at the recommendations for hardware deployment.

62.   Explain 'ASAP BPML.'

'**ASAP BPMLs (Business Process Master Lists)**' are MS-Excel Sheets generated by the ASAP Q&A Database for facilitating configuration and testing of the system, and development of end-user documentation. These lists become the central repository from which you build the individual master lists to manage the initial configuration, final configuration, final end-user integration testing, and any other end-user procedures including the documentation.

63.   What are 'BPPs' in ASAP?

'**ASAP BPP (Business Process and Procedures)**' are templates that typically walk you through a transaction in SAP and help you document them. The templates are replete with Best Practices or Standard Procedures for completing a particular transaction, which you can customize for end-user training. You will assign ASAP BPPS to the ASAP BPML.

64. Explain 'C-Maps.'

'C-Maps' or **C-Business Maps (Collaborative Business Maps)** represent a comprehensive portfolio of industry-specific and cross-industry process blueprints that show you how the mySAP.com e-business platform can help your business. These maps define the activities, roles, system interfaces, and business documents required for inter-enterprise collaboration. They also show which SAP Solutions and Services you need to make your organization a truly collaborative e-business.

C-Business Maps explain what happens when you deploy e-business solutions to integrate existing resources and transcend the borders of individual enterprises. They give you a complete picture of the benefits and advantages of collaborative business processes.

65. What is the advantage of SAP's 'Smart Implementations'?

'Smart Implementations' contain pre-configuration, documentation, installation, and configuration accelerators for specific mySAP components. Smart Implementations provide tools to assist with technical infrastructure planning, installation of necessary components, system configuration and integration into an existing SAP system landscape, and infrastructure management in a production system.

The Smart Implementation for the mySAP Workplace includes the following installation and configuration features:

- Easy system infrastructure configuration with the **Configuration Assistant**
- Automatic **mySAP Workplace** component installation
- Easy integration of multiple component systems
- Pre-configuration of all software components, including the Web server and Internet Transaction Server (ITS)
- Basis customization of the SAP R/3 System (Workplace Server)
- The **System Administration Assistant**, an easy-to-use tool providing a comprehensive administration concept to support the system administrator in important tasks.

66. What is the 'SAP Solution Architect'?

The 'SAP Solution Architect' is the portal that integrates all content, tools, and methodologies necessary for the solution-oriented evaluation, implementation, quick adaptation, and continuous improvement of the **mySAP.com e-Business platform**. It is fully integrated into the Customer Engagement Life Cycle (CEL), open to partner content, and an integral part of the SAP Service Infrastructure.

In one portal, the SAP Solution Architect integrates:

- **Best Practices** for mySAP.com to evaluate, implement, and extend e-Business solutions.
- Tried and tested implementation tools such as the **Implementation Guide (IMG)** and the **Test Workbench**.
- Access to **C-Business Maps** for in-depth information on collaborative business scenarios.
- The **ASAP** method for running mySAP.com projects.
- An authoring environment with which customers and partners can create their own pre-configured implementation solutions.
- Access to evaluation products such as the **E-Business Case Builder** and the **Solution Composer**.

The benefits of using the SAP Solution Architect include:

- Consistent access to all contents, tools, and methods for evaluating, implementing, adapting, and continuously improving your mySAP.com e-business solution.
- Rapid evaluation and implementation with Best Practices for mySAP. com.
- Tried and tested evaluation and implementation tools that have been enhanced specifically for use with mySAP.com.
- Improved project communication and efficiency through a central portal.
- A consistent and integrated approach that passes the business-oriented project definition from one phase to the next.
- Complete alignment with the ASAP Roadmap.
- Information about updates, training, and changes via the SAP Service Marketplace.

67. What is 'Configuration' in SAP?

'**Configuration**' is the process of maintaining settings (parameters) in the system to support specific/customized business requirements. Remember SAP is an 'all-encompassing' application which needs to be 'configured' to meet your specific requirements.

68.   What is the 'IMG'?

The '**IMG (Implementation Guide)**' in SAP provides you with the various configuration steps in a tree-like structure for easy access with the nodes at the bottom representing the configuration objects. This is the central repository for customizing, providing a step-by-step guide for carrying out various activities. Besides the steps/activities, the IMG also contains explanations concerning the order in which you need to make the customizations. When you execute an activity from the IMG, you are indirectly changing the values (parameters) in the underlying table.

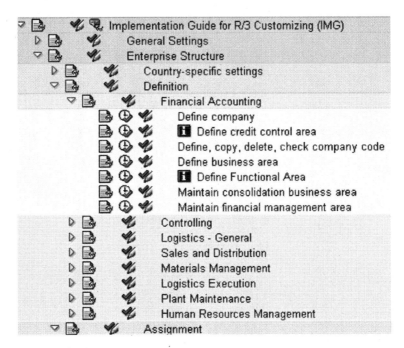

Figure 12: SAP R/3 IMG

The IMG is structured and arranged into four major logical groups:

1. **General Settings** (Country settings, currencies, calendar maintenance, time zones, field display characteristics, etc.)
2. **Enterprise Structure** (Definition, assignment, consistency check, etc.)

3. **Cross-Application Components** (ALE, Timesheet, CATT, CAD integration, DM-Document Management, EDI, Engineering Change Management (ECM), etc.)
4. **Functional Area Settings** (FI, CO, Logistics, PP, PM, QM, etc.)

Transaction
Code
SPRO

69.   Explain the various 'Types' of IMGs.

The **SAP Reference IMG** provides all the customizing steps for all functional areas of SAP. This, as the name suggests, is the 'reference IMG' from which you may create your own IMG to meet the exact requirements of the (1) enterprise and (2) project.

The **Enterprise IMG** is usually an exact copy of the 'SAP Reference IMG,' but limited to the countries where the implementation is carried out. From the Enterprise IMG, you may create your Project IMG, which will contain the application components/business processes required in the current project.

It is also possible to create the **Project IMG** by directly generating it from the SAP Reference IMG. In this case, the country selection is done when the Project IMGs are created.

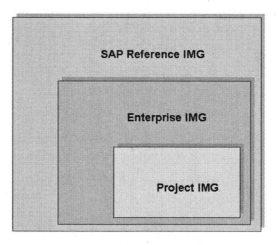

Figure 13: IMG (Reference, Enterprise, and Project)

70.   What are all the various ways of 'Customizing'?

You can customize SAP using:

- **IMG:** Just follow the IMG tree, step-by-step. No technical knowledge (about tables, views, etc.) is required.

  Example: To configure the 'Country Code,' just follow the IMG Menu Path 'General settings > Set countries > Define countries.'

- **Tables:** You need to know the name and structure of the tables where the parameters are directly entered. Technical knowledge of customizable objects is required.

  Example: To configure the 'Country Code,' use transaction code: **OY01**. Enter the details in Table **V_T005**.

71.   Why is the 'IMG' route of customizing easier than the 'Tables' route?

- IMG is a logical way to access data from multiple physical tables without knowing from where the data is flowing. This is because there are many transactions, which affect more than one table.
- There is no need to know the names of Tables and fields, though it always helps to know about the major tables.
- IMG offers a step-by-step way of progressing from one activity to the other. Also, you can classify the activities into various views such as 'mandatory/critical/optional,' 'Client-dependent/Client-independent,' etc., so that you can proceed per your requirements and time.
- Since IMG provides you with the functional view, it becomes easier to 'configure' and test immediately.

72.   What is known as the 'Go-Live Check'?

The '**Go-Live Check**' is done just before you cut over to 'live' (production) operation in a project. This is to test whether the system is properly configured to meet the requirements of the business. The check includes detecting problems in the (*a*) SAP R/3 Application, (*b*) Database, and (*c*) Operating System.

First, the **Go-live Check** involves an analysis of the major system components of the R/3 installation with regard to system consistency and reliability. For this, SAP experts log on to your R/3 system via a remote connection, inspect the configuration of individual system components, and provide valuable recommendations for system optimization. By analyzing the individual system components before production start up, SAP can considerably improve the availability and performance of the customer's live system. In addition, the technical application analysis provides information on how to speed up the core processes within R/3.

Secondly, the transactions with high resource consumption are searched for and necessary adjustments are made.

Thirdly, the changes from the two prior sessions are validated. This check is performed in the productive operation system.

After a system goes live, some fine tuning and eliminating of potential bottlenecks is still necessary. This is carried out four weeks after 'going live' with the R/3 System.

73.   When should you conduct 'Business Process Re-engineering' (BPR)?

Typically '**Business Process Re-engineering (BPR)**' needs to be completed well before the SAP implementation starts. This will help to identify any improvements that can be made prior to implementation and begin the process of change within the organization. Improvements that will be system-enabled will form part of the implementation and also help the project team to identify areas of change.

However, it is also possible (but not recommended if there are large areas requiring total process re-engineering) to do BPR during the business blueprint phase provided the project team works within the boundary of the initial scope provided.

74.   What are 'User Parameters'?

SAP provides a way of lessening your day-to-day data entry operations by facilitating default entries for fields, and bringing out the most suitable **Display Variant** for document display, document entry, open/line item processing, etc. The user parameters, also known as '**Editing Options**,' are a boon as they save time and result in greater accuracy as data entry errors are eliminated with the default values.

You can, among many alternatives, set:

1. The system to default the 'exchange rate' from the first line item.
2. A preference so that the user does not process any 'special GL transactions' or 'foreign currency transactions.'
3. That the document needs to be complete before it is 'parked.'
4. The system to calculate the tax component on the 'net' invoice and not on the 'gross.'
5. Your document currency either as the 'local currency' or as the one used in the last document.

6. The system to make a currency conversion if documents are to be fetched from 'archives.'

7. Documents to be displayed using a 'reference number.'

8. 'Payment reference' to be used as a selection item in open item processing.

9. To activate branch/head office 'dialogue' while processing line items.

Transaction Code
FB00

FINANCIAL
ACCOUNTING (FI)

FINANCIAL ACCOUNTING (FI)

GENERAL

75. Explain 'Financial Accounting (FI)' in SAP.

The **'FI (Financial Accounting)'** module of SAP is the back-bone, which records, collects, and processes financial transactions or information on a real-time basis to provide the necessary inputs for external (statutory) reporting. The module is integrated with other modules (such as Material Management (MM), Sales & Distribution (SD), Human Resources (HR), Production Planning (PP), Controlling (CO), etc.). The module FI has several submodules that are tightly integrated.

76. What are the 'Submodules' within FI?

- **FI-AA Asset Accounting**

  Integrated with FI-GL, FI-AR, FI-AP, CO, MM, PP and PM, this module manages the financial side (depreciation, insurance, etc.) of the assets throughout their entire lifecycle starting with procurement of assets and ending with scrapping or sales.

- **FI-AP Accounts Payable**

  Integrated with FI-GL, FI-AA, FI-TR and MM, this submodule manages vendor transactions by linking with material management, asset accounting, travel management, etc. Notable is the 'payment program' for making payments to vendors.

- **FI-AR   Accounts Receivable**

    Integrated with FI-GL, FI-AA, FI-TR, MM and SD, this submodule manages customers and receivables, and integrates with SD. It is well-known for credit management functionalities and the 'dunning' program.

- **FI-BL   Bank Accounting**
- **FI-FM   Funds Management**
- **FI-GL   General Ledger Accounting**

    This submodule is integrated with all other submodules within FI and outside FI.

- **FI-SL   Special Purpose Ledger**

    This submodule is used to provide the summary information from multiple applications at a level of detail that the user defines.

- **FI-LC   Legal Consolidations**

    This submodule helps in the central task of combining the financial operating results of the companies within a group to provide overall results for the group.

- **FI-TM   Travel Management**

77.   Name the submodules within FI, from which FI-GL gets simultaneous postings.

- Accounts Receivable (FI-AR)
- Accounts Payable (FI-AP)
- Asset Accounting (FI-AA)

78.   Name three distinct characteristics of FI-GL.

- Multi-currency capability
- Flexible real-time reporting
- Real-time transaction entries

GLOBAL AND ENTERPRISE SETTINGS

Before getting into the questions, please look into the FI organization structure depicted below. When moving through the questions, at any point in time if you need clarification on the arrangement of the various organizational elements, do visit this page again. To be successful as an FI/CO consultant you need to have a thorough grasp of this basic fundamental block in SAP FI/CO.

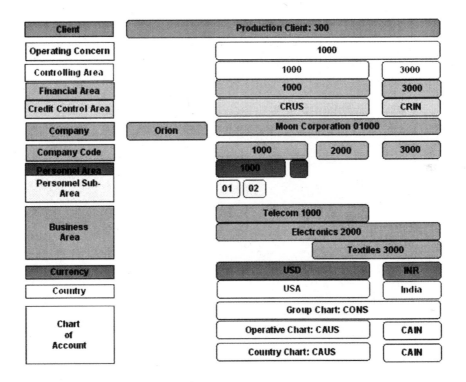

Figure 14: FI Organization Structure

79.   What do you mean by 'Organizational Units' in SAP?

The '**Organizational Units**' in SAP are the elements or structures representing business functions, and are used in reporting. For example, Client (across the various modules) Company Code (FI), Controlling Area (CO), Plant (logistics), Sales Organization (SD), Purchasing Organization (MM), Employee Group (HR), etc.

80. What are the important 'Organizational Units' in FI?

1. Company
2. Company Code
3. Business area

81. What is a 'Company'?

A **'Company'** in SAP is represented by a 5-character alphanumeric code and usually represents the enterprise or the group company. A Company can include one or more Company Codes. The creation of a Company, in SAP, is optional.

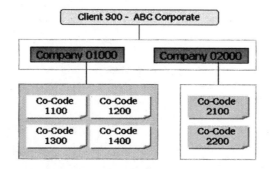

Figure 15: Company and Company Code

Company	9999M
Company name	Model Companies Worldwide
Name of company 2	Model Companies Worldwide
Detailed information	
Street	West Promenade
P.O.Box	
Postal code	60000
City	Frankfurt
Country	DE
Language key	DE
Currency	EUR

Figure 16: Define a Company

82. What is a 'Company Code,' and how is this different from a 'Company'?

A '**Company Code**' in SAP is the smallest organizational unit for which you can draw individual Financial Statements (Balance Sheet and Profit & Loss Account) for your external statutory reporting. It is denoted by a 4-character alphanumeric code. The creation of a Company Code is mandatory; you need to have at least one Company Code defined in the system, for implementing FI.

Company Code	9999
Company name	MODEL COMPANY

Additional data	
City	Frankfurt
Country	DE
Currency	EUR
Language	DE

Figure 17: Define a Company Code

You may define a Company Code by copying from an existing one (Copy, Delete, Check Company Code Option).

Transaction
Code
EC01

You may also define the Company Code anew (the second option in the following figure), from scratch.

Copy, delete, check company code

Edit Company Code Data

Figure 18: Options to define a Company Code

83.   What are the important 'Global Settings' for a Company Code?

General data:

- Company Code
- Company Name
- City
- Address
- Currency
- Country
- Language

Global data:

- Chart of Accounts
- Credit Control Area
- Fiscal Year Variant
- Field Status Variant
- Posting Period Variant

84.   Can you assign more than one 'Company Code' to a 'Company'?

All the Company Codes within a Company should use the same Chart of Accounts and the same Financial Year, though they all can have different Local Currencies.

85.   What is a 'Business Area'?

'Business Areas' correspond to specific business segments of a company, and may cut across different Company Codes (for example, product lines). They can also represent different responsibility areas (for example, branch units). The **Business Areas** are optional in SAP.

2000	Plant engineering & construct.
3000	Automotive
3400	Metal, Wood and Paper
3500	Aerospace & Defence
4000	Chemicals
4500	Engineering & Construction
5000	Consumer Products: Non-Food
6000	Pharmaceuticals
7000	Electronic Products

Figure 19: Business Area

The financial statements drawn per business area are for internal reporting purposes. You need to put a check in the check box in the configuration for the company for which you want to enable business area financial statements.

9990	India Inc.	Chennai
9999	MODEL COMPANY	Frankfurt

Figure 20: Enable Business Area Financial Statements

Transaction
Code
OB37

When transactions are posted in FI, you have the option of assigning the same to a Business Area so that the values are properly captured for internal financial statements.

86.   Can you attach a 'Business Area' to a Transaction?

Yes. The Business Area can also be derived from other account assignments; for example, cost center. But to do this, you need to define the Business Area in the master record of that particular cost center.

87.   How do you post Cross-company Code Business Area postings?

By using a cross-Company Code transaction, you should be able to post to different 'Business Areas' and cut across various Company Codes. Any number of 'Business Area–Company Code' combinations is possible.

88.   What is the 'Credit Control Area' in SAP?

The '**Credit Control Area**' in SAP helps administer credit management functions relating to customers. This organizational unit is used both in SD and FI-AR modules. By definition, you can have more than one credit control area in a Client, but each Company Code is assigned to one credit control area. However, it is true that you can attach many Company Codes to the same credit control area.

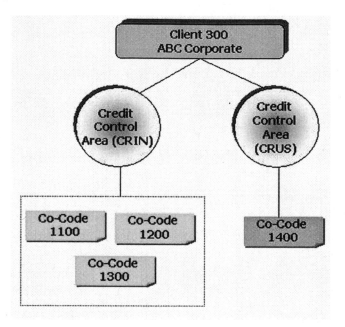

Figure 21: Credit Control Area

89.   What is a 'Chart of Accounts'?

A 'Chart of Accounts' is the list of GL accounts used in one or more Company Codes. All the GL accounts in a chart of accounts will have an account number, account name, and some control information. The control information decides how the GL account can be created.

90.   What are all the major components of a 'Chart of Accounts'?

A 'Chart of Accounts' includes the following components:

- Chart of account key
- Name
- Maintenance language
- The GL Account Number
- Controlling integration
- Group chart of accounts (consolidation)
- Block indicator

91.   What is an 'Operating Chart of Accounts'?

This chart is used for day-to-day postings and is also known as an **'Operative'** or **'Standard'** chart of accounts. Both FI and CO use a chart of accounts. It is mandatory that the chart of accounts be assigned to a Company Code.

92.   How does 'Group Chart of Accounts' differ from 'Operating Chart of Accounts'?

The **'Group Chart of Accounts,'** also known as the **Corporate Chart of Accounts**, is used for consolidating all Company Codes (with a dissimilar Operative Chart of Accounts) falling under a Company. This is the 'universe' of all-inclusive GL accounts from where the Operative Chart of Accounts is derived. A Company Code is not mandatory.

93.   What is a 'Country Chart of Accounts'? Why do you need this?

This chart of accounts, also known as an **Alternate Chart of Accounts**, contains the GL accounts necessary to meet the specific statutory/legal requirements of a company from which a Company Code operates. The assignment of this chart of accounts to a Company Code is also optional. It is possible that both the operative and the country chart of accounts are one and the same. In this case, you will not need two different charts of accounts.

In cases where the operative and country chart of accounts are different, a link needs to be established by entering the GL account number from the 'Country Chart of Accounts' in the GL master record (under the Company Code section) of the 'Operative Chart of Accounts' in the field 'Alternate Account Number.'

94.   Can one 'Chart of Accounts' be assigned to several Company Codes?

Yes. One chart of accounts can be assigned to several Company Codes. However, the reverse is not possible; i.e., you will not be able assign more than one chart of accounts to a single Company Code.

95.   What is a 'Fiscal Year' and 'Fiscal Year Variant'?

A 'fiscal year' is the accounting period, which normally spreads over 12 months. Financial statements are drawn for a fiscal year. The fiscal year, in SAP, is defined as a **'Fiscal Year Variant.'** All **Calendar Year Fiscal Year Variants**, in standard SAP, are denoted usually as K1, K2, etc.

FV	Description	Year-depend...	Calendar yr	Number of posti...	No.of special pe
F1	366 periods	☐	☐	366	
I4	Calendar year, 4 spec. periods	☐	☑	12	4
K0	Calendar year, 1 spec. period	☐	☑	12	
K1	Calendar year, 1 spec. period	☐	☑	12	1
K2	Calendar year, 2 spec. periods	☐	☑	12	2
K3	Calendar year, 3 spec. periods	☐	☑	12	3
K4	Calendar year, 4 spec. periods	☐	☑	12	4
Q1	Quarters	☐	☐	4	
R1	Short.fiscal year Jan-Sept.'94	☑	☐	12	4
UL	Special Purpose Ledger	☑	☐	100	
V3	Apr.- March, 4 special periods	☐	☐	12	4

Figure 22: Fiscal Year Variant

The fiscal year may or may not correspond to the calendar year. In the standard SAP system, the Non-Calendar Fiscal Year Variants are denoted V1, V2, etc.

V3	Apr.- March, 4 special periods	☐	☐	12	4
V6	July - June, 4 special periods	☐	☐	12	4
V9	Oct.- Sept., 4 special periods	☐	☐	12	4

Figure 23: Fiscal Year Variant (non-calendar year)

It is also possible that the fiscal year may be shorter than 12 months, and this is called a 'Shortened Fiscal Year' (R1, in Figure-1).

Transaction
Code
OB29

96.   How do you assign a 'Fiscal Year Variant' to a Company Code?

One 'Fiscal Year Variant' can be assigned to one or more Company Codes.

9990	India Inc.	K4	Calendar year, 4 spec. periods
9999	MODEL COMPANY	K4	Calendar year, 4 spec. periods

Figure 24: Assign Fiscal Year Variant to a Company Code

Transaction Code
OB37

97.   What is a 'Posting Period'?

A fiscal year, in SAP, is divided into various '**Posting Periods**,' with a start and end date defined for each of these periods. Any document posting is possible only when the 'posting periods' are in place in the system. Normally there will be 12 posting periods. A posting period consists of a month and year.

98.   How does the system identify a 'Posting Period'?

Based on the posting date entered into the system while posting a document, the system automatically determines the period by looking at the document date and the year. However, for this to occur you should have properly defined the fiscal year variant.

99.   What happens when you post to year 2006 when you are in 2007?

First of all, to post a document relating to a previous year, say 2006 when you are in 2007, the relevant posting period should be 'open' in the system. When such a posting is done, the system makes some adjustments in the background:

One: the carry-forward balances of the current year, already done, are updated in case the posting affects balance sheet items.

Two: if the posting is going to affect the Profit & Loss accounts, then the system adjusts the carried forward profit or loss balances to the Retained Earnings account(s).

100.   What do you mean by 'Opening/Closing' Posting Periods?

Postings in SAP are controlled by the '**opening**' or '**closing**' of posting periods. Normally, the current posting period is open for document posting and all other periods are closed. At the end of the period (month), this posting period is closed and the new one is opened for postings. This way it provides better control.

It is, however, possible to keep all the periods or select periods open.

Transaction Code
OB52

101. What is a 'Posting Period Variant'?

A 'Posting Period Variant' is useful in 'opening/closing' posting periods across many Company Codes at one time. You define a posting period variant and assign it to various Company Codes. Since the posting period variant is cross-Company Code, the opening and closing of the posting period is made simple. Instead of opening and closing individually for different Company Codes, you just need to open or close the posting period variant.

102. Can you selectively 'Open' and 'Close' accounts?

Yes. It is possible to selectively control the 'opening' and 'closing' for various types of accounts. Usually, a '+' is mentioned in the top-most entry indicating that all the account types are allowed for posting. Now, for the GL(S) accounts, you will need to specify the period which needs to be opened. This ensures that all the account types are open for the current period, indicated by '+,' and only the GL accounts are open for the previous period.

Select account types can also be opened or closed for a specific period; select accounts within an account type can also be opened or closed.

103. Why is it not possible to post to a customer a/c in a previously closed 'Period'?

When you want to selectively 'close' or 'open' the posting period of some accounts (account range), there will be no problem with that if you are doing it for GL accounts. But, if it is a subledger account (such as the customer), it has to be achieved via opening or closing the account interval of the **reconciliation account** of that account type.

104. Can you open a 'Posting Period' only for a particular user?

Yes. SAP allows you to open or close the posting period only for specific users. This can be achieved by maintaining an **authorization group** at the document header level.

105.   What is a 'Special Period'? When do you use it?

Besides the normal posting periods, SAP allows for defining a maximum four more posting periods, which are known as '**Special Periods**' as these are used for year-end closing activities. This is achieved by dividing the last posting period into more than one (maximum four) period. However, all the postings in these special periods should fall within the last posting period.

The special periods cannot be determined automatically by the system based on the posting date of the document. The special period needs to be manually entered into the 'posting period' field in the document header.

106.   What is the maximum number of 'Posting Periods' in SAP?

Under GL accounting, you can have a maximum of 16 posting periods (12 regular plus 4 Special Periods). However, you can have up to a maximum of 366 posting periods as is the case in '**special purpose ledgers.**'

107.   What is a 'Special Purpose Ledger'?

'**Special Purpose Ledgers**' (FI-SL) are used in reporting. These are basically user-defined ledgers, which can be maintained either as GL or subsidiary ones with various account assignment objects (with SAP-dimensions such as cost center, business area, profit center, etc., or customer-defined dimensions such as region, area, etc.).

Once defined, this functionality helps you to report at various levels. Ideally you collect the information, combine it, and create the totals. This is something such as an additional reporting feature, and use of this feature will have no effect on the regular functionalities of SAP.

108.   What variations are possible when defining a 'Fiscal Year'?

- ■ **The Fiscal Year is the same as a Calendar Year**

    The fiscal year starts on January 1 and there are 12 posting periods; the posting periods correspond to the calendar months; there is no need to define each of the posting periods.

Posting Period	Start Date	End Date
1	1-Jan	31-Jan
2	1-Feb	28/29 Feb

3	1-Mar	31-Mar
4	1-Apr	30-Apr
5	1-May	31-May
6	1-Jun	30-Jun
7	1-Jul	31-Jul
8	1-Aug	31-Aug
9	1-Sep	30-Sep
10	1-Oct	31-Oct
11	1-Nov	30-Nov
12	1-Dec	31-Dec

- **The Fiscal Year is NOT the same as a Calendar Year**

  In this case, you need to specify how many posting periods you want and how the system should derive the posting period. Since the posting period does not correspond to the calendar month, the start and end date of each of the posting periods need to be maintained.

109.   What is known as 'Year Shift/Displacement' in a Fiscal Year?

When the fiscal year is not the same as the calendar year, we need to define a **'displacement factor'** for each of the posting periods to correctly identify the number of posting periods.

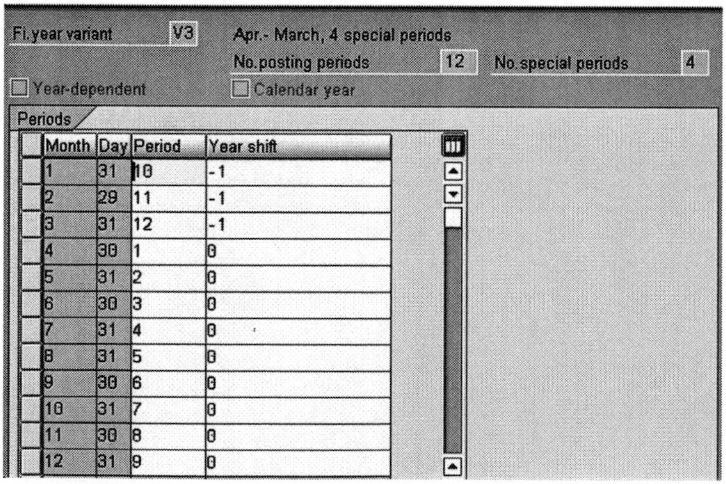

Figure 25: Year shift/displacement in Fiscal Year Variant

For example, consider the fiscal year variant V3 (Figure 25). The fiscal year starts on April 1st and ends on March 31st of the next calendar year so the displacement factor or year shift from April to December is '0,' and for January to March, it will be '-1'. By defining it this way, the system is able to recognize the correct posting period. A posting made on January 25th, 2006 will then be interpreted as the 10th posting period in fiscal year 2005.

110. Can you have 'non-Calendar' months as 'Periods' in a 'non-Calendar' Fiscal Year?

Yes. The '**non-calendar fiscal year**' can either correspond to calendar months or to non-calendar months.

In the case of non-calendar months as the posting periods, you need to specify the start and end date of these posting periods. Consider a fiscal year starting on April 16th, 2005 and ending on April 15th, 2006. Here, the posting period-1 starts on April 16th and ends on May 15th and so on. Note that the posting period-9 will have 2 displacements (0 and -1) as indicated below in the Table:

Posting Period	Start Date	End Date	Year	Year Displacement
1	16-Apr	15-May	2005	0
2	16-May	15-Jun	2005	0
3	16-Jun	15-Jul	2005	0
4	16-Jul	15-Aug	2005	0
5	16-Aug	15-Sep	2005	0
6	16-Sep	15-Oct	2005	0
7	16-Oct	15-Nov	2005	0
8	16-Nov	15-Dec	2005	0
9	16-Dec	31-Dec	2005	0
9	1-Jan	15-Jan	2006	-1
10	16-Jan	15-Feb	2006	-1
11	16-Feb	15-Mar	2006	-1
12	16-Mar	15-Apr	2006	-1

As a result, a posting made on December 27th, 2005, as well as the posting made on January 14th, 2006 are correctly identified as postings corresponding to period-9.

111. What is a 'Year-dependent' Fiscal Year?

A calendar year fiscal variant, when defined as '**year-dependent**,' is relevant and valid only for that year.

112. What precautions should you take while defining a 'Shortened Fiscal Year'?

Note that the '**Shortened Fiscal Year**' is always year-dependent. This has to be followed or preceded by a full fiscal year (12 months). Both the shortened and the full fiscal year, in this case, have to be defined using a single fiscal year variant.

113. Tell me more about a 'Shortened Fiscal Year.'

As mentioned already, a '**Shortened Fiscal Year**' is one containing less than 12 months. This kind of fiscal year is required when you are in the process of setting up a company, or when you switch over one fiscal year (e.g., calendar year) to another type of fiscal year (non-calendar).

114. How do you open a new 'Fiscal Year' in the system?

You do not need to 'open' the new fiscal year as a separate activity. Once you make a posting into the new fiscal year, the new fiscal year is automatically opened. Or, the new fiscal year is automatically opened when you run the '**balance carry-forward**' program.

However, you need to have (1) the relevant posting period already open in the new fiscal year, (2) completed the document number range assignment if you are following a year-dependent number range assignment, and (3) defined a new fiscal year variant if you follow the year-dependent fiscal year variant.

115. How do you 'Carry-Forward' account balances?

If you have already posted into the new fiscal year, you do not need to '**carry-forward**' the balances manually. But you can use the various 'carry-forward' programs supplied by SAP for this task.

116. Can you explain how 'Carry-Forward' happens in SAP?

Sure. For all the Balance Sheet items, the balances of these accounts are just carried forward to the new fiscal year, along with account assignments if any. This also true for customer and vendor accounts.

In the case of Profit & Loss accounts, the system carries forward the profit or loss (in the local currency) to the Retained Earnings account, and the balances of these accounts are set to '0.' No additional account assignments are transferred.

117.   Is there a prerequisite for 'Carry-Forward' activity?

Yes, for Profit & Loss accounts, you should have defined the Retained Earnings account in the system. Additionally, you should have also specified the '**Profit & Loss Account Type'** in the master record of each of these for Profit & Loss accounts.

There are no such requirements for GL accounts, customer and vendor accounts.

118.   How many 'Retained Earnings' a/c can be defined?

You can define as many '**Retained Earnings Accounts'** as you need. But normally, companies use only **one** retained earnings account. Remember, to define more than one, you should use the profit & loss account type.

119.   Can you have multiple 'Retained Earnings' a/c?

Normally it is sufficient if you use one '**retained earnings' account**. However, if you are configuring for a multinational company where the legal requirements require treating some of the tax provisions differently from other countries, then you will need more than one retained earnings account.

120.   How do you maintain 'Currency' in SAP?

'**Currency'** (the legal means of payment in a country) in SAP is denoted by a 3-character **Currency Code**, maintained per ISO standards. Example: USD (U.S. Dollars), INR (Indian Rupee), GBP (Great Britain Pound), etc. Each currency code in the system will have a validity defined.

A currency is defined in SAP using the IMG path: General settings > Currencies > Check exchange rate types.

121.   What is a 'Local Currency'?

When you define a Company Code, you also need to mention in which currency you will be maintaining the accounts/ledgers in financial accounting. This currency is called the '**Local Currency**.' This is also known as '**Company Code Currency**.'

122. What is a 'Parallel Currency'?

When defining the currencies for a Company Code, it is possible to maintain, for each of these company Codes, *two more currencies* in addition to the 'Local Currency.' These two currencies are called the '**Parallel Currencies**,' which can be the:

■ Group Currency
■ Hard Currency
■ Global Company Currency
■ Index-based Currency

To translate the values from one currency to the other, you will need to maintain an **exchange rate** for each pair of the defined currencies in the system. When parallel currencies are defined, the system maintains the accounting ledgers in these currencies as well, in addition to the local currency.

123. What is a 'Group Currency'?

This is the currency defined at the Client level.

124. What is the 'Global Company Code Currency'?

The currency defined for the Company (or the Consolidated Company) is called the '**Global Company Code Currency**.'

125. What is an 'Account Currency'?

When defining the GL accounts in the system, you are required to define a currency in which an account will be maintained, and this is called the '**Account Currency**.' This is defined in the 'Company Code' area of the GL master record, and is used for postings and account balance display.

126. What are all the prerequisites for posting in a 'Foreign Currency'?

The following are the prerequisites you need to consider before posting in a foreign currency:

- Local currency already defined for the Company Code (in the global parameters)
- Foreign currency defined in the currency code Table
- Exchange rate defined for the foreign currency and the local currency
- Translation Ratio maintained for the local and foreign currency

127. How are 'Exchange Rates' maintained in SAP?

An '**Exchange Rate**' is defined for each pair of currencies, and for each 'exchange rate type' defined in the system. The exchange rate is defined at the document header level.

128. What is an 'Exchange Rate Type'? List some of them.

The '**Exchange Rate Type**' is defined according to various purposes such as valuation, translation, planning, conversion, etc. The commonly used exchange rate types include:

B	Standard translation at bk.selling rate
G	Standard translation at bank buying rate
I	Intrastat exchange rate type
INT	Internal clearing exchange rate
M	Standard translation at average rate
P	Standard translation for cost planning

Figure 26: Exchange Rate Types

129. What is known as the 'Translation Factor'?

The relation between a pair of currencies per 'exchange rate type' is known as the '**Translation Factor**.' For example, the translation factor is 1 when you define the exchange rate for the currencies USD and INR:

$$\frac{USD}{INR} = \frac{1}{1}$$

130.   Is there an easy way to maintain Exchange Rates in SAP?

SAP offers a variety of tools to maintain exchange rates on an on-going basis. The tools include:

- Exchange Rate Spreads
- Base Currency
- Inversion

Use the SAP supplied program, **RFTBFF00**, for populating the exchange rate table automatically from an input file in a multi-cash format from a commercially available input file.

131.   What is known as an 'Exchange Rate Spread'?

The difference between the 'bank-buying rate' and the 'bank selling rate' is known as the **'Exchange Rate Spread,'** which remains almost constant. When you maintain the exchange rate spread, it is sufficient if you maintain the **'average rate'** for that currency in question in the system as you will be able to deduce the buying/selling rate by adding/subtracting the spread to/from the average rate.

132.   Explain the use of 'Direct' or 'Indirect Quotations.'

It is possible to maintain the exchange rates, in SAP, by either of these two methods. What determines the use of a particular type of quotation is the business transaction or the market standard (of that country).

SAP adopts two prefixes to differentiate direct and indirect quotes during entering/displaying a transaction:

- ''– Blank, no prefix. Used in Direct Quotation
- '/' – Used in Indirect Quotation

When there is no prefix entered, (blank), the quotation is construed as the 'direct quote' by the system. Possible scenarios include:

- The company in question is mainly using the **'Indirect Quotation.'**

  Use "(blank) as the prefix for default notation for indirect quotation. Use '*' as the prefix for the rarely used direct quotation. If someone tries entering a transaction using direct quotation, but without the '*' in the exchange rate input field, the system will issue a warning.

- The company in question is mainly using the **'Direct Quotation.'**

  You do not need any specific settings as the default is the "(blank) prefix for the direct quotation, and '/' for the indirect quotation. So, unless you make a transaction entry with '/' prefix, the system takes all the entries as that of direct quotation.

- There could be instances where you are required to configure in such a way that a prefix is mandatory irrespective of the type of quotation. In this case, define the direct quotation prefix as '*', and the indirect one as the system default '/' prefix. This necessitates a prefix each of the entries either by '*' or '/.' Otherwise, the user will get a warning to correct the entry.

133. Explain how 'Taxes' are handled in SAP.

SAP takes care of tax calculation, tax postings, tax adjustments, and tax reporting through the three FI components; namely GL, AP, and AR. The processing of the following kinds of taxes is possible:

1. Tax on Sales and Purchases
   (a) Input Taxes (Purchase Tax)
   (b) Output Taxes (Sales Tax)
2. Additional Taxes (these are country specific and in addition to the tax on sales and purchases)
3. Sales Tax
4. Withholding Tax
   (a) Classic Withholding Tax
   (b) Extended Withholding Tax

SAP allows taxation at three levels:

1. National level or federal level (Europe, South Africa, Australia, etc.)
2. Regional or jurisdiction level (USA)
3. National and Regional level (India, Canada, Brazil etc.)

134. How is Tax calculated in SAP?

SAP uses a technique called '**Condition Method**' to calculate taxes (except Withholding Tax) in the system. The system makes use of '**Tax (Calculation) Procedures**' defined in the system together with the **Tax Codes** for calculating the quantity of tax.

1. The **Tax Code** is the starting point in the tax calculation. The tax code is country specific, with every country having a country specific Tax Procedure defined in the standard system, which is used as the template for defining various tax codes. The system uses the tax code to verify the following:

Condit. type	AP1E A/P Sales Tax 1 Exp.	Access seq.	MWST Tax Classificati
			Records for a

Control data 1

Cond. class	D Taxes		Plus/minus
Calculat.type	A Percentage		
Cond.category	D Tax		
Rounding rule	Commercial		
StrucCond.			

Group condition

☐ Group cond.	GrpCond.routine
☐ RoundDiffComp	

Changes which can be made

Manual entries	No limitations		
☐ Header condit.		☑ Amount/percent	☐ Qty relation
☑ Item condition	☐ Delete	☑ Value	

Master data

valid from	Today's date	PricingProc	
Valid to	31.12.9999	delete fr. DB	Do not delete (set the
RefConType		☐ Condition index	
RefApplicatio			

Figure 27: Condition Type (Tax Processing)

   (a) Tax type
   (b) Amount of tax calculated/entered
   (c) GL account for tax posting
   (d) Calculation of additional tax portion, if any

2. **Tax Rates** are defined for each of the tax codes. The tax rates are then associated with **Tax Types**, which are included in the tax procedures. (Because of this relationship, it is technically possible that a single tax code can have multiple tax rates for various tax types.)

3. The tax code is assigned to a **Tax Procedure**, which is tagged to a GL master record. A particular tax procedure is accessed whenever that GL account is used in document processing.

Step	Cou	CTyp	Description	Fro	To	Man	Re	Stat	P	SuTo
100	0	BASB	⊙se Amount			☐	☐	☐		
110	0	MWAS	Output Tax	100		☐	☐	☐		
120	0	MWVS	Input Tax	100		☐	☐	☐		
130	0	MWVN	Non-deduct.Input Tax	100		☐	☐	☐		
140	0	MWVZ	Non-deduct.Input Tax	100		☐	☐	☐		
150	0	MWAL	Sumptuary Tax	100		☐	☐	☐		
160	0	MWAA	Clearing Tax	110		☐	☐	☐		
170	0	NLXA	Acqu.Tax Outgoing	100		☐	☐	☐		
180	0	NLXV	Acquisition Tax Deb.	100		☐	☐	☐		
190	0	NLXN	Non-deduct.Input Tax	170		☐	☐	☐		
200	0	NLNA	Non-deduct.Input Tax	170		☐	☐	☐		

Figure 28: Steps in Tax processing

A Tax Procedure contains the following:

- **Steps** - To determine the sequence of lines within the procedure.
- **Condition Types** - Indicates how the tax calculation model will work (whether the records are for fixed amount or percentages and whether the records can be processed automatically, etc.)
- **Reference Steps** - Where the system obtains the amount/value it uses in its calculation (for example, the base amount)
- **Account/Process Keys** - Provide the link between the tax procedure and the GL accounts to which tax data is posted. This helps in automatic tax account assignments. To enable that these keys have the necessary information for automatic assignment, you need to define the following:
  - **Posting keys** (unless you have a specific requirement, it will be sufficient to use the GL posting keys: Debit: 40, Credit: 50)
  - **Rules** to determine on which fields the account determination is to be based (such as the tax code or country key)
  - **Tax accounts** to which the postings need to be made

SAP comes with a number of predefined account/process keys, and it is recommended that the standard keys be used.

4. The **Access Sequence** helps in identifying the sequence of Condition Tables to be used and identifying which field contents are the 'criteria' for reading the **Condition Tables** (a group of Condition Types).

5. The tax amount so calculated is normally posted to the same side as the GL posting that contains the tax code. When exchange rate differences occur (due to tax adjustments in foreign currencies) these differences are generally posted to the specific account(s) for exchange rate differences.

However, it is possible to specify (per Company Code) that the exchange rates for tax items can also be entered manually or determined by the posting or the document date, and the resulting differences posted to a special account.

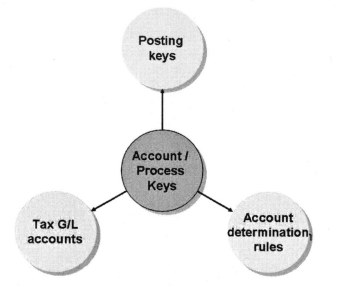

Figure 29: Account/Process Key for tax processing

6. R/3 has a number of predefined account keys, and it is recommended that the standard keys be used.

135. Explain the Configurations required for Taxes in SAP.

You need to define the following to customize SAP for this purpose:

1. **Base Amount for Tax Calculation**

   For each Company Code you need to define whether the **Base Amount** includes the cash discount as well. If the base amount includes the discount, then the tax base is called '**Gross**,' otherwise, it is '**Net**.' You may also define a similar base amount for calculating the '**Cash Discount**.' This also has to be maintained for each of the Company Codes.

2. **Tax Codes**

   The **Tax Code** is a 2-digit code specifying the percentage of tax to be calculated on the base amount. While defining the tax code, you will also specify the '**Tax Type**' to classify a tax code relating to either '**Input Tax**' or

'**Output Tax**.' The tax types are country specific and determine how a tax is calculated and posted.

3. **Tax Rate**

The **Tax Rate** is the percentage of tax to be calculated on a base amount. You will be able to define tax rates for one or more tax types when you define a single tax code.

4. **Check Indicators**

By using the check indicators, you configure the system to issue **Error/Warning Messages** when the tax amount entered manually is incorrect.

136. What is a (Tax) 'Jurisdiction Code'?

A '**Jurisdiction Code**,' used in countries such as the United States, is a combination of the codes defined by tax authorities. It is possible to define up to four tax levels below the federal level. The four levels can be the:

- Sub-city level
- City level
- Country level
- State level

Before you can use the jurisdiction codes for tax calculation, you need to define the following:

1. Access Sequence (to include the country/tax code/jurisdiction fields)
2. Condition Types (which references the access sequence as defined above)
3. Jurisdiction Codes

The tax rates are defined in the tax code by jurisdiction. When posting taxes with a jurisdiction code, note that the taxes may be entered per jurisdiction code or per tax level.

137. Tell me about the 'Tax Reports' in SAP.

SAP comes delivered with country-specific default '**Tax Reports**' to meet your tax-reporting requirements. However, it is not uncommon to use third-party software for the same purpose. As a process, it is recommended that the 'closing operations' are completed before running the tax reports. This will ensure that the system makes relevant adjustment entries (between payables and receivables, exchange rate differences, etc.) so that the correct tax amounts are reported.

138.   How is 'Master Data' different from 'Transaction Data'?

There are three kinds of data residing in any SAP system:

1. Table Data
2. Transaction Data
3. Master Data

Table Data refers to the customized information for a particular Client. This includes data such as payment terms, discounts, pricing, tolerance limits, etc., which you do not normally change on a day-to-day basis.

Transaction Data is the day-to-day recording of business information such as purchase orders, sales returns, invoices, payments, collections, etc. This includes both system-generated data (tax, discount, etc., automatically calculated by the system during document posting) as well as user-generated data.

Master Data is the control information required to decide how transaction data gets posted into various accounts (such as customers, vendors, GL, etc.). The master data is usually shared across modules (for example, customer master records are common both to FI and SD in SAP) obviating the need for defining it in various application areas. The master data remains in the system for fairly a long period.

In the case of GL Master Records, the data is created in two areas:

1. **Chart of Accounts Area** (common to all Company Codes: Chart of accounts, GL account number, account name (short and long text), B/S or P&L indicator, account group, etc.).

2. **Company Code Area** (specific to that particular Company Code: Company Code, tax code, currency, open item management, line item display, sort key, etc.).

In the case of the **Customer/Vendor Master Record**, the data is created in two areas:

1. **Client Specific** (general data such as account number, name, telephone, bank information, etc., which is common to all the Company Codes using this master).

2. **Company Code Specific** (valid only for the Company Code, this includes: terms of payment, dunning procedure, reconciliation account, sort key, sales area, purchasing information, etc.).

139.   Can you post an a/c document if the 'Credit' is not equal to the 'Debit'?

In general, unless the 'debits' equal the 'credits' in a document, you will not be able to post the document. However, the system allows you to post some of the documents, even if this not true, which includes the following:

■ **Noted items:** this will contain only a debit or credit. Since there is no updating of accounting entries, the system will allow you to go ahead with the posting of these items.

GENERAL LEDGER ACCOUNTING

140.   What is a 'Document' in SAP?

SAP is based on the **'document principle'** meaning that a document is created out of every business transaction in the system. The **Document** is the result of a posting in accounting in SAP, and is the connecting link between various business operations. There are two types of documents:

1. **Original Documents:** these documents relate to the origin of business transactions such as invoices, receipts, statement of accounts from bank, etc.

2. **Processing Documents:** These include **'accounting documents'** generated from postings in the system, **'reference documents,' 'sample documents,'** etc. The processing documents other than the accounting ones are also known as **'special documents'** and they aid in the simplification of document entry in the system.

Every document consists of:

■ A Document Header

■ Two or more Line Items

Before attempting to enter a document, call up the relevant document entry function as the system provides a variety of ready-made document entry templates suited to different transactions such as regular GL entry, customer invoice posting, etc. The details entered in a document can be simulated and displayed before the document is actually posted in the system. You may also choose to 'park' the document and post it later.

141.   What is a 'Document Header'?

The **'Document Header'** contains information that is valid for the whole document such as:

■ Document Date

■ Document Type (Control Information)

■ Document Number

■ Posting Date

- Posting Period
- Company Code

Besides the above, the document header also has information (editable, later on) such as (*a*) trading partner, (*b*) document header text, (*c*) reference, (*d*) cross-Company Code number, etc.

142. What is a 'Document Type'?

SAP comes delivered with a number of '**Document Types**,' which are used in various postings. The document type helps to classify an accounting transaction within the system, and is used to control the entire transaction and determine the account types a particular document type can post to. For example, the document type '**AB**' allows you to post to all the accounts, whereas type 'DZ' allows you to post only the customer payments. Every document type is assigned a number range.

The common document types include:

Doc. Type	Description	Doc. Type	Description
AA	Asset posting	KG	Vendor credit memo
AB	Accounting document	KN	Net vendors
AF	Depreciation postings	KR	Vendor invoice
DG	Customer credit memo	KZ	Vendor payment
DR	Customer invoice	KG	Vendor credit memo
DZ	Customer payment	SA	GL account document
X1	Recurring entry doc.	X2	Sample document

Transaction Code
OBA7 (Define)
OBAB (Change)

143. How is 'Account Type' connected to 'Document Type'?

The '**Document Type**' is characterized by a 2-character code such as AA, DG, etc., whereas an '**Account Type**' is denoted by a 1-character code such as A, D, etc., specifying which accounts a particular document can be posted to. The common account types include:

- **A**   Assets

- **D**   Customer (Debtor)
- **K**   Vendor (Creditor)
- **M**   Materials
- **S**   GL

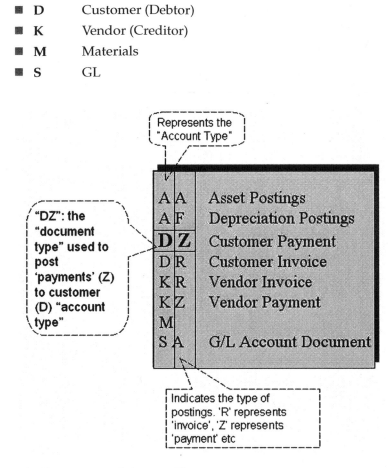

Figure 30: Document and Account Types

144. What do you mean by 'Net' Postings?

Usually, when a transaction is posted, for example, a vendor invoice (document type: KR), the system posts the 'Gross' amount with the 'tax' and 'discount' included. However, SAP provides you the option of posting these items as 'Net.' In this case, the posting excludes 'tax' or 'discounts.' Remember to use the special document type **KN**. (Similarly, you will use the document type **DN** for 'customer invoice–Net' compared to the normal invoice postings for the customer using the document type **DR**.) For using this 'net method' of posting you should have activated the required settings in the customization.

145. Explain the various 'Reference Methods.'

SAP recommends '**Reference Methods**' as a 'document entry tool' to facilitate faster and easier document entry into the system, when you are required to enter the same data time and again. Besides making the document entry process less time-consuming, this also helps in error-free document entry.

The various Reference Methods used in SAP include:

1. Reference Documents
2. Account Assignment Models
3. Sample Documents

146. What is the 'Document Change Rule'?

The functionality '**Document Change Rules**' configured in the system maintains the information relating to 'what fields can be changed?' and 'under what circumstances?.' As you are already aware, SAP's **document principle** does not allow changing the 'relevant' fields once a document is posted; any changes can only be achieved through 'Reversal' or additional postings. Fields such as company code, business area, account number, posting key, amount, currency, etc., can never be changed once the document is posted. However, SAP allows changing some of the fields in the line items such as payment method, payment block, house bank, dunning level, dunning block, etc. These can be changed document by document or by using '**mass change**' for a number of documents in a single step.

The changes to 'master data' are tracked and stored per user for an 'audit trail.'

147. Differentiate between 'Account Assignment Model,' 'Recurring Entries,' and 'Sample Document.'

'**Account Assignment Model**' is a 'reference method' used in document entry when the same distribution of amounts to several Company Codes, cost centers, accounts, etc., is frequently used. Instead of manually distributing the amount among accounts or Company Codes, you may use **equivalence numbers** for distributing both the credit and debit amounts. A cross-Company Code account assignment model can also be created.

The account assignment model may contain any number of GL accounts. The GL account items need not be complete. The model can be used across several Company Codes, and can even include Company Codes from non-SAP systems.

PK	CoCd	G/L acct	Tx	Jurisdictn code	BA	Cost ctr	Amount	Equiv
40	1000	416100	V0		9900	1000	1,000.00	20
40	1000	416100	V0		9900	2100	1,500.00	30
40	1000	416100	V0		9900	2100	2,500.00	50
50	1000	113105			9900		5,000.00	100

Acct assgnmt model UTILITY22
Utility Payments model — Company code 1000
Currency EUR
Debit distribution 5,000.00 — Credit distribution 5,000.00

Account assignment model items

Figure 31: Account Assignment Model

- You can use the account assignment model while 'parking' a document (but you cannot use a 'reference document' for 'parking').

- The use of account assignment models is limited to GL accounts.

Unlike a '**Sample Document**,' an account assignment model may be incomplete and can be completed during document entry by adding or deleting or changing the data already saved in the model.

Transaction Code
FKMT

The '**Recurring Entry**' original document is used by the system as a 'reference document' for enabling posting of periodically recurring postings such as loan repayments, insurance premium payments, rent, etc. Since this document is not an accounting document, the account balances are not affected. In a recurring entry original document, you will not be able to change the (a) posting key, (b) account, and (c) amount. The **recurring entry documents** are defined with a special number range (**X1**). Unlike an account assignment model, these documents cannot be used for cross-Company Code postings.

The **recurring entry document** does not update transaction figures, per se, but acts only as a reference and as the basis for creating accounting documents. The SAP program **SAPF120** creates the accounting documents from the recurring entry original document. There are two ways to set the exact date when this document should be posted to:

- **Posting frequency:** enter the day of the month and the period (in months) between two postings.
- **Scheduled run:** configure the 'run schedule' specifying the calendar days on which the program should post these documents.

A **Sample Document** is like a template, which is created and stored so that the information contained therein can be easily copied into new documents and posted in the system. But once a sample document is created note that you will not be able to change the 'line items' already contained in that document; all you can do is change the amounts in that sample document. But you can overcome this by defining a new sample document that can contain other line items or you may add new line items to the FI document, which is created by copying from the original sample document.

Sample documents have separate number ranges (**X2**).

148. What is a 'Line Item'?

The '**Line Items**' contain information relating to account number, amount, debit/ credit, tax code, amount, etc. SAP allows a maximum of 999 line items in a single document. Besides the one entered by you during an document entry, the system may also create its own line items called '**system generated line items**,' such as tax deductions, etc. Irrespective of the number of line items entered, ensure that the total of these is always zero (that is, total debits should equal total credits). Otherwise, the system will not allow you to post the document.

149. What is a 'Posting Key'?

A '**Posting Key**' in SAP is a 2-digit alphanumeric key that controls the entry of line items. SAP comes with many posting keys for meeting the different business transaction requirements: **40** (GL debit), **50** (GL credit), **01** (customer invoice), **11** (customer credit memo), **21** (vendor credit memo), **31** (vendor payment), etc.

The posting key determines:

1. What account can be posted to
2. Which side of the account (debit or credit) to be posted to, and
3. What 'layout' screen needs to be used for that particular transaction.

Transaction Code
OB41

It is a normal practice not to change any of the default posting keys in the system, as you would very rarely require additional posting keys.

150.   Differentiate between the 'Parking' and the 'Holding' of documents.

The **'Parking of a Document'** in SAP is one of the two **preliminary postings** (the other being the 'Holding' of documents) in the system and refers to the storing of incomplete documents in the system. These documents can later be called on for completion and posting. While 'parking' a document, the system does not carry out the mandatory 'validity checking.' The system does not also carry out any automatic postings (such as creating tax line items) or 'balance checks.' As a result, the transaction figures (account balances) are not updated. This is true in the case of all financial transactions except in the area of **TR-CM (Cash management)** where 'parked' documents will update the transactions.

The parking of documents can be used to 'park' data relating to customers, vendors, or assets (acquisition only). When a cross-Company Code document is 'parked,' only one document is created in the initial Company Code; when this 'parked' document is posted all other documents relevant for all other Company Codes will also be created. However, it is to be noted that **substitution** functionality cannot be used with document 'parking,' as substitution is activated only on transaction processing.

The added advantage is that a document 'parked' by an accounting clerk can be called on for completion by someone else. The 'parked' documents can be displayed individually or as a list from where the required document can be selected for completion and posting. The number of the 'parked' document is transferred to the posted document. The original 'parked' document, if necessary, can be displayed even after it has been posted to.

During a transaction when you do not have a piece of required information, you can **'Hold the Document'** and complete it later. As in the case of 'parked' documents, here also the document does not update the transaction figures.

The essential difference between these two types of preliminary postings can be summarized as follows:

Attribute	'Park' document	'Hold' document
View the document in 'Account Display'?	Yes	No
Changes to the document?	Any user can access, view, and/change the document	No other user, except the creator, will be able to access, view, and/change the document

Document number?	System assigned	Manually entered by the user
Use of data in the document for evaluation purposes?	Possible	Not possible

151.   What is an 'Automatic Posting'?

When you post documents in SAP, there are instances where the system also adds some more line items (such as tax, cash discount, gain/loss from foreign exchange transactions, etc.) besides the ones you have entered in the document. This helps to reduce your work as the system calculates these automatically. However, you need to define accounts you want the system to automatically post to; this will ensure that no manual posting is allowed to any of these accounts.

152.   What is 'Clearing'?

'**Clearing**' in SAP refers to squaring-off open debit entries with that of open credit entries. Clearing is allowed in GL accounts maintained on an 'open item' basis and in all customer/vendor accounts. The clearing can either be manual or automatic. In the case of **manual clearing**, you will view the open items and select the matching items for clearing. In the case of **automatic clearing**, a program determines what items need to be cleared based on certain pre-determined open item selection criteria and proposes assignments before clearing these assigned items. Whatever the type of clearing, the system creates a **clearing document** with the details and enters the 'clearing number' against each of the cleared open items. The **clearing number** is derived from the document number of the clearing document.

You will also be able to do a '**partial clearing**' when you are unable to match open items exactly; in this case, the balance amount not cleared is posted as a new open item. You may also configure **clearing tolerance** and also define rules on how to tackle the situation where the net amount after clearing is not zero (such as, writing off, posting the difference to a separate 'clearing difference' account, etc.).

In the case of customers who are also vendors, you will be able to clear between these two provided it is duly configured in the relevant master data (by entering the customer number in the vendor master record and the vendor number in the customer master record).

153.   Explain 'Reversal of Documents' in SAP.

If you need to change some of the accounting information relating to an already posted document, you can only achieve this by '**Reversing**' the original document and posting a new one with the correct information. However, reversal is possible only when:

- The origin of the document is in FI (not through SD or MM, etc.)
- The information such as business area, cost center, etc., is still valid (that you have not deleted these business objects)
- The original document has no cleared items
- The document relates only to the line items of customer/vendor/GL

While reversing, the system automatically selects the appropriate document type for the reversal, and defaults the relevant posting keys. (Remember that the document type for the **reversal document** would have already been configured when the document type was defined in the configuration.) Also note that if you do not specify the posting date for the reversal document, the system defaults to the posting date of the original document.

154.   Explain 'True Reversal.' How is it different from regular 'Reversal'?

As you are aware, any reversal results in opposite postings to the credit/debit sides of the original posting, leading to an increase in the account balances and the 'trial balance' is automatically inflated on both the sides. This is against the law in some countries such as France where it is required that even after reversal, there should not be an increased account balance. As a result, SAP came out with '**True Reversal**' which overcomes this problem by '**negative postings**' to the same line item(s) during reversal. The account balance, which was originally increased, is restored to the actual balance during the reversal:

Type of Reversal	Type of Posting	Account 100000		Account 200000	
		Debit	Credit	Debit	Credit
Traditional Reversal	Original Posting	$2500			$2500
	Reversal		$2500	$2500	
'True' Reversal	Original Posting	$2500			$2500
	Reversal	-$2500			-$2500

155.   What is 'Fast Entry'?

Instead of the regular document entry screens, SAP provides **'Fast Entry'** screens for facilitating a quick way of entering repetitive line items in a transaction. For achieving this, you need to define a **Fast Entry Screen Layout**, which will specify what fields you will require for data entry, and in what order. You may configure these fast entry screen layouts for GL account line items, credit memos, and customer/vendor invoices. Each of these fast entry screen layouts will be denoted by a 5-character screen variant in the system. Fast entry screens are used in **complex (general) postings**.

SAP's **enjoy postings** are also meant for similar data entry screens, but the difference is that in the case of 'fast entry' you will start from scratch when identifying the fields, positioning them in the line item, etc., whereas in enjoy postings, the system comes with all the fields activated and you will select the fields that you do not want to be made available for data entry.

156.   How do you create 'GL Account Master Data'?

'GL Account Master Data' can be created using any one of the following methods:

1. Manually
2. Creating with reference
3. Through Data Transfer Workbench
4. Copying from existing GL accounts

The **Manual Creation** of GL account master records is both laborious and time consuming. You will resort to this only when you can't create master records using any of the other methods listed above.

You will follow the second method, **Creating With Reference**, when you are already in SAP and have an existing Company Code (Reference Company Code) from which you can copy these records to a new Company Code (Target Company Code). You will be able to do this by accessing the Menu: 'General Ledger Accounting > GL Accounts > Master Data > GL Account Creation > Create GL Accounts with Reference.' While doing this, you can copy the **'account assignments'** as well ensuring that the integration of GL with other applications is intact. SAP facilitates so that you can (i) limit the number of GL records thus copied to the target Company Code, (ii) create new records if necessary, and (iii) change the account number/name.

When your GL accounts are in a non-SAP system and you feel that these accounts will meet your requirements you will then use the **'Data Transfer Workbench'** of SAP to transfer these records into SAP, and change them to suit the

SAP environment. Since this will not have 'Account Assignment' logic as defined in SAP, you need to be careful when defining these assignments.

You will resort to the last option of **Copying from Existing GL Accounts** only when you feel that there is a Chart of Accounts in the system that meets your requirements 100%. Otherwise, follow the second method described above.

157.   What is 'Collective Processing' of GL accounts?

'**Collective Processing**' helps you to make systematic changes to a number of GL accounts in a single step. For example, you have used the '**creating with reference**' method to create GL accounts in a new Company Code and you want to change the account names as well as the 'GL account type' (P&L or B/S). Then you will use the **mass processing method**. You can make changes to:

1. Chart of accounts data
2. Company Code data

Use Menu Path: 'Accounting > Financial accounting > General ledger accounting >Master records > Collective processing.' This can be achieved in IMG through: 'Financial Accounting > General Ledger Accounting > GL Accounts > Master Data > GL Account Creation > Change GL Accounts Collectively.'

Remember that the 'collective processing' helps only to edit and you cannot use this method if you need to create new master records.

158.   What is 'Individual Processing' of GL accounts?

In contrast to the 'collective processing' of GL accounts where you edit a number of accounts in a single step, **Individual Processing** helps to edit or create GL account master records one at a time. Here you can edit (including display, change, block, unblock, and delete) or create a new GL account in three different ways:

1. **Centrally:** You will be editing or creating a GL account master record in both the Chart of Accounts area and Company Code area in one step. This is also known as '**one-Step**' **GL creation**.

2. **In the Chart of Accounts area:** you first edit or create the record here before doing it in the Company Code area.

3. **In the Company Code area:** you edit or create the record here after it has been done in the Chart of Accounts area.

Put together, steps 2 and 3 relate to the 'step-by-step' creation of GL account master records.

159. Is it possible to change an existing B/S GL a/c to the P&L type?

Technically, you will be able to change all the fields, except the account number, of a GL account in the Chart of Accounts area. However, in this particular instance when you change the 'GL account type' from 'B/S' to 'P&L,' make sure that you again run the 'balance carry-forward' program after saving the changes so that the system corrects the account balances suitably.

160. Why doesn't the system allow you to change the 'Tax Category' in a GL a/c master?

You will be able to change the '**Company Code**' related fields such as tax category, currency, etc., provided that there has not been any posting to these accounts. Pay attention to the following:

1. If you need to denote an existing GL account to later be managed on an 'open item basis' or vice versa, then make sure that the account balance is zero in either case.

2. If you are trying to change an existing 'reconciliation account' (to a regular GL), then make sure that the account has not been posted to.

3. If you are attempting to denote an existing ordinary GL account into a 'reconciliation account,' ensure that the account has a zero balance.

161.   What is an 'Account Group'?

The 'Account Group' (or GL Account Group), a 4-character alphanumeric key, controls how the GL account master records are created in the system. This helps to 'group' GL accounts according to the 'functional areas' to which they must belong. Account group is mandatory for creating a master record. The same account groups can be used by more than one more Company Code if they all use the same Chart of Accounts. Each GL account is assigned to only one account group.

The Account Group determines:

1. The **number interval** that is to be used while creating the master record.
2. The **screen layout** that is to be used while creating the master record in the Company Code area.

While defining the account groups in the system, you also need to define the corresponding field status for each of these groups. Otherwise, you will not be able to see any fields as all these would be hidden by default.

SAP comes delivered with a number of 'account groups' such as:

- **SAKO** (GL accounts general)
- **MAT.** (Materials Management accounts)
- **FIN.** (Liquid Funds accounts)

INT	MA60	AR60/Materials manag.accounts	10000000	10999999
INT	MAT	Materials management accounts		999999999
INT	MAT.	Materials management accounts		999999999
INT	PL	P&L accounts		999999999
INT	PL60	AR60/Income statement accounts	15000000	15999999
INT	RECN	Recon.account ready for input		999999999
INT	SA60	AR60/General G/L accounts	10000000	15999999
INT	SAKO	General G/L accounts		999999999

Figure 32: GL Account Group

Transaction Code
OBD4

In most situations, you will not require additional groups other than the ones already available in the standard system. However, if you need to create a new one, it is easier to copy an existing one and make modifications to it instead of creating one from scratch.

162.   Describe 'Number Range Interval.'

A 'Number Range' refers to a number interval defined in the system so that when documents are posted, the system assigns a number from this range. You will define different number ranges for different document types. Each document in SAP is uniquely identified by the combination of (*a*) document number, (*b*) company code, and (*c*) fiscal year.

The number range for a document type can be defined:

1. Per fiscal year or
2. Until a fiscal year in future.

If defined to last only one fiscal year, then the number range needs to be defined every year. When number ranges are defined every year, the system starts from the first number in the range for that particular year, which helps to prevent reaching the upper limit too fast.

NR Object	Accounting document			
Subobject	0001			

Intervals

No	Year	From number	To number	Current number	Ext
01	1993	0100000000	0199999999	0	☐
01	1999	0100000000	0199999999	100000001	☐
01	2007	0100000000	0199999999	0	☐
01	9999	0100000000	0199999999	100000569	☐
02	1992	0200000000	0299999999		☑
02	1993	0200000000	0299999999		☑
02	1999	0200000000	0299999999		☑
02	2007	0020000000	0029999999	0	☐
02	9999	0200000000	0299999999	0	☐

Figure 33: Document Number Range

If you specify the fiscal year as '9999,' then the document number range is valid forever (well, almost!) and you do not have to do this exercise of maintaining number ranges every fiscal year. But every year the system starts from the last number used up in the previous year and if a small number range is defined for a document type, you could easily run out of the number range fast.

The document numbers can either be:

1. **Internally** assigned by the system or
2. **Externally** input when the same is created.

The number ranges can be defined in such a way that the system generates the number automatically when a document is created. This is known as '**internal number assignment**.' Under this, the system stores the 'last number' used for a document in the 'Current Number' field and will bring up the next number when another document is created.

If '**external numbering**' is used, the user needs to input a document number every time a document is created in the system. Since the user supplies the number every time, the subsequent numbering may not be sequential. Unlike an internal numbering, the system does not store the 'last number' in the 'Current Number' field.

The numbers in a number range can either be **numeric** or **alphanumeric**. If numbers are numeric, the system will prefix the number with the required zeros to make the number length uniform at 10 digits. If you are using alphanumeric numbering, then the number is padded with zeros from the right. If you are following 'year-specific' numbering, it is better not to mix numeric and alphanumeric numbering for a particular document type in various fiscal years.

The system creates a minimum of one document when a transaction is created /completed. SAP recommends 'filing' original documents (under the number of the processing document (the document generated in SAP)). The best practice is to enter the (external) number of the 'original document' in the 'Reference' field of the document created in the SAP system. For easy cross-reference, the SAP document number thus created needs to be noted on the 'original document.'

The following are the activities you need to complete for configuring the number ranges properly in the system:

1. Defining the number ranges
2. Copying the number ranges to Company Code(s)
3. Copying the number ranges to fiscal year(s)

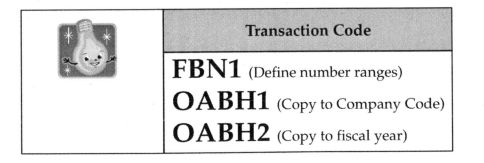

	Transaction Code
	FBN1 (Define number ranges) **OABH1** (Copy to Company Code) **OABH2** (Copy to fiscal year)

163. What is a 'Screen Layout'?

The 'account group' determines which **Screen Layout** should be used while creating a GL account master record. For each of the account groups, you can define different screen layouts, which essentially determine the **Field Status** of a field.

The field status refers to whether the field is:

1. **Suppressed** (field is invisible, hidden from display)
2. **Required** (display on, entry mandatory)
3. **Optional** (display on, entry not mandatory)

	Suppress	Req. Entry	Opt. Entry
Due date	●	○	○
Value date	○	○	●
Payment terms	●	○	○
Cash discount deduction	●	○	○
Own Bank	○	○	●
Bank Business Partners	○	○	●

Figure 34: Field Status

All the above three are shown as 'radio buttons' against each of the fields in the screen layout, and you should select any one to set the status to that field; by default all the fields are 'suppressed.'

There are two levels of controls of field status:

1. Field status at the account group level
2. Field status at the activity (create/change/ display) level (i.e., at the transaction level).

You may also have the field status defined for posting keys (40-debit and 50-credit for the GL account postings). Also remember to define the field status for 'reconciliation accounts' as you will not be able to define any such status in the subledger accounts (for example, customer or vendor).

SAP has built-in rules, called **link rules**, to link these two levels and to decide the final status of a field in the 'screen layout.' The link rules also help to overcome the field-status setting differences arising out of different settings at the Client level (field status for posting keys) and the Company Code level (field status settings at the account group level).

164.   What is a 'Field Status Group'?

The 'field status' of an individual field or a group of fields is marked in a **'Field Status Group,'** which is then assigned to individual GL account master records. You may attach field status groups to a field status variant so that the **'field status groups'** are used in various Company Codes.

	Field status variant	0001	Field status for 0001

	Field status group	Text
	G001	General (with text, allocation)
	G003	Material consumption accounts
	G004	Cost accounts
	G005	Bank accounts (obligatory value date)
	G006	Material accounts

Figure 35: Field Status Variant (FSV)

The Field Status Variant is named similar to the Company Code. For example, if your Company Code is 1000, the field status variant is also named 1000, and it is assigned to the Company Code.

Co...	Company Name	City	Fld stat.var.
BLUE	Blue Fish	New York	1000

Figure 36: Assign a FSV to Company Code

165.   What do you mean by 'Balances in Local Currency' only?

When you create GL account master records, it is necessary to decide whether you want an account to have the transactions updated only in local currency. You will set this indicator accordingly in the 'Company Code area' of the master record. Make sure to set this indicator for **clearing accounts** such as:

- Cash discount clearing accounts
- GR /IR clearing accounts

Note that you need to set this indicator 'on' for all the 'clearing accounts' where you use the local currency to clear the line items in various currencies so that the transactions are posted without posting any exchange rate difference that otherwise might arise.

Example: Consider an invoice for USD 1,000, which on that day translates into an amount of INR 45,000 with an exchange rate of I USD = INR 45. Imagine that when the goods are received, the exchange rate was 1 USD = INR 44.

- If the indicator is set, the system ignores the exchange rate as if the line items have been maintained only in the local currency (INR), and the items are cleared.

- If the indicator is NOT set, the system makes a posting for the 'exchange rate difference' (INR 1, 000) before clearing the two line items.

166. What is 'Line Item Display'?

To display line items of an account, you need to set the indicator '**Line Item Display**' to 'on' in that account's master record. This is mandatory for customer and vendor accounts. The line items can be displayed using the classical display or the SAP List Viewer (ALV). You can also use several '**display variants**' to display various fields when you feel that the Standard Variant is not meeting your requirements.

167. What is 'Archiving'? How does it differ from 'Deletion'?

'**Archiving**' refers to deleting data from the documents in the database and storing the data in a file, which can be transferred to an 'archiving system' later on. Archiving does not physically delete the documents. '**Deletion**' actually removes the documents from the database. To proceed with archiving and deletion you need to:

1. **Block** posting to these archived master records.
2. **Mark** (the master records) **for deletion:** Mark for deletion at the 'Chart of Accounts area' to delete the records from all the Company Codes. However, if you do not want to delete from all the Company Codes, but only from one or more Company Codes then do the same in the 'Company Code area' of the master record(s).
3. **Archive** all the transaction figures from the relevant documents.
4. Call up a special program to '**delete**' the records: The program will check whether that particular document could be deleted. If yes, it will proceed to 'archive' and then to 'deletion.'

168.   Tell me the two uses of 'Blocking' an account.

You may use '**Blocking**' to:
1. Block an account from further postings.
2. Block the creation of the account itself (at the Company Code level or Chart of Accounts area).

169.   How do you configure the GL a/c for the 'House Bank'?

A '**House Bank**' is defined using transaction code **FI12**. A '**bank key**' represents the bank. The house bank can contain several accounts; for each of these accounts you need to maintain a GL account. The bank determination, for an automatic payment program, is configured using the Transaction Code **FBZP**.

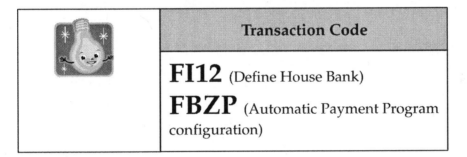

Transaction Code
FI12 (Define House Bank)   **FBZP** (Automatic Payment Program configuration)

170.   What is an 'Intermediate Bank'?

'**Intermediate Banks**' are used in SAP in addition to the house banks and partner banks for making or receiving payments from business partners abroad. The payment processing, involving an intermediate bank, makes use of the '**bank chain**,' which may consist of a house bank, a partner bank, and a maximum of intermediate banks.

171.   Explain 'Intercompany Postings.'

'**Intercompany Postings**' arise when a Company Code, for example, in a centralized procurement, pays for itself and on behalf of other Company Codes. When posted, the transaction results in three documents: (1) one for the paying Company Code (say, 1111) (2) one for the other Company Codes (say, 2222 and 4444), and (3) one for the intercompany transaction itself.

Before making intercompany transactions, you need to configure both 'intercompany payables' and 'intercompany receivables.' For each combination of these Company Codes, you will be required to maintain a 'clearing account,' which must be referenced in each of these Company Codes. You will also be able to configure whether you manually input the transaction number or allow the system to automatically assign the numbers. In the case of system-generated transaction numbers, this 16-digit number consists of (1) a 10-digit document number (1222222222) of the paying Company Code, followed by (2) 4 digits representing this paying Company Code (1111), and (3) 2 digits representing the last two digits of the financial year (07) (for example, 1222222222**1111**07).

172. How can you manually 'clear' 'Open Items'? When?

Under '**Manual Clearing**,' you will select the open items, based on the incoming payment so that the selected 'open items' are 'cleared' (knocked-off). In cases like refunds from a vendor or transactions involving bank sub-accounts and clearing accounts, etc., you will use manual clearing. When cleared, the system flags these line items as 'cleared,' creates a **clearing document**, and enters the clearing document number and clearing date in these open items. Besides the clearing document, the system may also generate 'additional documents' in cases such as **partial** or **residual processing**, and for posting the loss/gain to the assigned GL account.

While doing this, if there is a **payment difference**, it can be treated the way it is configured in the system:

- If the difference is within the tolerance limit, defined in the system using the tolerance groups (defined at the Company Code level), the cash discount is adjusted or the system automatically posts the difference to a gain/loss GL account.

- When the payment difference exceeds the limits of defined tolerance, then the incoming amount may be processed as a partial payment (the original open item is not cleared, but the incoming payment is posted with a reference to that invoice) or the difference is posted as a residual item (the original open item is cleared and a new open item is created by the system for the difference amount) in the system.

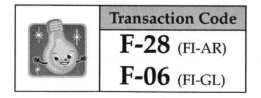

Transaction Code
F-28 (FI-AR)
F-06 (FI-GL)

You may also use the Menu Path: Accounting > Financial Accounting > Account Receivable > Document entry > Incoming payment > Post or Accounting > Financial Accounting > GL > Document entry > Incoming payment > Post

173. How do you perform 'Period Closing' in SAP?

You do a '**(Period) Closing**' in SAP in three steps:

- Completing the Pre-closing activities
- Financial Closing
- Managerial Closing

174. What is 'Pre-closing'?

You need to ensure the following as part of the '**Pre-closing**' activities:

1. Post all the Recurring Entries for expenses and accruals.

2. Ensure that all the interfaced programs have been run so that the required data have been transferred to the system.

3. Post all the depreciation, material receipts, invoices, salaries, etc. In short, ensure that all the transactions for the period in question have been duly recorded and posted into the system.

175. Explain 'Financial Closing.'

'**Financial Closing**' involves completing the following activities and taking out the financial statements for the period concerned:

1. **Revaluate/Regroup:**
   - **Revalue** Balance Sheet items managed in foreign currencies – use the report **RFSBEW00** to valuate GL Balance Sheet Accounts managed in a foreign currency. (The report generates a Batch Input session to post the revenue or expense resulting from any exchange rate differences.)
   - Clear Receivables or Payables with the 'exchange rate difference.'
   - Valuate all the Open Items using the report **SAPF100**. This is used to valuate all the open receivables and payables, using the period-end exchange rates. Here also, the report generates a Batch Input session to post the entries resulting from any exchange rate differences.
   - **Regroup** GR/IR using the program **RFWERE00** to allocate the net balance (depending on whether the balance is a net debit or credit) in the GR/IR

Account to one of two GL Accounts (created to actually depict the net effect of the balance in the GR/IR Account).

2. **Ensure accounting accuracy:**

   Use the program **SAPF190** to compare the totals created by the system in the (1) indexes (customers, vendors, and GL) and documents (customers, vendors, and GL) with that of the (2) account balances (customers, vendors, and GL) to ensure the transaction accuracy.

3. **Run required reports:**

   Generate the **financial statements** (balance sheet and profit & loss account) using the **financial statement versions**. You may also generate the key figure/ratio reports (use the GL account information system).

176. What is a 'Financial Statement Version'?

A '**Financial Statement Version**' helps to define the Financial Statements (both the **Balance Sheet** and **Profit & Loss statements**). When you copy the settings from an existing Company Code to a new one, you will also be copying the financial statement version defined for the 'source' Company Code.

Fin.Stmt.version	Financial Statement Version Name
BAIT	Commercial balance sheet (Italy)
BAJP	Financial statement (Japan)
BAKR	Financial Statement (Korea)
BANK	Bank financial statements
BANL	Commercial balance sheet (Netherlands)
BANO	Commercial balance sheet (Norway)
BAPT	Commercial balance sheet (Portugal)
BAR2	Commercial balance sheet for Russian Fed. (Form 2)
BARU	Commercial balance sheet (Russia)
BASE	Commercial balance sheet for Sweden (BAS90)
BASG	Commercial balance sheet (Singapore)
BATW	Financial Statement Version (Taiwan)
BAUC	Commercial balance sheet (CANA)
BAUS	Commercial balance sheet USA
BAZA	Commercial balance sheet (South Africa)
BICH	Commercial balance sheet (Switzerland)
BSUS	Commercial balance sheet USA

Figure 37: Financial Statement Versions

You may also define a new financial statement version and build the financial statements from scratch. You may create the financial statements both for external reporting (Company Code financial statements) and internal reporting (business area financial statements).

You may also create the balance sheets for a group of Company Codes using FI-SL (Special Purpose Ledgers). The financial statements may be defined to provide information from a period accounting point of view (GL account groups wise) or a cost of sales point of view (functional area financial statements).

All the above statements can be configured and defined to provide different levels of detail:

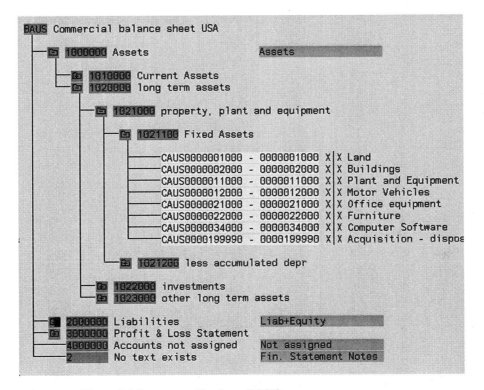

Figure 38: Financial Statement Version - BAUS

A financial statement version can have a maximum of 10 hierarchy levels, with each level assigned with an item (account category). As you go down the hierarchy, you define the account categories in more detail, with the lowest level being represented by the GL accounts. The system displays the relevant amount for each of these items.

177. What items are required in a 'Financial Statement Version'?

Irrespective of the details you require in a 'Financial Statement Version,' it is mandatory that you have, at least, the following items defined:

1. **Assets**
2. **Liabilities**
   (a) Net Result: Profit
   (b) Net Result: Loss
3. **P/L result** (during annual closing, when you run the program **RFBILA00**, the system calculates the profit or loss by subtracting the 'total liabilities' from 'total assets' and updates the relevant Net Result item - Profit or Loss).
4. **Not assigned** (posted amounts but not yet assigned to any of the account groups).

178. How do you ensure 'correct' balances in the 'Financial Statement Version'?

In order to have a balanced statement (Profit & Loss and Balance Sheet) you need to ensure that the accounts are correctly and completely assigned to the nodes of the **Financial Statement Version**. You may do this by resorting to the necessary assignments at the account balance level or node balance level.

At the **account balance level**, you need to ensure that the account is shown in two different nodes, but you will turn "ON" the 'debit indicator' of the account on one node and turn "ON" the 'credit indicator' on the other node. Imagine that you have a bank current account 10001000. When you turn "ON" the debit indicator, this account shows only the debit balances and is construed as the asset. On the other hand, when the credit indicator is turned "ON," the balances on this node now indicate that you owe to the bank (overdraft).

You may also use the **node-level assignment**. In this case, the system uses the 'debit/credit shift' and shows only the 'effective' balance at the node and not at the individual account level.

179. How do you perform 'Annual Closing' in SAP?

'Annual Closing' is like any other 'period closing' and you will be performing all the activities that are required for a period-end-close. In addition to those activities, you will also:

- Carry forward Vendor and Customer accounts
- Carry forward the GL account balances of all the Balance Sheet items

- Close the Profit & Loss Accounts and carry forward the balance (profit or loss) to the retained earnings account(s)

    For a GL account 'carry forward,' use the program **SAPF011**.

180. Explain 'Managerial Closing.'

In '**Managerial Closing**' you will:

- Do a preliminary Controlling period closing
- Settle/re-allocate costs across Controlling organization
- Draw and review internal reports
- Re-open the Controlling period
- Correct and adjust the accounting data, if required
- Reconcile FI and CO by running the FICO Reconciliation Ledger
- Run re-adjustment programs to ensure that the Business Areas and the Profit Centers are balanced
- Draw reports and analyze

181. What is the 'New FI-GL' in FI in ECC?

The traditional or '**Classic FI-GL accounting**' in FI has been focused on providing comprehensive external reporting by recording all business transactions in the system. However, to meet modern-day requirements, this has now been enhanced, called the '**New FI-GL**,' and includes the following:

- **Parallel accounting:** Maintaining several parallel ledgers to meet different accounting principles.
- **Integrated legal and management reporting:** Unlike the traditional GL, the 'New FI-GL' enables you to perform internal management reporting along with legal reporting. So you are in a position to generate Financial Statements for any dimension (for example, profit center) in the business.
- **Segment reporting:** With the introduction of the Segment dimension, SAP now enables you to produce Segment Reports based on **IFRS (International Financial Reporting Standards)** and the **GAPP (Generally Accepted Accounting Principles)** accounting principles.
- **Cost of sales accounting:** It is now possible to perform cost of sales accounting in the 'New FI-GL.'

However, the following functions are not yet supported in the 'New FI-GL':

- Transfer Price

- SKF (Statistical Key Figure)
- Euro Translation
- AIS (Audit Information System)
- Archiving
- Data Retention Tool

The 'New FI-GL' needs to be activated in the system before you start using the IMG Menu Path: > Financial Accounting (New) -> Financial Accounting Global Settings (New)/General Ledger Accounting (New).

In the standard system, the tables from 'classic general ledger accounting' (**GLT0**) are updated as well as the tables in 'New FI-GL' during the activation. This enables you to perform a 'ledger comparison' during the implementation of 'New FI-GL' to ensure that your 'new GL accounting' has the correct settings and is working correctly. To compare ledgers, in Customizing choose Financial Accounting Global Settings (New) -> Tools -> Compare Ledgers.

It is recommended that you 'deactivate' the update of tables for 'classic GL accounting' once you have established that 'New FI-GL' is working correctly. To do this, in Customizing choose Financial Accounting Global Settings (New) -> Tools -> Deactivate 'Update of Classic General Ledger.'

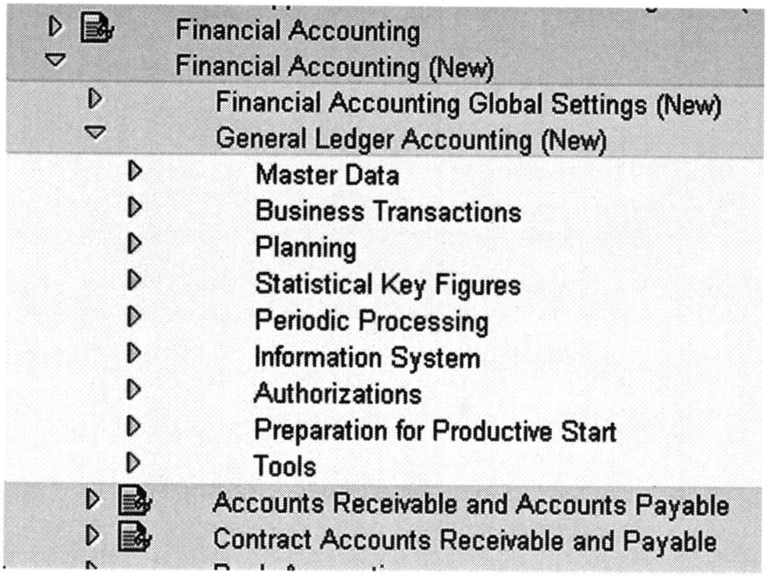

Figure 39: New FI-GL

ACCOUNTS RECEIVABLE

182. Explain 'Customer/Vendor Master Records.'

There are three categories of data maintained in a typical master record for a customer:

- General Data
- Company Code Data
- Sales Area Data (for customers)/Purchasing Organization Data (for vendors)

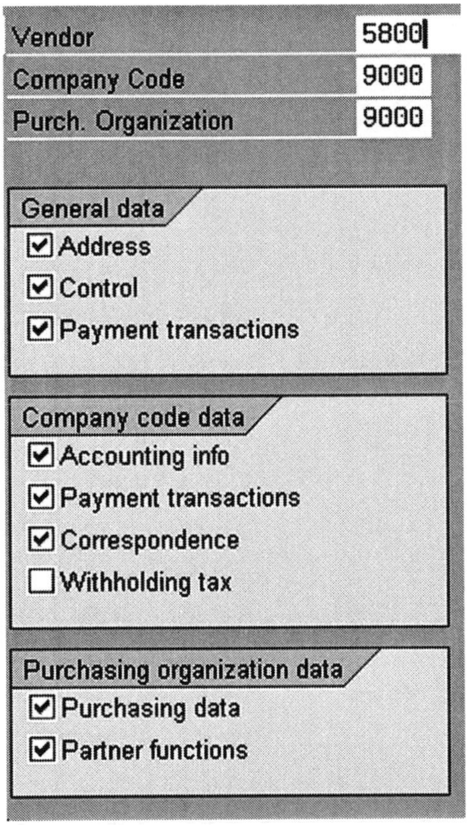

Vendor	5800
Company Code	9000
Purch. Organization	9000

General data
- ☑ Address
- ☑ Control
- ☑ Payment transactions

Company code data
- ☑ Accounting info
- ☑ Payment transactions
- ☑ Correspondence
- ☐ Withholding tax

Purchasing organization data
- ☑ Purchasing data
- ☑ Partner functions

Figure 40: Vendor Master - Various Data

General Data includes general information such as account number, name, telephone, bank information, trading partner, vendor (if the customer is also a vendor), group key, bank key, bank account, alternate payee, etc., which are common to all the Company Codes using this master.

Company Code Data comprises terms of payment, payment methods, tolerance group, clearing with vendor, dunning data (dunning procedure, dunning recipient, dunning block, dunning clerk, etc.), reconciliation account, sort key, sales area (purchasing organization in the case of vendor master), head office, etc. Except for sales (purchasing) related information, all other details are usually maintained for the finance people who can also access the sales data when the master is maintained 'centrally.'

Sales Area Data in the Company Code area of a Customer master record contains the following:

- Order-related data (sales district, sales office, sales group, customer group, etc.)
- Price-related data (pricing group, pricing procedure, etc.)
- Shipping data (shipping strategy, delivery priority, etc.)
- Billing data (payment terms (different from the payment terms maintained at the Company Code level), account assignment group, etc.)

Purchasing Organization Data in the Company Code area of a Vendor master record contains the following:

- Conditions (order currency, payment terms, Incoterms, minimum order value, etc.)
- Sales data (a/c with Vendor)
- Control data (as in the screen shot below)

During creation of a master record, the system checks for 'duplicates' for the same customer which is achieved by the system through the 'Search-Id' (Match Code) configured on the customer's address information.

As in the case of the GL account master record, the creation of the customer/vendor master record is also controlled by the 'Account Group,' which is called **'Customer Account Group/Vendor Account Group'** (CPD/CPDL/KREDI/LIEF) and controls the numbering of customer/vendor master records, field status, whether an account is a regular one or a **'One-Time' account**, etc.

	Transaction Code
	As in the table below:

Activity	In Accounting		Centrally	
	Customer	Vendor	Customer	Vendor
Create	FD01	FK01	XD01	XK01
Change	FD02	FK02	XD02	XK02
Display	FD03	FK03	XD03	XK03
Block/Unblock	FD05	FK05	XD05	XK05
Mark for Deletion	FD06	FK06	XD06	XK06

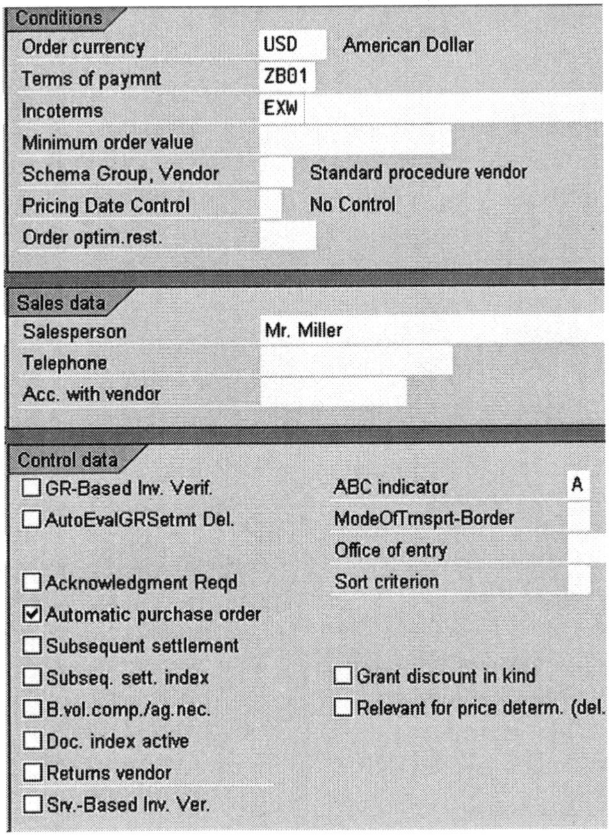

Figure 41: Purchasing Data

183. Who is an 'Alternate Payee'?

A customer who pays on behalf of another customer is known as an '**Alternate Payee**' (or **Alternate Payer**). Though the alternate payee pays on behalf of another, the system maintains all the transaction details in the account of the original customer. Designating 'alternate payee' does not absolve the customer of his/her obligation for payment.

The 'alternate payee' can be maintained in Client-specific data or in the Company Code area. When maintained in the Company Code area you can use that payer only in that Company Code; if defined at the Client level you can use it across all Company Codes.

There are three ways to 'select' the alternate payee when an invoice is processed:

1. The alternate payee (say, 1000) entered in the customer master record is the one selected by the system as the default.

2. When there is more than one alternate payer (say, 1000, 1900, 2100, etc.) defined for a single customer in the master record (you will do this by clicking on the **'allowed payer'** button and create more than one payer), you may select a payer (say, 2100) (other than the default, 1000) while processing the invoice. Now the system will ignore the alternate payer (1000) coming from the master record.

3. If you have put a check mark in the 'individual entries' check box in the 'alternate payer in document' section in the customer master record, then this will allow you to propose a new alternate payer, say, 3000 (other than those already defined in the system). Now, after defining this alternate payer you can use it to process the invoice. In this case, the alternate payer (3000) takes precedence over the payers (1000 and 2100) in step 1 and 2 above.

184. What is the 'Trading Partner' concept?

The **'Trading Partner'** concept is used to settle and reconcile 'inter-company transactions,' both sales and purchases. This is generally achieved by entering the Company-ID (not the Company Code) to which a customer belongs in the 'trading partner' field under the tab 'Account Control' in the customer master record. You can do a similar entry in the vendor master record.

185. Explain 'Tolerance' in transaction processing.

'Tolerances' are defined in the system to facilitate dealing with the differences arising out of accounting transactions and to instruct the system on how to proceed further. Normally, you define tolerances (either in 'absolute terms' or in 'percentages') beyond which the system will not allow you to post a document should there be a difference.

In SAP, tolerances are defined per Company Code and there are several types:

- Employee tolerance
- Customer/vendor tolerance
- GL account clearing tolerance

You will define an 'employee tolerance group' in the system and assign the employees to these groups. While defining the tolerance group you will specify:

1. **Upper limits for various posting procedures**

   - Amount per document
   - Amount per open account item
   - Cash discount, in percentage

2. **Permitted payment differences**

How much over or under payment an employee is allowed to process. This is defined both in absolute values and in percentages.

Group				
Company code	4400	Thailand		Bangkok
Currency	THB			

Upper limits for posting procedures	
Amount per document	฿11.291.881.196,22
Amount per open item account item	5.112.918.811,96
Cash discount per line item	5,000 %

Permitted payment differences	Amount	Percent	Cash discnt adj.to
Revenue	511,29	10,0 %	5,11
Expense	511,29	10,0 %	5,11

Figure 42: FI Tolerance Group for Users

Besides defining the above two, at the Company Code level, you will also define similar tolerances for **customer/vendor tolerance group**. Once defined, each of the customers (vendors) is assigned to one of these groups. Here also, you define the '**permitted payment differences**':

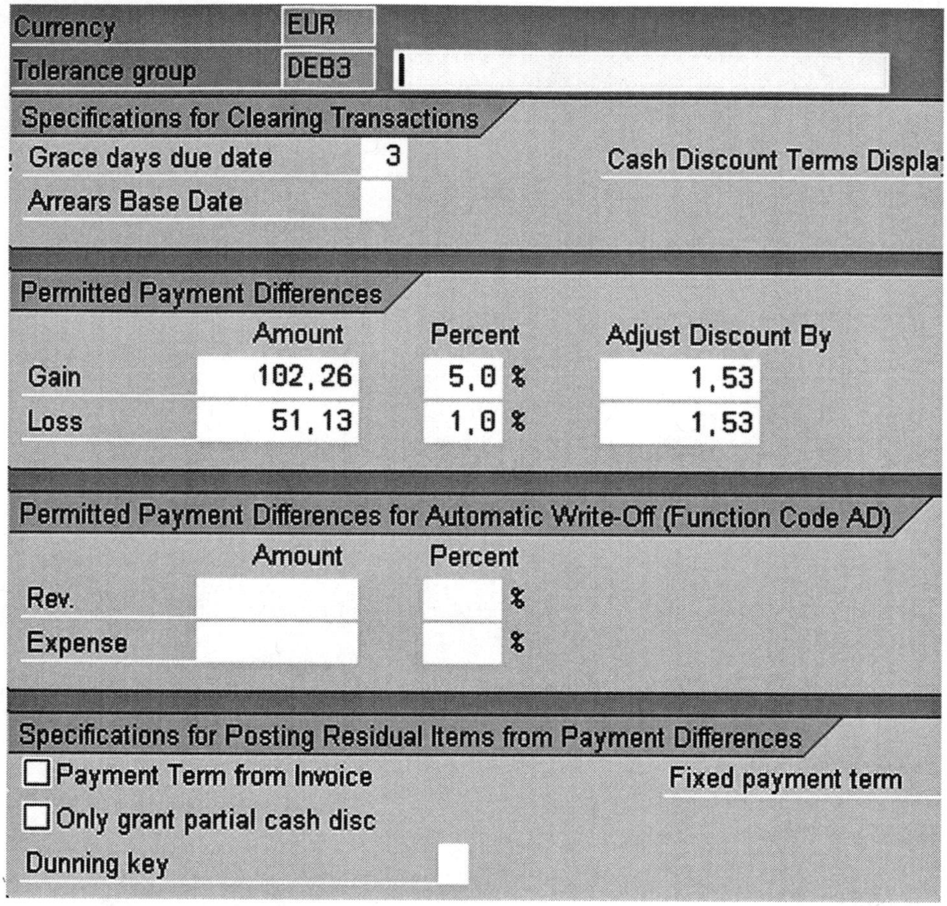

Currency	EUR	
Tolerance group	DEB3	

Specifications for Clearing Transactions

Grace days due date	3		Cash Discount Terms Displa:
Arrears Base Date			

Permitted Payment Differences

	Amount	Percent	Adjust Discount By
Gain	102,26	5,0 %	1,53
Loss	51,13	1,0 %	1,53

Permitted Payment Differences for Automatic Write-Off (Function Code AD)

	Amount	Percent
Rev.		%
Expense		%

Specifications for Posting Residual Items from Payment Differences

☐ Payment Term from Invoice   **Fixed payment term**

☐ Only grant partial cash disc

Dunning key

Figure 43: Customer/Vendor Tolerances

While processing, the system compares the tolerance of an employee against the customer tolerance (or vendor tolerance or the GL) and applies the most restrictive of the two.

186. What is 'Dual Control' in master records?

'**Dual Control**' helps to prevent unauthorized changes to the important and 'sensitive' fields in the master records in the system. (All such sensitive fields are defined in the Table **T055F** when customizing the application. And these fields are defined per Company Code and per Client.) Consider, for example, a sensitive field such as '**payment block**' in a vendor master record. When a user changes this field's content, the system requires another user (usually of higher authority) to approve this change and an **audit trail** is maintained of all such changes. Unless the change is approved, in this example, this particular master is blocked by the system for considering the same in the next '**payment run.**'

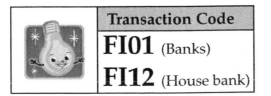

Transaction Code
As in the table below:

Activity	Customer	Vendor
Display changes (accounting area)	FD04	FK04
Display changes (centrally)	XD04	XK04
Confirm changes, individually	FD08	FK08
Confirm changes, in a list	FD09	FK09

187. What is a 'Bank Directory' in SAP?

SAP stores the master data (details such as bank key, bank name, bank country, bank address, and so on) relating to the banks in the '**Bank Directory**' (Table: **BNKA**). Remember, the 'bank masters' are not created in the application but in the implementation side using the IMG. (Of course, you can also create the bank master in the application side in **FI-TR** and not in FI-GL or AP or AR.) However, if you are in the process of creating a master record for a vendor or a customer and you enter some bank details, which the system does not find in the 'Bank Directory,' then the system automatically brings in the relevant screens for you to maintain and update the bank details in the bank directory.

You may create the bank directory in two ways:

1. **Manually** (IMG path: Financial Accounting > Bank Accounting > Bank Accounts > Define 'House Banks')
2. **Automatically** (by importing the bank details using a special program)

Transaction Code
FI01 (Banks)
FI12 (House bank)

188.   What is a 'House Bank'?

A **'House Bank'** is the bank (or financial institution) in which the Company Code in question keeps its money and does the transactions from. A house bank in SAP is identified by a 5-character alphanumeric code. You can have any number of house banks for your Company Code, and the details of all these house banks are available in the **'bank directory.'**

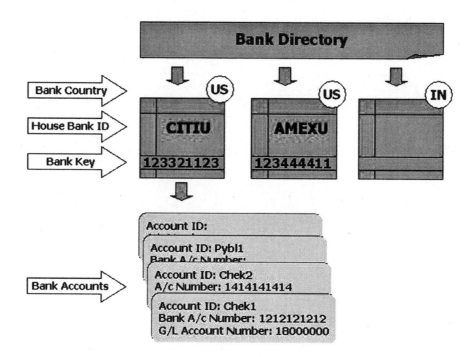

Figure 44: Bank directory

Each 'house bank' in the system is associated with a **country key** (U.S., IN, etc.) representing the country where the bank is located, and a unique country specific code called a 'bank key.' The system makes use of both the 'country key' and the 'bank key' to identify a 'house bank.'

- For each of the 'house banks,' you can maintain more than one bank account; each such account is identified by an **account ID**; i.e., Chek1, Check2, Pybl1, etc. Here, 'Chek1' may denote Checking account 1, 'Pybl1' may denote Payables account 1, and so on. You may name the accounts in a way that it is easily comprehensible. The 'Account ID' is referenced in the customer/vendor master record and it is used in the payment program by the system.

■ For each 'account ID' you will also specify the **bank account number** (maximum length of this identifier is 18 characters). You may name this in such a way that it is also easily comprehensible.

■ For each 'bank account number' so defined in the 'house bank,' you need to create a GL account master record, and while doing so you will incorporate the 'house bank id' and the 'account id' in that particular GL master record.

189.   Explain a 'Sales Cycle' in SAP.

A '**Sales Cycle**' comprises all activities including quotation/inquiry, sales order, delivery, billing, and collection. The following are the various processes within SAP that complete a sales cycle:

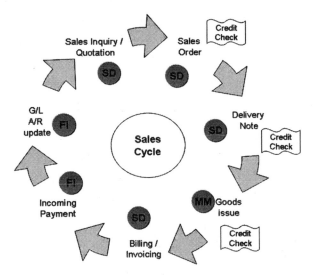

Figure 45: Sales Cycle

Typically, the following are the documents created during a sales cycle:

■ Inquiry

■ Quotation

■ Sales Order

■ Delivery Note

■ Goods Issue

■ Order Invoice

■ Credit/Debit Note

190. Explain 'Automatic Account Assignment' in SD.

During goods issue in the sales cycle, the system is usually configured to update the relevant GL accounts automatically and to create the relevant accounting documents. This customization in IMG is also called **material account assignment** and is achieved through a number of steps as detailed below:

1. Determine 'valuation level' (Company Code or plant).

2. Activate 'valuation grouping code' and link it with the 'chart of accounts' for each 'valuation area.'

3. Link 'valuation class' with 'material type' (FERT, HAWA, HALB, etc.) with the 'account category reference' (combination of valuation classes).

4. Maintain 'account modification codes' for 'movement types.'

5. Link 'account modification codes' with 'process keys' (transaction/event keys).

6. Maintain a GL account for a given combination of 'chart of accounts' + 'valuation grouping code '+'account modification code '+'valuation classes.'

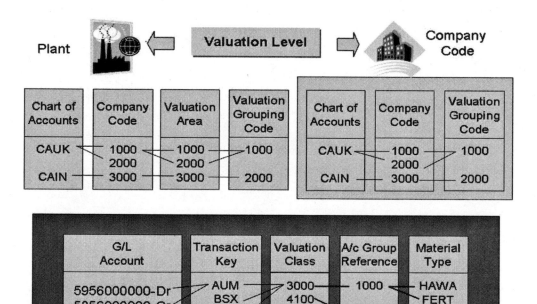

Figure 46: Automatic account determination in a sales cycle

The process of **Automatic Account Determination** is as follows:

1. Depending on the 'plant' entered during goods issue (GI), the 'Company Code' is determined by the system which in turn determines the relevant 'Chart of Accounts.'

2. The plant thus entered in goods issue determines the 'valuation class' and then the 'valuation grouping code.'

3. The 'valuation class' is determined from the 'material master.'

4. Since the 'account modification code' is assigned to a 'process key' which is already linked to a 'movement type,' the 'transaction key' (DIF, GBB, AUM, BSX, etc.) determines the 'GL account' as posting transactions are predefined for each 'movement type' in 'inventory management.'

191. Explain 'Revenue Account Determination' in SD.

The billing documents created during the sales cycle results in automatic postings to GL accounts on the FI side. In general, '**Account Determination**' is based on the following five factors:

1. Chart of accounts

2. Sales organization

3. Account assignment group of the customer

4. Account assignment group of the material

5. Account key

The system determines the '**chart of accounts**' from the company code in the '**billing document**,' and the '**sales organization**' is determined from the corresponding '**sales order**.' The '**account assignment group**' is taken from the respective masters of customer/material. The '**account key**' helps the user to define the various GL accounts, and this key is assigned to the '**condition type**' (KOFI) in the '**pricing procedure**.'

These **GL accounts** are automatically determined when you make the following configuration in the system:

1. Assigning an 'account determination procedure' to a 'billing document type'

2. Assigning this 'account determination procedure' to a 'condition type'

3. Assigning this 'condition type' to an 'access sequence'

4. Configuring the 'condition tables'

Table	Description
001	Customer grp/Material Grp./AccKey
002	Cust. Grp/AccKey
003	Material Grp/Acc Key
004	General
005	Acc Key

Application	Condition Type	Chart of a/c	Sales Org	AcctAsg Grp	Acc Asgmnt	A/c Key	GL a/c
001	Customer grp/Material Grp./AccKey: Details						
V	KOFI	COMP	1000	01	10	ERL	5012100000
V	KOFI	COMP	1000	01	10	ERS	5012100000
V	KOFI	COMP	1000	02	10	ERL	5012200000
V	KOFI	COMP	1000	02	10	ERS	5012200000
V	KOFI	COMP	2000	01	20	ERL	5013100000
V	KOFI	COMP	2000	01	20	ERS	5013100000
V	KOFI	COMP	2000	02	20	ERL	5013200000
V	KOFI	COMP	2000	02	20	ERS	5013200000
005	Acc Key: Details						
V	KOFI	COMP	1000			MWS	2470000000
V	KOFI	COMP	2000			MWS	2470000000

Figure 47: Revenue account determination

192. Outline 'Credit Management' in SAP.

'**Credit Management**' helps to determine credit limits of customers, aids in the creation of '**credit check**' policies, as well as helps companies monitor and evaluate their customers. This is a cross-functional responsibility in SAP, covering both the Sales and Distribution and Financial Accounting modules.

As in the case of any automated process such as dunning, payment, etc., credit management in SAP requires certain prerequisites be defined beforehand:

1. **Customer master data** has been created both in SD and FI.
2. **Credit control area** has been defined and assigned to a Company Code.

SAP makes use of the concept '**credit control area**' for credit management. As explained elsewhere, the credit control area is an organizational element defined to which one or more Company Codes are attached. In the case of customers defined under more than one Company Code, they may fall under different credit control areas. But note that:

- A Client can have more than one credit control area, but the converse is not true: one credit control area cannot be assigned to more than one Client.
- A credit control area can be assigned to more than one Company Code, but the converse is not true: one Company Code cannot be assigned to more than one credit control area.

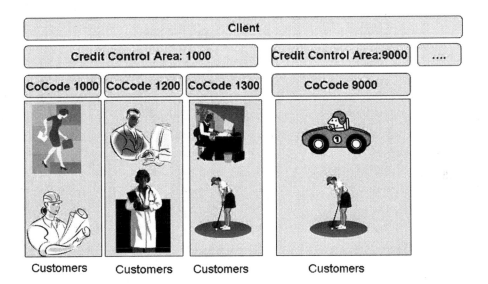

Figure 48: Client – Credit Control Area – Company Code – Customer

While defining the credit limit for a customer:

- You will define a maximum limit per credit control area (Example: Credit Control Area AAAA -> USD 500,000, Credit Control Area BBBB -> USD 200,000)
- You will define a global maximum limit for all credit control areas put together (USD 600,000)

3. **Credit data** (per credit control area 'maximum limit' as well as the 'total' for all areas, in the control data screen) for the customer has been created.

4. **Risk categories** have been defined and assigned to customers.

5. **Credit groups** (document credit group) for document types have been defined. Document credit groups combine order types and delivery types for credit control.

6. Defined, in SD, at what time (when order is received or when a delivery is made, etc.) the **credit check** should happen.

The **credit management process** starts when a sales order is entered in SD. Imagine that this results in exceeding the credit limit defined for the customer. Now:

(a) The system creates three **comparison totals** considering (1) open receivables, (2) sales order values, value of goods to be delivered and the billing document value from SD, and (3) special GL transactions (e.g., 'down payments' and 'bills of exchange').

(b) Based on (a) above the system throws an (1) error message and prevents saving the order or (2) a warning message, and the system does not prevent saving, but the order is 'blocked.'

(c) The **Credit representative**, using **information functions** (SD information system, FI information system, credit overview, credit master list, early warning list, oldest open item, last payment, customer master, account analysis, etc.), processes this blocked order either (1) from the 'blocked SD documents list' or (2) the mailbox, and releases the order, if necessary.

(d) Delivery is created, the billing document is generated and posted, and A/R is updated.

(e) Customer pays the invoice and A/R is posted.

193.   What is a 'Credit Check'?

A '**Credit Check**' is defined for any valid combination of the following:

- Credit control area
- Risk category
- Document credit group

194.   Differentiate 'Static Credit Check' from 'Dynamic Check.'

Under '**Static Credit Check**,' the system calculates the credit exposure of a particular customer as the total of:

- Open order (delivery not yet done)
- Open delivery (value of deliveries yet to be invoiced)
- Open billing documents (not transferred to accounting)
- Open items (AR item not yet settled by the customer)

  Customer's credit exposure is not to exceed the established credit limit.

The '**Dynamic Credit Check**' is split into two parts:

- **Static limit:** Total of open items, open billing, and open delivery values.

- **Dynamic limit** (Open Order Value): The value of all undelivered and partially delivered orders totalled and stored on a time-scale in the future (10 days, 1 week, etc.) known as a '**horizon date**.'

During the 'dynamic credit check,' the system will ignore all orders beyond the 'horizon date.' The sum total of 'static' and 'dynamic' limits should not exceed the credit limit established for the customer.

195.   List the Reports in 'Credit Management.'

SAP provides you with the following **Reports in Credit Management**:

- **RFDKLI10**   Customers with missing Credit Data
- **RFDKLI20**   Re-organization of Credit Limit for Customers
- **RFDKLI30**   Short Overview of Credit Limit
- **RFDKLI40**   Overview of Credit Limit
- **RFDKLI41**   Credit Master Sheet
- **RFDKLI42**   Early Warning List (of Critical Customers)
- **RFDKLI43**   Master Data List
- **RFDKLI50**   Mass change of Credit Limit Data
- **RVKRED06**   Checking Blocked Credit Documents
- **RVKRED08**   Checking Credit Documents which reach the Credit Horizon
- **RVKRED09**   Checking the Credit Documents from Credit View
- **RVKRED77**   Re-organization of SD Credit Data

196.   How does 'Partial Payment' differ from 'Residual Payment'?

When processing the '**incoming payment**' to apply to one or more of the 'open items' of a customer, there may be a situation where the incoming payment is more than the '**tolerances**' allowed. In this case, you can still go ahead and process the payment by resorting either to a Partial Payment or a Residual payment.

A **Partial payment** results in posting a credit to the customer's 'open item,' but leaves the original item intact. As a result, no open item is cleared. During partial payment, the system updates the '**invoice reference**' and '**allocation**' fields.

In contrast to a partial payment, the **Residual payment** clears the particular 'open item' against which the payment is applied. However, since there are not enough amounts to clear the entire open item, the system creates a new open item, which is the difference between the original invoice item and the payment applied. Note that the new invoice/open item created by the system will have the new document date and new baseline date though you can change these dates.

197. What is 'Payment Advice'?

'**Payment Advice**' helps in the automatic searching of 'open items' during the 'clearing' process to find a match for an 'incoming payment.' This is possible because you can use the 'payment advice' number instead of specifying parameters in the '**selection screen**.' A typical payment advice may contain details such as document number, amount, currency, reason for underpayment, etc. The payment advices are of various categories; the first 2 digits of the payment advice number help to differentiate one payment advice from another:

- Bank advice
- EDI advice
- Lockbox advice (created during the clearing process, available in the system whether clearing was successful or not)
- Manual advice
- Advice from a bank statement

Most of the payment advices are deleted as soon as the clearing is successful in the system.

198. Describe 'Lockbox' processing.

'**Lockbox**' processing (configured in the FR-TR module) of incoming payments is used predominantly in the United States. Here, the bank receives the checks from customers as incoming payments, creates payment advice for each of these customer check payments, and informs the payee of the payment, in BAI file format. This lock box file is sent to the payee who imports the details into the system using this electronic file. The system updates the payments into the GL by way of 'batch input' processing.

199. How can 'Reason Codes' help with incoming payment processing?

'**Reason Codes**' configured in the system help to handle the 'payment differences' of individual open items in an invoice (either using payment or advice or in the normal course). To each of the reason codes, you will define the 'posting rules' and the GL accounts in the IMG.

Once done, when there is a payment difference against a particular open item, the system looks for the reason code:

- When the '**charge-off indicator**' has been set for that reason code, then the system posts the payment difference to a GL account. When this indicator is not set, then a new open item is created for the payment difference.

- When '**disputed item indicator**' has been set, then the system ignores these line items when counting for the customer's credit limit.

200.   What is 'Dunning' in SAP?

The SAP System allows you to 'dun' (remind) business partners automatically. The system duns the open items from business partner accounts. The **dunning program** selects the overdue open items, determines the **dunning level** of the account in question, and creates **dunning notices**. It then saves the **dunning data** determined for the items and accounts affected. You can use the dunning program to dun both customers and vendors. It may be necessary to dun a vendor in the case of a debit balance as a result of a credit memo.

   Dunning is administered through a Dunning Program, which uses a **dunning key** (to limit the dunning level per item), a **dunning procedure**, and a **dunning area** (if dunning is not done at the Company Code level).

Dunn.key	Max.level	Print sep	Text
1	1	☐	Triggers maximum dunning level 1
2	2	☐	Triggers maximum dunning level 2
3	3	☐	Triggers maximum dunning level 3
Z		☑	Payment has been made, separate item display

Figure 49: Dunning Key

Transaction Code
F150

201.   What is a 'Dunning Procedure'?

SAP comes equipped with a number or '**Dunning Procedures**,' which you can copy, or you can create your own:

Procedure	Name
0001	Four-level dunning, every two weeks
0002	Four-level dunning, every month
0003	Payment reminder, every two weeks
FVVD	Four-level dunning, every two weeks (loans)
IMMO	Four-level dunning, every two weeks (real estate)

Figure 50: List of Dunning Procedures

A **dunning procedure** controls:

- **Dunning interval**/frequency
- **Grace days**/minimum days in arrear
- Number of **dunning levels** (at least one level)

Dunn.Procedure	0001			
Name	Four-level dunning, every two weeks			
Dunning level	1	2	3	4
Days in arrears/interest				
Days in arrears	2	16	30	44
Calculate interest?	☐	☐	☑	☑
Print parameters				
Always dun?	☐	☐	☐	☑
Print all items	☐	☐	☑	☑
Payment deadline			10	7
Legal dunning procedure				
☐ Always dun in legal dunning proc.				

Figure 51: Dunning Levels

- Transactions to be dunned
- Interest to be calculated on the overdue items

■ Known or negotiated leave, if any, which needs to be considered when selecting the overdue items

■ Company Code data such as (*a*) Is dunning per 'dunning area'? (*b*) Is dunning per 'dunning level'? (*c*) Reference Company Code, (*d*) Dunning Company Code, etc.

■ **Dunning forms**/media to be selected for the **dunning run**

Dunn.Procedure	0001	
Name	Four-level dunning, every two weeks	

General data		
Dunning Interval in Days	14	
No.of dunning levels	4	
Total due items from dunning level		
Min.days in arrears (acct)	6	
Line item grace periods	2	
Interest indicator	01	Standard itm int.cal
Public hol.cal.ID		
☑ Standard transaction dunning		
☑ Dun special G/L transactions		

Reference data		
Ref.Dunning Procedure for Texts	0001	Four-level dunning, every two weeks

Figure 52: Control Information in a Dunning Procedure

202.   What is the 'Dunning Area'?

The '**Dunning Area**' is optional and is required only if dunning is not done at the Company Code level. The Dunning area can correspond to a sales division, sales organization, etc.

203.   Describe the 'Dunning' process.

The '**Dunning Process**' involves three major steps:

1.   Maintaining the **parameters** for the **dunning run**

2.   Creating/editing the **dunning proposal** generated by the system

3. Printing **dunning notices**

1. Maintaining Dunning Parameters

As the first step in dunning, you need to maintain certain parameters, which identify the current dunning run. Entering the date of execution and the dunning run identifier is the starting point, after which you will continue to maintain other parameters such as:

(*i*)   Dunning date to be printed on the notice

(*ii*)   Document posted up to

(*iii*)   Company Code

(*iv*)   Account restrictions (optional)

Now, you can save the parameters and display the log generated (to see if there were any errors), the dunning list (list of accounts and items), and some dunning statistics (blocked accounts/items, etc.).

2. Creating a Dunning Proposal

Once scheduled, the 'dunning program' prepares the 'dunning proposal' as described below:

(*a*)   The Dunning Program determines which accounts to dun:

(*i*)   System checks the fields **'Dunn.procedure'** and **'Last dunned'** in the customer master record to determine whether the arrears date or the date of the last dunning run lies far enough back in the past.

(*ii*)   Checks whether the account is blocked for dunning according to the dunning block field in the customer master record.

(*iii*)   Program processes all open items relating to the accounts thus released in (*ii*) above that were posted to this account on or before the date entered in the field **'Documents posted up to.'**

(*iv*)   Program checks all the open items, as released in (*iii*) above, in an account to decide:

■ Is the item blocked?

■ Is it overdue according to the date of issue, the base date, the payment conditions, and the number of grace days granted?

(*v*)   Program then proceeds to process all open items thus released in (*iv*):

■ How many days the item is overdue

■ Which 'dunning level' for a particular open item

(*vi*)   The program determines the highest 'dunning level' for the account based on (*v*) above. The highest 'dunning level' determined is stored in the master record of the account when you print the letters. This 'dunning level' determines the 'dunning text' and a 'special dunning form,' if defined.

(*vii*) The program then proceeds to check each account:

- Does the customer/vendor have a debit balance with regard to all open overdue items selected?
- Is the total amount to be dunned and the percentage of all open items more than the minimum amount and percentage defined in the 'dunning procedure'?
- Is the 'dunning level' for the account or the overdue items higher than it was for the last 'dunning run'? If not, are there new open items to be dunned (with a previous dunning level of 0)? If not, does the 'dunning procedure' for this level specify that dunning be repeated?

(*b*) The program creates the **dunning proposal list**

(*c*) Edit **dunning proposal list**

(*i*) You can edit the Dunning Proposal to:

- Raise or lower the 'dunning level' of an item
- Block an item from being dunned
- Block an account for the current 'dunning run' or remove the block
- Block an account in the master record for dunning or remove the block
- Block a document for dunning or remove the block

(*ii*) You can view the sample print out to ascertain how the printed notice will look (a maximum of 10 notices can be seen on the screen).

(*iii*) You may also display 'logs' to see the changes made in the editing earlier, as a confirmation of what you wanted to change in the system-generated proposal earlier. If necessary, you can go back and change the proposal.

3. Print Dunning Notices

You can use a 'single form' or 'multiple forms,' which will have different text, based on the 'dunning levels.' There may also be a requirement to use a completely different form for **legal dunning**.' Once the print option is activated, the program prints the notices, and the dunning related information such as 'dunning level,' 'last dunned,' etc., are updated in the customer/vendor masters. SAP provides the option of optically 'archiving' the notices as the system prints the dunning notices. There is also a provision to re-start the printing if it is interrupted before completing the printing.

204.   Can you 'dun' customers across 'Clients' in a single 'Dunning Run'?

No. All the data processing is carried out per Client.

205.   What differentiates one 'Dunning Level' from another?

The '**Dunning Level**' determines the 'dunning text' and (if one is required) a 'special dunning form.' The 'dunning program' determines what 'dunning level' should be used in the 'dunning run.' The dunning level so determined is stored in the master record of the account when the 'dunning letter' is printed. The dunning level may also determine whether there will be some 'dunning charges.'

206.   How many 'Dunning Levels' can be defined?

You may define up to nine dunning levels. If there is only one dunning level, then it is called a '**payment reminder**.'

ACCOUNTS PAYABLES

207.   Explain the 'Account Payables' submodule.

'**Accounts Payables**,' a submodule under Financial Accounting (FI), takes care of vendor-related transactions as the module is tightly integrated with the purchasing transactions arising from the '**Procurement Cycle**.' The module helps in processing outgoing payments either manually or automatically through the '**Automatic Payment Program**.' It also helps in '**Vendor Evaluations**.'

208.   What documents result from 'Procurement Processes'?

In **Materials Management** (MM):
- **PR:** Purchase Requisition (manual or automatic using MRP)
- **PO:** Purchase Order

In **Financial Accounting** (FI):
- Invoice Verification
- Vendor Payment (manual or automatic)

Both MM and FI areas:
- Goods Receipt

You may also group these documents into (1) Order documents, (2) GR (Goods Receipt) documents, and (3) IR (Invoice Receipt) documents. While GR/IR documents can be displayed both in MM and FI views, the order documents can only be viewed in MM view.

209.   Describe a 'Purchase Cycle.'

A **'Purchase Cycle or Procurement Cycle'** encompasses all activities including purchase requisition, purchase order, goods movement, goods receipt, invoicing, invoice verification, payment to vendors, and ends with the updating of vendor account balances.

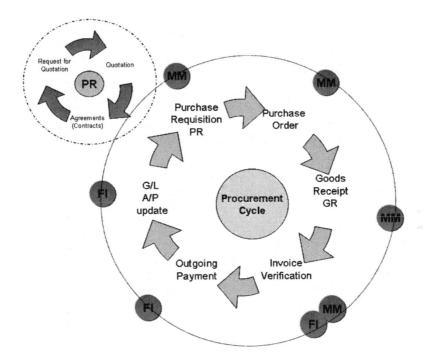

Figure 53 : Procurement Cycle

210.   What is a 'Purchase Requisition' (PR)?

A 'Purchase Requisition,' PR, is the document that outlines a company's purchasing needs of a material/service from vendor(s). A PR, typically an internal document that can be created automatically or manually, identifies the demand for a product and authorizes the purchasing department to procure it. In the automatic creation of a PR, this is done as a result of **MRP (Material Requirements Planning)**. The PR, after identifying the vendor, is processed further to result in a **RFQ (Request for Quotation)** or directly to a **Purchase Order (PO)**.

211. What is a 'Request for Quotation' (RFQ)?

A 'RFQ (Request for Quotation),' which can be created directly or with reference to another RFQ or a PR or an Outline Agreement, is actually an invitation to vendor(s) to submit a 'quotation' for supplying a material or service. The RFQ will contain the terms and conditions for supply. You may send the RFQ to single or multiple vendors, and you can monitor it by sending reminders to those who have not responded to the RFQ.

212. What is an 'Outline Agreement'?

An 'Outline Agreement,' a declaration binding both the buyer and seller, is the buyer's intention to purchase a material/service with certain terms and conditions agreed to by both parties. The essential difference between the 'outline agreement' and 'quotation' is that the outline agreement does not contain details such as delivery schedule or quantities. Outline agreements can be **contracts** or **scheduling agreements**.

213. What is a 'Contract'?

A 'Contract,' also referred to as a 'Blanket Order,' is a long-term legal agreement between the buyer and the seller for procurement of materials or services over a period of time. The contract, created directly or with reference to a PR/RFQ or another contract, is valid for a certain period of time with start and end dates clearly mentioned. There are two types of contracts: **Quantity Contracts** and **Value Contracts**.

214. What is a 'Release Order'?

A 'Release Order' is a 'purchase order' created against a Contract. The release orders usually do not contain information on quantities or delivery dates and are also called 'Blanket Releases,' 'Contract Releases,' or 'Call-Offs.'

215.   What is a 'Scheduling Agreement'?

A 'Scheduling Agreement' is also a long-term agreement with the buyer and seller for procurement of certain materials or services subject to certain terms and conditions. These agreements can be created directly or with reference to other documents such as another scheduling agreement, or an RFQ or PR. These agreements help in promoting **Just-In-Time (JIT)** deliveries, less paperwork, they reduce supply lead times, and ensure low inventory for the buyer.

216.   What is a 'Quotation'?

A 'Quotation' contains information relating to the price and other conditions for supply of a material or a service by a vendor, and is the vendor's willingness to supply the same based on those conditions. You will be able to compare the data from quotations using a **Price Comparison List** and will help in identifying the most reasonable vendor for supply of that item(s). After you receive the quotations, you will typically enter the quotation data (pricing/delivery) in RFQ. The SAP system can easily be configured to automatically print '**Rejections**' for vendors whose quotation are not selected.

217.   What is a 'Purchase Order' (PO)?

A 'Purchase Order' (PO) is a legal contract between a vendor and a buyer concerning the material/service to be purchased/procured on certain terms and conditions. The order mentions, among other things, the quantity to be purchased, price per unit, delivery related conditions, payment/pricing information, etc.

A PO can be created:

(1) Directly or

(2) With reference to a PR/RFQ/contract or another PO. Remember, all items on a PO should relate to the same Company Code.

218.   What is a 'PO History'?

The 'Purchase Order History' (PO History) lists all the transactions for all the items in a PO such as the GR/IR document numbers.

219.   Will the FI document be created with the Purchase Order (PO)?

No. There will not be any document created on the FI side during creation of a PO.

However, there can be a document for posting a 'commitment' to a Cost Center in CO. (The offsetting entry is posted at the time of GR.)

220. Explain FI-MM Integration.

FI-MM Integration is based on the following:

- Movement Types
- Valuation Class
- Transaction Keys
- Material Type

The **Movement Type** is the 'classification key' indicating the type of material movement (for example, goods receipt, goods issue, physical stock transfer). The movement type enables the system to find pre-defined posting rules determining how the accounts in FI (stock and consumption accounts) are to be posted and how the stock fields in the material master record are to be updated.

MvT	Movement Type Text
101	GR goods receipt
102	Reversal of GR
103	GR into blocked stck
104	Rev. GR to blocked
105	GR from blocked stck
106	Rev.GR from blocked
107	GR to Val. Bl. Stock
108	GR to Val. Bl. Rev.
109	GR fr. Val. Bl. St.
110	GR fr. Val. Bl. Rev.

Figure 54 : Movement Types

The **Valuation Class** refers to the assignment of a material to a group of GL accounts. Along with other factors, the valuation class determines the GL accounts that are updated as a result of a valuation-relevant transaction or event, such as a goods movement. The valuation class makes it possible to:

- Post the stock values of materials of the *same* material type to *different* GL accounts.
- Post the stock values of materials of *different* material types to the *same* GL account.

The **Transaction Key** (also known as the '**Event Key** or **Process Key**') allows users to differentiate between various transactions and events (such as physical inventory transactions and goods movements) that occur within the area of inventory management. The transaction/event type controls the filing/storage of documents and the assignment of document numbers.

The **Material Type** groups together materials with the same basic attributes, for example, raw materials, semi-finished products, or finished products. When creating a material master record, you must assign the material to a material type. The material type determines:

- Whether the material is intended for a specific purpose, for example, as a Configurable Material or Process Material.
- Whether the material number can be assigned internally or externally.
- The Number Range from which the material number is drawn.
- Which screens appear and in what sequence.
- Which user department data you may enter.
- What Procurement Type the material has; that is, whether it is manufactured in-house or procured externally, or both.

Together with the plant, the material type determines the material's inventory management requirement, that is:

- Whether changes in quantity are updated in the material master record.
- Whether changes in value are also updated in the stock accounts in financial accounting.

221.   What happens, in SAP, when you post a 'Goods Receipt'?

When you post a **'Goods Receipt' (GR)**, the stock account is debited (stock quantity increases) and the credit goes to the **GR/IR Clearing Account**, which is the intermediate processing account, before you actually process the vendor invoice or payments to the vendor:

Debit: Inventory Account

Credit: GR/IR Clearing Account

During this (1) a material document is created, (2) an accounting document to update the relevant GL account is created, (3) PO order history is updated, and finally (4) the system enables you to print the GR slip.

222.   Explain 'Invoice Verification' (IV) in SAP.

'Invoice Verification' involves:

1. Validating the accuracy of the invoices (quantity, value, etc.).
2. Checking for 'blocked' invoices (which vary to a great extent from that of the PO).

3. Matching of invoices received from vendors with that of the Purchase Order/ Goods Receipt. At this point in time, the PO History is updated for the corresponding PO Line Item(s) of the matched invoice.

4. Passing of matched invoices to the FI module. The system posts the following entries:

   Debit: GR/IR Clearing Account

   Credit: Vendor a/c (Accounts Payable open line item)

   Credit: GL Reconciliation Account

The different scenarios in invoice verification include:

1. GR-based Invoice Verification indicator is **not** set in the PO detail screen:

   Although this setting enables you to post the invoice referenced to a PO prior to making a GR, the system will block the invoice for payment (this kind of posting results in a **Quantity Variance** as there has not been a GR).

2. GR-based Invoice Verification indicator is set in the PO detail screen:

   When the PO number is referenced the system brings up all the unmatched items of GR in the selection screen. You will not be able to post the invoice for its full value, unless the PO has been fully received.

223. How do you deal with 'Tax' when you post an invoice?

When you enter an invoice, based on the configuration settings, the system checks the Tax Code and calculates the applicable tax or validates the Tax Amount entered by you:

1. **Manual Entry:** Input the **Tax Code** and the **Tax Amount**. The system will validate and issue a message in case it does not find the tax code or if the amount is different.

2. **Automatic Entry:** Leave the Tax Code and Tax Amount fields blank. Check the 'Calculate Tax' indicator. The system picks up the corresponding tax code and calculates the tax amount automatically.

224. What 'Variances' do you come across in Invoice Verification?

The system needs to be configured properly with 'Tolerances' so that you are not hampered with variances when you try Invoice Verification. You need to define the lower and upper limits for each combination of the Company Code and the tolerance key defined for the various variances. The system then checks these tolerance limits and issues warnings or prevents you from proceeding further when you process an invoice.

'**Variances**' arise because of mismatch or discrepancies between the invoice and the PO against which the invoice has been issued. Normally you will encounter:

1. **Price variances:** If there is a discrepancy in invoice price and PO item prices.

2. **Schedule variances:** If the planned delivery date is later than the invoice postings.

3. **Quantity variances:** If the delivered quantity (or delivered quantity less the previously invoiced quantity) is not the same as that of the invoiced quantity. When the invoiced quantity is more than the GR, the system requires more GRs to square off the situation.

225.   Outline 'Vendor Payments' in the SAP system.

The payments to single or multiple vendors can either be handled in a manual process or through an '**Automatic Payment Program**.' The open liability item created for the vendor during the invoice verification will be squared off when you make the vendor payment or when you run the automatic payment program. The payment program in SAP is designed to allow you to enjoy the maximum discount allowed by that vendor.

226.   Explain 'Automatic Payment Program.'

The '**Automatic Payment Program**' in SAP helps to process payment transactions both with customers and vendors. AR/AP/TR/Bank Accounting uses the payment program.

The 'automatic payment program' helps in determining:

- **What is to be paid?** To do this, you specify rules according to which the open items to be paid are selected and grouped for payment.

- **When is payment to be carried out?** The due date of the open items determines when payment is carried out. However, you can specify the payment deadline in more detail via configuration.

- **To whom the payment is made?** You specify the payee (the vendor or the alternate payee as the case may be).

- **How the payment is made?** You determine rules that are used to select a payment method.

- **From where the payment is made?** You determine rules that are used to select a bank and a bank account for the payment.

227. Explain 'Automatic Payment Program' Configuration.

Before you are ready to run the '**Automatic Payment Program**,' the following should have been defined/configured in the system:

- **House Bank** and the corresponding **bank accounts**.
- **Payment Methods** to be used for the Company Code. SAP comes with predefined payment methods, both for AR and AP. The following payment methods are available for you to select from depending on the requirements:

  (a) Accounts Payable
  - Check (S)/Transfer/Postal Giro transfer/Bill of exchange

  (b) Accounts Receivable
  - Bank collection/Bank direct debit/Refund by check/Refund by bank transfer/BE payment request

- **Bank Chain** defined, if necessary. Bank chains are used to make payment via more than one bank, for example, via the correspondence banks of the house bank, the recipient bank, or the intermediary banks. You can define up to three banks.
- **Payment Forms** defined. SAP delivers standard forms, which can be modified, or new forms can be created for use.

Transaction Code
FBZP

Customizing: Maintain Payment Program

- All company codes
- Paying company codes
- Pmnt methods in country
- Pmnt methods in company code
- Bank determination
- House banks

Figure 55: Customizing Automatic Payment program using FBZP

You may do most of the configurations by using the Transaction Code **FBZP** and branching to individual sections thereon. Or you may use the following Transaction Codes for individually doing it:

1. **(Sending) Company Code specifications**

Transaction Code **OBVU**

(*a*) Sending the Company Code – if Company Code 'A' is making payments on behalf of 'B,' then 'B' is the Sending Company Code. Otherwise, the sending Company Code is considered the paying Company Code (both are one and the same).

(*b*) Tolerance days

(*c*) Paying Company Code specifications

- Minimum amounts for incoming and outgoing payments.
- Forms for payment advice and EDI.
- Bill of Exchange parameters

2. **Payment Methods/Country and Bank determination**

Transaction Code **OBVCU**

(*a*) Payment Methods/ Country

- Payment Method for outgoing/incoming?
- Payment Method classification
- Master data requirements
- Posting details – document types
- Payment medium details - Print programs
- Permitted currencies (leave blank to allow all currencies)

(*b*) Bank Determination

- Ranking Order
  - Per Payment Method:
    - ◆ Which bank should be used first, second, etc.
    - ◆ Currency
    - ◆ Bill of Exchange

- Bank accounts
- Available amounts
    - Per House Bank and Payment Method combination:
        - Offset a/c for subledger posting
        - Available funds in each bank
        - Clearing accounts for Bill of Exchange
- Value date
- Charge

3. **Payment methods per Company Code**

Transaction Code
OBVU

(*a*) For each Payment Method and Company Code you need to define:
- Minimum/maximum payment amounts
- Whether payment abroad or in foreign currency is allowed
- Payment Media
- Bank optimization

4. **House Bank**

Transaction Code
FI12

---

228. How do you execute an 'Automatic Payment Program'?

The following are the series of events happening in the system when you try to execute an '**Automatic Payment Program**':

1. **Maintain Payment Parameters**

   To start with, you need to maintain the parameters required such as date of execution of 'payment run,' 'payment run identifier,' etc. Once this is done, you need to specify the 'posting date' of these payments, the 'document date' up to which the program should consider the items, the paying Company Code, payment methods to be considered, the 'next posting date,' is there certain accounts which need to be excluded from the run, etc. The payment run then needs to be scheduled either immediately or at a specified time/date.

2. **Payment Proposal**

The system creates a 'payment proposal' based on the payment parameters maintained in (1) above. The system selects the eligible **Open Items** based on the following sequence:

(*a*) **Due date** is determined via the **Base Line Date** and the **Terms of Payment** for each of the line items.

(*b*) Program calculates the **Cash Discount Period** and due date for the **Net Payment**.

(*c*) **Grace Periods** are then added to this due date.

(*d*) Which **Special GL** accounts are to be included, based on what you have already maintained as the parameters in (1) above.

(*e*) The system will determine whether to include an item during the current run or for the future one based on the specifications you made in (1).

(*f*) **Blocking** an item.

The payment proposal can be displayed for further processing; the 'log' can be checked to see the system messages, and the exception list can be generated for further evaluation.

3. **Payment Proposal**

With the payment proposal available, you can now edit the proposal to:

(*a*) Change House Bank, from what was maintained earlier

(*b*) Change Payment Method, if necessary

(*c*) Change Payment Due Date to relax or restrict certain open items

(*d*) Block/Unblock line items

4. **Payment Run**

After the payment proposal has been edited, you can run the **Payment Program** that creates the payment documents and prepares the data for printing the forms or creating the tape or disk. Before printing the forms, check the logs to determine that the payment program run was successful.

5. **Print Run**

Payment Medium Programs use the data prepared by the payment program to create forms (payment advice, EDI accompanying sheet, etc.) or files for the data media. The data created by the payment program is stored in the following tables:

REGUH	Payee or Payment Method data
REGUP	Individual Open Items data
REGUD	Bank Data and Payment Amounts data

You need to define **Variants** for print programs, which need to be defined:

(*a*) Per Payment Method per country -> assign a Print Program

(*b*) To run the Print Program ->at least one Variant per Print Program per Payment Method

Transaction Code
F110

229. Can you pay a vendor in a currency other than the invoice currency?

With release 4.5A, you can pay a vendor in a currency that is different from that of the transaction/invoice currency. This is achieved by entering the required currency code directly in the open item. Prior to this release, to pay in a different currency, you had to manually process the payment.

230. What is a 'Payment Block'?

A '**Payment Block**' prevents you from paying an open item of a vendor. The payment block is entered in the '**Payment Block**' field in a vendor master record or directly in the open line item.

Use the payment '**Block Indicators**' to define the '**Payment Block Reasons.**' You may use the SAP delivered payment block indicators (**A, B, I, R**, etc.) or create your own. An indicator such as '*' is used when you want to skip the particular account, and a blank indicator indicates that the account/item is free for payment. However, for each of these 'block indicators,' you need to configure whether changes would be allowed while processing the payment proposal. Then, it is also possible to block a payment or release a blocked one while processing the '**Payment Proposal.**'

You may also propose a 'payment block indicator' while defining Terms of Payment.

231. How do you release 'Blocked invoices for payments'?

The system will **block an invoice** if it comes across with an item with a '**Blocking Reason**.' The blocking reason may be due to variances or inspection-related issues. When the system blocks an invoice for payment, the 'payment block' field is checked by the system.

You will use an '**Invoice Release Transaction**' to select the blocked invoices for processing further. The 'release' of blocked invoices for payments can be handled either manually or automatically.

232. What is the 'Account Assignment Category'?

The '**Automatic Account Assignment**' logic takes care of posting to the correct GL accounts for '**Stock Material**' with the '**Material Type**' permitting inventory management, and the material master contains information as to which GL account needs to be updated. But there are material line items ('**Non-Stock**' materials) created manually in the Purchase Requisition/Purchase Order/Outline Agreement for which someone needs to decide the account assignment data and manually enter it in the Purchase Requisition. Here, the **Account Assignment Category** determines where to allocate the costs relating to such materials. The account assignment category helps you to define the type of account assignment (Sales Order-C, Project-P, Cost Center-K, etc.) and which accounts are to be posted to when GR/IR is posted to.

233. What is a 'Credit Memo'?

A '**Credit Memo**' is issued by a vendor who has earlier supplied you some services or materials. The occasion is necessitated when the delivered goods are damaged or you have returned some of the goods back to the vendor. The system treats both the invoices and the credit memo in the same way, except that the postings are done with the opposite sign.

If the credit memo is for the entire invoiced quantity, the system generates the credit memo automatically. However, if the credit memo relates to a portion of the invoiced quantity, you need to process it manually in the system.

234. What are 'Special GL Transactions'?

'**Special GL Transactions**' are not directly posted to the GL (Reconciliation Accounts) though these are related to subledger accounts such as AR/AP. The transactions to these accounts are shown separately in the balance sheet. There are specific posting keys/indicators defined in the system to regulate the postings to these items. You need to specify a **Special GL Indicator** (such as a **F**-Down Payment Request, **A**-Down Payment) for processing such a transaction. And the system will make use of the specially defined posting keys (09-customer debit, 19-customer credit, 29-vendor debit, and 39-vendor credit) for posting these special GL transactions.

There are three types of Special GL transactions:

■ Free Offsetting Entries (Down Payment)

■ Statistical Postings (Guarantee)

■ Noted Items (Down Payment Request)

A	Down payment on current assets
B	Financial assets down payment
D	Discount
E	Unchecked invoice
F	Down payment request
G	Guarantee received
H	Security deposit
I	Intangible asset down payment
M	Tangible asset down payment
O	Amortization down payment
P	Payment request
S	Check/bill of exchange
V	Stocks down payment
W	Bill of exch. (rediscountable)

Figure 56: Special GL Indicators

235. Differentiate 'Free Offsetting Entry' from a 'Statistical Posting.'

'Free Offsetting Entry' postings are part of the regular postings but with a freely definable offsetting entry, and relate to the **On-Balance Sheet Items**. On the other hand, in a **Statistical Posting**, you will always be posting to the same offsetting entry, and these are all the **Off-Balance Sheet Items**.

236. What is a 'Noted Item'?

'Noted Items' are never displayed on Financial Statements as they serve only as reminders of a financial obligation such as outstanding payments to be made or due to us, such as a **'Down Payment Request.'** This kind of posting does not update any GL account in the system but helps to keep track of such obligations for easy follow-up. This is also sometimes referred to as a **'Memo Entry.'**

It is interesting to note that while the Special GL Indicator for a Down Payment Request is **'F,'** you need to enter the indicator **'A'** as the target Special GL indicator while you are in the **Down Payment Request Entry Screen**. When you post this entry, the system creates a one-sided memo entry for the customer or vendor but does not update the GL.

ASSET ACCOUNTING

237.   Explain 'Asset Accounting' (FI-AA).

The '**Asset Accounting' (FI-AA)** submodule in SAP manages a company's fixed assets, right from acquisition to retirement/scrapping. All accounting transactions relating to depreciation, insurance, etc., of assets are taken care of through this module, and all the accounting information from this module flows to FI-GL on a real-time basis.

Figure 57: FI-AA integration with other modules

You will be able to directly post (the goods receipt (GR), invoice receipt (IR), or any withdrawal from a warehouse to a fixed asset) from MM or PP to FI-AA. The integration with FI-AR helps in direct posting of sales to the customer account. Similarly, integration with FI-AP helps in posting an asset directly to FI-AA and the relevant vendor account in cases where the purchase is not routed through the MM module. You may capitalize the maintenance activities to an asset using settlements through the PM module. FI-AA and FI-GL has real-time integration where all the transactions such as asset acquisition, retirement, transfer, etc., are recorded simultaneously in both the modules. However, batch processing is required to transfer the depreciation values, interest, etc., to the FI module.

The FI-AA and CO integration helps in:

- Assigning an asset to any of the **Controlling Objects** such as cost center, internal order/maintenance order, or an activity type. **Internal Orders** act as a two-way link to the FI-AA: (i) they help to collect and pass on the capital expenditure to assets, and (ii) they collect the depreciation/interest from FI-AA to controlling objects. (Note that when there is a situation where the asset master record contains an internal order and a cost center, the depreciation is *always* posted to the internal order and not to the cost center.)

- The depreciation and the interest are passed on to the cost/profit centers.

238.   What is a 'Lean Implementation' in FI-AA?

A 'Lean Implementation' is the scaled-down version of the regular FI-AA configuration in IMG, with minimal configuration required to enable asset accounting. This is suitable for small companies using the standard functionalities of asset accounting, and also in situations where the Asset Catalog is not that large.

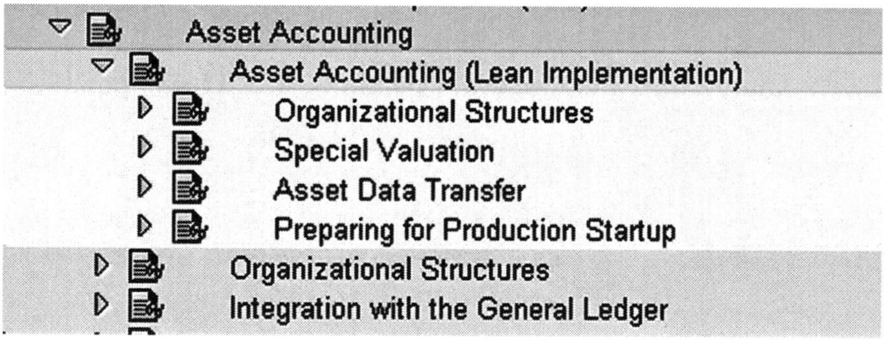

Figure 58: Lean implementation in FI-AA

You should not opt for lean implementation if:

- You need more than Depreciation Areas
- You need to Depreciate In Foreign Currencies as well
- You have Group Assets

- You need to define your own Depreciation Keys/Transaction Types/Reports
- You need a Group Consolidation

Transaction Code
OASI

239.   What are the kinds of 'Assets' in SAP?

An asset can be a **Simple Asset** or **Complex Asset**. Depending on the requirement, assets are maintained with **Asset Main Numbers** and **Asset Subnumbers**. A complex asset consists of many **Sub-Assets**; each of them identified using an asset subnumber. You may also use the concept **Group Asset** in SAP.

240.   Explain 'Complex Assets' and 'Asset Subnumbers.'

A '**Complex Asset**' in SAP is made up of many master records each of which is denoted by an '**Asset Subnumber**.' It is prudent to use asset subnumbers if:

- You need to manage the 'subsequent acquisitions' separately from the initial one (for example, your initial acquisition was a PC, and you are adding a printer later).
- You want to manage the various parts of an asset separately even at the time of 'initial acquisition' (for example, an initial purchase of a PC where you create separate asset master records for the monitor, CPU, etc.).
- You need to divide the assets based on certain technical qualities (keyboard, mouse, etc.).

When you manage a complex asset, the system enables you to evaluate the asset in all possible ways such as (*i*) for a single subnumber, (*ii*) for all subnumbers, and (*iii*) for select subnumbers.

241.   What is a 'Group asset' in SAP? When you will use this?

A 'Group Asset' in SAP is almost like a normal asset except that it can have (any number of) **sub-assets** denoted by **Asset Subnumbers**. The concept of group asset becomes necessary when you need to carry out depreciation at a group level, for some special purposes such as tax reporting. Remember that SAP's way of depreciation is always at the individual asset level. Hence, to manage at the group level, you need the group asset. Once you decide to have group assets, you also need to have 'special depreciation areas' meant for group assets; you will not be able depreciate a group asset using a normal depreciation area.

Unlike **Complex Assets**, you can delete a group asset only when all the associated subnumbers have been marked for deletion.

242. What is a 'Asset Super Number' in SAP?

The concept of '**Asset Super Number**,' in FI-AA, is used only for reporting purposes. Here, you will assign a number of individual assets to a single asset number. By using this methodology, you will be able to see all the associated assets with the asset super number as a single asset (for example, brake assembly line) or as individual assets (for example, machinery, equipment in the brake assembly line).

243. What is a 'Chart of Depreciation'? How does it differ from a 'Chart of Accounts'?

A '**Chart of Depreciation**' contains a list of country-specific depreciation areas. It provides the rules for the evaluation of assets that are valid in a given country or economic area. SAP comes supplied with default charts of depreciation that are based on the requirements of each country. These default charts of depreciation also serve as the 'reference charts' from which you can create a new chart of depreciation by copying one of the relevant charts. After copying, you may delete the depreciation areas you do not need. However, note that the deletion must be done before any assets are created.

You are required to assign a chart of depreciation to your Company Code. Remember that one Company Code can have only one chart of depreciation assigned to it, even though multiple Company Codes can use a single chart of depreciation.

The chart of accounts can be global, country specific, and industry specific based on the needs of the business. The chart of depreciation is only **country specific**. The charts are independent of each other.

Chart of Depreciation	Chart of Accounts
Established by FI-AA.	Established by FI.
A chart of depreciation is a collection of country specific depreciation areas.	The chart of accounts is a list of GL accounts used in a Company Code. The chart of accounts contains the chart of accounts area and the Company Code area.

The chart of depreciation is country specific. Usually you will not require more than one chart of account. SAP comes delivered with many country specific charts of depreciation as 'reference charts' which can be copied to create your own chart of depreciation.	Depending on the requirement you may have an 'operating chart of accounts,' 'country specific chart of accounts,' 'global chart of accounts,' etc.
One Company Code uses only one chart of depreciation.	One Company Code uses only one chart of accounts.
Many Company Codes, in the same country, can use the same chart of depreciation.	Several Company Codes within the same country can use the same chart of accounts.

244. How do you create an 'Asset Accounting Company Code'?

(*i*) Define the Company Code in FI configuration, and assign a chart of accounts to this Company Code.

(*ii*) Assign a chart of depreciation to this Company Code in FI-AA configuration.

(*iii*)   Add necessary data for the Company Code for use in FI-AA, and your 'asset accounting Company Code' is now ready for use.

245. What is 'Depreciation'? Explain the various types.

'**Depreciation**' is the reduction in the **book value** of an asset due to its use over time ('decline in economic usefulness') or due to legal framework for taxation reporting. The depreciation is usually calculated taking into account the **economic life** of the asset, **expected value** of the asset at the end of its economic life (**junk/scrap value**), **method of depreciation calculation** (straight line method, declining balance, sum of year digits, double declining, etc.), and the defined percentage decline in the value of the asset every year (20%, or 15%, and so on).

The depreciation can either be planned or unplanned.

Planned depreciation is one which brings down the value of the asset after every planned period; say every month, until the asset value is fully depreciated over its life period. With this method, you will know what the value of the asset at any point of time in its active life.

On the contrary, **unplanned depreciation** is a sudden happening of an event or occurrence not foreseen (there could be a sudden break out of a fire damaging an asset, which forces you to depreciate fully as it is no longer useful economically) resulting in a permanent reduction of the value of the asset.

In SAP, you will come across three types of depreciation:

1. **Ordinary depreciation**, which is nothing but 'planned depreciation.'

2. **Special depreciation**, which is over and above 'ordinary depreciation,' used normally for taxation purposes.

3. **Unplanned depreciation**, which is the result of reducing the asset value due to the sudden occurrence of certain events.

246. Define 'Depreciation Areas.'

Fixed assets are valued differently for different purposes (business, legal, etc.). SAP manages these different valuations by means of '**Depreciation Areas**.' There are various depreciation areas such as book depreciation, tax depreciation, depreciation for cost-accounting purposes, etc.

Chart of dep.	1IN	Sample chart of depreciation: India			

Define Depreciation Areas

	Ar.	Name of depreciation area	Real	G/L	Trg
	1	Book depreciation	☑	1	
	15	Depreciation as per Income Tax Act 1961	☑	0	
	20	Cost-accounting depreciation	☑	3	
	30	Consolidated balance sheet in local currency	☑	0	
	31	Consolidated balance sheet in group currency	☑	0	
	32	Book depreciation in group currency	☑	0	
	41	Investment support deducted from asset	☑	0	
	51	Investment support posted to liabilities	☑	1	

Figure 59: Depreciation Area

A depreciation area decides how and for what purpose an asset is evaluated. The depreciation area can be 'real' or a 'derived one.' You may need to use several depreciation areas for a single asset depending on the valuation and reporting requirements.

The depreciation areas are denoted by a 2-character code in the system. The depreciation areas contain the depreciation terms that are required to be entered in the **asset master** records or **asset classes**. SAP comes delivered with many depreciation areas; however, the depreciation area **01 – Book Depreciation** is the major one.

Chart of dep.	1IN	Sample chart of depreciation: India
Deprec. area	1	Book depreciation
		Book deprec.

Define Depreciation Areas

Real Depreciation Area	☑

Posting in G/L	Area Posts in Realtime
Target Ledger Group	
Different Depreciation Area	
Cross-syst.dep.area	

Value Maintenance

Acquisition value	Only Positive Values or Zero Allowed
Net book value	Only Positive Values or Zero Allowed
Investment grants	Only Negative Values or Zero Allowed
Revaluation	No Values Allowed
Ordinary depreciat.	Only Negative Values or Zero Allowed
Special Depr.	No Values Allowed
Unplanned Depreciat.	Only Negative Values or Zero Allowed
Transfer of reserves	No Values Allowed
Interest	No Values Allowed
Revaluation ord.dep.	No Values Allowed

Figure 60 : Details of 01-Book Depreciation

The other depreciation areas are:

- Book depreciation in group currency
- Consolidated versions in local/group currency
- Tax balance sheet depreciation
- Special tax depreciation
- Country-specific valuation (e.g., net-worth tax or state calculation)
- Values/depreciations that differ from depreciation area 01 (for example, cost-accounting reasons)
- Derived depreciation area (the difference between book depreciation and country-specific tax depreciation)

247.   How do you set up 'Depreciation Area postings' to FI from FI-AA?

You need to define how the various depreciation areas need to post to FI-GL. It can be any one of the following scenarios:

- Post depreciation through 'periodic processing.'
- Post both the APC (Acquisition and Production Costs) and depreciation through periodic processing.
- Post the APC in 'real time' but depreciation through periodic processing.
- No values are posted.

However, you need to ensure that at least one depreciation area is configured to post values automatically to the FI-GL. Normally, this depreciation area will be 01 (book depreciation). For the rest of the depreciation areas, it may be configured that they derive their values from this area and the difference thus calculated is automatically posted to FI-GL. There may also be situations where you may define depreciation areas just for reporting purposes, and these areas need not post to the GL.

248.   What is an 'Asset Class'?

An '**Asset Class**' in SAP is the basis for classifying an asset based on business and legal requirements. It is essentially a grouping of assets having certain common characteristics. Each asset in the system needs to be associated with an asset class.

Class	Short Text	Asset class description
1100	Buildings	Buildings
2000	Machines decl. depr.	Machines declining depr.
2100	Machines str.-line	Machines straight-line-depr.
2200	Group assets	Group assets (USA/Canada only)
3000	Fixture and fitting	Fixture and fittings
3100	Vehicles	Vehicles
3200	Personal computers	Personal computers
4000	Assets under Constr.	Assets under construction
4001	AuC for Measures	Assets under construction in investment me
5000	LVA (individ. mgmt.)	Low value assets (individual management)
5001	LVA (collect. mgmt.)	Low value assets (collective management)
6000	Leased assets	Leased assets
6001	Leased assets	Leased assets
9000	Leasing objects	Leasing objects
9360	Adm Purchasing	Administration Purchasing

Figure 61: Asset Class

An asset class is the most important configuration element that decides the type of asset (such as land, buildings, furniture and fixtures, equipment, assets under construction, leased assets, low-value assets, etc.), the document number range, data entry screen layout for asset master creation, GL account assignments, depreciation areas, depreciation terms, etc. An asset class is defined at the Client level and is available to all the Company Codes of that Client.

The asset class consists of:

- A **header** section - control parameters for master data maintenance and account determination.

- A **master data** section - default values for administrative data in the asset master record.

- A **valuation** section - control parameters for valuation and depreciation terms.

The asset class can be:

- Buildings
- Technical assets
- Financial assets
- Leased assets
- AuC (assets under construction)
- Low value assets

249.   Why do you need 'Asset Classes'?

An '**Asset Class**' is the link between the asset master records and the relevant accounts in the GL. The **account determination** in the asset class enables you to post to the relevant GL accounts. Several asset classes can use the same account determination provided all these asset classes use the same chart of accounts and post to the same GL accounts.

250.   What is an 'Asset Class Catalog'?

An '**Asset Class Catalog**' contains all the asset classes in an enterprise and is therefore valid across the Client. Since an asset class is valid across the Client, most of the characteristics of the asset class are defined at the Client level; however, there are certain characteristics (such as the depreciation key, for example), which can be defined at the chart of depreciation level.

251.   Is it possible to create 'Asset Classes' automatically?

One of the benefits of lean implementation configuration is the ability to create asset classes automatically from the asset GL accounts. This tool selects only necessary system settings so that the asset classes are created automatically in a very short time. During the process of creation, the system allows you to delete all the existing objects (i.e., asset classes, number ranges, account allocations, field selections, etc.) before creating the new ones.

The prerequisites for automatic asset class creation include:

- Company Code must be assigned to a chart of depreciation
- Depreciation areas have already been defined
- GL account number is not more than 8 digits (otherwise you need to assign the classes manually)

Also note that you may need to maintain the GL account for 'accumulated depreciation' manually. The system maintains the necessary account assignment only with regard to the depreciation area 01 (book depreciation). If you need more areas, you may need to do that manually in the IMG.

252.   What is an 'Asset Value Date'?

The '**Asset Value Date**' is the start date of depreciation for the asset. The 'planned depreciation' is calculated by the system based on this depreciation start date and the selected 'depreciation term' for that asset. Be careful with the posting date and asset value date. Both dates need to be in the same fiscal year.

253.   What is an 'Asset Master'?

An '**Asset Master**' can be created by copying an existing asset in the same Company Code or another Company Code; it can also be created from scratch when it is done for the first time. Again, while creating the master, SAP allows you to create multiple assets in one step, provided all such assets are similar (having the same asset class and all belonging to the same Company Code).

From Release 4.5, the transaction codes for creating an asset master have been changed to the AS series instead of the earlier AT series (for example, create asset is code **AS01** (**AT01** before), change asset is **AS02** (**AT02** before), and so on. If you are more comfortable with the creation of assets using the conventional screen than with the 'tab' feature available now in the AS transaction series, you can do so, but you cannot find these transactions under 'ASMN'!

Each asset master contains the necessary information to calculate the depreciation:

- Capitalization date/acquisition period
- Depreciation areas relevant for the asset
- Depreciation key
- Useful life/expired useful life
- Change over year, if any
- Scrap value, if any
- Start date of (ordinary depreciation)

254. Explain the two ways used to create 'Asset Masters.'

- Copy an existing asset as a reference for creating the new one.
- From an existing asset class create a new asset so that this asset class provides the default control parameters for the new asset.

255. Is it possible to create multiple assets in a single transaction?

SAP enables you to create multiple (but similar) assets in one transaction. What you need to know is that all these assets should belong to the *same* asset class and the *same* Company Code. Enter the number of assets you need to create in the **'Number of similar assets'** field. After creating the assets, you will be able to change the individual descriptions/inventory numbers when you are about to save the master records. When you save the master records, the system assigns a range of asset numbers.

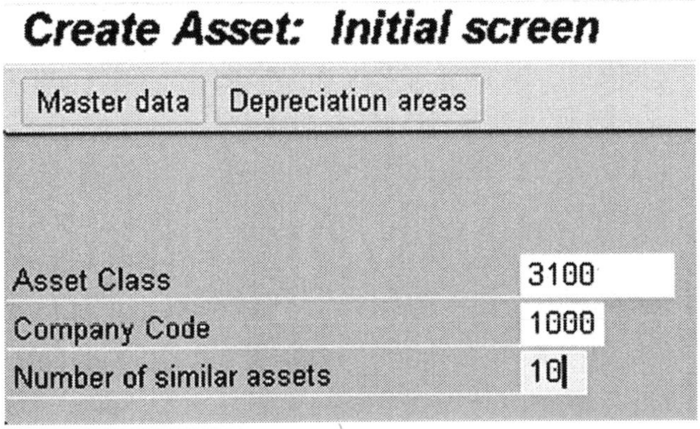

Create Asset: Initial screen

Master data	Depreciation areas

Asset Class	3100
Company Code	1000
Number of similar assets	10

Figure 62: Create multiple assets

Transaction Code
AS01

The only drawback of using this method of creating assets in bulk is that you will not be able to create **long text** for any of these assets.

256. What is the 'Time-dependent Data' in an asset master?

All the cost accounting assignment-related data such as cost center, internal orders or investment projects, etc., need to be maintained as 'Time-dependent Data' in asset masters. Additionally, the information related to **asset shut-down** and **shift operation** also needs to be maintained as time dependent. SAP maintains all the time-dependent data for the entire life span of the assets.

257. Explain 'Asset Acquisition.'

'Asset Acquisition' can be through any one of the following three routes:

1. **External Acquisition through Purchase**

   External acquisition of assets will be primarily from vendors, who are either your business partners or third parties. It can also be from your affiliated companies (use **Transaction Code: ABZP**). The external asset acquisition can be done several ways:

   (i) The asset can be posted in the MM module.

   (ii) The asset can be created in FI-AA with automatic clearing of the offsetting entry (Transaction Code: ABZON). This can be achieved either of the following ways:

   (a) The posting is made initially in FI-AP and the clearing account cleared when the posting is made to the asset (FI-AA).

   (b) Post the asset with the automatic offsetting entry (FI-AA) and then clear the clearing account through a credit posting by an incoming invoice (FI-AP).

   (iii) When *not* integrated with FI-AP, you may acquire the asset in FI-AA with an automatic offsetting entry without referencing a Purchase Requisition (PR). This kind of acquisition is necessary when:

   (c) You have not yet received the invoice or

   (d) When the invoice has already been posted in FI-AP

(*iv*) When integrated with FI-AP, acquire the asset in FI-AA using an incoming invoice but without a reference to a Purchase Order (PO).

2. **In-house Production/Acquisition**

   In-house Asset Acquisition is primarily the capitalization of goods/services produced by your company. The costs associated with the complete or partial production of the goods/services from within the company needs to be capitalized into separate asset(s). Usually, the capitalization is done as follows:

   (*i*) Create an order/project (in Investment Management) to capture the production costs associated with the goods/services produced in-house.

   (*ii*) Settle the order/project to an AuC (Asst under Construction).

   (*iii*) Distribute/Settle the AuC so created into new asset(s).

   You will be using the **Transaction Type 110** for asset acquisition from in-house production.

3. **Subsequent Acquisition**

   When the asset/vendor accounts are posted, the system updates the corresponding GL accounts (FI-AP and FI-AA) through relevant account determinations. SAP uses various kinds of 'transaction types' to distinguish the different transactions. During acquisition the system makes the following entries in the asset master data:

   - Date of initial acquisition/period and year of acquisition.
   - Capitalization date of the asset.
   - Start date for ordinary depreciation (the start date is determined from the asset value date/period/year of acquisition).
   - Vendor is automatically entered in the 'origin.'

258. What are automatically set in the asset masters during 'Initial Acquisition'?

- Date of capitalization
- Acquisition period
- Posting date of original acquisition
- Depreciation start date (per depreciation area)

259. Why it is necessary to 'Block' an asset master record?

In case you decide that you do not want to post any more acquisitions to an existing asset, then it is necessary for you to set the **Block Indicator** in the asset master record. This is usually the case with AuC, where after the capitalization you no longer want any further additions to the asset. The block indicator prevents only further postings but not transfers or retirements or depreciation; even after an asset is blocked, you can continue to depreciate it as in the case of other assets.

260. How do you 'Delete' an asset master?

You can '**Delete an Asset Master**' record from the system only when there are no transactions posted to it. The system will not allow you to delete the master record if there are transactions against the asset, even if you reverse all the previous transactions pertaining to the asset and bring down the asset value to zero. However, unlike FI-AR, FI-AP, or FI-GL where **archiving** is a prerequisite to delete the master records, you may delete the asset master records without archiving. When deleted, the system also deletes the asset number.

261. What is an '(Asset) Transaction Type' in FI-AA?

'**Transaction Types**' in FI-AA identify the nature of an asset transaction (acquisition or transfer or retirement) to specify what is updated, among (a) Depreciation area, (b) Value field, and (c) Asset accounts (in B/S).

TTy	Transaction type name
020	Acquisition:Cost-accounting area only
030	Acquisition in the group area
040	Acquisition in the tax area only
060	Acq. areas 01, 02, 20
100	External asset acquisition
101	Acquisition for a negative asset
105	Credit memo in acquis. year
106	Credit memo in invoice year to affiliated
110	In-house acquisition
115	Acquisition from settlement from CO to
116	Acquisition from settlement of order / W
120	Goods receipt
121	Goods receipt for production order
122	Goods receipt from affiliated company (
130	Goods issue (External production)
131	Goods issue (In-house production)
140	Incidental costs without capitalization
145	Gross interco.transf.acq. curr-yr.acq. af
146	Gross interco.transf.acq. curr-yr.acq. af
147	Gross interco.transf. acquis. of prior-yr
148	Gross interco.transf.acquis. of current-y
150	Acquisition from an affiliated company

Figure 63: (Asset) Transaction types

The following are some of the common transaction types used:

- **100**   Asset Acquisition – Purchase
- **110**   Asset Acquisition – In-house Production
- **200**   Asset Retirement – Without revenue
- **210**   Asset Retirement – With revenue

The transaction type is extensively used in most asset reports, including the **asset history sheet**, to display the various asset transactions differentiated by the transaction types. SAP comes with numerous transaction types, which will take care of almost all your requirements. However, should there be a specific case, you may also create your own transaction type.

Every transaction type is grouped into a **Transaction Type Group** (for example, 10 -> Acquisition), which characterizes the various transaction types (for example, transaction types 100 and 110) within that group. The system makes it possible to limit the transaction type groups that are associated with certain asset classes.

262.   Explain 'Assets under Construction' (AuC) in SAP.

The goods and/or services produced, in-house, can be capitalized into asset(s). But, there are two distinct phases during this process:

1. Construction phase (AuC)
2. Utilization phase (useful or economic life phase)

It then becomes necessary to show the assets under these two phases in two different balance sheet items:

The 'construction phase' is one in which you start producing or assembling the asset but it is not yet ready for economic utilization. SAP categorizes these kinds of assets into a special asset class called '**Assets under Construction**' (**AuC**).

The AuC is managed through a separate asset class with a separate asset GL account. SAP allows posting 'down payments' to AuC. It is also possible to enter credit memos for AuC even after its complete capitalization, provided you are managing this asset class and allowing negative **APC** (**Acquisition and Production Costs**). The **IM** (**Investment Management**) module helps to manage internal orders/projects for AuC. It is necessary to use the **depreciation key** '0000' to ensure that you are not calculating any depreciation for AuC. But you can continue to have **special tax depreciation** and **investment support** even on these assets.

263.   How do you capitalize AuC in SAP?

An '**Asset under Construction**' can be managed in two ways as far as the asset master is concerned:

- As a 'normal' asset.
- As an asset with 'line item management.'

Later on, the AuC is capitalized and transferred to regular asset(s) by 'distribution'/'settlement.' While doing so, the system, with the help of different **transaction types,** segregates the transactions relating to the current year with that of the previous years. The capitalization can be:

1. Lump sum capitalization.
2. With line item settlement (when capitalized using line item settlement, it is not necessary to settle all the line items and 100% in a particular line item).

In the case of integration with SAP-IM (Investment Management), capital investments can be managed as an AuC by:

- Collecting the production costs associated with an order/project.
- Settling the collected costs to an AuC.
- Capitalizing the AuC into new assets by distribution/settlement.

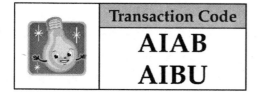

Transaction Code
AIAB
AIBU

264. What do you mean by 'Low Value Assets'?

SAP uses the term '**Low Value Assets**' to denote assets that will be depreciated in the year of purchase or in the period of acquisition. This categorization usually follows the statutory requirements of the country of the Company Code, wherein you define a monetary limit and consider all those assets falling below the value, say $1,000, as low value assets. You have the flexibility of managing these assets either on an individual (**individual check**) basis or a collective basis (**quantity check**).

SAP uses a special **depreciation key** called LVA, and the expected useful life of such an asset is considered to be one period (month).

265. Explain 'Asset Transfer' in SAP.

There are two types of '**Asset Transfers**,' namely:

1. Inter-company asset transfer
2. Intra-company asset transfer

Inter-company Asset Transfer is between Company Codes, resulting in the creation of the new asset in the target Company Code (the receiving one). The transaction posts the values per the 'posting method' selected during the transfer. In doing so the system:

- Retires the asset in the source/sending Company Code by **asset retirement**.
- Posts acquisition in the new/target Company Code by **asset acquisition**, and creates the new asset in the target Company Code.
- Posts inter-company profit/loss arising from the transfer.
- Updates FI-GL automatically.

An inter-company asset transfer is usually necessitated when there is a need for physically changing the location from one company to the other or there is an organization restructuring and the new asset is to be attached to the new Company Code. You may use the standard **Transfer Variants** supplied by SAP. The selection of a suitable transfer variant will be based on the legal relationship among the Company Codes and the methods chosen for transferring the asset values.

Inter-company asset transfers can be handled:

- Individually using the normal transaction for a single asset.
- For a number of assets using the '**mass transfer**.'

If you need to transfer assets cross-system, you need to use ALE functionality.

Intra-company Asset Transfer is the transfer of an asset within the same Company Code. This would be necessitated by:

- Change in the asset class or business area, etc.
- Settlement of an AuC to a new asset.
- Transfer of stock materials into an asset (by posting a GI to an order through MM or settlement of a production order to an asset).
- Splitting an existing asset into one or more new assets.

Transaction Code
ABUMN

266. What is a 'Transfer Variant'?

A '**Transfer Variant**' is dependent on whether the Company Codes involved are legally dependent or independent. Transfer variants specify how the transferred asset will be valued at the receiving Company Code and the type of transaction (acquisition or transfer) used for the transaction.

Vari...	Name
1	Gross method
2	Net method
3	Revaluation method
4	Transfer within a company code
5	Summary settlement from CO
6	Line item settlement from CO or from AuC
7	Gross variant (affiliated company)
8	Gross variant (non-affiliated company)
FIN	Finland - Transfer assets EVL depreciation

Figure 64: Transfer variant

267.   Explain 'Asset Retirement' in FI-AA.

'Asset Retirement' is an integral part of asset management. You may retire an asset by sale or by scrapping. In the case of sales, it can be with revenue or without revenue; again, the asset sale can be with the customer or without the customer.

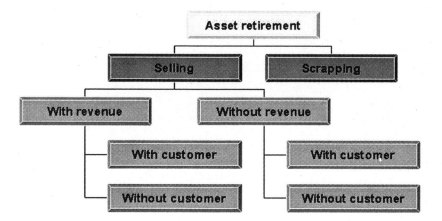

Figure 65: Asset Retirement

During asset sales transactions, the system removes the **APC (Acquisition and Production Costs)** and also the corresponding **accumulated depreciation**, then the **profit or loss** arising from the sale is recorded in the system. Even in the case of 'partial retirement' or 'partial sales,' the system records the proportionate gain/ loss arising from the transaction. Any tax posting arising from the transaction is automatically created by the system.

SAP provides various ways of posting retirement in the system, which includes:

- Mass retirement
- Asset retirement with revenue
  - With customer (involving integration with FI-AR)
    - Debit customer, credit assets
  - Without customer
- Asset retirement without revenue
  - With customer
    - Debit clearing account, credit asset
    - Debit customer in A/R, credit the clearing account
- Asset retirement using GL document posting

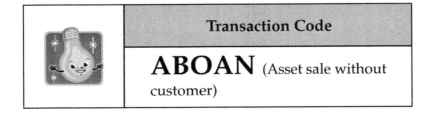

	Transaction Code
	ABOAN (Asset sale without customer)

268. Describe transfer of 'Legacy Asset Data' to SAP.

One of the challenges in the implementation of FI-AA is the transfer of '**Legacy Asset Data**' from your existing systems to SAP FI-AA. Though SAP provides multiple options and appropriate tools to carry out this task, you need a carefully planned strategy for completing this task. You may have to transfer the old asset values through any one of the following ways:

- Batch data inputs (large number of old assets)
- Directly updating the SAP Tables (very large number of old assets)
- Manual entry (few old assets)

Normally, you will not have to use the manual process as it is time consuming and laborious; however, you may do this if you have a very limited number of assets. Otherwise, you may use either of the other two options, though batch data input with error handling is the preferred way of doing it. You need to reconcile the data transferred, if you resort to any of the two automatic ways of transferring the data. You may also use **BAPIs (Business Application Programming Interface)** to link and process the asset information in SAP FI-AA from non-SAP systems.

The transfer can be done at the end of the last closed fiscal year, or during the current fiscal year following the last closed fiscal year. You will be able to transfer both master data as well as accumulated values of the last closed fiscal year. If required, you can also transfer asset transactions, including depreciation, during the current fiscal year. It is important to note that the GL account balances of the old assets need to be transferred separately.

269. Outline 'Automatic Transfer of Old Assets.'

SAP provides you with the necessary interfaces for converting your 'legacy asset data' into prescribed formats for upload into the SAP system. The **data transfer workbench** allows you to control the entire data transfer process.

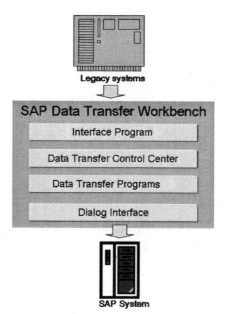

Figure 66: Legacy asset transfer to SAP FI-AA

(*i*) These interface programs convert the data so that it is compatible with SAP data dictionary tables such as **BALTD** for master data and **BALTB** for transactions. If you have more than 10 depreciation areas, then you need to change the transfer structures for both **BALTD** and **BALTB**.

(*ii*) The converted data is stored in sequential files.

(*iii*) Use the data transfer program **RAALTD01** (for batch input) or **RAALTD11** (direct table update) for transferring the data to SAP.

- Do a **test run**. This will help to correct errors if any.
- Do a **production run**, with a few asset records, to update the relevant tables in FI-AA.
- Reset the values in the asset Company Code.
- Continue with the production run for all the assets.

(*iv*) All the asset records without errors will be updated immediately through background processing in relevant tables such as **ANLH, ANLA, ANLB, ANLC**, etc.

(*v*) The records with errors will be stored in a separate batch input session, which can be processed separately.

270. What is an 'Asset Transfer Date'?

The '**Asset Transfer Date**' refers to the 'cut-off' date for the transfer of old assets data from your existing system. Once established, you will not be able to create any old assets in SAP before this reference date. Any transaction happening after the transfer date but before the actual date of asset transfer needs to be created separately in SAP after you complete the old asset transfer.

271. Describe 'Mass Change.' How do you achieve this?

'**Mass Change**' enables you to make changes (such as mass retirements, changes to incomplete assets, etc.) in FI-AA to a large number of asset master records at one time. The mass change functionality is achieved through **work lists**, which are FI-AA standard tasks pre-defined in the system. These tasks are assigned with 'work flow objects,' which can be changed according to your specific requirements. The work lists are created in several ways from asset master records, asset value displays, from the asset information system, etc.

To make a mass change you need to:

1. Create a **substitution rule(s)** in which you will mention what fields will be changed. This rule will consist of an 'identifying condition' (for example, if the cost center = 1345), and a 'rule to substitute' new values (for example, replace the 'field' cost center with the 'value' '1000').
2. Generate a list of assets that need to be changed.
3. Create a 'work list' to carry out the changes.
4. Select the appropriate 'substitution rule' (defined earlier in step 1 above).

5. Process the 'work list.' You may also release it to someone else in the organization so that he/she can complete the task.

6. Run a 'report' to verify the changes.

272. What is 'Periodic Processing' in FI-AA? Explain.

'**Periodic Processing**' in FI-AA relates to the tasks you need to carry out at periodic intervals to plan and post some transactions. The tasks include:

■ Depreciation calculation and posting.

   As you are aware, SAP allows automatic posting of values from only one depreciation area (normally 01 – book depreciation). For all other depreciation areas, including the derived ones, you need to perform the tasks periodically so that FI is updated properly.

■ Planned depreciation/interest for CO primary cost planning.

■ Claiming and posting of 'investment support' (either 'individually' or through 'mass change').

273. What is a 'Depreciation Key'?

Depreciation is calculated using the '**Depreciation Key**' and **Internal Calculation Key** in the system. Depreciation keys are defined at the chart of depreciation level, and are uniform across all Company Codes, which are attached to a particular chart of depreciation. The depreciation key contains all the control amounts defined for

Chart of dep.	1IN	Sample chart of depreciation: India	
DepKy	**Name for whole depreciation**		**Status**
0000	No depreciation and no interest		Active
DG20	Declining balance 2 x		Active
DG25	Declining balance 2.5 x		Active
DG30	Declining balance 3 x		Active
DIG4	Sum-of-the-years-digits dep. 4 years		Active
GD10	Buildings decl.bal.10.0/ 5.0 / 2.5 %		Active
GD35	Buildings decl.bal.3.5/ 2.0 / 1.0 %		Active
GD50	Buildings decl.bal. 5.0 / 2.5 / 1.25 %		Active
GD70	Buildings decl.bal. 7.0 / 5.0 / 2.0 / 1.25 %		Active
GL20	Buildings straight-line 2%		Active
GL25	Buildings straight-line 2.5%		Active
GWG	LVA 100 % Complete depreciation		Active
IN1	Tax Depreciation - 5% - India		Active

Figure 67: Depreciation Key

the calculation of planned depreciation. The system contains a number of pre-defined depreciation keys (such as **LINA**, **DWG**, **DG10**, etc.) with the controls already defined for calculation method and type. A depreciation key can contain multiple internal calculation keys.

274.   What is an 'Internal Calculation Key'?

'Internal Calculation Keys' are the control indicators within a 'depreciation key.' Together with the depreciation key, these calculation keys help in determining depreciation amounts. Each internal calculation key contains:

1. Depreciation type (ordinary or unplanned)
2. Depreciation method (straight-line or declining balance)
3. Base value
4. Rate of percentage for depreciation calculation
5. Period control for transactions (acquisition, retirement, etc.)
6. Change-over rules (in case of declining/double declining methods of calculation)
7. Treatment of depreciation after useful life period

275.   What is known as a 'Depreciation Run' in SAP?

The 'Depreciation Run,' an important periodic processing step, takes care of calculating depreciation for assets and posting the corresponding transactions in both FI-AA and FI-GL. The depreciation calculation is usually done in sessions, and the **posting session** posts the different depreciation types, interest/revaluation, and also writing-off/allocating special reserves. The depreciation run should be started with a 'test run' before making it the **'production run**,' which will update the system. The system will restart a run session should there be problems in the earlier run. The depreciation run needs to be completed per period. During every depreciation run, the system will create summarized posting documents per business area and per account determination; no individual posting documents are created.

276.   Explain the various steps in a 'Depreciation Run.'

1. Maintain the parameters for the depreciation run on the initial screen of the Transaction **AFAB** (Company Code, fiscal year, and posting period).
2. Select a 'reason' for the posting run (repeat run, planned posting run, restart run, or unplanned run).

3. Select the appropriate check boxes in the 'further option' block if you need a list of assets, direct FI posting, test run, etc. Please note that it is a good practice to select the 'test run' initially, see and satisfy the outcome of the depreciation run, then remove this 'check box' and go for the 'productive run.'

4. Execute the test run (if the assets are less than 10,000, you may then do the processing in the foreground; otherwise execute the run in the background).

5. Check the results displayed.

6. Once you are convinced that the test run has gone as expected, go back to the previous screen, uncheck the 'test run' check box, and execute (in the background).

7. Complete the 'background print parameters,' if prompted by the system. You may also decide to schedule the job immediately or later. The system uses the 'depreciation-posting program' **RABUCH00**, for updating the asset's values and generating a batch input session for updating FI-GL. The 'posting session' posts values in various depreciation areas, interest, and revaluation, besides updating special reserves allocations and writing-off, if any. If there are more than 100,000 assets for depreciation calculation and posting, you need to use a special program, **RAPOST00**.

8. Process the 'batch input session' created by the system in step-7 above. You may use the Transaction Code **SM35**. Again, you have the option of processing the session in the foreground or in the background.

9. System posts the depreciation in FI-GL.

277. How does the system calculate 'Depreciation'?

1. The system takes the 'depreciation terms' from the asset master record and calculates the annual depreciation for the asset taking into account the 'useful life' and the 'depreciation key.' The start date for depreciation is assumed to be the first date of acquisition of the asset.

2. The system may also calculate other values such as interest, revaluation, etc.

3. The depreciation and other values are calculated for each of the depreciation areas.

278. Explain 'Derived Depreciation.'

'Derived Depreciation' is a separate depreciation area that is 'derived' from two or more 'real depreciation' areas using a pre-determined rule. You may use this to calculate something such as **special reserves** or to show the difference in valuation between local and group valuation, etc. Since the values are derived, the system does not store any values in the database, but updates the derived values whenever there are changes in the real depreciation area or its depreciation terms. You may also use the derived depreciation only for reporting purposes.

279.   What is known as a 'Repeat Run' in the depreciation process?

A '**Repeat Run**' is normally used at the end of the fiscal year to carry out posting adjustments or corrections that may arise due to changes in depreciation terms or manual depreciation calculations. However, you can also use this to repeat but within the same posting period. The 'repeat run' also provides the flexibility to restrict the calculations to specific assets.

280.   What does 'Restart a Depreciation Run' mean?

Restart Depreciation Run is used only when there has been a problem with the previous run resulting in the termination of that run. To make sure that all the steps in a depreciation run are completed without errors, the system logs the status at every stage of the processing and provides 'error logs' to find the problem. This 'restart' option is not available during the 'test run' mode.

281.   What is 'Depreciation Simulation'?

'**Depreciation Simulation**' refers to a 'what if' valuation of assets. This is achieved by changing and experimenting with the 'parameters' required for depreciating the assets. The simulation helps you to 'foresee' the depreciation should there be changes in various 'depreciation terms.' You may simulate to see the valuation for future fiscal years. **Sort versions** and options for **totals report** are also available in simulation. The depreciation simulation can be applied to a single asset or your entire asset portfolio.

282.   What is a 'Sort Version'?

A '**Sort Version**' defines the formation of groups and totals in an asset report. You can use all the fields of the asset master record asset group and/or sort criteria for defining a sort version. The sort version cannot have more than five **sort levels**.

283.   Can you select 'Direct FI Posting' for a 'Depreciation Run'?

If the check box to enable '**Direct FI Posting**' is clicked then the system will not create the 'batch input session' for a depreciation posting; instead, the FI-GL is posted directly. Be careful when checking the Direct FI Posting check box because there will not be an opportunity to correct mistakes, if any, in accounts and account assignments such as business area, cost objects, etc., when you execute the depreciation run. Also, you will not be able to check and correct postings. Note that if this option is selected during a depreciation run, and if the run is terminated for any reason and needs to be restarted, this has to be kept checked during that time as well.

The standard system comes with the document type '**AF**' (number range defined as 'external numbering') configured to be used in 'batch input.' Hence, with this default configuration, you will get an error when you try a depreciation posting run by selecting the option 'direct FI posting.' You can, however, overcome this by not restricting the same FI-AA customization. (Use Transaction Code **OBA7** and remove the check mark from 'Batch input only' check box.)

284. Explain 'Year Closing' in FI-AA.

The year-end is closed when you draw the final balance sheet. But, to reach this stage, you need to ensure that the depreciation is posted properly; you can achieve this by checking the 'depreciation list' and also the 'asset history sheets.' After this is done, draw a test balance sheet and profit and loss statement and check for the correctness of the depreciation. Correct the discrepancies, if any, with adjustment postings. You need to re-run the depreciation posting program if you change any of the depreciation values.

When you now run the '**Year-End Closing Program**,' the system ensures that the fiscal year is completed for all the assets, depreciation has fully posted, and there are no errors logged for any of the assets. If there are errors, you need to correct the errors before re-running the year-end program. When you reach a stage where there are no errors, the system will update the last closed fiscal year, for each of the depreciation areas for each of the assets. The system will also block any further postings in FI-AA for the closed fiscal year. If you need to re-open the closed fiscal year for any adjustments postings or otherwise, ensure that you re-run the year-end program so that the system blocks further postings.

285. Explain 'Asset History Sheet.'

SAP comes delivered with country-specific '**Asset History Sheets**,' which meet the legal reporting requirements of a specific country. The asset history sheet is an important report that can be used either as the **year-end report** or the intermediate report whenever you need it. Asset history sheets help you to freely define the report layout, headers, and most of the history sheet items.

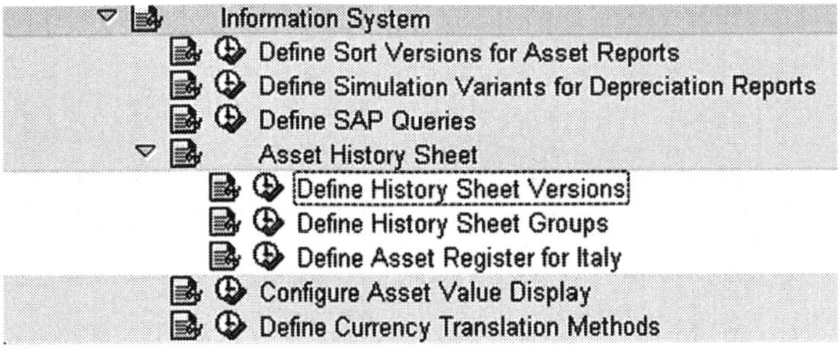

Figure 68: Configuring Asset History Sheet

You may create various versions of the Asset History Sheet:

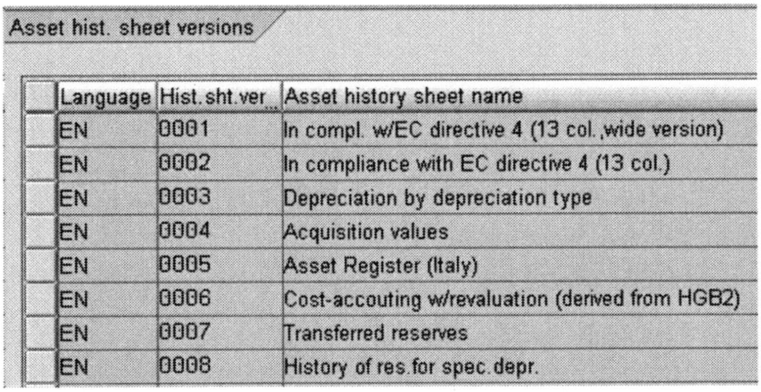

Asset hist. sheet versions

Language	Hist.sht.ver...	Asset history sheet name
EN	0001	In compl. w/EC directive 4 (13 col.,wide version)
EN	0002	In compliance with EC directive 4 (13 col.)
EN	0003	Depreciation by depreciation type
EN	0004	Acquisition values
EN	0005	Asset Register (Italy)
EN	0006	Cost-accouting w/revaluation (derived from HGB2)
EN	0007	Transferred reserves
EN	0008	History of res.for spec.depr.

Figure 69: Asset History Sheet Versions

For each of the versions, you will be able to define various columns according to your requirements:

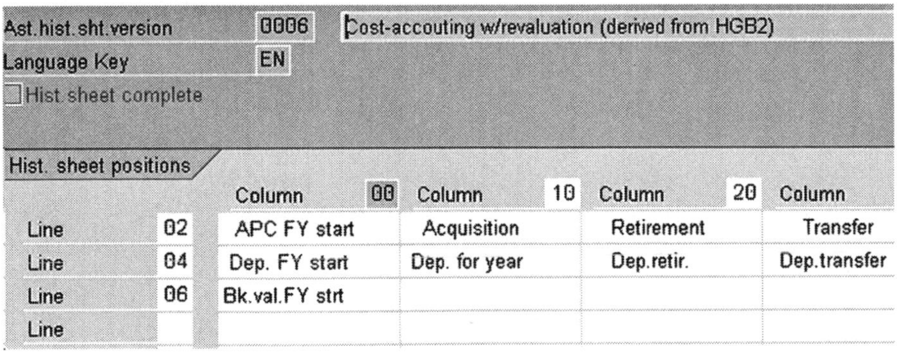

Ast.hist.sht.version 0006 Cost-accouting w/revaluation (derived from HGB2)
Language Key EN
Hist.sheet complete

Hist. sheet positions

		Column 00	Column 10	Column 20	Column
Line	02	APC FY start	Acquisition	Retirement	Transfer
Line	04	Dep. FY start	Dep. for year	Dep.retir.	Dep.transfer
Line	06	Bk.val.FY strt			
Line					

Figure 70: Field Positions in an Asset History Sheet Version

286.   What is an 'Asset Explorer'?

'**Asset Explorer**' is a handy and convenient single interface transaction that helps you to display asset values, depreciation details, etc., in a very user friendly way. Gone are the days where you had to move to different pages and re-enter the same transaction many times to display the details of different assets.

Using asset explorer you have the convenience of:

- Moving from one asset number to the other effortlessly.
- Displaying asset values, both planned and posted, for any number of depreciation areas from the same page but in various tab pages.
- Jumping to the asset master or cost center master or GL account master.
- Calling up various asset reports.
- Currency converted views.
- Looking at the various transactions relating to an asset.
- Looking up all the values for different fiscal years.
- Distinguishing between real and derived depreciation areas with two differentiating symbols.
- Displaying the **depreciation calculation function**, and if necessary, recalculating depreciation.

Asset explorer is designed for easy navigation, with the following sections:

1. **Asset values window**

    The top-left area/window is the 'asset values' window, which is in a tree-like structure expanding to various depreciation areas such as 01, 03, 10, etc. By selecting any one of these depreciation areas, you will be able to view the value of an asset in the 'asset value details window.'

2. **Objects related to asset window**

    This is also on the left-hand side of the display page, just below the 'asset values window.' With a drill-down tree-like structure you will be able to navigate between cost centers and GL accounts relating to the asset.

3. **Asset value detail window** (with tab pages)

    This is the main window on the right, usually occupying most of the page area. Here, you will see information such as Company Code, asset number selected, fiscal year, etc. This window is made of two components that are completely re-sizeable: the top area displaying the asset values and the bottom showing the asset transactions.

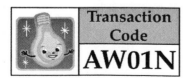

Transaction Code
AW01N

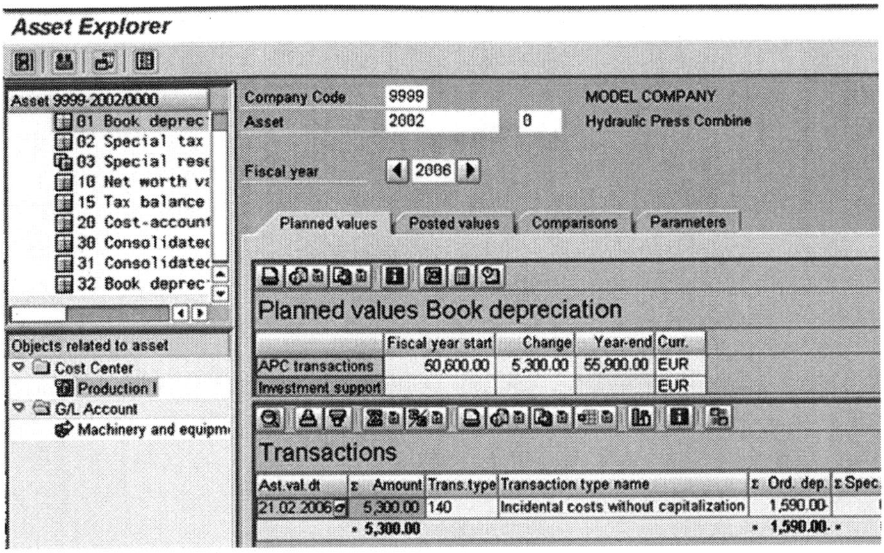

Figure 71: Asset Explorer

287. Explain 'Production Set-up' in FI-AA.

The '**Production Set-up**' is a collection of logical steps in FI-AA to ensure that all the required configuration and activities are in place for making the asset accounting Company Code 'productive.' This includes:

(*i*) **Consistency check**

This will enable you to analyze errors, if any, in FI-AA configuration in the charts of depreciation, assignment of Company Code to the chart of depreciation, definition of depreciation areas, asset classes, GL account assignments, etc.

(*ii*) **Reset Company Code**

As you will have test data, before the Company Code becomes productive, resetting the company is necessary to delete all this data. Note that this is possible only when the Company Code is in 'test' status. All the master records and values will be removed only from FI-AA. You need to remove all the FI and CO values separately as the resetting of the asset account Company Code does not remove these. Resetting will not remove any configuration settings of FI-AA.

(*iii*) **Reset posted depreciation**

This step is required when there had been errors during a previous depreciation run. This is also possible only when the asset Company Code is in test status.

(*iv*) **Set/reset reconciliation accounts**

Define the GL accounts for FI-AA reconciliation, if not done already. You may also reset already defined reconciliation accounts in the case of wrong account assignments earlier.

(*v*) **Transfer asset balances**

Transfer the asset balances to the GL accounts that have been defined as the asset reconciliation accounts.

(*vi*) **Activate asset accounting Company Code**

This is the last step in the production set-up. All the previous statuses of the Company Code (test status/transfer status) become invalid now. No more transfer of old asset data is allowed when the asset Company Code becomes productive.

CONTROLLING (CO)

CONTROLLING (CO)

GENERAL CONTROLLING

288. Explain 'Controlling (CO)' in SAP.

SAP calls **managerial accounting 'Controlling'** and the module is commonly known as **'CO.'** The CO module is, thus, primarily oriented towards managing and reporting cost/revenue and is mainly used in 'internal' decision-making. As with any other module, this module also has configuration set-up and application functionality.

The controlling module focuses on internal users and helps management by providing reports on cost centers, profit centers, contribution margins and profitability, etc.

289. What are the important 'Organizational Elements of CO'?

The important organizational structure of controlling includes:

- **Operating Concern** (the top-most reporting level for profitability analysis and sales and marketing controlling).
- **Controlling Area** (central organization in 'controlling,' structuring internal accounting operations).
- **Cost Centers** (lower-most organizational units where costs are incurred and transferred).

290. What is a 'Controlling Area'? How is it related to a Company Code?

A 'Controlling Area' is the central organizational structure in 'controlling' (CO) and is used in cost accounting. The controlling area, as in the case of a Company Code, is a self-contained cost accounting entity for internal reporting purposes. The controlling area is assigned to one or more Company Codes to ensure that the necessary transactions, posted in FI, are transferred to controlling for **cost accounting** processing.

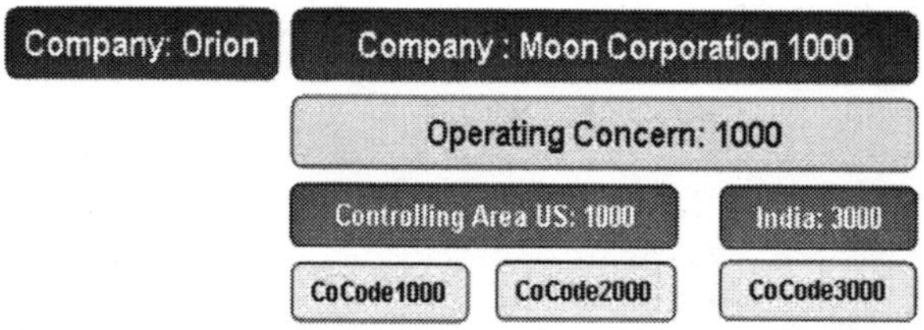

Figure 72: Operating Concern, Controlling Area, and Company Code

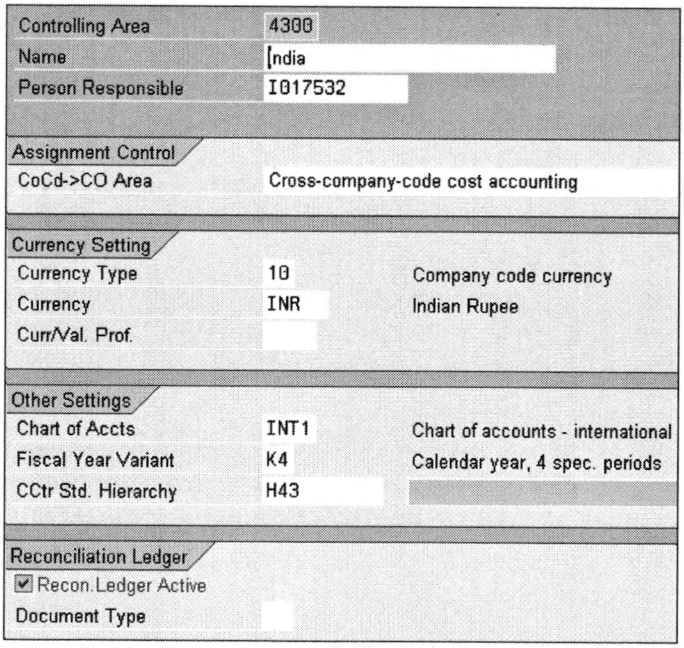

Figure 73: Controlling Area - Details

- One controlling area can be assigned one or more Company Codes.
- One chart of accounts can be assigned to one or more controlling areas.

- One or more controlling areas can be assigned to an operating concern.
- One Client can have one or more controlling areas.

291.   Outline 'Company Code – Controlling Area' assignments.

There are two types of assignments possible between the Company Code and a controlling area:

- **One-to-one:** Here, one Company Code corresponds to one controlling area.
- **Many-to-one:** More than one Company Code is assigned to a single controlling area.

292.   Explain the different types of 'Controlling Area/Company Code' assignments.

Controlling area -Company Code assignment	1:1 assignment	1: many assignments (cross-Company Code cost accounting)
Chart of accounts	The chart of accounts should be the same between the controlling area and the Company Code.	The 'operative chart of accounts' of the Company Codes, and the controlling area should be the same.
Fiscal year variant (special and posting periods)	The number of special periods may be different between the Company Code and the controlling area, but the number of posting periods should be the same. Also, the period limits of posting periods should be identical.	
Controlling area currency	Same as the Company Code currency.	You may use the same currency as that of the Company Code.
		You may also use another currency in controlling
Object currency	Additional currency, besides the controlling area currency, can be used for each account assignment objects in CO.	You can choose any object currency if all the assigned Company Codes have the same currency that are the same as the controlling area currency. Otherwise, the system automatically assigns the Company Code currency to the account assignment object as an object currency.

Transaction currency	Documents are posted in CO in the transaction currency.	
Allocations	Cross-Company Code cost allocation in CO is not possible.	Cross-Company Code allocation in CO is possible.

293.   What are the 'Components of Controlling'?

There are three major submodules in CO and each of these submodules has many components as detailed below:

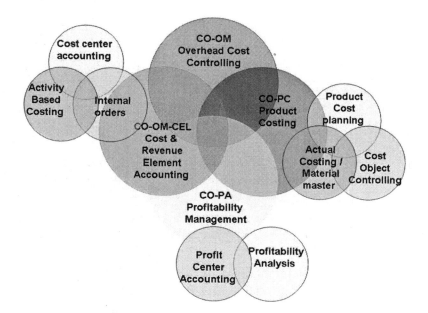

Figure 74: Controlling Module's Components

- Cost Element Accounting
- Cost Controlling
- Cost Center Accounting
- Internal Orders
- Activity-Based Costing
- Product Cost Controlling
- Profitability Analysis
- Profit Center Accounting

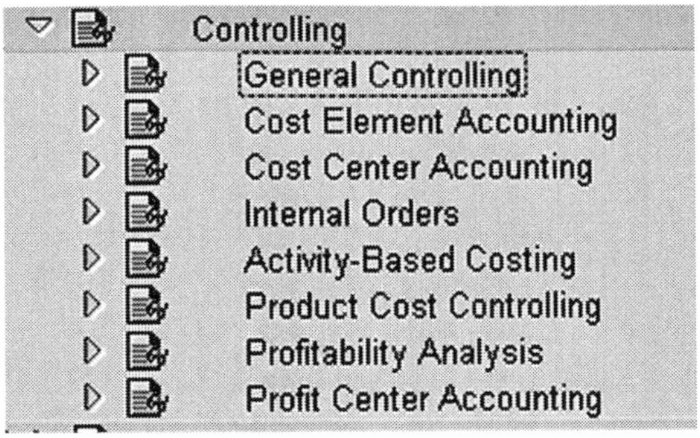

Figure 75: Controlling Components

294.   Why do you need 'Cost Element Accounting'?

'Cost Element Accounting' (CO-OM-CEL) helps you to classify costs/revenues posted to CO. It also provides you the ability to reconcile the costs between FI and CO. CO-OM-CEL provides the structure for assignment of CO data in the form of cost/revenue carriers called **cost elements** or **revenue elements**.

295.   Explain 'Cost Center Accounting.'

'Cost Center Accounting' deals with the difficult task of managing 'overheads' within your organization. Since **overhead costs** are something that you cannot directly associate with a product or service, which can be difficult to control, cost center accounting provides you with the necessary tools to achieve this.

296.   What is 'Activity-Based Costing'?

'Activity-Based Costing,' popularly known as **ABC**, helps you to view overhead costs from the point of business processes. The result is you will be able to optimize costs for the entire business process. As a single business process, activity-based costing will cut across several cost centers and will give you an enhanced view of the costs incurred.

297.   What is 'Product Cost Controlling' (CO-PC)?

'Product Cost Controlling' (CO-PC) deals with estimating the costs to produce a product/service. CO-PC is divided into two major areas:

(i) Cost of materials

(*ii*) Cost of processing

With CO-PC, you can calculate:

(*a*) Cost of goods manufactured (COGM)

(*b*) Cost of goods sold (COGS)

CO-PC is tightly integrated with **Production Planning** (PP) and **Materials Management** (MM), in addition to FI. The functionality helps to:

- Calculate Standard Costs of manufactured goods
- Calculate the Work-In-Progress (WIP)
- Calculate the Variances, at period-end
- Finalize settlement of product costs

Note that CO-PC deals only with production costs as it deals only with the production.

298. What is 'Profitability Analysis' (CO-PA)?

'Profitability Analysis' (CO-PA) helps you determine how profitable (denoted by the **'contribution margin'**) your market segments are. The analysis is on the external side of the market. You will be able to define what segments, such as customer, product, geography, sales organization, etc., of the market are required for analyzing 'operating results /profits.' With multi-dimensional 'drill-down' capability, you have all the flexibility you need for reporting.

299. How is 'Profit Center Accounting' (EC-PCA) different from CO-PA?

Unlike CO-PA where the focus is on external market segments' profitability, **'Profit Center Accounting' (EC-PCA)** focuses on profitability of internal areas **(profit centers)** of the enterprise. Profit center accounting is used to draw internal balance sheets and profit & loss statements. You may use EC-PCA in place of **business area** accounting.

Attribute	Profitability Analysis (CO-PA)	Profit Center Accounting (EC-PCA)
Focus	External market segments	Internal responsibility centers
Reporting	Any point of time	During period-end
	Margin reporting	Profit & Loss statements
Accounting	Cost of sales	Period-based

Both CO-PA and EC-PCA serve different purposes, and are not mutually exclusive. You may need them both in your organization.

300.   Explain 'Integration of CO' with its components and other SAP modules.

The CO module is integrated with FI, AA, SD, MM, PP, and HR:

- FI is the main source of data for CO. All expenses, posted in FI, flow to CO through the 'primary cost elements' to the appropriate 'cost centers.' Similarly, postings in Asset Accounting (such as depreciations) are also passed on to CO.

- Revenue postings in FI would result in postings in CO-PA and also in EC-PCA.

- The SD, MM, and PP modules have many integration points in CO. Goods issue (GI) to a controlling object or goods receipt (GR) from a 'production order' are some examples of integration. These modules are tightly integrated as consumption activities, cost of goods issued, overhead charges, material costs, etc., which are passed on to production objects such as PP production order or sales order. The WIP (Work-In-Progress) and the variances, at period ends, are settled to CO-PA, CO-PCA, and also to FI. Revenues are directly posted when you generate billing documents in SD, if the sales order is a cost object item.

- The HR module generates various types of costs to be posted in CO. Planned HR costs can also be passed on for CO planning.

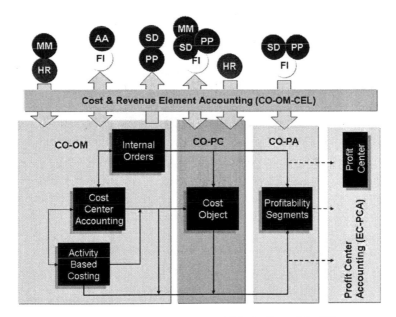

Figure 76: Integration of CO components within and outside CO

The following table illustrates how the various components of CO are integrated:

	Overhead Cost Controlling
CO-OM	External costs can be posted to cost centers/internal orders from other SAP modules.
	Cost centers can then allocate costs to other cost centers, orders, and business processes in Activity-Based Costing (ABC).
	Internal orders can settle costs to cost centers, other internal orders, and to business processes in ABC.
	ABC, in turn, can pass on costs to cost centers and orders.
	Product Cost Controlling
CO-PC	Direct postings from FI to cost objects (such as production orders).
	Costs from cost centers can be posted to the production orders as overhead cost allocation.
	Costs settled from internal orders can be passed on to production orders.
	Statistical cost postings from all CO components
CO-PA	Cost assessments from cost centers/ABC.
	Costs settled from internal orders.
	Production variances from CO-PC.

301. What is a 'Cost Object'?

A '**Cost Object**,' also known as a **CO Account Assignment Object**, in SAP denotes a unit to which you can assign objects. It is something like a repository in which you collect costs, and, if necessary, move the costs from one object to another. All the components of CO have their own cost objects such as cost centers, internal orders, etc.

The cost objects decide the nature of postings as to whether they are real postings or statistical postings. All the objects that are identified as statistical postings are *not* considered cost objects (for example, profit centers).

302. Differentiate between 'Real' and 'Statistical Postings' in CO.

The CO account assignment objects decide the type of postings allowed. They can be real or statistical postings.

'**Real Postings**' allow you to further allocate/settle those costs to any other cost object in CO, either as 'senders' or as 'receivers.' The objects that are allowed to have real postings include:

- Cost Centers
- Internal Orders (Real)
- Projects (Real)
- Networks
- Profitability Segments
- PP – Production Orders (make-to-order)

'**Statistical Postings**,' on the other hand, are only for information purposes. You will not be able to further allocate/settle these statistical costs to other cost objects. Examples of such objects include:

- Statistical (Internal) Orders
- Statistical Projects
- Profit Centers

303. How do you define 'Number Ranges' in CO?

You will be required to define, for each of the controlling areas, the '**Number Ranges**' for all transactions that will generate documents in CO. Once done for a controlling area, you may copy from one controlling area to other controlling areas when you have more than one such area.

To avoid too many documents, SAP recommends grouping multiple but similar transactions, and then assigning number ranges to this group. Further, you may create different number ranges for plan and actual data. As in FI, the number ranges can be **internal** or **external**. The document number ranges in CO are independent of fiscal years.

304. How does 'Master Data' differ from 'Transaction Data' in CO?

The '**Master Data**' remain unchanged over a long period, whereas '**Transaction Data**' are short-term. The transaction data are assigned to the master data.

Though you normally create the master data from transactions, note that you will be able to create these records from the configuration side as well. When you need to create a large number of master data, you may use the '**collective processing**' option to create related master records in one step. SAP puts master data in 'groups' for easy maintenance.

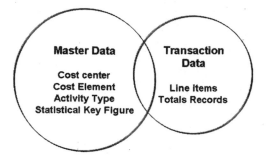

Figure 77: Master and Transaction Data in CO

In the case of master data of cost center/cost elements/activity types, once they are created, you will not be able to change the date. SAP calls this feature the '**time dependency**' of master data. If necessary, you can extend the 'time' by creating a new one and attaching it to the existing objects. In the case of **resources**, the master data are time-dependent and the system will allow you to delete these objects. **Statistical Key Figures (SKF)** are not time-dependent; once defined they are available in the system forever.

COST ELEMENT ACCOUNTING

305. What is a 'Cost Element'?

'**Cost Elements**' represent the origin of costs. There are two types of cost elements:

- Primary Cost Elements
- Secondary Cost Elements

306. What is a 'Primary Cost Element'?

'**Primary Cost Elements**' represent the consumption of production factors such as raw materials, human resources, utilities, etc. Primary cost elements have their corresponding GL accounts in FI. All the expense/revenue accounts in FI correspond to the primary cost elements in CO. Before you can create the primary cost elements in CO, you first need to create them in FI as GL accounts.

Note that SAP treats **revenue elements** also as primary cost elements in CO processing. The only difference is that all the revenue elements are identified with a negative sign while posting in CO. The revenue elements correspond to the revenue accounts in FI and they fall under the **cost element category**, category 01/11.

307. What is a 'Secondary Cost Element'?

'**Secondary Cost Elements**' represent the consumption of production factors provided internally by the enterprise itself, and are present only in the CO. They are actually like cost carriers, and are used in **allocations and settlements** in CO. While creating these elements, you need to mention the cost element category, which can be any of the following:

- Category 21, used in **internal settlements**
- Category 42, used in **assessments**
- Category 43, used in **internal activity allocation**

308. What is a 'Cost Element Category'?

All the cost elements need to be assigned to a '**Cost Element Category**,' to determine the transactions for which you can use the cost elements.

Example:

- Category 01, known as the '**general primary cost elements**,' is used in standard primary postings from FI or MM into CO.
- Category 22 is used to settle order/project costs, or cost object costs to objects outside of CO (such as assets, materials, GL accounts, etc.).

309. How do you automatically create 'Cost Elements'?

You will be able to create 'cost elements' automatically by specifying the cost element, the cost element interval, and the cost element category for the cost elements. All these are achieved by creating **default settings**. The creation of cost elements is done in the background.

The **primary cost elements** can be created only when you have the corresponding GL accounts in the chart of accounts of the Company Code. Even though the GL account names are used as the names of the primary cost elements thus created by the system, you have the option of changing these names in CO. All the **secondary cost elements** are created in CO; the name of these cost elements comes from the **cost element category**.

COST CENTER ACCOUNTING

310. Define 'Cost Center Accounting (CO-OM-CCA).'

'Cost Center Accounting (CO-OM-CCA)' helps you to track where costs are incurred in your enterprise. All the costs, such as salary and wages, rent, water charges, etc., incurred are either assigned or posted to a cost center.

311. What is a 'Cost Center'?

A 'Cost Center' is an organizational element within a **controlling area**.

You may define cost centers according to your specific needs; the most common approach is to define a cost center for each of the bottom-most organizational units that are supposed to manage their costs. So, typical cost centers could be canteen, telephone, power, human resources, production, etc.

There are other ways of designing cost centers; you may create cost centers representing geographical requirements or responsibility areas or activities/ services produced, etc.

After defining individual cost centers, you will assign each one of the cost centers to one of the **cost center categories**. All cost centers of a controlling area are assigned to a **standard hierarchy**.

312. What is a 'Cost Center Category'?

A 'Cost Center Category' is an indicator in the cost center master record that identifies what kind of activities a particular cost center performs. SAP comes delivered with default categories such as administration, production, logistics, marketing, development, management, etc. If necessary, as in other cases, you may create your own categories. The categorization is useful for assigning certain standard characteristics to a group of cost centers performing similar activities.

SAP also allows you to store **special indicators** (such as **lock indicators**) for each of the cost center categories. These special indicators serve as defaults when you create a new cost center.

Cost center categories

CCtC	Name	Qty	ActPri	ActSec	ActRev	PlnPri	PlnSec	PlnRev	Cm
1	Production	☑	☐	☐	☑	☐	☐	☑	
2	Service cost center	☑	☐	☐	☑	☐	☐	☑	
3	Sales	☐	☐	☐	☑	☐	☐	☑	
4	Administration	☐	☐	☐	☑	☐	☐	☑	
5	Management	☑	☐	☐	☑	☐	☐	☑	
6	Research & Develop.	☑	☐	☐	☑	☐	☐	☑	
7	Services	☑	☐	☐	☑	☐	☐	☑	
9	Allocation cost ctr	☐	☐	☐	☑	☐	☐	☑	
C	Consulting	☐	☐	☐	☑	☐	☐	☑	
E	Development	☐	☐	☐	☑	☐	☐	☑	
F	Production	☑	☐	☐	☑	☐	☐	☑	
G	Logistics	☐	☐	☐	☑	☐	☐	☑	
H	Service cost center	☑	☐	☐	☑	☐	☐	☑	
L	Management	☐	☐	☐	☑	☐	☐	☑	
M	Material	☐	☐	☐	☑	☐	☐	☑	

Figure 78: Cost Center Category

313.   What is a 'Standard Hierarchy'?

A tree-like hierarchy structure grouping all the cost centers (of all the Company Codes belonging to a single controlling area) so defined is known as the '**Standard Hierarchy**' in CO. This is the SAP method of grouping all the cost centers in a controlling area, which helps in analyzing the cost summary at the end of the nodes of the hierarchy (cost center or cost center groups or at the top level). A cost center can be attached to any number of cost center groups, but you cannot assign the same cost center more than once within a cost center group.

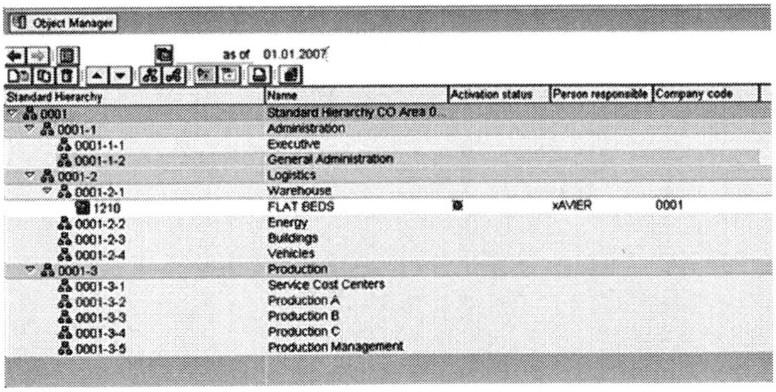

Figure 79: Standard Hierarchy Sample

The standard hierarchy helps in easy maintenance of the cost centers / cost center groups for creation of new ones or changing existing ones. It supports drag-drop functionality.

You may use **alternate hierarchies** to group cost centers according to your internal reporting requirements. You can have any number of alternate hierarchies but it is mandatory that you have one standard hierarchy. The alternate hierarchy is also known as the **master data group**.

314. Explain posting of costs to 'Cost Centers.'

When you create accounting transitions in FI/FI-AA/MM, you typically post to one or more GL accounts. While doing so, provided you have already configured in such a way, you also require the user to input the cost center for that transaction, so that when the transaction is posted the values (costs) flow not only to the GL but also to CO to the appropriate cost center. The system will create two posting documents: one for FI and another for CO.

Additionally, you will also be able to post non-financial information such as direct labor hours from HR or PP modules to cost centers in CO.

315. What is an 'Activity Type'?

'**Activity Type**' helps you do define the service/action (for example, human labor, machine labor, repair hours, etc.) performed or provided by a cost center. It forms the 'basis' for allocating costs to other cost centers or internal orders, etc. You may assign an activity type to an operation so that they are reflected in PP; a CO document is created with the costs of the operation allocated from the cost center that produced the operation to a production order, when the operation is completed in PP.

You may group activity types into **activity type groups** for easy maintenance.

You need to arrive at the **activity price**, which needs to be attached to that particular activity type for planning or recording the actual. The activity price is calculated by dividing the total costs by the total planned/actual activity quantity (hours, units, etc.).

It is not necessary that all the cost centers have activity types associated with them. If there is no output from a cost center, then there will be no activity type for that cost center.

316. Where do you assign Activity Type in Cost Centers?

There is no direct assignment. You plan the output for a cost center first by using **Transaction KP26**. Then, plan the value of that cost center with the budget for a period in **Transaction KP06**. 'Planned Activity expenditure'/'Planned Activity Quantity' gives the 'planned activity rate,' which you can use to valuate your activity confirmations in manufacturing orders. You can also define your activity prices on your own, but you have to run the 'price revaluation' if you want to revaluate your actual activity prices.

	Transaction Code
	KP26
	KP06

317. What is a 'Resource' in CO?

'**Resources**' are goods/services, consumed by CO objects such as cost center/internal order/WBS element, which are supplied (internally or externally) to an organization in order to produce business activities. The resources are used only in planning and not for tracking the actual.

There are three types of resources:

- Type **B** (used in base planning object)
- Type **M** (refers to a material)
- Type **R** (exists only in CO-OM)

318. What is a 'Statistical Key Figure' (SKF)?

The '**Statistical Key Figure (SKF)**' is used as the basis (**tracing factor**) for making allocations (**assessments/distributions**). They are the statistical data such as number of employees, area in square meters, etc. You will make use of a SKF when you are faced with a situation where it is not possible to use any other conventional method or measure to arrive at the share of costs to be allocated to cost centers.

Suppose that you are incurring a monthly expense of USD 5,000 in the cost center cafeteria, the cost of which needs to be allocated to other cost centers. You can achieve this by the SKF. Imagine that you want this to be allocated based on the 'number of employees' working in each of the other cost centers such as administrative office (50 employees) and the factory (200 employees). You will now use the number of employees as the SKF for allocating the costs. The following illustration helps you to understand how SKF is used:

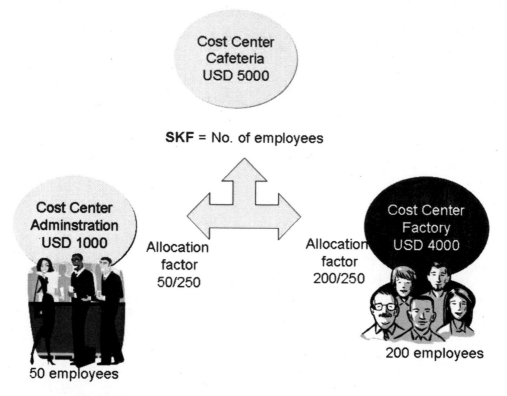

Figure 80: Statistical Key Figure

Transaction Code
KK01

In SKF allocation, you have the flexibility of using two different **SKF Categories**; namely, **Total value** or **Fixed value**. You will use fixed values in situations where the SKF does not change very often, as in the case of the number of employees, area, etc. You will use total values in situations where the value is expected to change every now and then, as in the case of power use or water consumption and the like.

319. Explain the 'Planning' steps in CO-OM-CCA.

The three steps involved in planning in cost center accounting include:

■ Configuration required for planning

- Configure a **Plan Version**
- Create or Copy **Plan Layouts**
- Create **Plan Profile**
- Insert Plan Layouts into Plan Profile
- Inputting the planned data
- Completing the planning activity

320. What is a 'Plan Version'?

A '**Plan Version**' is a collection of planning data. The version controls whether the user will maintain plan data or actual data or both. You may create as many versions as you need, though SAP provides you with the necessary versions in the standard system.

Each version has information stored in the system per fiscal year period. The version '000' is automatically created for a period horizon of five years, and is normally the final version as this allows for storing actual information as well. You will be using the data in version '000' for all the planned activity price calculation. Once planning is completed, you need to 'lock' that version so that no one will be able to modify the plan data.

321. What is 'Integrated Planning' in CO-OM-CCA?

'**Integrated Planning**' helps you to transfer data from other SAP modules such as PP, HR, FI-AA, etc. If you have planned data in these modules and just transfer these into CO, without making any changes, then you do not need plan again in cost center accounting. Before using integrated planning, you need to activate the integration in the planning menu.

Note that integrated planning is possible only when there has been no data planned on that version before activating the integrated planning.

322. Explain 'Plan Layout.'

A '**Plan Layout**' is nothing but a data entry screen or template that you use to input plan data.

In most situations, it would be more than sufficient to use SAP supplied planning layouts; however, you may create your own by copying one of the existing layouts and altering it with the help of **report painter**. While creating a custom layout, note that you have the flexibility to create up to nine **lead columns** (giving the details the nature of the data associated with the value columns), and any number of **value columns** (plan data such as amount, unit, etc., corresponding to the lead column).

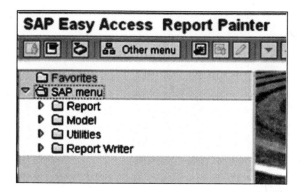

Figure 81: Report Painter

You also have the option of using MS-Excel spreadsheets as the data input screen in lieu of the SAP plan layouts; but to achieve this you need to activate the 'integrating with Excel option' while assigning the layout(s) to a planner profile in IMG.

You need to define a plan layout for each of the three planning areas in CO, namely:

(i) Primary Cost and Activity Inputs

(ii) Activity Output/Prices

(iii) Statistical Key Figures

323. Explain a 'Plan Profile.'

A '**Plan Profile**' (or **Planning Profile**) helps in controlling the whole process of planning by logically grouping the various plan layouts together. It determines the timeline for planning. You can have more than one planning layout per plan profile.

Before you actually start inputting the data, you need to set the plan profile so that the system knows what layout needs to be used for the planning exercise.

324. How do you copy 'Plan Data' from one period to another?

SAP allows you to copy planning data, created manually earlier, from one fiscal year to the other or from one period to a different period within the same fiscal year. You have the option of copying existing plan data to a future period as new plan data or copying actual data from one period to another as plan data.

325.   What is the recommended Planning Sequence, in CO?

SAP recommends three steps in the planning. In all three steps, the planning can be carried out **manually** or **automatically**. You may use assessment, distribution, and indirect activity allocation or inputted costs for planning. You can also have **centralized planning** (cost element planning for all the cost centers) and **decentralized planning** (planning for individual cost centers) in your organization.

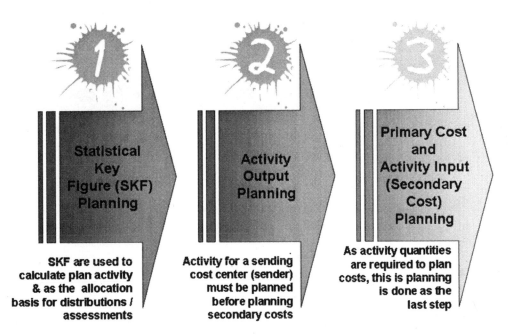

Figure 82: Planning Sequence for Cost Center Accounting

326.   What are the two options for entering Plan Data?

SAP provides you with a choice of two options to enter your plan data. You may use **Form-based entry** or **Free entry**.

In **form-based entry**, all you need to do is fill in the plan data in the rows corresponding to the characteristic values (cost centers, cost element, etc.) displayed on the screen. But, in **free entry**, you have the freedom of inputting even the characteristic values.

327.   What are 'Distribution Keys'?

The SAP system uses '**Distribution Keys**' to distribute planned values across various periods. With the standard distribution keys supplied by SAP, you will be able to achieve the type of distribution you need:

- **DK1** (equal distribution)
- **DK2** (distribution as done earlier)
- **DK5** (copy values to period where there is no value)

For example, if you have a planned annual value of 12,000, by using **DK1** you will be able to distribute 1,000 each as the monthly values. If you had plan values for last year which were something like 1,000 for January to June, 500 for July, 1,500 for August, and 1,000 each for September to December, then by using **DK2**, you will be able to copy the same amounts to the next fiscal year. **DK5** will copy values to future periods only if there are no values already available for those periods.

328.   Differentiate 'Activity-Dependent 'and 'Activity-Independent' Costs.

As you might be aware of already, there are two types of costs; namely, **variable costs** and **fixed costs**.

Variable Costs, such as material costs, factory labor, etc., are always dependent on an activity, and will vary depending on the activity. The higher the activity the more will be the expenditure towards variable costs. In short, these costs are directly proportional to the level of activity. In SAP CO, these costs are known as '**Activity-Dependent Costs**.'

In contrast to the variable costs, '**Activity-Independent Costs**' or **fixed costs** do not usually vary with the level of activity. And you may need to incur these costs irrespective of whether there is an activity. Costs such as costs towards security, insurance premiums, etc., fall under the category of fixed costs.

329.   What is a 'Mixed Cost'?

There are instances where you will come across a costing situation where the costs cannot be strictly segregated into either fixed or variable costs. These costs are known as **semi-fixed costs** or **semi-variable costs** or **mixed costs**, because a portion of the total costs is fixed and the remaining portion is a variable cost.

The classic example is the charges for electricity in a production environment, where there is a basic minimum charge payable to the electricity provider (or towards heating requirements of the buildings) which remains fixed whether there is some production activity or not. When there is production, you will use more electricity, which varies with the level of production.

330. Explain 'Manual Primary Cost Planning.'

'**Manual Primary Cost Planning**' is used to plan for costs associated with the external procurement of goods and services. You will plan both fixed and variable costs, and also mixed costs, if necessary. You will plan costs such as salaries, wages, etc., as activity-dependent costs; the costs towards security, etc., will be planned as activity-independent costs.

You need to note that planning fixed primary costs is not vastly different from that of planning for variable primary costs. When you plan for the variable primary costs you need to mention the activity type associated with that. You may further break down this cost into fixed and variable proportions. The 'fixed primary costs' or 'activity-independent primary costs' are planned using the primary cost elements on various cost centers, based on the activity performed on a particular cost center.

You may use any of the following SAP supplied planning layouts:

- **1-101** – Activity-independent or activity-dependent primary costs
- **1-103** – Activity-independent costs
- **1-152** – Activity-independent costs (on a quarterly basis)
- **1-153** – Cost-element planning (two versions simultaneously)
- **1-154** – Cost-element planning (previous year's actual displayed in the lead column)
- **1-156** – Central planning (Cost element planning from Cost center perspective)

331. Explain 'Automatic Primary Cost Planning.'

SAP provides you with two ways of handling **Primary Costs Planning**; namely:

- Inputted Costs Calculation
- Distribution

Inputted Costs Calculation is used to smooth one-time costs (bonus, incentives, etc.) incurred by spreading them over a period of time though it is posted on the FI side at the end of the year. You again have two methods of processing these costs: (*i*) when there is no corresponding costs equivalent on the FI side such as the inputted family labor or inputted rent, etc., and (*ii*) when there is a corresponding cost equivalent on the FI side such as festival bonus, etc.

Distribution helps in planning primary costs from one cost center to the other. The cost center from where the costs are distributed is known as the **sender** (or **pooled cost center** or **clearing cost center**) and the other cost centers to which the costs are distributed or where the costs are received are known as **receivers**.

Note that you will be able to distribute planned/actual primary costs only. Also note that the pooled cost center does not incur any of these costs but acts only as the 'clearing center' for distribution to other cost centers. During the process, you will use the SKF or the regular percentage method as the **distribution rule** for achieving the distribution. The **distribution cycle** helps to carry out the whole planning exercise.

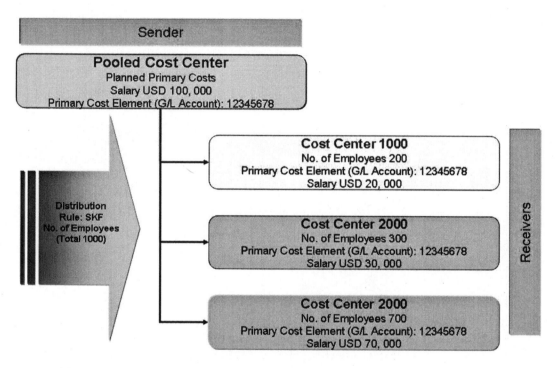

Figure 83: Distribution (Automatic Primary Costs Planning)

332. Explain 'Manual Secondary Cost Planning.'

'Manual Secondary Cost Planning' is required when you need to plan consumption quantities of a sender cost center's planned activity from the point of view of the receiving cost center. The activity inputs may be planned either as the activity-dependent costs (variable) or as activity-independent costs (fixed).

The 'activity-dependent primary cost planning' is used only when you need the services such as repair hours on a specified activity type. On the other hand, you will use 'activity-independent primary cost planning' when you need services such as maintenance hours, which are not restricted to a particular activity.

The system uses the 'planned calculated activity price' for posting the secondary cost. It is possible to carry out 'manual secondary cost planning' for activity types categorized as Category-1 (manual entry/manual allocation). Note that it is important that you perform reconciliation of planned consumption of an activity at the receiver cost center to the volume planned at the sender's level; otherwise, you will get a warning message when the system calculates the activity price.

333. Explain 'Assessment' in Secondary Cost Planning.

'**Assessment**' is one of the methods used in 'automatic planning of secondary costs' in cost center accounting. You will typically use this method when you need to allocate costs from one cost center to other cost centers. The original costs, even if they are primary, from the cost center are grouped and reclassified as secondary while allocating the same to other cost centers (imagine that you are collecting primary costs such as postage, telephone, courier expenses, fax charges, etc., into a cost center called 1000, now group these costs for assessment using a secondary cost element to receiver cost centers: 2000 and 3000).

You need to define an **assessment rule** (either 'percentage' or 'SKFs' or 'fixed amounts') for affecting assessment. You would have now noticed that this is similar to the distribution used in 'primary cost planning.'

So, why do you need an assessment? Assessment is required when you need to allocate secondary costs, and when you do not need the details you would otherwise get from distribution.

334. What is an 'Allocation Structure'?

You need to define or use a secondary cost element, called the 'assessment cost element,' while you carry out the 'assessment' in 'automatic secondary cost planning.' Instead of defining individual assessment elements (for a group of primary cost elements) in individual segments, every now and then, you may define various assessment elements in an '**Allocation Structure**,' and use them repeatedly.

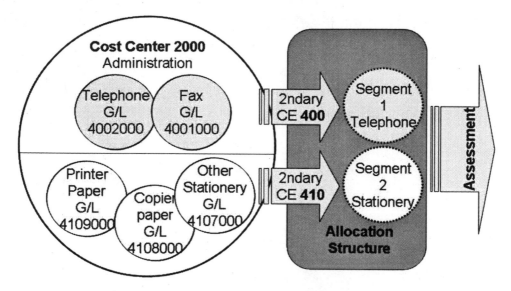

Figure 84: Assessment (Automatic Secondary Cost Planning)

335. Explain 'Segments' and 'Cycles.'

A '**Segment**' is one processing unit required to complete an automated allocation of distribution or assessment or reposting of planned/actual costs in controlling in SAP. A segment is made up of (*a*) allocation characteristics – to identify the sender/ receiver, (*b*) values of the sender – plan/actual, type of costs to be allocated, and (*c*) values of the receiver – the basis for allocation, for example, the **tracing factor** such as SKF, percentages, etc.

When you combine multiple segments into a single process, then you call that the '**Cycle**.' A Cycle helps you to process various segments in a chain-like fashion one after another. A Cycle consists of header data (valid for all Segments in a Cycle) and one or more Segments, with summarized rules and settings enabling allocation. The Segments within a 'cycle' can be processed iteratively (one segment waits for the results of another) or non-iteratively (all the segments are processed independently) or cumulatively (to take care of variations in receiver Tracing Factors or sender amounts).

Typically, when you start the cycles you will start them in a 'test' mode to see the allocations before actual postings. Technically, you can run the cycles in 'production' mode at any point of time, but the system will carry out the allocation postings only on the first day of a period. The utility of the cycle lies in the fact that you can run these period after period.

336.   What is 'Iterative Processing' of Cycles?

'**Iterative Processing**' is nothing but the repetitive processing of sender/receiver relationships until the sender's entire cost is transferred to the receiver(s). During iterative processing, you will not be able to use 'fixed amounts' as the 'sender rules'; you will also not be able to define a percentage to remain on the sender. You will be able to use both plan and actual data while using the iteration.

337.   What is 'Splitting'? Explain the 'Splitting Structure.'

'**Splitting**' is a process used to assign 'activity-independent' plans/actual costs, both primary and secondary, of a cost center to the individual activity types within that cost center. But the important requirement is that you will use this when there is no account assignment to the activity types.

You may either use the **Splitting rules** or the **Equivalence number** to achieve this. When you split the costs from a cost center, the cost center temporarily becomes more than one cost center for the purpose of allocation but again becomes a single cost center when posting happens in the subsequent period.

If you need to assign different cost elements or cost element groups to activities in more than one way, then you need to define a '**Splitting Structure**' containing 'splitting rules' to determine the criteria of splitting 'activity-independent' costs to an activity type. If you have created the splitting structure in customizing and assigned the same to a cost center, then the system uses the splitting structure for cost apportioning; otherwise, it will use the equivalence number.

The '**splitting rules**' determine the amount or the proportion of costs to be allocated to various activity types of a cost center and is based on the consumption of these activity types. The costs thus allocated may be a fixed sum, or a percentage, or it can even be based on the tracing factors or SKFs.

The '**equivalence number**' is a basic method for splitting the costs when you manually plan for each of the activity types. By this, you will plan all activity-independent costs according to the equivalence numbers (the default is 1).

338.   What is an 'Activity Price Calculation'?

You will be completing the planning process only when you perform the '**Activity Price Calculation**,' which is based on planned activities and costs. By doing this you are valuating the planned secondary costs at receiving cost centers. If you do not want to use activity price thus calculated, you are free to use the **political price** for the activity type.

As you are aware, the activity price is used for planned/actual allocation and is determined by using either the political price or the system-calculated activity price.

339. How does the system calculate the 'Activity Price'?

The system calculates the '**Activity Price**,' for each activity type and cost center, by following the underlying rule:

$$\text{Planned Activity Price} = \frac{\text{Planned Primary Costs} + \text{Planned Secondary Costs}}{\text{Planned Activity Type Volume}}$$

Note that the system will continue to calculate the activity price even if you have set the price indicator of an activity type to the '**political price**.'

340. What is known as the 'Political Price' for an activity type?

The '**Political Price**' is the price determined outside the SAP system, which is used in manual input using the required planning layout in planning.

341. What is 'Allocation Price Variance'?

'**Allocation Price Variance**' is the difference between the 'political price' of an activity type and the 'system calculated activity price' of the same activity type.

342. What is 'Budgeting'?

'**Budgeting**' is used to augment the planning process at the cost-center level. While planning is considered the '**bottom-up**' approach, budgeting is regarded as the '**top-down**' method to control costs.

Budgeting usually comes 'down' from the 'top (management)' and is used to guide the planning process at the cost-center level. Note that budgeting is *not* integrated with postings; you will get an error when the system comes across a posting that will result in the actual values exceeding the budget for that cost center.

343. What are the 'Direct Allocation' methods of posting in CO?

The '**Direct Allocation**' of posting in CO may be an actual cost entry or a transaction-based posting.

The **actual cost entry** is the transfer of primary costs from FI to CO, on a real-time basis, through the primary cost elements. You may also transfer transaction data by making the cost accounting assignment to cost objects from other modules such as FI-AA, SD, and MM:

- FI-AA: Assign assets to a cost center (to post depreciation, etc.)
- MM: Assign GR to a cost center/internal order
- SD: Assign or settle a sales order to a cost center or internal order

Note that during actual cost entry, the system creates two documents. When you post the primary costs from FI to CO, the system will create a document in FI and a parallel document in CO, which is summarized from the point of the cost object/element.

Transaction-based postings are executed within the CO, again on a real-time basis, enabling you to have updated cost information on the cost centers at any point in time. You will be able to carry out the following transaction-based postings in CO:

- Reposting
  - Line items
  - Transactions
- Manual cost allocation
- Direct activity allocation
- Posting of Statistical Key Figures
- Posting of sender activities

344. What is the 'Indirect Allocation' method of postings in CO?

The '**Indirect Allocation**' of postings in CO may be used at the end of a period as a periodic allocation. This is done after you have completed all the primary postings. You may post the following periodic allocations using indirect allocation:

- Periodic Reposting
- Distribution
- Assessment
- Accrual Cost Calculation (Inputted Cost Calculation)
- Indirect Activity Allocation

345. Explain 'CO Automatic Account Assignment.'

For transferring primary costs to CO, on a real-time basis, you need to have '**Automatic Account Assignments**' defined in the system. By doing this, you will always be able to post a particular cost to a specified cost center. You can also use this assignment for automatically posting the exchange rate differences (gain or loss), discount, etc., to CO.

You may also have additional account assignment at different levels such as:

- Controlling area/account/Company Code in the customizing
- Controlling area/account/cost element in the master record
- Controlling area/account/Company Code/business area/valuation area in customizing

The system always goes through the route of customizing first, then to the cost element master record while accessing the account assignment rules.

346.   How does 'Validation' differ from 'Substitution'?

SAP uses validations and substitutions to check the integrity of data entered before posting a document. When you have both substitutions and validations defined, the system first completes the substitution then goes on to validate the entries. Note that only one validation and one substitution can be activated at a time for a controlling area per 'call-up point.'

A 'Validation' uses Boolean logic for **checking** any type of combination of specified criteria (such as account type/cost center combination) for ensuring the validity before allowing you to post a document.

Example:

- **Validation Rule:** If the cost element is '120000,' then the cost center is '1200.'
- **Document:** You try posting a document containing the cost element as '120000' and the cost center is '1400.'
- **System Response:** The system will throw an 'error message' after checking that the cost center value does not match the cost center value of the criteria for that given cost element value.

In contrast to validation which just checks for validity, **substitution** ensures that the system replaces a value assigned to one or more fields based on predetermined criteria, using, again, '**Boolean logic**.'

Example:

- **Substitution Rule:** If the cost element is '120000,' then the cost center is '1200.'
- **Document:** You try posting a document containing the cost element as '120000' and the cost center as '1400.'
- **System Response:** The system will replace the entered cost center value of '1400' with that of the correct value '1200.'

347. What is a 'Call-up Point'?

A '**Call-up Point**' is a particular point in transaction processing that triggers an action such as substitution or validation.

348. What is 'Boolean Logic'?

'**Boolean Logic**' is based on simple logic to determine if a given statement is true or false. The logic works on the basic principle that a statement can either be true or false. In a complex statement (created using operators 'and '/ 'or '/ 'nor,' etc.) with many parts, the logic goes by assigning true or false from part to part, and then determines at the end whether the combination is true or false.

349. Explain 'Reposting' in Cost Center Accounting.

'**Reposting**' is one of the 'transaction-based postings' in Cost Center Accounting used to reallocate costs that were incorrectly posted to another cost center earlier. Also called **internal reposting**, there are two types:

■ Line Item Reposting
■ Transaction Reposting

Use **Line Item Reposting** only when a certain line item, from the original posting, needs to be reposted. Under this reposting, at the end of the transaction, the system creates a new CO document, but keeps the original FI document unchanged. In the new CO document created, the original FI number is referenced.

You will resort to the entire **Transaction Reposting** when the original posting was incorrect. Here, the original FI documents are not referenced to in the new CO document created, though the original FI document remains unchanged.

350. Is 'Periodic Reposting' different from 'Reposting'?

'**Periodic Reposting**,' a method under 'indirect allocation,' is used to correct multiple postings made to cost centers during a particular period. As such, this is similar to **multiple reposting** under 'transaction-based postings.'

Periodic reposting is also similar to **distribution**, when you use this, at the period end, to transfer all costs from a 'pooled cost center' to other receivers. (Note that the 'distribution' is meant primarily for cost allocation, but periodic reposting is meant for correcting the posting errors.)

351. Explain 'Manual Cost Allocation.'

'**Manual Cost Allocation**' – one of the 'transaction-based postings' – is used to post both primary and secondary actual costs (*not* the planned costs), and also to transfer external data. You may also use this to correct secondary costs that were incorrectly posted earlier. In the process of manual cost allocation, remember that you can use any type of cost element except 43, as this is meant exclusively for activity allocation.

You may use this among cost centers, internal orders, networks, network activities, sales orders, sales order items, WBS elements, etc., identifying these cost objects as senders/receivers.

352. What is 'Direct Activity Allocation'?

'**Direct Activity Allocation**' – one of the 'transaction-based postings'– is used to record activities performed by a cost center and to allocate simultaneously to 'receiving cost centers.' You will use this 'direct activity allocation' only when you know the activity volumes of both the sender and the receiver. If not known, then use the **indirect activity allocation** at the period end.

You need to input the activity quantity, sender/receiver cost center and date to enable the system to allocate the costs; the system will automatically determine the **allocation cost element** and the **activity price** (either the planned price or the actual price). The system multiplies the activity consumed with that of the activity price to arrive at the allocated cost.

353. How do you calculate 'Accrued Costs'?

SAP provides two methods for calculating the **Inputted** or **Accrued Costs** in CO:
- Target = Actual method
- Cost Element Percent method

354. Describe the 'Reconciliation Ledger.'

The '**Reconciliation Ledger**' is used to keep track of all cross-Company Code transactions between FI and CO, as there is every chance that there may be some imbalance between the CO totals and FI totals when more than one Company Code is attached to a controlling area. This is because you may try to allocate costs from one cost center to another assigned to a different Company Code.

The reconciliation ledger records the Company Code, business area, functional area, amount, cost objects, cost element, currency (Company Code and controlling area), etc. You can make reconciliation postings at the end of a period to synchronize FI and CO with the configuration settings to automatically post the differences to FI.

While configuring the reconciliation ledger, you may use **extended account assignments** besides the normal account assignment for automatic transfer of reconciled postings. The extended account assignment helps make more comprehensive assignments to the relevant reconciliation accounts, with the option and flexibility of specifying any field in the reconciliation ledger (Company Code, cost element, functional area, etc.) for checking the 'substitution rules.'

To aid in determining possible reconciliation postings, you can opt for selecting individual cost flows from all the relevant cost flows. This is accomplished by running the relevant report and looking for the relevant 'data block' (such as total cost flows, basic overview list, and detailed list).

355.   What is 'Variance Analysis' in CO-OM-CCA?

'Variance Analysis' is the determination and interpretation of the difference(s) between the actual and planned (target) costs (within a cost center/cost center group) in cost center accounting. The analysis is intended to provide important clues to top management to plan better later.

356.   What are the 'Categories of Variances' in CO-OM-CCA?

SAP helps to classify all variances into two categories:

- Input Variance
- Output Variance

357.   Explain the 'Input Variance.'

The 'Input Variance' is the result of the mismatch of amounts/quantities of inputs planned and actually used. You will be able to identify the following **input side variances** in the system:

- **Quantity variance** – when there is a difference between planned and actual quantity of activity consumption. The inference is that there is some production inefficiency leading to more consumption or there is some loss/shrinkage in the quantities.
- **Price variance** – when there is a difference between the planned and actual price of an activity. The inference will be that you may need to change the suppliers looking for lower prices or it is just a market condition.

- **Resource (use) variance** – when there is use of an unplanned cost element or there has not been a posting of a planned cost element. The inference is that there are some unidentified costs that may be planned in the next planning cycle, or just plain errors in postings.
- **Remaining (input) variance** – these are all miscellaneous variances where the system is not able to categorize a variance.

358.   What is an 'Output Variance'?

An '**Output Variance**' is the result when the actual costs allocated from a cost center differ from the planned (or target) cost allocation from the cost center. The variances on the 'output side' may be any one of the following:

- **Volume variance** – this variance occurs with actual and planned activities (in terms of activity quantity and/or the activity itself). It can arise in either or both situations described below:
  - Volume variance = Plan Activity Cost – (Actual Activity Quantity * Planned Activity Price)
  - Volume variance = Plan Activity Price * (Planned Activity Quantity – Actual Activity Quantity)
- **Output price variance** – this variance occurs when the activity price used in the actual allocation is a political activity price (manually entered or plan price) differing from the system calculated activity price (target price).
- **Output quantity variance** – this kind of variance occurs only on the actual side, when there is a difference between the actual activity quantity (manually) entered in the sender cost center, and the actual activity quantity allocated from that sender cost center.
- **Remaining variance** – this reflects the miscellaneous variance, at the cost center level, identified by the system on the output side but remains not categorized into any of the above three types. The possible reason can be that you have deactivated the output variances in the **variance variant** configuration or the output variance is less than the 'minor difference' you have defined in the 'variance variant.'

359.   How do you deal with 'Variances'?

Though the system identifies and calculates variances, they are not automatically dealt with by the system. Hence, these variances will remain at the cost center as a **period-end balance** and you need to act on that in one of the following ways:

- You may do actual activity price calculation to revalue all internal allocations with a newly calculated price (as against the initial planned activity price), and post the difference to all the cost centers which initially received the allocations. This will help you in clearing all or a portion of output price variances.

■ You may 'transfer' the variance balance to other modules (such as CO-PA) for further analysis.

■ You may make additional automated allocations within CO-OM-CCA to one or more cost center.

360.   What are all the 'Standard Reports' in CO?

SAP comes delivered with a number of '**Standard Reports**' in the CO module. The reports are grouped under:

■ Planning reports

■ Comparison reports

■ Line item reports

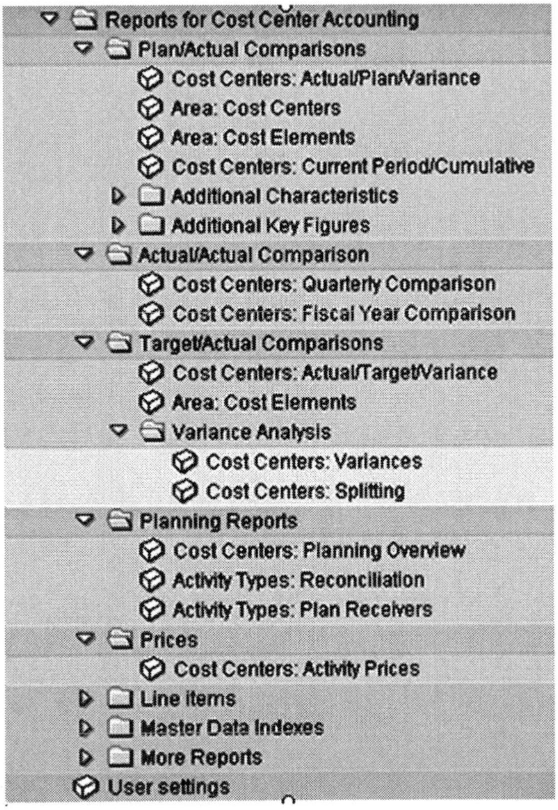

Figure 85: Report Tree in CO

- Report for activity prices
- Reports for variance analysis
- Master data reports
- Document display

All the reports are arranged in a '**report tree**' with a hierarchical arrangement of reports under various nodes. Note that you will not be able to change the standard report tree supplied by SAP; if you need to you can copy it, define your own reports, and then attach these newly defined ones to the new report tree you just defined.

361. What is 'Summarization' in CO?

'**Summarization**' helps to condense and store the transaction data at the 'cost center group' level. You may do the summarization for the highest node of the standard hierarchy or any of the 'alternate hierarchies.' Once summarized, you will be able to create a vast number of reports with report run-time vastly reduced as all the data of the nodes are readily available from the summarized table.

INTERNAL ORDERS

362. What is an 'Internal Order'?

An '**Internal Order**' is a cost object used mainly for recording costs associated with certain events taking place within the company. The events are unique such as marketing campaigns, repairs, trade exhibitions etc. Unlike the cost centers where you typically post only the costs, you will be able to post both cost and revenue information to internal orders. You can plan, monitor, collect, and settle costs/revenue on internal orders.

The internal orders can be classified as a **Single order/Individual order** or a **Standing order**. The orders can also be a **Real internal order** or a **Statistical internal order**.

363. How does an 'Individual Order' differ from a 'Standing Order'?

An '**Individual (Internal) Order**' is meant for collecting and settling costs of a one-time and unique business activity such as a new product launch. You will be settling the order in full at the end of the activity. Typically, this type of order is used for advertising campaigns, R & D costs, assets produced in-house, etc.

A '**Standing (Internal) Order**,' on the other hand, is used in the case of repetitive operations, the costs of which are generally smaller compared to one-time orders. You will settle the costs and form these orders on a 'periodic basis' (say, at the end of every month) and will keep the order open to receive future costs. You will use this type of order for tracking costs on routine maintenance, telephone use charges, etc. These orders do away with the need to create a new order every time you need such a tracking; they are similar to standing instructions.

364.   What are the 'Groups' of Internal Orders?

Internal Orders can be grouped into the following categories/groups:

- **Overhead orders**

   Associated with monitoring of overhead costs incurred for a specific purpose such as tracking repair work, painting the factory, conducting an exhibition, etc. Overhead cost orders are used only in the CO area.

- **Investment orders**

   Tracking the costs incurred on fixed assets (assets under construction) such as construction of a warehouse, etc. These are also called **capital investment orders**.

- **Accrual orders**

   You will use accrual orders when you need to make an offsetting posting of accrued costs to a cost center in CO.

- **Orders with revenue**

   These orders help you carry out cost accounting functionality of SAP SD (customer orders) when you have not implemented the SD module. By doing this, you will be able to track costs and revenues.

365.   How do 'Statistical Internal Orders' differ from 'Real Orders'?

A '**Statistical Internal Order**' is used to collect costs for the purpose of information and reporting, as the costs 'collected' on this order are never settled to a cost object. When you want to create such an order, you will be required to specify that the order is 'statistical' in its master record. However, to make a posting to this kind of order, you need to have a 'real' or 'true' cost object specified during the transaction.

A '**Real Internal Order**' is always used to settle costs to other cost objects. So, even if you specify a real cost object while making a posting to a real order, the system will consider that cost object a statistical one as the internal order itself is a real cost object.

LOGISTICS

LOGISTICS

SALES & DISTRIBUTION (SD)

Depicted below is the broad organizational structure of logistics, which will help you understand how the various units of SD as well as MM modules are linked to FI:

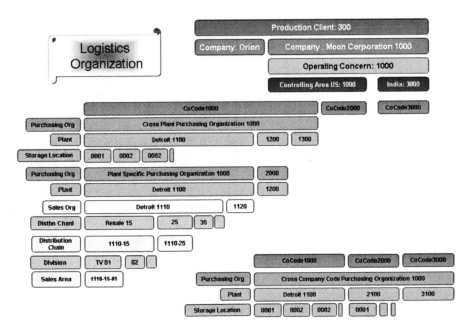

Figure 86: Logistics organizational structure in SAP

366.   What are the components of the SAP SD module?

The important **Components** in SAP Sales & Distribution module include:

- Master data
- Basic functions
- Sales (including foreign sales and sales support)
- Shipping and transportation
- Billing
- Sales support
- Information systems

367.   What are the important organizational elements of SAP SD?

The important **Organizational Elements** in SAP Sales & Distribution include:

- Sales organization
- Distribution channel
- Division
- Sales area
- Sales group
- Sales person

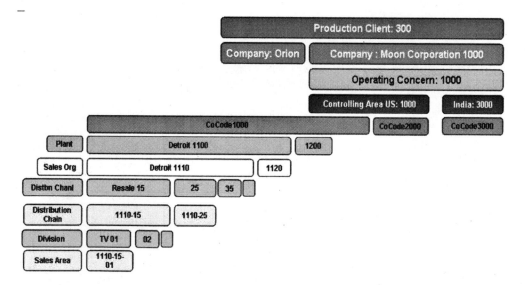

Figure 87: SD Organizational Structure

368.   Explain the 'Sales Organization.' How it is assigned to a 'Plant'?

The **'Sales Organization'** is the top-most organizational element in SD. It represents and takes care of all the transactions relating to the selling and distribution of products or services. A **distribution channel** is assigned to one or more sales organization. The customer master can be maintained with different sales organization views.

The sales organization, identified by a 4-character code, is assigned to one or more plants. These plants are, in turn, assigned to a Company Code. So, it follows that any number of **sales areas** can be brought under a single Company Code.

Even though it is possible that you may have any number of sales organizations, it is recommended that you have a minimum number of these units in your set-up. Ideal recommendation is for a single sales organization per Company Code. If you are selling the same product or service from more than one sales organization, then there is a clear indication that you have more sales organizations defined than what would ideally be required.

369.   What is a 'Distribution Channel'?

A **'Distribution Channel'** depicts the channel through which the products or services reach the customers after they are sold (for example, wholesale, retail, direct sales, etc.). Represented by a 2-digit identifier, the distribution channel is assigned to one or more **sales areas**. As a result, one customer may be serviced through more than one distribution channel. Such as in a **sales organization**, the customer master data may have different distribution channel views.

370.   What is a 'Distribution Chain'?

A **'Distribution Chain'** represents the possible combinations of **sales organization**(s) and **distribution channel**(s). In Figure 89, Detroit 1110-Resale 15 forms a distribution channel and is normally denoted '1110-15.'

371.   What is a 'Division'?

A **'Division'** depicts the product or service group for a range of products/services. For each division, you may define and maintain customer-specific parameters such as terms of payment, pricing, etc. The division may come under one or more distribution channels.

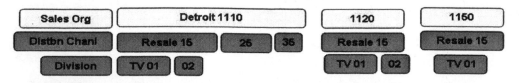

Figure 88: Sales Organization – Distribution Channel – Division Assignment

372.   Explain the assignments among Organizational Units in SD.

1 Company Code		>1 Plant
1 Sales Area		> 1 Plant
> 1 Sales Area	is assigned to	1 Company Code
1 Distribution Channel		> 1 Sales Area
1 Customer		>1 Distribution Channel
>1 Division		>1 Distribution Channel

373.   What is a 'Sales Area'?

A **'Sales Area'** is a combination of the **sales organization, distribution channel,** and **division**. From Figure 91 you can derive sales area 1110-15-01, which in fact represents that the product 'TV' is sold through the 'resale' distribution channel from sales organization 'Detroit.' Usually, you will use sales areas for reporting purposes.

374.   Explain how 'Human Elements' are organized in SD.

There are three distinct organizational units in SD from the human angle:

- Sales Office
- Sales Group
- Sales Person

The **Sales Office** represents the geographical dimension in sales and distribution. A sales office is assigned to a **sales area**. The staff of a sales office may be grouped into **Sales Groups**. This corresponds to sales divisions. A **Sales Person** is assigned to a sales group. This assignment is done at the personnel master record level.

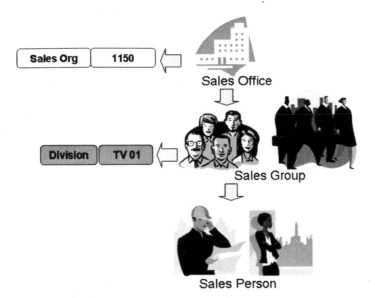

Figure 89: Sales office - Sales group - Sales person structure

375. Where and how is a 'Business Area Assignment' done?

Business area assignment is done at two levels:

- Plant level
- Valuation area level

    The 'business area' is assigned to the combination of 'plant'/'valuation area' and the 'division.'

376. A 'Plant' is assigned to which of the entities in the SD Organization?

A **Plant** is assigned to:

- Company Code
- Combination of Sales Organization & Distribution Channel
- Purchasing Organization

377. How is the 'Shipping Point' determined by the system?

The '**Shipping Point**' is determined by the combination of **shipping condition, loading group,** and **plant** assigned to a shipping point.

378. What are the important 'Customer Master Records'?

Some of the important customer records are:

- Sold-to-Party record
- Ship-to-Party record
- Bill-to-Party record
- Payer record

379. What are the various sections of the 'Customer Master Record'?

The different sections in a master record are:

- **General data**

  You will be able to create general data such as addresses, telephones, contact persons, unloading points, etc., either from the accounting side or from the sales side.

Transaction Code
VD01
XD01

- **Company Code data**

  You will be able to create data in account management (credit management, payment details, taxations, insurance, etc.) that pertains to the Company Code in which the customer is created. You do this from the accounting side.

Transaction Code
XD01

- **Sales & Distribution data**

  The data for pricing, shipping, etc., comes under this category of information. You will create this from the SD area. You can have data for different sales areas for a single customer.

Transaction Code
VD01

380. What is a 'Customer-Material Information Record'?

The information relating to a material that applies only to a specific customer is known as **'Customer-Material Information.'** This is nothing but the description of your 'material by the customer,' and you record this customer-specific information in the customer-material information record.

Transaction Code
VD51

381. What is a 'Sales Order'?

A **'Sales Order'** is a contract between your Sales Organization and a Customer for supply of specified goods and/services over a specified timeframe and in an agreed upon quantity or unit. All the relevant information from the customer master record and the material master record, for a specific sales area, are copied to the sales order. The sales order may be created with reference to a 'preceding document' such as a quotation, then all the initial data from the preceding document is copied to the sales order.

The 'sales order' contains:

- **Organizational data** (sales organization, distribution channel, division, sales document type, pricing procedure, etc.).

- **Header data** (sold-to-party, sales office, sales group, pricing date, document date, order reason, document currency, price group, sales district, customer group, shipping condition, incoterms, payment terms, billing schedule, PO number, etc.).

- **Item data** (item category, order quantity, material, batch number, product hierarchy, plant, material group, shipping point, route, delivery priority, customer material, item number, etc.).

- **Schedule line data** (schedule line, schedule line number, delivery date, order quantity, confirmed quantity, material availability date, loading date, proposed goods issue date, transportation date, movement type, shipping point, etc.).

382. Explain the process flow for a 'Standard Sales Order.'

Starting with the quotation, a **'Standard Sales Order'** goes through the following process:

Figure 90: Standard Sales Order – Process Flow

383. Outline the process flow for 'Sales Returns.'

Starting with the quotation, a **'Sales Return'** goes through the following process:

Figure 91: Sales Returns – Process Flow

384. Describe the process flow for a 'Credit Memo.'

The following diagram depicts a typical process flow for a **'Credit Memo'**:

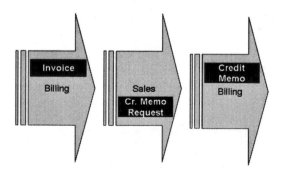

Figure 92: Credit Memo – Process Flow

385. What are the 'Special Sales Document Types'?

- **SO**   Rush Order
- **G2**   Credit
- **RE**   Return Order
- **KN**   FoC (Free-of-Charge) Subsequent Delivery Order
- **RK**   Invoice Correction Request

386. What is the 'Consignment Stock Process'?

In the **'Consignment Stock Process,'** you allow your stock or material to be at the customer's site. You may also allow your stock or material to be made available at your site, but reserved for a particular customer. And you will allow the customer to sell or consume as much stock as he wants from this. You will then bill the customer only for the quantities that he has consumed or sold.

You will monitor the consignment stock – also known as **special stock** - in your system customer-wise and material-wise. You will use the standard sales order document type **KB** and standard delivery type **LF** for processing a **consignment sales order.**

387. Explain 'Sales Document Blocking.'

You may be required to **block** a specific sales document type from further processing, when you want to block undesirable customers. You can achieve this for a specific customer or for a specific document type. You may also block it, in the customer master record, for a single sales area or for all the sales areas attached to the customer.

The blocking is done in customizing by assigning **blocking reasons** to the sales document types. Then in the customer master record do the necessary document block.

388. Can you 'block' a transaction for a material that is 'Flagged for Deletion'?

When you set the **'deletion flag'** for a material at the plant level, you will still be able to enter an order even though the system will 'warn' you that the material has been flagged for deletion. If you need to block any transaction for a material, then you need to use the **'Sales Status'** field in the **'Sales Organization View'** of the material master.

389. Can items in a 'Sales Order' belong to different 'Distribution Channels'?

No. The various items in a **'Sales Order'** should belong to a single **distribution channel** only. However, the various items in a **delivery** can belong to different distribution channels.

390. Can the items in a 'Billing Document' belong to different 'Distribution Channels'?

No. The various items in a **'Billing Document'** should belong to a single **distribution channel** only.

391. Differentiate between a 'Sales Area' and a 'Sales Line.'

A **'Sales Area'** is comprised of sales organization, distribution channel, and division whereas a **Sales Line** is the combination of the sales organization and the distribution channel.

392. Can a 'Sales Area' belong to different Company Codes?

No. A **'Sales Area'** can belong to only one Company Code.

393. What is the 'Storage Location Rule'?

The **'Storage Location Rule'** assigned in the Delivery Document type determines the Storage Location, even when the storage location is entered during delivery creation. This is based on the following rules:

- **MALA:** Shipping Point/Plant/Storage condition
- **RETA:** Plant/Situation/Storage condition
- **MARE:** MALA then RETA

394. How do you configure the 'Partner Determination Procedure' in SD?

The **'Partner Determination Procedure'** is configured as outlined in the following steps:

- Create an account group
- Create and assign a number range to that account group

- Create and assign the partner functions to the account group
- Create a partner determination procedure
- Assign the partner functions to the partner determination procedure
- Finally, assign the partner determination procedure to the account group

395. Where do you define 'Unloading Points' and 'Goods Receiving Hours'?

The **'Unloading Points'** and **'Goods Receiving Hours'** are defined in the Customer Master > General Data > Unloading Points tab.

396. Where do you define the 'Terms of Payment' for a customer?

The **'Terms of Payment'** for a specific customer is defined in the Customer Master > Company Code Data > Payment Transactions Tab, and also in the Billing Document Tab in the Sales Area Data of the Customer Master.

MATERIAL MANAGEMENT (MM)

397. What functions are supported in the SAP 'Material Management' (MM)?

The MM module of SAP supports the following functions:

- MRP (Material Requirements Planning)
- Procurement
- Inventory Management
- Inventory Valuation
- Invoice Verification

398. What is 'MRP'?

'MRP (Material Requirements Planning)' is nothing but the determination of which materials are required, when and in what quantities, based on current information and forecasts.

399.   Explain the basic 'Organizational Structure' in MM.

The major **Organizational Elements** of MM include:

- Purchasing Organization
- Plant
- Storage Location

The **Purchasing Organization** is typically attached to one Company Code. But a single Company Code can have one or more purchasing organizations. One or more **Plants** are attached to a purchasing organization. One or more **Storage Locations** are attached to a plant. One or more plants are assigned to a Company Code, but one plant is attached to only one Company Code.

Depending on how the purchasing organization has been structured, you may come across three types of structures as detailed below:

- **Cross-plant purchasing organization**

  The purchasing organization caters to more than one plant of the same Company Code.

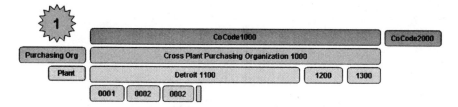

Figure 93: Cross-Plant Purchasing Organization

- **Plant-specific purchasing organization**

  Each Plant has it is own purchasing organization.

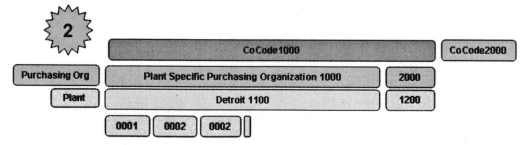

Figure 94: Plant-specific Purchasing Organization

■ **Cross-company code purchasing organization**

A single purchasing organization is responsible for the procurement activities of more than one Company Code. The plants attached to this purchasing organization are also cross-Company Code. In this case, the purchasing organization is *not* attached to any of the Company Codes; instead, the various plants are attached to the purchasing organization. This kind of purchasing organization is known as a **central purchasing organization**. This kind of organizational structure is essential in the case of centralized procurement in an enterprise.

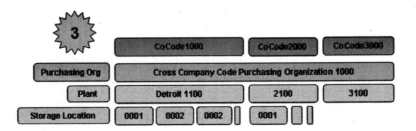

Figure 95: Cross-Company Code Purchasing Organization

400. Define 'Plant' in SAP.

'**Plant**' in SAP can denote a manufacturing location, distribution center, or a warehouse. With unique numbers identifying each of the plants, though these are all not all necessarily financial entities, they can still be linked to a **Business Area**. The Plant is the place where you normally valuate the inventory in SAP. The system, however, checks for the inventory either at the Plant or Plant/Storage Location during an Order entry.

401. Explain the 'Storage Location' in SAP.

A sub-division of a plant, the '**Storage Location**,' defines a location for materials that can be a warehouse, bin, or a **storage area** of raw materials/WIP/finished product. You will manage the physical inventory, material movement, picking, cycle counting, etc., at the storage-location level. In **Warehouse Management**, the storage location is further subdivided.

402. Explain the 'Purchasing Organization' in SAP.

This refers to the organizational structure in SAP that is responsible for procurement of materials. The '**Purchasing Organization**' is the top-most organizational element in MM, and this can take any one of three forms such as (1) **Cross-plant purchasing organizations** (catering to more than one plant but within the same Company Code), (2) **Plant-specific purchasing organizations** (with a 1:1 relationship with the plant), and (3) **Cross-company code purchasing organizations** (catering to more than one Company Code). Entrusted with the activity of negotiating the price, delivery conditions, etc., of materials from vendors, the Purchasing Organization can further be subdivided into **purchasing groups.**

403. Explain the 'Purchasing Group' concept in MM.

The **'Purchasing Group'** carries out the actual activities of purchasing, and is assigned to a material in the material master. The activities of several purchasing organizations can be done by one purchasing group.

404. Explain the 'Valuation Area' concept in MM.

The valuation of a material is done at the **'Valuation Area,'** which can either be at the **Company Code** level or the **Plant** level. The level at which the valuation needs to happen is defined in the customizing. Note that once it is defined, you will not be able to change it later!

When the valuation is at the Company Code level, then the valuation of a material is uniform across the plants attached to that Company Code. On the other hand, if the valuation is at the plant level, then the value of the material is plant-specific and will vary from one plant to another. If you are using **PP (Production Planning)/MRP** in your company, then the valuation has to be at the plant level.

405. What is a 'Factory Calendar'?

A **'Factory Calendar'** is a calendar that is country-specific with a list of **public holidays** (maintained via the **Holiday Calendar**) and **working days,** which are Client-independent. The factory calendar helps in controlling goods issues/receipts. Each **plant** is assigned a factory calendar, and the calendar must be activated (through 'CTS functionality') before using it.

406. Explain how SD and MM are connected in SAP.

The goods/services from a **plant** can be sold by one or more **sales organizations.** It is also possible that single sales organizations sells goods/services for several plants. When the sales organizations sells for more than one plant belonging to one or more Company Codes, then this is called **inter-company sales**, and will require you to make some special configurations in the system. A sales organization, attached to a **Company Code**, is further divided into **distribution channels** and **divisions** in SD. A division typically represents a product line, and is assigned to a material in the material master.

407. Outline the functions supported by 'Material Master.'

The **'Material Master'** is the central master record catering to various business functions in **Logistics**. The data stored in this master support a variety of business functions and operations such as:

- Production Planning
- MRP
- Procurement
- Invoice Verification
- Inventory Management
- Product Costing
- Sales and Distribution
- Quality Management

The data is stored, within a material master, at different organizational levels. The **general data** is valid for all the Company Codes at the Client level. The purchasing information is valid at the plant level. The **sales information** is valid at the sales organization/distribution channel. Lastly, when **Warehouse Management** is activated, the data is maintained at the warehouse number/storage type level.

408. Explain why a 'Material Master' is divided into 'Views.'

Since the information in a material master needs to be maintained by a number of users across several modules, SAP has structured the master into a number of **Views** for facilitating easier access and updating of data. The views include:

- Basic Data
- Classification
- Sales
- Purchasing
- Purchase Order text
- Accounting
- Foreign Trade

- Work Scheduling
- Forecasting
- Storage
- Costing
- Plant/Storage Location stock
- MRP

409. What information is available in the 'Accounting View' of a 'Material Master'?

The most important information maintained in the **'Accounting View'** of a material master is the **valuation class**, which needs to be assigned to individual materials. The valuation class, in turn, helps in determining the relevant GL accounts for posting valuation-relevant transactions such as GR, GI, etc.

You will maintain the **price control indicator** in the accounting view, which enables determining how the stock of a material is to be valued (at **Standard price (S)** or **Moving average price (V)**).

410. Why do you need 'Material Types' in MM?

One way to group materials is by **'Material Type'** (the other being by 'Industry Sector'). This grouping helps determine what information or data is to be made available at the material master level for a particular material.

The material type (for example, FERT, HAWA, HALB, ROH, and so on) is used to control:

- Which Views can be maintained on the master record
- Which Fields are mandatory, optional, or for 'display only' in the material master
- What kind of Procurement is allowed for that material (internal or external or both)
- How to Number (Internal/External) and what Number Range is allowed
- Whether Quantity and/or Value updating should be done in a particular Valuation Area
- Which GL Accounts will be posted to (via the Valuation Class) during goods movement
- The default Item Category Group (S&D)

■ The default Price Control Indicator (S or V) and

■ Whether the default Price Control Indicator is changeable during material master maintenance

411. Explain the 'Price Control Indicator.'

The **'Price Control Indicator'** is used by SAP to determine how a material will be valuated, by default. The indicator can be set to:

■ Standard Price **(S)** or

■ Moving Average Price **(V)**

When you set the indicator to **'S,'** the system carries out all the **inventory postings** at the standard price. The **variances** □ due to a different price of a material in goods movement or invoice receipts □ if any, are all posted to **price difference accounts**. As a result, the standard price remains the same, unless it is changed intentionally by manual processing. This will be necessary only when the difference between the standard and moving average prices becomes very large. (While updating the price difference accounts, however, the system also updates the moving average price with these variances, so that you get a chance to adjust the standard price should the difference between the standard and moving average prices becomes very substantial.)

Example:

■ *1st April 2007*

- Initial Stock   : 1000 units
- (Standard) Price /unit (A)   : $5
- Initial Stock Value (B)   : $5,000

■ *20th May 2007*

- Goods Receipt   :1000 units
- GR Price/unit (A1)   : $6
- Stock A/c (Dr.) (C)   : $5,000 (=1000 X $5)
- Price Difference A/c (Dr.)   : $1,000 (=1000 X $1)

    The amount of $1,000 posted to the 'price difference' A/c represents the 'variance' reflecting the difference between the new price (A1) and the standard price (A).

- GR/IR A/c (Cr.)   : $6,000 (= 1000 X $6)
- Stock Value, now (B1)   : $10,000 (= B+C) (i.e., 2000 units @ $5)

■ *29th May 2007*

- ● Goods Issue   : 100 units
- ● Price/unit (same as that of A) : $5

On the other hand, when you set the indicator to **'V'** then all the goods receipts (GR) will be at the GR value. The system will then adjust the price in the material master by the GR price. However, if there is a difference between the moving average price of the material and the goods movement/invoice receipt, then the price difference is moved to the stock account, and the price of the material in the material master is adjusted accordingly.

Example:

■ *1st April 2007*

- ● Initial Stock   : 1000 units
- ● (Moving Average) Price /unit (A)   : $5
- ● Initial Stock Value (B)   : $5,000

■ *20th May 2007*

- ● Goods Receipt   :1000 units
- ● GR Price/unit (A1)   : $6
- ● Stock A/c (Dr.) (C)   : $6,000 (= 1000 X $6)
- ● GR/IR A/c (Cr.)   : $6,000 (= 1000 X $6)
- ● Stock Value, now (B1)   : $11,000 (= B+C) (= 2000 units @ $5.50)

At this point, the price on the material master is adjusted upward from $5 (A) to $5.5 (A2) by the system automatically, to reflect the new stock value.

- ● New Moving Average Price (A2)   : $5.50 (= B1/2000)

■ *29th May 2007*

- ● Goods Issue   : 100 units
- ● Price/unit (A2)   : $5.50

412. Explain 'Prices Maintenance' for materials transferred from 'Legacy' to SAP.

Before you transfer the initial inventory from a legacy system to SAP, you need to create the relevant master data for the materials.

If you are planning to maintain a **standard price** for the materials, then you will create the material masters with 'S' as the price control indictor in SAP. With this control, when you enter the material inventory, the system valuates this stock with the standard price defined. In this case, you enter a new price and the system posts the price difference (between the standard price and the new price you entered) to a price difference account.

Similarly, if you are planning to maintain a **moving average price** for materials, then you will create the material masters with 'V' as the Price Control Indictor in SAP. With this control, when you enter the material inventory, the system valuates this stock with the moving average price defined. In this case, you enter a new price and the system adjusts the moving average price accordingly. If you enter only the quantity, and not any new price, the system continues to valuate the stock at the original moving average price, and the price of the material does not change.

413. What is the 'Material Status'?

The **'Material Status'** is a 2-digit code enabling you to control the usability of material for various MM and PP applications. This status key also controls warehouse management, transfers order instructions, quality inspection instructions, decides how the system behaves when a product cost estimate is created, and so on.

The material status can be maintained as (1) Plant-specific material status, (2) Cross-plant material status, and (3) Distribution material status.

414. What is the 'EAN'?

The **'EAN (International Article Number),'** equivalent to the **UPC (Universal Product Code)** of the United States, is an international standard number for identifying a material, which SAP allows you to assign (done in the 'Eng./Design or Units of Measure' screen) to the materials. The EAN is normally assigned to the manufacturer of a material. Made up of a prefix (to identify the country or company from where the material originates), article number, and a check digit (ensures correctness of an EAN number so that no incorrect entries are scanned or entered into the system).

415. What are some of the 'Partner Functions' of a 'Vendor'?

Through the definition of **'Partner Functions'** in the Vendor Master, SAP helps to designate vendors for different roles. The partner role is designated by a 2-digit code.

- **VN**   Vendor
- **PI**   Invoice Presented by

- **OA**   Ordering Address
- **GS**   Goods Supplier
- **AZ**   Payment Recipient

A **partner schema** (also known as a **partner procedure**) is assigned to a **vendor account group**. The procedure specifies which partner roles are 'allowed'/ 'mandatory'/'can be changed' for a vendor master with that account group. You may assign three different partner schemas to an account group, one for each level of purchasing data, i.e., one at the purchase organization level, one at the VSR level, and one at the plant level. This enables maintaining different partners at different organizational levels.

416.   What is a 'Batch' in the context of 'Batch Management'?

Representing a quantity of material with a homogenous set of properties/ characteristics produced during a particular cycle of manufacturing, a **'Batch'** is a subset of inventory quantity, which cannot be reproduced again with the same properties. A batch is linked to the **classification system**, and you can use it only when the classification system has been set up properly for **batch management.**

A batch is unique for a single material, and is unique at the Client level as well. That is, you will be able to use a batch number only once in the Client regardless of the plant and material. The batch will be known only in the plant where it was created. The batch numbers can either be manually assigned or system generated.

417.   What are the possible values for 'Procurement Types'?

The possible values for **'Procurement Types'** are:

- No procurement
- External procurement
- In-house production
- Both procurement types

418.   What are the 'prerequisites' for an 'MRP Run'?

The following are the **'prerequisites'** for an MRP Run:

- MRP activated
- Valid MRP data for the material

- Valid MRP type
- Valid material status

419. What is an 'MRP Area'?

An **'MRP Area'** is not an organizational structure, but a unit for which you can carry out **Consumption-based MRP**. The MRP area is used to carry out MRP for the components provided to a sub-contractor. There are three types of MRP areas that you will come across:

- MRP Area for Storage Locations
- MRP Area for Subcontracting Vendor Stock
- MRP Area for the Plant

420. What is an 'MRP List'?

An **'MRP List'** displays the results of the last 'planning run.' Using a 'collective display' format, you will be able to display planning details for a number of materials for a given set of 'selection parameters.'

421. Explain the 'Re-Order Point' procedure.

The **'Re-Order Point'** is the level of inventory that triggers material procurement. Once the inventory falls below this level, you need to create the **order proposal** either manually or automatically by the system.

In the case of the **manual re-order point** procedure, you will define the re-order point and the **safety stock** in the material master. On the other hand, in the **automatic re-order point** procedure, the system will calculate the re-order point and the safety stock based on the next period's consumption pattern.

422. Explain the 'Inventory Management' submodule.

The **'Inventory Management'** submodule deals with the GR/GI of materials from/into the inventory. It also manages the transfer of materials from one storage location to another. As an important element of MM, this module is integrated with SD, PP, QM, and PM modules.

423. What is 'Goods Movement'?

'Goods Movement' represents an event causing a change in the stock, with the change being value or status, stock type, or quantity. It also represents the physical movement of stock from one location to another. Goods movement is classified into:

- Receipt of goods/services
- Issue of materials
- Stock transfers

424. What is a 'Goods Receipt'?

A **'Goods Receipt (GR)'** results in an increase in the quantity/value of the stock in a plant/warehouse. A GR may be **'with/without reference to a Purchase Order.'** A GR leads to:

- A Material document
- An Accounting document (not always)
- GR Slip printing
- GL Account update
  - Consumption Account
  - Stock Account
- Quantity updating
  - Stock quantity
  - Consumption statistics
  - Vendor Evaluation
- Other updates (if applicable)
  - Cost Center
  - Project
- A Stock Transfer Order
- Purchase Order History updates

425. Explain the 'accounting' side of GR.

When you post a GR with reference to a purchase order:

- **GR before Invoice Receipt:**
  - A posting will be made to the stock account (stock value increases)
  - An offsetting entry is made to the GR/IR clearing account
    - ◆ Once the invoice is received, the GR/IR clearing account is cleared

◆ A posting is made to the A/P account for the vendor (payables increase)

■ **Invoice Receipt (IR) before the GR**

● A posting is made to the A/P account for the vendor (payables increase)

● A posting is made to the GR/IR clearing account

◆ Once the goods are received, the GR/IR clearing account is cleared

◆ A posting will be made to the stock account (stock value increases)

When the GR is for a consumable material, the initial posting will go to the 'consumption account' (expense account) instead of a 'stock account.' However, the offsetting entry will still go to the GR/IR 'clearing account.' The value of the posting to the stock account will depend on which type of 'price control' is being used.

426. What happens during a 'Goods Issue'?

The **'Goods Issue (GI)'** results in a reduction in the stock quantity/value. The GI can be **Planned** (via sales order, production order, return delivery, delivery for internal, use etc.) or **Unplanned** (drawing a stock for a sample, scrapping, etc.).

The GI results in:

■ Creation of a Material/Accounting document

■ Update of Reservation for the issue (if any)

■ Update of GL accounts

■ Update of 'points of consumption' if applicable (cost center, project, etc.)

■ Update of Stock quantity

427. Explain 'Stock Transfers.'

The physical movement of stock between locations is called a **'Stock Transfer,'** which can be within a plant or between plants. Stock transfers can be carried out either in a single step or in two steps. The stock transfer may be from:

■ Company to Company

■ Plant to Plant

■ Storage Location to Storage Location

If there is a logical change in the stock type/status, then this kind of 'transfer' is called a **'transfer posting.'** The transfer posting may be from:

■ Product to Product

- Quality Inspection to Unrestricted Use
- Consignment Store to Storage Location

428.   What is a 'Stock Type'?

Used in the determination of available stock of a material, the **'Stock Type'** is the sub-division of inventory at a storage location based on the use of that inventory. In SAP, there are many kinds of stock types:

- **Unrestricted (use) stock** (the physical stock that is always available at a plant/storage location)
- **Restricted (use) stock**
- **Quality inspection stock** (not counted for unrestricted use and may be made available for MRP)
- **Stock-in transfer**
- **Blocked stock** (not to be counted as unrestricted stock and is not available for MRP)

Besides all of the above, which are all known as **valuated stocks**, you will also come across one more type called **'GR blocked stock,'** which is a **non-valuated stock.**

The **GR-blocked stock** denotes all the stock accepted 'conditionally' from the vendors. This stock is not considered available for 'unrestricted use.' You will use the **Movement Type 103** for the GR-blocked stock and **Movement Type 101** is used for a normal GR.

429.   Explain 'Return Delivery.'

You will use **'Return Delivery'** when you return goods to the supplier (vendor) for reasons such as damaged packaging, etc. Note that the **'reason for return'** is mandatory as this will help you, later on, to analyze problems with a vendor. The system uses the **Movement Type 122**, and will create a **return delivery slip**, which will accompany the goods being returned.

If the 'return' is from a 'GR-blocked stock,' you need to use a different **Movement Type: 104**.

430.   What are all the various types of 'Physical Inventory'?

The following are the different types of **'Physical Inventory'** in SAP MM:

- **Periodic inventory** (All the stocks are physically counted on a 'key date' (balance sheet date), and all the stock movements are blocked during physical counting)

- **Cycle counting** (Physical counting is done at periodical intervals)

- **Sampling** (Randomly selected stocks are counted physically, and the system uses this information to 'estimate' stock value on a given date)

- **Continuous** (Stocks are tracked continuously throughout the fiscal year, with physical stock taking once a year, at least!)

431. What is a 'Material Ledger'?

A **'Material Ledger'** is nothing but a tool for inventory accounting that provides new methods for 'price control' for 'material valuation' (you can store the material inventory values in more than one currency). It makes it possible to keep the 'material price' constant over a period of time (say, over the life of a production order). The **moving average price** field is used to store a 'periodic price.' This periodic price stays constant and is the price used for valuation until you close the material ledger. At closing, the periodic price is updated based on the actual value of invoice receipts received for that material during the period.

432. Explain 'Split Valuation.' Why is it necessary?

'Split Valuation' allows substocks of the same material to be managed in different stock accounts. This allows substocks to be valuated separately, and every transaction is carried out at the substock level. So, when processing a transaction, it is necessary to mention the substock.

The 'split valuation' is necessary if the material has:

- Different Origins
- Various Levels of Quality
- Various Statuses

It is also required in situations where you need to make a distinction between 'in-house produced materials' and 'materials procured externally,' or if there is a distinction between 'different deliveries.'

433. Explain the basic steps in 'Configuring Split Valuation.'

The five basic steps for **'Configuring Split Valuation'** are:

1. Activate 'Split Valuation'

2. Define 'Global Valuation Types'

For each 'valuation type' you need to specify: (*a*) whether 'external' purchase orders are allowed, (*b*) whether production orders are allowed, and (*c*) the account category reference.

3. Define 'Global Valuation Categories'

For each valuation category specify: (*a*) default 'valuation type' to be used when purchase orders are created and whether this default can be changed, (*b*) default valuation type to be used when production orders are created and whether this default can be changed, and (*c*) whether a 'valuation record' should be created automatically when a GR is posted for a valuation type for which no record yet exists.

4. Allocate 'Valuation Types' to the 'Valuation Categories'

5. Define which of the 'Global Categories/Types' apply to which 'Valuation Areas'

434. Outline 'Stock Valuation Methods' for material revaluation.

There are three methods with which you can revaluate your stock for Balance Sheet purposes. Irrespective of the method you select, you will be able to valuate your stock either at the **Company Code** level or at the **Valuation Area** level:

1. **LIFO (Last-In-First-Out):** This method is based on the assumption that the materials received last were the ones issued/consumed first. The valuation is based on the initial receipt.

2. **FIFO (First-In-First-Out):** Here the assumption is that the materials received first are the ones consumed/issued first. So, the valuation is based on the most recent receipt. The FIFO method can also be used in conjunction with the **lowest value method**. By this you can determine whether the system should make a comparison between the FIFO determined price and the **lowest value price**. You can also determine whether the FIFO price should be updated in the material master record.

3. **Lowest Value Method:** Here, the stocks are valued at their original price or the current market price whichever is lower. This method is suitable when the inventory needs to be valued to take into account material obsolescence, physical deterioration, or changes in price levels.

435. How does 'Automatic Account Assignment' work in MM?

1. 'GL accounts' are assigned to 'Transaction Keys' (BSX, WRX, PRD, UMG, GBB, etc.).

2. Transaction Keys identify which GL Accounts are to be debited or credited.

3. Transaction Keys are assigned to 'Value Strings' (for example, WA01).

4. 'Movement Types' (for example, 901) are associated with a 'Value String.'

436. Explain 'Automatic Account Assignment' configuration in MM.

There are four steps required to complete the **'Automatic Account Assignment'** configuration settings for MM:

1. Finalize the **'valuation level.'**

2. Activate the **'valuation grouping code'** option. (For this you need to group **valuation areas** using valuation grouping codes.)

3. Maintain **'valuation classes'** and **'account category references'** and their linkage to **'material types.'**

4. Maintain the **'GL accounts'** for each combination of **Chart of accounts, valuation grouping code, valuation class,** and **transaction key.**

You may use the **'automatic account determination wizard'** to complete the configuration settings, as the wizard guides you step-by-step.

437. Explain the 'Transaction Keys' in MM.

Also known as **'process keys,'** the **'Transaction Keys'** are pre-defined in the system to enable transaction postings in Inventory Management and Accounting (Invoice Verification). For each of the **movement types** in MM, there is a **value string** that stores these possible transactions.

The pre-defined **transaction keys** are:

- **BSX** (used in Inventory Postings)
- **WRX** (used in GR/IR Clearing Postings)
- **PRD** (used to post Cost/Price differences)
- **UMB** (used to post Revenue/Expenses from revaluation)
- **GBB** (used in offsetting entries in Stock postings)

BSX, WRX, and **PRD** are examples of transaction keys that are relevant for a GR with reference to a purchase order for a material with standard price control. The transaction key **UMB** is used when the standard price has changed and the movement is posted to a previous period. Likewise, **GBB** is used to identify the GL account to post to as the offsetting entry to the stock account (when not referencing a purchase order) such as miscellaneous goods receipts, goods issues for sales orders with no account assignment, and scrapping.

438.   How does the system determine the correct 'GL a/c' for a posting?

Imagine that you are posting a goods movement.

- Since the goods movement is from a **plant**, and the plant is assigned to a Company Code, the goods movement identifies the relevant Company Code.

- As the **Company Code** has already been assigned to the **Chart of Accounts**, the system is able to identify the **GL accounts.**

- The plant also determines the **valuation area** (and the optional **'valuation grouping code'**).

- Since each **movement type** is assigned to a **'value string'** which in turn is identified with a **transaction key**, the goods movement determines the correct transaction key.

- Since each of the **transaction keys** is associated with the relevant **GL accounts**, through the value string, the movement type now identifies the relevant GL Account, and the transaction is posted.

PRODUCTION PLANNING (PP)

439.   Explain how the PP module is organized in SAP.

The **PP** module is made up of the following **components:**

- **PP-BD**   Basic Data
- **PP-SOP**   Sales and Operations Planning
- **PP-MP**   Master Planning
- **PP-CRP**   Capacity (Requirements) Planning
- **PP-MRP**   Material Requirements Planning
- **PP-SFC**   Production Orders
- **PP-KAN**   Kanban
- **PP-REM**   Repetitive Manufacturing
- **PP-PI**   Production Planning for Process Industries
- **PP-PDS**   Plant Data Collection
- **PP-IS**   Information Systems

440. Explain how 'PP' is 'integrated' with other modules.

'PP' is one of the modules in SAP R/3 that is complex as the functions cut across many modules. The following modules are tightly **integrated** with PP:

- **CO**   Controlling
- **FI**   Financial Accounting
- **MM**   Materials Management
- **SD**   Sales & Distribution
- **PS**   Project Systems
- **PD**   Personnel Planning and Development

441. What is a 'BOM'?

A '**BOM (Bill of Material)**' is nothing but a structured list of components (with the object number, quantity, and unit of measure) that go into the making of a product or an assembly. Depending on the industry sector, they may also be called **recipes** or lists of ingredients. The structure of the product determines whether the bill of material is **simple** or very **complex**.

442. What are the 'BOM Categories' supported by SAP?

The following are the various **Categories of BOM:**

- Equipment BOM
- Material BOM
- Sales Order BOM
- Document Structure
- Functional Location BOM
- WBS BOM

443. What are all the 'Technical Types of BOM'?

There are two '**Technical Types of BOM**' supported in SAP:

- Variant BOM
- Material BOM

444. Differentiate 'Variant BOM' from 'Multiple BOM.'

While a **'Variant BOM'** groups together several BOMs that describe *different* objects (for example, different models of a car) with a high proportion of identical parts, a **Multiple BOM** groups together several BOMs that describe *one* object (for example, a product) with different combinations of materials for different processing methods.

The Variant BOMs are supported for the following BOM categories:

- Material BOMs
- Document structures
- Equipment BOMs
- Functional location BOMs

Multiple BOMs are only supported for Material BOMs.

445. Is it possible to convert a 'Multiple BOM' into a 'Variant BOM'?

No. You can only create a **'Variant BOM'** from a simple Material BOM. No multiple BOMs can exist for a material.

446. What is a 'Work Center' in PP?

A **'Work Center'** in PP (PP-BD-BOM) is an organizational unit that can be a combination of machines or groups of craftsmen, people, and production lines, wherein certain operations are carried out to produce some output. Each of the work centers is assigned to a cost center. A work center can be assigned to a work center in SAP-HR, which will enable assignment of employees, qualifications, etc.

447. What is a 'Routing' in PP?

A **'Routing'** in PP (PP-BD-RTG) is used to define the sequence of operations (work steps) and resources required to perform certain operations in order to produce a material with or without reference to an order. The standard values of planned time for the various operations need to be entered into the routing.

There are two different types of routing:

- Routing
- Rate routing

(A similar concept exists in PS where you define a **'task list,'** which is similar to 'routing' in PP.)

448. What are all the 'Sub-components' of Production Orders?

The following are the **'Sub-components of Production Orders'** (PP-SFC):

- Order Planning
- Order Execution
- Order Close

449. What is a 'Product Hierarchy'?

Used in pricing, a **'Product Hierarchy'** is an alphanumeric character string consisting of a maximum of 18 characters. It thus defines the product and its composition.

Example:

A product hierarchy represented by '00050002000300040005.' The first four characters '0005' could indicate that the product is a car. The next four characters '0002' could indicate the plant in which the car is manufactured. The third set of characters could indicate the color of the car. The next set may determine its engine capacity and so on. Thus, the product hierarchy helps in defining the product composition.

450. Define 'BOM Group.'

A **'BOM Group'** is a collection of BOMs that lets you describe a product or a number of similar products. The value in the BOM group field uniquely identifies the BOM group. You can use the BOM group as an alternative way of accessing the BOM. A BOM group comprises either all the alternatives of a multiple BOM or all the variants of a variant BOM.

When you create a BOM group, the system checks the special characters you use. Apart from the usual alphanumeric characters, you can use the following special characters: ' - ', ' / ', ' _ .' You cannot use blanks.

451. Define 'SOP' (Sales & Operations Planning).

Suitable for long/medium-term planning, with an aim to streamline a company's **'Sales and Operational Planning, SOP'** is a forecasting tool enabling you to set up sales, production, and other supply chain targets based on existing, future, or historical data. SOP is most suitable for planning finished goods, and not for material component planning.

SOP plans are passed on to **Demand Management (DEM)** in the form of independent requirements, which in turn is fed into **MPS (Master Production Scheduling)** and **MRP (Material Requirements Planning)**. The results of SOP can be passed on to profitability analysis, cost center accounting, and activity-based costing.

SOP contains two application components; namely, **Standard SOP (PP-SOP)** and **Flexible Planning (LO-LIS-PLN)**. The Standard SOP comes pre-configured with the system. Flexible planning can be configured in a variety of ways.

452. What is known as 'Demand Management'?

'Demand Management' (PP-MP-DEM) helps in determining the requirement quantities and delivery dates for finished goods assemblies. It uses the **planned independent requirements** and customer requirements (customer requirements come from sales orders). **Planning strategies** help in deciding the kind of demand program. If production is triggered by sales orders, then it is known as **'Make-to-Order'** production; if is not then it is known as **'Make-to-Stock'** production.

453. What is 'Capacity Planning'?

'Capacity Planning' aims at economic use of resources. It is integrated with SD, PM, PS, and CS. There are two components within capacity planning: **Capacity evaluation** and **Capacity levelling**. Capacity planning supports short-term detailed planning, medium-term planning, and long-term rough-cut planning.

454. Explain 'MRP' (Material Requirements Planning).

'MRP' aims to guarantee **material availability**; it is used to procure/produce the required quantities on time (both for internal purposes and for sales and distribution). This involves monitoring of stocks and, in particular, the automatic creation of 'procurement proposals' for purchasing and production. PP-MRP assists and relieves MRP Controllers (who are responsible for all the activities from specifying when, what, type, etc., of material requirements) in their area of responsibility. With the automatic planning run in MRP, it is possible to determine any shortages so as to create procurement elements. With the system generating messages for critical parts and unusual situations, you can rework the planning results in the specific area with problems.

The material requirements can be planned at **plant level** or for different MRP areas. With MRP at the plant level, the system adds together stocks from all of the individual storage locations, with the exception of individual customer stocks, to determine total plant stock. In the case of material requirements planning on an **MRP area level**, only the stocks from the storage locations or subcontractor assigned to the respective MRP areas are taken into account.

455.   What are the three 'MRP Procedures'?

- Materials Requirements Planning **(MRP)**
- Master Production Scheduling **(MPS)**
- Consumption-based Planning

456.   What is 'MPS' (Master Production Scheduling)?

Executed as that of an MRP, **'MPS'** is nothing but a special form of MRP, which aims to **reduce storage costs** and to **increase planning stability**. With MPS you can flag materials that greatly influence company profits or take up critical resources as **master schedule items** and check and plan them separately with a series of special tools.

457.   What is 'Consumption-based Planning'?

Using past consumption data, **'Consumption-based Planning'** aims at determining future requirements. In the process, it makes use of **material forecasts** or any other 'static' planning procedures. The 'net requirements' calculation is triggered when the stock level falls below a **reorder point**. The net requirements can also be calculated by **forecast requirements** from a historical consumption pattern.

MISCELLANEOUS

MISCELLANEOUS

458. Explain 'Cash Management' in SAP.

The 'Cash Management' submodule takes care of the following by integrating bank-related accounting with the respective subledger accounting:

- Check Deposit
- Cash Position
- Cash Concentration
- Bank Statement
- Liquidity Forecast
- Cash Concentration
- Money Market

459. What is the 'Cash (Management) Position'?

The 'Cash Management Position' helps to reproduce the activities of bank accounts. With input controls for preventing data duplication, parallel management of foreign currencies, and with the required documentation for revision of all planning activities, you will be able to view up-to-date activities in bank accounts and forecast cash position or daily liquidity. The cash management position is set up using **groupings**, which determine the levels and accounts to be displayed.

The data required for this activity is supplied from (a) FI postings in cash management relevant GL accounts, (b) payment advices entered manually, and (c) cash-flow transactions transferred from the Treasury Management module.

The data can be displayed using any of the following formats:

- Aggregated, either as account balance (K) or as individual values of inflow/outflow(D)
- For any data in the past, present, or future
- In increments (days, weeks, etc.)

460. Explain 'Groupings' and 'Levels.'

'**Groupings**' determine how to summarize the data, with various 'groups' and 'levels' defined. A **Group** adds up various bank accounts and contains a number of 'levels.'

A **Level**, thus, denotes the sources of data or account transactions. Below the levels are the **line items**, which are displayed using a 'list display.'

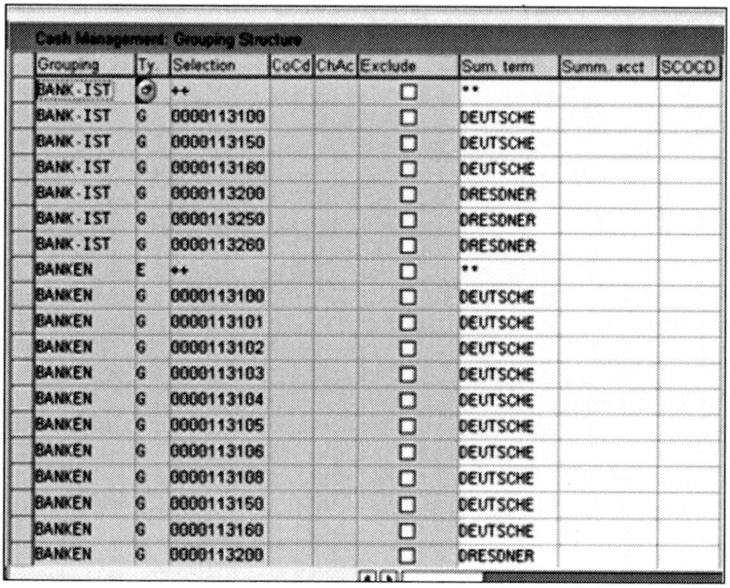

Cash Management: Grouping Structure

Grouping	Ty	Selection	CoCd	ChAc	Exclude	Sum. term	Summ. acct	SCOCD
BANK-IST		++			☐	**		
BANK-IST	G	0000113100			☐	DEUTSCHE		
BANK-IST	G	0000113150			☐	DEUTSCHE		
BANK-IST	G	0000113160			☐	DEUTSCHE		
BANK-IST	G	0000113200			☐	DRESDNER		
BANK-IST	G	0000113250			☐	DRESDNER		
BANK-IST	G	0000113260			☐	DRESDNER		
BANKEN	E	++			☐	**		
BANKEN	G	0000113100			☐	DEUTSCHE		
BANKEN	G	0000113101			☐	DEUTSCHE		
BANKEN	G	0000113102			☐	DEUTSCHE		
BANKEN	G	0000113103			☐	DEUTSCHE		
BANKEN	G	0000113104			☐	DEUTSCHE		
BANKEN	G	0000113105			☐	DEUTSCHE		
BANKEN	G	0000113106			☐	DEUTSCHE		
BANKEN	G	0000113108			☐	DEUTSCHE		
BANKEN	G	0000113150			☐	DEUTSCHE		
BANKEN	G	0000113160			☐	DEUTSCHE		
BANKEN	G	0000113200			☐	DRESDNER		

Figure 96: Grouping Structure in Cash Management

461. Explain 'Liquidity Forecast.'

The '**Liquidity Forecast**' helps to reproduce the activities in subledger accounts by (*a*) linking to all the 'system resident' data such as customer open items in a customer account, (*b*) receipts and disbursements form FI/SD/MM, and (*c*) maintaining items such as reversal, document change, open item clearing, etc., automatically.

The liquidity forecast helps to identify the liquidity trends in the subledger accounts based on the information on expected payment flows. The incoming and outgoing payments per open item, from FI-AR and FI-AP, form the basis of the liquidity forecast. You will be able to branch to FI-AR or AP information systems from the liquidity forecast.

462. How do you set up 'Cash Management' in SAP?

Under customizing, you need to define the 'Cash Management Groups' and assign these groups to **planning levels**. In customer/vendor master records, you need to enter the cash management groups to enable the system to transfer data between customer/vendor accounts and the liquidity forecast. The cash management groups help to differentiate customers/vendors based on certain characteristics such as behavior (whether the customer takes a cash discount), risk (credit rating), etc.

463. Explain 'Bank Statement' in Cash Management.

'**Bank Statement**' (manual or electronic) functionality runs on the same principle as **Check Deposit Processing**. Note that it is not necessary for Cash Management to be active for bank statement processing.

During processing, customer payments (except checks) are first posted to the bank clearing account; then customer open items are cleared when balancing the bank clearing account. Similarly, vendor payments are posted to a bank clearing account for outgoing payments where the balancing is done from the entries made from the payment program. Other payments such as bank charges, bank interest, etc., are posted to the respective GL accounts, and they will not go through the bank clearing accounts. In the case of unidentified payment transactions, you will post them first to the bank clearing accounts and then 'clear' them when you have the appropriate information.

464. What are the configurations for 'Bank Statement Processing'?

Before you make use of the '**Bank Statement Processing**' functionality in SAP, you need to have the following defined or configured in your system:

- Start Variant
- Search ID

■ Processing Type
■ Internal Bank Determination

Dialog Structure	Define Posting Rules												
☐ Create Account Syr	Posti	Pos	Po	S	Acct (Debit)	Compre	Pos	S	Acct (Cre	Compre	Doc.	Po	On
☐ Assign Accounts to	0001	1	40	✍	BANK	☐	50		GELDEINGA	☐	SA	1	
☐ Create Keys for Po:	0001	2	40		GELDEINGANG	☐				☐	DZ	8	
☐ Define Posting Rule	0002	1	40		BANK	☐	50		SCHECKEII	☐	SA	1	
	0003	1	40		SCHECKEINGANG	☐	50		SCHECKVEI	☐	SA	1	
	0003	2	40		SCHECKVERRECHNG	☐				☐	DZ	8	
	0004	2	40		SCHECKEINGANG	☐				☐	DZ	8	
	0005	1			SCHECKAUSGANG	☐	50		BANK	☐	SA	4	
	0006	1			GELDAUSGANG	☐	50		BANK	☐	SA	4	
	0007	1	40		GELDAUSGANG	☐	50		BANK	☐	KZ	1	
	0007	2				☐	50		GELDAUSGA	☐	KZ	7	
	0008	1			SONSTIGE	☐	50		BANK	☐	SA	4	
	0009	1	40		BANK	☐			SONSTIGE	☐	SA	5	
	0010	1	40		GEBÜHREN	☐	50		BANK	☐	SA	1	
	0011	1	40		SONSTIGE	☐	50		BANK	☐	SA	1	
	0012	1	40		BANK	☐	50		SONSTIGE	☐	SA	1	
	0013	1	40		GELDAUSGANG	☐	50		BANK	☐	DZ	1	

Figure 97: Bank Statement Configuration

465. Differentiate 'Manual Check Deposit' from 'Electronic Check Deposit.'

The '**Manual Check Deposit**' function enables you to enter all 'checks' received by posting the entries in two steps: in GL and in subledger accounts. It also helps to 'clear' customer invoices. You may also make use of additional functions for additional processing of checks thus entered.

The '**Electronic Check Deposit**,' in contrast to the 'manual check deposit' function, enables you to process data even from an external data entry system provided the data is delivered in the SAP defined format. You will be able to enter check deposit details electronically so that you may complete and post individual data later with manual check deposit processing.

466. Explain 'Travel Management' in SAP.

The '**Travel Management**' submodule of FI, FI-TR, helps you to plan travel and travel-related activities (such as calculating trip costs, trip reimbursements, etc.) for the enterprise's human resources.

FI-TR transfers the travel expenses to the FI, which in turn makes use of FI-AP to reimburse employees. Employees are reimbursed for travel expenses using the 'payment program' (automatic/manual) in Financial Accounting. In order for the reimbursement process to work, a vendor master record has to be created for every employee who travels. Use **Transaction PRAA** to automatically create (through Bach Data input) vendor records for the employees.

If you are using SAP-HR, then you will use **HR master data** to store an employee's information; otherwise, you will create a **mini-master** record (a scaled down version of HR master) where you will save such as personal information, address, bank details, etc. You will also define personal action, travel privileges, and travel preferences.

467. What is a 'Personal Action'?

A '**Personnel Action**' includes all **infotypes** that are processed as part of a personal procedure, such as hiring, organizational change, promotion, and so on. To ensure that no important information is forgotten, the relevant infotypes are made available for processing one after another. Each completed action is entered in the 'action' infotype so that the 'actions' infotype has a log of all procedures completed for this person.

Personnel actions are normally completed in SAP-HR. If SAP-HR is not implemented, FI-TV offers two 'actions' for maintaining FI-TV mini-master records:

- **Create TV mini-master records.** (When completing the 'Create TV mini-master record' action, the infotype's 'measures,' 'organizational assignment,' 'personal information,' and 'travel privileges' are made available.)
- **Organizational change.** (When using the 'organizational change' action, only the infotype's 'actions' and 'organizational assignment' are made available.)

468. What is an 'Infotype'?

HR master data normally contain large volumes of information (personal as well as employment related) per employee in the organization. Since the data volume is so large, this information is stored in data groups, in SAP. An '**Infotype**' is one such data group. (For example, since city, street, and street number are part of the address of an employee's bank, they are saved (along with other data) in the Infotype Bank.)

IType	Infotype text
0000	Actions
0001	Organizational Assignment
0002	Personal Data
0003	Payroll Status
0004	Challenge
0005	Leave Entitlement
0006	Addresses
0007	Planned Working Time
0008	Basic Pay
0009	Bank Details
0010	Capital Formation
0011	External Transfers
0012	Fiscal Data D
0013	Social Insurance D
0014	Recurring Payments/Deductions
0015	Additional Payments
0016	Contract Elements
0017	Travel Privileges
0019	Monitoring of Tasks
0020	DEUEV

Figure 98: Infotypes in SAP

469. Explain 'Travel Manager' in SAP.

'Travel Manager,' in SAP, helps employees have an overview of travel and travel-related items/objects (such as travel requests, travel plans, and travel reimbursements). He or she will be able to create:

A 'travel request' notifying the company about his/her forthcoming business trip, based on the workflow configuration, which then moves to the internal travel office for further approval and processing.

The employee (or the designated travel agent of the company) makes use of the object **travel plan** to plan the details of the **trip**. The system retrieves the **travel preferences** from the 'infotype' and helps book the means of travel.

The permitted **travel expenses** are configured in the system and are country specific. This configuration helps in **reimbursement processing** when the employee puts through the travel reimbursement claim to the internal travel office. After a trip is completed, the employee enters the travel expenses manually in the system or they can be obtained from the travel plans and corrected later. Again, SAP provides the flexibility so that travel expenses can either be entered by employees or by the travel office's representative.

For reimbursement settlement of the expenses, the system determines the total amount to be paid based on the travel plan, travel information, settlement rules, and reimbursement records (for previous payments). The **settlement information** is sent to FI, where the payment is made though FI-AP's payment program.

470. What is a 'Value Pricer'?

The '**Value Pricer**' tool, in SAP-HR, helps to compare the selected bookings (of a flight) and compares the price of it with that of other carriers, for the same route(s), and recommends the lowest cost fares for the travel plan.

471. What is a 'Schedule Manager'?

The SAP '**Schedule Manager**' helps you to organize, execute, and monitor complex and repetitive business transactions (such as month-end processing) from an easy-to-use workspace, which resembles an all-in-one 'organizer' type of utility containing:

- User notes window
- Task overview window
- Calendar window
- Daily overview window

The **information window** provides the details of what and how you can achieve the tasks by providing useful information with hyperlinks to processes and steps within a process. This appears to the left of all other windows. Depending on the requirement, this can be 'switched-on' or 'switched-off.'

The **task overview window** provides a complete 'drill-down' facility in a tree-structure of all tasks entered and monitored by you. The tasks are grouped into an upper level task list, which can be scheduled, released, and monitored using the 'daily overview' window. Remember that the tasks maintained in the task overview window need to be properly scheduled/released for execution; the mere listing of tasks here will not start a transaction or a program or a report.

The **daily overview window** is similar to an appointment column of any organizer, with fully customizable time intervals (in increments of 30 minutes, 45 minutes, etc.). Ideally, the tasks appearing in the task list in the 'task overview' window, when scheduled/released, will appear here against the appropriate time slot. By selecting a task here you can monitor it using the 'monitor' icon or from the menu. A look at this daily overview window, at the beginning of a day, will remind you of the tasks scheduled for that day.

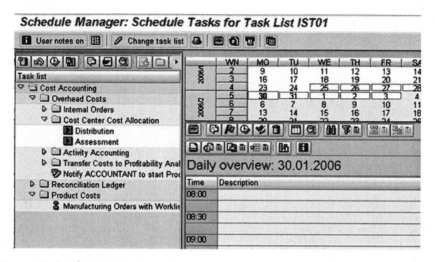

Figure 99: Schedule Manager

The **calendar window** is a calendar utility to help you organize. However, this goes beyond the regular calendar by displaying, in different colors such as yellow and green, a particular date indicating the status of tasks scheduled for that day. A 'green' background indicates that everything is OK, but a 'yellow' background indicates that there are some warnings.

Transaction
Code
SCMA

472. How do you use the 'Schedule Manager' in SAP?

The Schedule Manager has **three distinct functionalities** built in:

1. **Processes**

   This functionality helps you to define the **task list** (also called a **task group**) and the individual **tasks** (a task is essentially a transaction or a program/report), which are later on 'scheduled'/'released' and 'monitored' using the special '**monitoring**' function. Any number of task lists can be created and these lists are shown in a tree format for easy navigation. A task list may contain another task list or a **chain of tasks** within and tasks are grouped into a task list.

While defining the task itself, you can maintain the owner of the task, when it needs to be executed, etc. The scheduling of tasks is also possible by simply dragging them into the appropriate time slots in the 'daily overview' window. You may also use the **'job wizard'** while scheduling. A task, by mere scheduling, is not started automatically unless it is properly **'released.'** The tasks/task lists defined can be moved in the hierarchy up/down or deleted from a list. The tasks can also be documented using MS-Office Word or Excel, etc.

2. **Scenarios**

   The schedule manager gives you **three options** for scheduling and monitoring:

   (*a*) **Start transaction/program/report online and schedule the jobs (tasks) in the scheduler:** Here, you can create or select a new task list in the schedule, enter these in the 'daily overview,' and monitor and control the task's execution in the 'monitor.'

   (*b*) **Start transaction/program/report online and schedule the jobs (tasks)/ job chain (task chain):** This is similar to (*a*) above except that you have the option of inserting a **'job chain'** defined in **'flow definition'** into the task list.

   (*c*) **Start transactions/reports online, schedule job or job chain, work-list:** Here, you can also execute and monitor a complete work-list involving several processing steps with all the step sequences. Besides scheduler, monitor, and flow definition, you can use the **'work-list monitor'** for monitoring the processing status.

3. **Help Functions**

   Schedule Manager supplements with useful functions such as:

   ■ Run-time analysis

   ■ Working with variables

   ■ Releasing jobs

SAP TABLES

SAP TABLES

FINANCIAL ACCOUNTING (FI)

Sl. No.	Are you looking for:	Table
1	Account Assignment Templates for GL Account items	KOMU
2	Account Master (Chart of Accounts)	SKA1
3	Accounting Correspondence Requests	BKORM
4	Accounting Data – A/R and A/P Information System	RFRR
5	Accounting Document Header	BKPF
6	Accounting Document Header (docs from External Systems)	EBKP
7	Accounting Document Header	BKPF
8	Accounting Document Segment	BSEG
9	Accounting secondary index for customers	BSID
10	Accounting secondary index for customers – cleared items	BSAD
11	Accounting – Secondary Index for GL Accounts	BSIS
12	Accounting – Secondary Index for GL Accounts - cleared items	BSAS
13	Accounting secondary index for vendors	BSIK
14	Accounting secondary index for vendors – cleared items	BSAK
15	Accounts Blocked by Dunning Selection	MAHN
16	Asset Accounting – Basic Functions	FI-A
17	Asset Class: Depreciation Area	ANKB
18	Asset classes – Description	ANKT

19	Asset Classes – Field Cont Dependent on Chart	ANKP
20	Asset Classes – General Data	ANKA
21	Asset Classes – Insurance Types	ANKV
22	Asset down payment settlement	ANEV
23	Asset Line Items	ANEP
24	Asset Master Record Segment	ANLA
25	Asset Master Record Segment	ANLX
26	Asset Master Record User Fields	ANLU
27	Asset Periodic Values	ANLP
28	Asset Texts	ANLT
29	Asset Type Text	ANAT
30	Asset Types	ANAR
31	Asset Value Fields	ANLC
32	Bank Master Record	BNKA
33	Business Partner Master (General Data)	BP000
34	Cash Management Line Items in Payment Requests	FDZA
35	Create GL account with reference	TSAK
36	Credit Management – FI Status data	KNKK
37	Customer/Vendor Linking	KLPA
38	Customer master – general data	KNA1
39	Customer master – partner functions	KNVP
40	Customer master – sales data	KNVV
41	Customer master – sales request form	KNVD
42	Customer Master (Company Code)	KNB1
43	Customer Master Bank Details	KNBK
44	Customer Master Credit Management – Central Data	KNKA
45	Customer Master Credit Management – Control Area Data	KNKK
46	Customer Master Dunning Data	KNB5
47	Customer Master Special GL Transactions Figures	KNC3
48	Customer Master Transaction Figures	KNC1
49	Customer Payment History	KNB4
50	Depreciation Terms	ANLB
51	Document Header Asset Posting	ANEK
52	Document Header for Document Parking	VBKP

53	Document Header Supplement for Recurring Entry	BKDF
54	Document Type Texts	T003T
55	Dunning Data (Account Entries)	MHNK
56	Electronic Bank Statement Line Items	FEBEP
57	Financial Accounting 'Basis'	FBAS
58	GL Account Master (Chart of Accounts – Description)	SKAT
59	GL Account Master (Chart of Accounts – Key Word list)	SKAS
60	GL Account Master (Chart of Accounts)	SKA1
61	GL Account Master (Company Code)	SKB1
62	General Ledger Accounting – Basic	FI-G
63	General Ledger Accounting – Basic	FI-G
64	Global Settings for Payment Program for Payment Requests	F111
65	Index for Vendor Validation of Double Documents	BSIP
66	Insurable Values (Year Dependent)	ANLW
67	Inter Company Posting Procedure	BVOR
68	Main Asset Number	ANLH
69	Management Records for the Dunning Program	MAHNV
70	Name of Transaction Type	AT10T
71	One-Time Account Data Document Segment	BSEC
72	Payment Medium File	PAYR
73	Payment Requests	PAYR
74	Pre-numbered Check	PCEC
75	Pricing Communication Header	KOMK
76	Run Date of a Program	FRUN
77	Secondary Index, Documents for Material	BSIM
78	Settings for GL Posting Reports	FIGL
79	Substitutions	GB92
80	Tax Code Names	T007S
81	TemSe – Administration Data	REGUT
82	Time Dependent Asset Allocations	ANLZ
83	Transaction Activity Category – Description	AT02T
84	Transaction Code for Menu TIMN	AT02A
85	Transaction type	AT10
86	Validation/Substitution User	GB03

87	Validation	GB93
88	Vendor Master (Company Code Section)	LFB1
89	Vendor Master (General Section)	LFA1
90	Vendor Master Bank Details	LFBK
91	Vendor Master – Dunning Data	LFB5
92	Vendor Master Dunning Data	LFB5
93	Vendor Master Record – Purchasing Data	LFM2
94	Vendor Master Record – Purchasing Organization Data	LFM1
95	Vendor Master Transaction Figures	LFC1

CONTROLLING (CO)

Sl. No.	Are you looking for:	Table
1	Activity Type Master	CSLA
2	Actual Line Items for Reconciliation	COFIS
3	Assignment of Work Center to Cost Center	CRCO
4	Basic Settings for Versions	TKA09
5	Characteristic Values	AUSP
6	CO Object: Control Data for Activity Type	COKL
7	CO Object: Control Data for Cost Center	COKA
8	CO Object: Control Data for Primary Cost Element	COKP
9	CO Object: Control Data for Secondary Cost Element	COKS
10	CO Object: Control Data for Statistical Key Figure	COKR
11	CO Object: Document Header	COBK
12	CO Object: Line Items (by Fiscal)	COEJ
13	CO Object: Line Items (by Period)	COEP
14	CO Object: Line Items for Activity Types	COEPL
15	CO Object: Line Items for Activity Type	COEJL
16	CO Object: Line Items for Prices	COEJT
17	CO Object: Line Items for Prices	COEPT
18	CO Object: Line Items for SKF	COEJR
19	CO Objects: Assignment	COSC
20	CO Period Locks	KAPS
21	CO Versions	TKVS

22	Controlling Areas	TKA01
23	Cost Center/Activity Type	CSSL
24	Cost Center/Cost Element	CSSK
25	Cost Center Master Data	CSKS
26	Cost Center Texts	CSKT
27	Cost elements – data dependent on chart of accounts	CSKA
28	Cost elements – data dependent on controlling area	CSKB
29	Cost elements texts	CSKU
30	Dependent on Material and Receiver	A141
31	Dependent on Material Group	A143
32	Dependent on Material	A142
33	Distribution Rules Settlement Rule Order Settlement	COBRB
34	Document Header Controlling Object	BPBK
35	Document Header for Settlement	AUAK
36	Document Segment: Transactions	AUAV
37	EC-PCA: Actual Line Items	GLPCA
38	EC-PCA: Object Table for Account Assignment Elements	GLPCO
39	EC-PCA: Plan Line Items	GLPCP
40	EC-PCA: Transaction Attributes	GLPCC
41	Line Item Annual Values Controlling Object	BPEJ
42	Line Item Period Values Controlling Object	BPEP
43	Line Item Total Values Controlling Object	BPEG
44	Object –Control Data for Cost Elements	COKA
45	Object – Cost Totals for External Postings	COSP
46	Object – Cost Totals for Internal Postings	COSS
47	Object Table for Reconciliation L	COFI01
48	Order Master Data	AUFK
49	PCA – Totals Table	GLPCT
50	Price per Company Code	A138
51	Price per Controlling Area	A136
52	Price per Cost Center	A132
53	Price per Country/Region	A137
54	Price per Profit Center	A139
55	Profit Center Master Data Table	CEPC

56	Profit Center Master Data Table	CEPC
57	Profit Center Master Data	CEPCT
58	Settlement Document: Distribution	AUAB
59	Settlement Document: Receiver Segment	AUAA
60	Settlement Rule for Order Settlement	COBRA
61	Settlement Rules per Depreciation	AUAI
62	Single Plan Items for Reconciliation	COFIP
63	Totals Record – Reconciliation Ledger	COFIT
64	Totals Record for Annual Total Controlling Object	BPJA

SALES & DISTRIBUTION (SD)

Sl. No.	Are you looking for:	Table
1	Billing Document Header	VBRK
2	Billing Document Item	VBRP
3	Condition for items	KNOP
4	Condition for transaction data	KNOV
5	Customer Master – Co. Code Data (payment method, recon. acct)	KNB1
6	Customer Master – Dunning info	KNB5
7	Customer Master Bank Data	KNBK
8	Customer Master Credit Control Area Data (credit limits)	KNKK
9	Customer Master Credit Mgmt.	KNKA
10	Customer Master Ship Data	KNVS
11	Customer Master Tax Indicator	KNVI
12	Customer Payment History	KNB4
13	Customer/Vendor Link	KLPA
14	Customers, General Data	KNA1
15	Delivery document – header data	VBAK
16	Delivery document – item data	VBAP
17	Delivery Document Header data	LIKP
18	Delivery due index	VEPVG
19	Delivery header data	LIKP
20	Delivery item data	LIPS
21	Document Flow	VBFA

22	Handling unit – Header table	VEKP
23	Header Status and Administrative Data	VBUK
24	Item Status	VBUP
25	Output type	KNVD
26	Packing – handling unit item (contents)	VEPO
27	Partner Function key	KNVP
28	Partners	VBPA
29	Sales Area Data (terms, order probability)	KNVV
30	Sales document – business data	VBKD
31	Sales document – header data	VBAK
32	Sales document – header status and administrative data	VBUK
33	Sales document – item data	VBAP
34	Sales document – item status	VBUP
35	Sales document – partner	VBPA
36	Sales document – release order data	VBLB
37	Sales document – schedule line data	VBEP
38	Sales document flow	VBFA
39	Sales Document Schedule Line	VBEP
40	Sales Requirements: Individual Records	VBBE
41	Schedule line history	VBEH
42	SD document – delivery note header	VBLK
43	Shipping Unit Header	VEPO
44	Shipping Unit Item (Content)	VEKP

MATERIALS MANAGEMENT (MM)

Sl. No.	Are you looking for:	Table
1	Account Assignment in Purchasing Document	EKKN
2	Document Header – Reservation	RKPF
3	Document Segment – Material	MSEG
4	General Material Data	MARA
5	Header – Material Document	MKPF
6	Header – Physical Inventory Document	IKPF
7	Help Texts for Movement Types	T157H

8	History per Purchasing Document	EKBE
9	Lists what views have not been created	MOFF
10	Material Groups	T023
11	Material Consumption	MVER
12	Material Descriptions	MAKT
13	Material to BOM Link	MAST
14	Material Valuation	MBEW
15	Movement Type	T156
16	Number range intervals	NRIV
17	Physical Inventory Document Items	ISEG
18	Plant Data for Material	MARC
19	Plant/Material	A501
20	Purchase Requisition Account Assignment	EBKN
21	Purchase Requisition	EBAN
22	Purchasing Document Header	EKKO
23	Purchasing Document Item	EKPO
24	Purchasing Groups	T024
25	Purchasing Info Record – General Data	EINA
26	Purchasing Info Record – Purchasing Organization Data	EINE
27	Release Documentation	EKAB
28	Reservation/dependent requirements	RESB
29	Sales Data for materials	MVKE
30	Scheduling Agreement Schedule Lines	EKET
31	Storage Location Data for Material	MARD
32	Texts for Purchasing Document Types	T161T
33	Texts for Purchasing Document Types	T161T
34	Vendor Master (Company Code)	LFB1
35	Vendor Master (General section)	LFA1

PRODUCTION PLANNING (PP)

Sl. No.	Are you looking for:	Table
1	BOM Explosion Structure	STPF
2	BOM Group to Material	MAST

3	BOM Header Details	STKO
4	BOM History Records	STZU
5	BOM Item Details	STPO
6	BOM Item Selection	STAS
7	BOM Sub Items (designators)	STPU
8	Capacity Header	KAKO
9	CAPP Sub-operations	PLPH
10	Characteristic Allocation to Class	KSML
11	Characteristic Detail	CABN
12	Characteristic Value Texts	CAWNT
13	Characteristic Values	AUSP
14	Characteristic Values	CAWN
15	Class Detail	KLAH
16	Component Allocation	PLMZ
17	Confirmation Pool	AFRV
18	Confirmations – Defaults for Collective Confirmation	AFRD
19	Confirmations – Goods Movements with Errors	AFFW
20	Confirmations – Header Info for Confirmation Pool	AFRH
21	Confirmations – Incorrect Cost Calculations	AFRC
22	Confirmations – Subsequently Posted Goods Movements	AFWI
23	Customer and Priority	AENR
24	Hierarchy Header	CRHH
25	Hierarchy Structure	CRHS
26	Independent Requirements by Material	PBIM
27	Independent Requirements Data	PBED
28	Inspection Characteristics	PLMK
29	Intervals of Capacity	KAZY
30	LIS – Material Use	S026
31	LIS – Reporting Point Statistics	S028
32	LIS – Run Schedule Quantities	S025
33	LIS – Stock/Requirements Analysis	S094
34	Maintenance Package Allocation	PLWP
35	Material Allocation to Class	KSSK
36	MRP Document Header Data	MDKP

37	MRP Firming Dates	MDFD
38	MRP Table Structure (no data)	MDTB
39	Order Batch Print Requests	AFBP
40	Order Completion Confirmations	AFRU
41	Order Header	AFKO
42	Order Item Detail	AFPO
43	Order Operations Detail	AFVC
44	Order PRT Assignment	AFFH
45	Order Sequence Details	AFFL
46	Planned Orders	PLAF
47	Planning File Entries	MDVM
48	Planning Scenario (Long-term Planning)	PLSC
49	PRT Allocation	PLFH
50	Relationships – Standard Network	PLAB
51	Reporting Point Document Logs	CEZP
52	Reporting Points – Periodic Totals	CPZP
53	Reservations/Dependent Requirements	RESB
54	Revision Numbers	AEOI
55	Routing Header Details	PLKO
56	Routing Link to Material	MAPL
57	Routing Operation Details	PLPO
58	RS Header Master Data	SAFK
59	Task List – Selection of Operations	PLAS
60	Workcenter Capacity Allocation	CRCA
61	Workcenter Cost Center Assignment	CRCO
62	Workcenter Header Data	CRHD
63	Workcenter Text	CRTX

SAP TRANSACTION CODES

SAP TRANSACTION CODES

Below are some of the important Transaction Codes (T-Codes), listed module-wise, for easy reference. The notable feature of these lists is the way these Transaction Codes have been arranged: it is not an alphabetical list because such a list would not help if you do not know the Transaction Code but are looking with some description in mind. The Transaction Codes are arranged based on their functionality or use or task so that it is easier to search. Look for keywords in the second column of the table ('**are you looking for**'), and then look at the corresponding Transaction Code under the '**T-Code**' column.

All the Transaction Codes are stored in the system in tables **TSTC** and **TSTCT**.

It is not practical to list all the Transaction Codes of SAP. As you get to know SAP, you will learn to look for Transaction Codes by going through the **Transaction Code SE93**. Should you want to know those Transaction Codes that are not listed in the following pages, use the **Transaction Code SE93** to find them. Here is a short tutorial on how to look for Transaction Codes in the system:

Transaction Code
SE93

1. Enter the '**Maintain Transaction**' transaction by Transaction Code SE93:

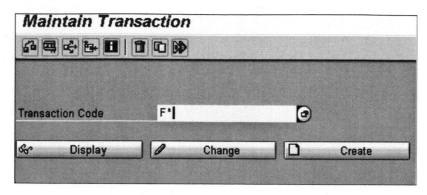

Figure 100: Maintain Transaction – Initial Screen

2. If you know some information about the Transaction Code you are looking for, you may enter it in the 'Transaction Code' field. For example, assume that you are trying to list all the Transaction Codes starting with 'F.' Then you would enter 'F*' as indicated in Figure 101 and click the ![button] button. The system will now bring out the list as indicated in Figure 102:

Repository Info System: Transactions Find (200 Hits)	
Transaction Code	**Short text**
F-01	Enter Sample Document
F-02	Enter G/L Account Posting
F-03	Clear G/L Account
F-04	Post with Clearing
F-05	Post Foreign Currency Valuatio
F-06	Post Incoming Payments
F-07	Post Outgoing Payments
F-18	Payment with Printout
F-19	Reverse Statistical Posting
F-20	Reverse Bill Liability
F-21	Enter Transfer Posting
F-22	Enter Customer Invoice
F-23	Return Bill of Exchange Pmt Re
F-25	Reverse Check/Bill of Exch.
F-26	Incoming Payments Fast Entry
F-27	Enter Customer Credit Memo
F-28	Post Incoming Payments

Figure 101: List of Transactions starting with 'F'

3. If you don't know what Transaction Code you are searching for, you may still find it if you try searching through the 'package or application

components, short description,' etc. In step-2 above, instead of entering

the search string in the 'Transaction Code' field, click the button and you will be taken to the following 'Find Transaction' selection screen:

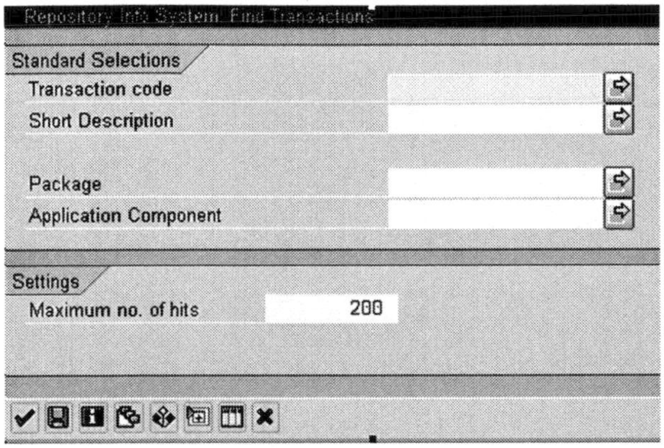

Figure 102: Standard Selection Screen to find Transactions

4. Maintain any of the known information under 'Standard Selections.' Assume that you are planning to search by 'Application Component': then

    click the button to the right of the 'Application Component' field. Now the system takes you to the '**Select Application Componen**t' pop-up screen:

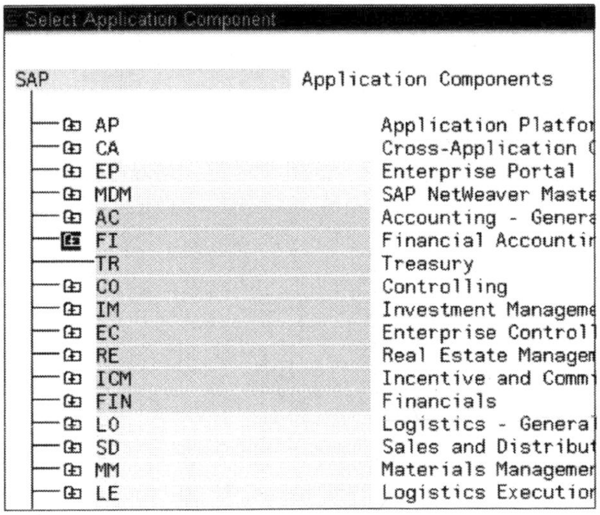

Figure 103: Select 'Application Component'

5. Expand the 'Application Components' tree to reach the 'specific 'functionality'or the 'component' you are looking for. Suppose that you are looking for Transaction Codes relating to 'Basic Functions' in FI-AR:

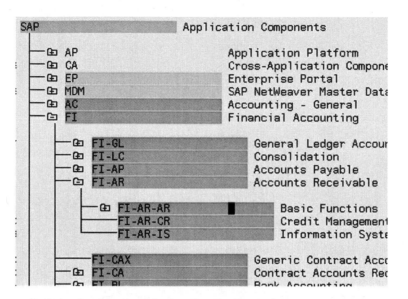

Figure 104: Selecting the specific Application Component

6. Double-click on 'FI-AR-AR,' and you are taken back to the initial selection screen:

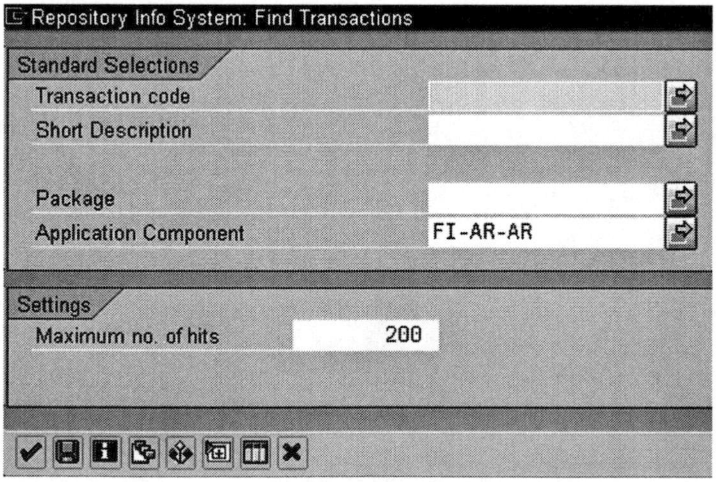

Figure 105: Standard Selection with FI-AR-AR under 'Application Component'

7. Press ☑, and the system will now bring the list of Transaction Codes of all 'Basic Functions' under FI-AR:

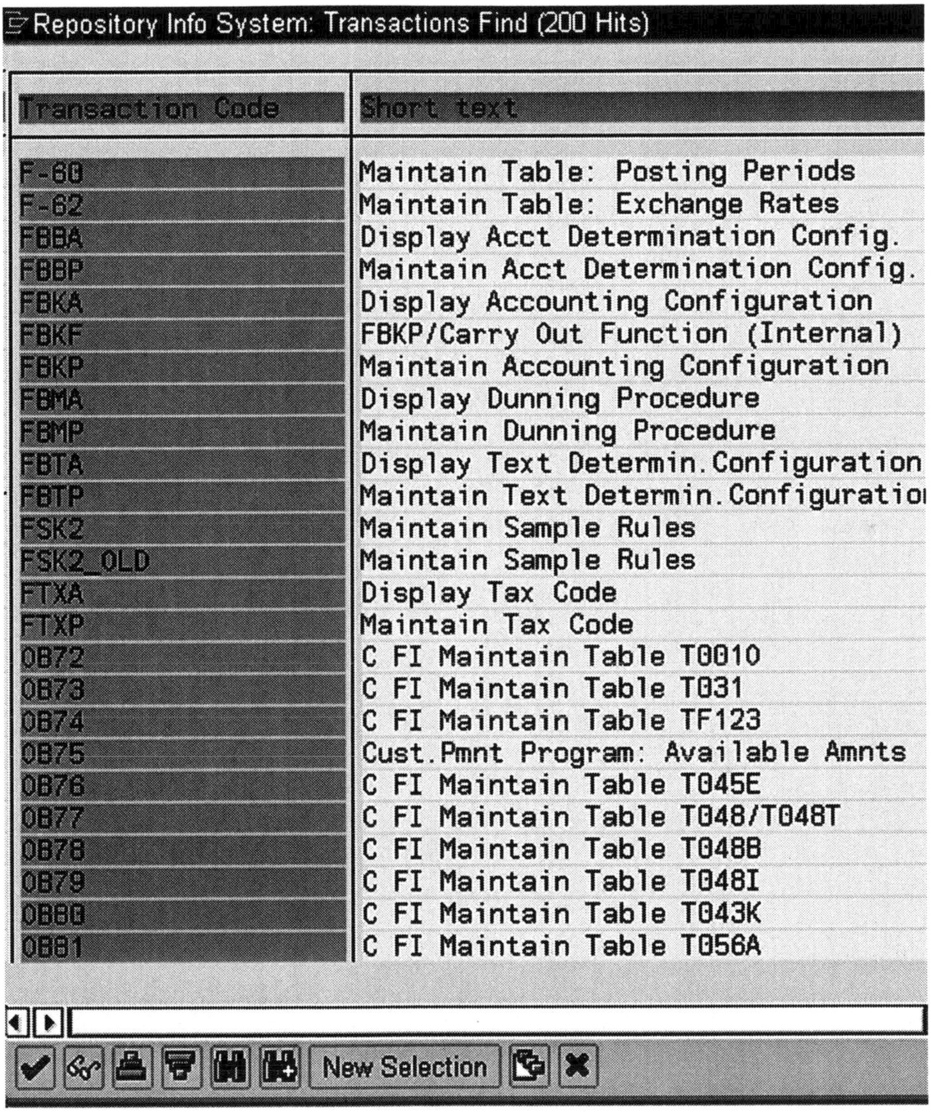

☞ Repository Info System: Transactions Find (200 Hits)

Transaction Code	Short text
F-60	Maintain Table: Posting Periods
F-62	Maintain Table: Exchange Rates
FBBA	Display Acct Determination Config.
FBBP	Maintain Acct Determination Config.
FBKA	Display Accounting Configuration
FBKF	FBKP/Carry Out Function (Internal)
FBKP	Maintain Accounting Configuration
FBMA	Display Dunning Procedure
FBMP	Maintain Dunning Procedure
FBTA	Display Text Determin.Configuration
FBTP	Maintain Text Determin.Configuratior
FSK2	Maintain Sample Rules
FSK2_OLD	Maintain Sample Rules
FTXA	Display Tax Code
FTXP	Maintain Tax Code
OB72	C FI Maintain Table T0010
OB73	C FI Maintain Table T031
OB74	C FI Maintain Table TF123
OB75	Cust.Pmnt Program: Available Amnts
OB76	C FI Maintain Table T045E
OB77	C FI Maintain Table T048/T048T
OB78	C FI Maintain Table T048B
OB79	C FI Maintain Table T048I
OB80	C FI Maintain Table T043K
OB81	C FI Maintain Table T056A

◀ ▶

☑ 🔍 🖨 ☷ 💾 💾 [New Selection] 🗗 ❌

Figure 106: Transaction Codes of Basic Functions under FI-AR

Basis & ABAP

Sl. No.	Are you looking for:	T-Code
1	ABAP Editor	SE38
2	ABAP Function Modules	SE37
3	ABAP Objects Run-time Analysis	SE30
4	ABAP Program analysis	AL21
5	ABAP Repository Information System	SE86
6	ABAP Text Element Maintenance	SE32
7	ABAP/4 Dialogue Modules	SE35
8	ABAP/4 Reporting	SA38
9	ABAP/4 Repository Information System	SE85
10	ABAP: Extended Program Check	SLIN
11	Analyze User Buffer	SU56
12	Application Hierarchy	SE81
13	Background Job Overview	SM37
14	Background Processing Analysis Tool	SM65
15	Batch Input Monitoring	SM35
16	Batch Request	SM36
17	Business Navigator – Component View	SB01
18	Business Navigator – Process Flow View	SB02
19	CCMS	SRZL
20	Client Administration	SCC4
21	Client Copy	SCC0
22	Client Copy Log	SCC3
23	Client Delete	SCC5
24	Client Export	SCC8
25	Client Import	SCC6
26	Client Transport	SCC2
27	Computer Aided Test Tool (CATT)	SCAT
28	Context Builder	SE33
29	Convert Data Dictionary Tables on Database Level	SE14
30	Current Customizing	SPRM
31	Customer Enhancement Simulation	SE94

32	Customer Measurement	USMM
33	Customizing	SPRO
34	Customizing Organizer	SE10
35	Data Dictionary Display	SE12
36	Data Dictionary Maintenance	SE11
37	Data Modeler	SD11
38	Data Transfer Workbench	SXDA
39	Development Class Overview	OY08
40	Development Coordination Info System	SE88
41	Display and Delete Locks	SM12
42	Display Output Requests	SP02
43	Display Own Jobs	SMX
44	Display SAP Directories	AL11
45	Display Table Content	SE16
46	Display Users	SU01D
47	Download to Early Watch	AL10
48	Dynamic Menu	SMEN
49	Early-Watch Report	AL07
50	Enhancements	CMOD
51	Environment Analyzer	SE02
52	Execute Logical Commands	SM49
53	Generate Enterprise IMG	SCPF
54	Generate Table Display	SE17
55	Generate Table View	SE54
56	Global User Manager	SUMM
57	Installation Check	SM28
58	Integrated User Maintenance	SUPF
59	Job administration	SM68
60	Job analysis	SM39
61	Job scheduling	SM67
62	LAN Check with Ping	OS01
63	Language Import Utility	SMLI
64	List for Session Manager	SU54
65	List of SAP Servers	SM51

66	Local Client Copy	SCCL
67	Lock Transactions	SM01
68	Logical databases	SE36
69	Logon to Online Service System (OSS)	OSS1
70	Maintain Area Menu	SE43
71	Maintain Authorization Profiles	SU02
72	Maintain Authorizations	SU03
73	Maintain Internet Users	SU05
74	Maintain Logon Group	SMLG
75	Maintain Messages	SE91
76	Maintain Organization Levels	SUPO
77	Maintain Own User Parameters	SU52
78	Maintain PC Work Directory	SO21
79	Maintain Technical Settings (Tables)	SE13
80	Maintain Transaction Codes	SE93
81	Maintain Trees in Information System	SE89
82	Maintain User	SU01
83	Maintain User Parameter	SU2
84	Mass Changes to User Master	SU10
85	Mass Changes to User Master Records	SU12
86	Menu Painter	SE41
87	Modification Browser	SE95
88	Monitor Current Workload	AL05
89	Number Range Objects	SNRO
90	Object Navigator	SE80
91	OLE Applications	SOLE
92	Performance Monitoring	STUN
93	Performance, SAP Statistics, Workload	ST03
94	Performance: Upload/Download	AL06
95	Queue Maintenance Transaction	SM38
96	Quick-Viewer	SQVI
97	R/3 Documentation	SE61
98	R/3 Repository Information System	SE84
99	Record Batch Input	SHDB

100	Remote Client Copy	SCC9
101	Reporting: Change Tree Structure	SERP
102	Repository Browser	SEU
103	Repository Info System	SE15
104	Repository Info System	SUIM
105	SAP Alert Monitor	AL01
106	SAP Enhancement Management	SMOD
107	SAP Query: Language Comparison	SQ07
108	SAP Query: Maintain Functional Area	SQ02
109	SAP Query: Maintain Queries	SQ01
110	SAP Query: Maintain User Groups	SQ03
111	SAP Web Repository	SMW0
112	SAPoffice: Inbox Overview	SOY5
113	SAPoffice: Outbox	SO02
114	SAPoffice: Private Folders	SO03
115	SAPoffice: Shared Folders	SO04
116	SAPoffice: User Master	SO12
117	SAPscript Font Maintenance (revised)	SE73
118	SAPscript Form	SE71
119	SAPscript Format Conversion	SE74
120	SAPscript Settings	SE75
121	SAPscript Styles	SE72
122	SAPscript Translation Styles	SE77
123	SAPscript: Form Translation	SE76
124	SAPscript: Graphics administration	SE78
125	SAPscript: Standard Texts	SO10
126	Screen Painter	SE51
127	Split-screen Editor: Program Compare	SE39
128	Spool and Relate Area	SP00
129	Spool Control	SP01
130	Spool Management	SPAD
131	SQL Trace	ST05
132	Start Report Immediately	SC38
133	System Administration Assistant	SSAA

134	System Log	SM21
135	System Log Analysis	SM23
136	System Messages	SM02
137	System Trace	ST01
138	Table History	OY18
139	Table Maintenance	SM31
140	Transport and Correction System	SE01
141	Transport Management System	STMS
142	Transport System Status Display	SE07
143	Transport Utilities	SE03
144	Update Program Administration	SM14
145	User Overview	SM04
146	Users Logged On	AL08
147	View/Table Comparison	SCMP
148	View-cluster Maintenance Call	SM34
149	Web Object Administration	SIAC1
150	Work Process Overview	SM50
151	Workbench Organizer (Initial Screen)	SE09
152	Workflow Definition	SWDC

Financial Accounting (FI): Customizing

Sl. No.	Are you looking for:	T-Code
1	Activate Functional Area Substitution	OBBZ
2	Activate Validations	OB28
3	Allocate a Company Code to Sample Account Rule Type	OB67
4	Assign Chart of Depreciation to Company Code	OAOB
5	Assign Country to Tax Calculation Procedure	OBBG
6	Assign Employee Groups to Credit Representative Groups	OB51
7	Assign GL Accounts to Reason Codes	OBXL
8	Assign Posting Keys to Document Types	OBU1
9	Assign Reference Interest Rates to Interest Indicators	OB81

10	Assign Tax Codes for Non-Taxable Transactions	OBCL
11	Assign Treasury Transaction Types to House Banks	OT55
12	Assign Users to Tolerance Groups	OB57
13	Automatic Account Assignment for Interest Calculation	OBV1
14	Automatic Account Assignment, Cross-Company Code	OBYA
15	Automatic Account Assignment, MM	OBYC
16	Automatic Postings Documentation	OBL1
17	Bank Chain Determination	FIBB
18	Cash Management Implementation Tool	FDFD
19	Configuration: Maintain Display Format	FAKP
20	Configuration: Show Display Format	FAKA
21	Configure Days in Arrears Calculation	OB39
22	Configure the Central TR-CM System	FF$X
23	Copy Chart of Accounts	OBY7
24	Copy Chart of Depreciation	EC08
25	Copy Company Code	EC01
26	Copy GL Accounts from Chart of Accounts to the Company Code	OBY2
27	Copy Vendor Master Records Creation Program	FK15
28	Copy Vendor Master Records Upload Program	FK16
29	Define Treasury Groupings	OT17
30	Define Additional Local Currencies	OB22
31	Define Asset Classes	OAOA
32	Define Base Method	OAYO
33	Define Cash Discount Accounts	OBXI
34	Define Cash Management Account Names	OT16
35	Define Check Lots	FCHI
36	Define Company Code (Create/Check/Delete)	OX02
37	Define Company Code Global Parameters	OBY6
38	Define Countries	OY01
39	Define Credit Control Areas	OB45
40	Define Credit Representative Groups	OB02
41	Define Credit Risk Categories	OB01

42	Define Currency Translation Ratios	GCRF
43	Define Customer Account Groups	OBD2
44	Define Customer Tolerance Groups	OBA3
45	Define Data Transfer Rules for Sample Accounts	FSK2
46	Define Depreciation Key	AFAMA
47	Define Document Types	OBA7
48	Define Financial Statement Versions	OB58
49	Define GL Account Groups	OBD4
50	Define GL Number Ranges	FBN1
51	Define House Banks	FI12
52	Define Line item Layouts	O7Z3
53	Define Lockbox Accounts	OB10
54	Define Number Range for Payment Request	F8BM
55	Define Number Ranges for Depreciation Postings	FBN1
56	Define Number Ranges for Master Classes	AS08
57	Define Number Ranges of Vendor Account Groups	OBAS
58	Define Number Ranges for Vendor Account Groups	XKN1
59	Define Posting Keys	OB41
60	Define Posting Period Variant	OBBO
61	Define Posting Rules for Electronic Bank Statement	OT57
62	Define Reason Codes	OBBE
63	Define Reference Interest Rates	OBAC
64	Define Screen Layouts for Asset Depreciation Areas	AO21
65	Define Sort Variants	O757
66	Define Source Symbols, for Treasury	OYOS
67	Define Special Fields	OBVU
68	Define Specify Intervals and Posting Rules	OAYR
69	Define Tax Accounts	OB40
70	Define Tax Codes for Non-Taxable Transactions	OBCL
71	Define Tax Codes for Sales/Purchases	FTXP
72	Define Tax Jurisdiction Codes	OBCP
73	Define Tolerance Groups	OBA4
74	Define Vendor Account Groups	OBD3
75	Define Void Reason Codes for Checks	FCHV

76	Define Sample Account Rules	OB15
77	Depreciation Keys	OAYO
78	Determine Depreciation Areas in Asset Classes	OAYZ
79	Define Planning Groups for Treasury	OT13
80	Display Accounting Configuration	FBKA
81	Document Change Rules	OB32
82	Fast Entry Screens	O7E6
83	FI Configuration Menu (instead of IMG)	ORFB
84	Field Status Variants	OBC4
85	Integration with GL	AO90
86	Interest Indicator (Arrears Interest) for Int. Calculation Program	OB82
87	Internal Number Range for Payment Orders	FBN2
88	Loans Customizing	FDCU
89	Maintain Accounting Configuration	FBKF
90	Maintain Accounting Configuration	FBKP
91	Maintain Bank Chains for Account Carry-over	FIBTU
92	Maintain Bank Chains for House Banks	FIBHU
93	Maintain Bank Chains for Partner	FBIPU
94	Maintain Bank Chains for Partner	FIBPU
95	Maintain Business Area	OX03
96	Maintain Client-Dependent User Exits	GCX2
97	Maintain Currency Translation Type	FDIC
98	Maintain Currency Translation Type	FGIC
99	Maintain Currency Translation Type	FKIC
100	Maintain Dunning Procedure	FBMP
101	Maintain Fiscal Year Variant	OB29
102	Maintain Functional Areas	OKBD
103	Maintain Key Figures	FDIK
104	Maintain Lockbox Control Parameters	OBAY
105	Maintain Lockbox Posting Data	OBAX
106	Maintain Payment Program Configuration	FBZP
107	Maintain Substitutions	GGB1
108	Maintain Text Determination Configuration	FBTP

109	Maintain Validations	GGB0
110	Map Internal Reason Codes to External Reason Codes	OBCS
111	Real Estate Implementation Guide	FEUI
112	Retained Earnings Variant	OB53
113	Scenarios for Bank Chain Determination	FIBC
114	Specify Round Up Net Book Valuation	OAYO
115	Structure for Tax Jurisdiction Codes	OBCO
116	Transaction Types for Electronic Bank Statement	OBBY
117	Transport Chart of Accounts	OBY9
118	Treasury Planning Levels	OT14

Financial Accounting (FI): Transactions

Sl. No.	Are you looking for:	T-Code
1	A/P: Account Balances	F.42
2	A/P: Account List	F.40
3	A/P: Balance Interest Calculation	F.44
4	A/P: Evaluate Info System	F.46
5	A/P: Open Items	F.41
6	A/R Summary	FCV1
7	A/R Dunning Run	F150
8	A/R: Account Balances	F.23
9	A/R: Account List	F.20
10	A/R: Balance Interest Calculation	F.26
11	A/R: Evaluate Info System	F.30
12	A/R: Interest for Days Overdue	F.24
13	A/R: Open Item Sorted List	F.22
14	A/R: Open Items	F.21
15	A/R: Periodic Account Statements	F.27
16	Accounting Editing Options	FB00
17	Accounts Detailed Listing from OI Account Accum. Audit Trail	F.5C

18	Accumulated Classic Audit Trail: Create Extract (RFKLET01)	F.59
19	Accumulated Details from Historical Accum. Balance Audit Trail	F.5A
20	Accumulated OI Audit Trail: Create Extract (RFKLET01)	F.5B
21	Acquisition from Purchase with Vendor	F-90
22	Advance Tax Return	F.12
23	Archive Bank Master Data	F041
24	Archive Customer	F043
25	Archive Transaction Figures	F046
26	Archiving Bank Data Storage	F66A
27	Archiving Banks	F61A
28	Archiving Check Data	FCHA
29	Archiving GL Accounts	F53A
30	Archiving Payment Request	F8BO
31	Archiving Vendors	F044
32	Asset Acquisition to Clearing Account	F-91
33	Asset Depreciation Run	AFAB
34	Asset Explorer	AW01
35	Asset Master Creation	AS01
36	Asset Retirement from Sale With Customer	F-92
37	Asset Scrapping	ABAVN
38	Asset Transfer	ABUMN
39	Asset, Create Sub-Asset	AS11
40	Automatic Clearing: ABAP/4 Report	F.13
41	Balance Sheet- ABAP/4 Report	F.01
42	Balance Sheet Adjustment: ABAP/4 Reporting	F101
43	Balance Sheet/P&L with inflation	FJA3
44	Bill of Exchange List	F.25
45	Bill of Exchange Payment	F-36
46	Bill of Exchange Payment Request Dunning	F.70
47	Bill of Exchange Payment – Header Data	F-40
48	Bill of Exchange Presentation – International	FBWE

49	Block Customer (Accounting)	FD05
50	Block Vendor (Accounting)	FK05
51	Cash Concentration	FF73
52	Cash Journal Document Number Range	FBCJC1
53	Cash Journal	FBCJ
54	Cash Management and Forecast – Initial Screen	FF72
55	Cash Management Position/Liquidity Forecast	FF70
56	Cash Management Summary Records	FF-3
57	Cash Position	FF71
58	Change Bank	FI02
59	Change Check/Payment Allocation	FCHT
60	Change Check Information/Cash Check	FCH6
61	Change Credit Limits	FD24
62	Change Current Number Range Number	FI07
63	Change Customer (Accounting Data)	FD02
64	Change Customer Credit Management	FD32
65	Change Customer Line Items	FBL6
66	Change Document	FB02
67	Change GL Account Line Items	FBL4
68	Change Intercompany Document	FBU2
69	Change Last Adjustment Dates	FJA2
70	Change Line Items -Customer/Vendor/Asset/GL	FB09
71	Change Parked Document (Header)	FBV4
72	Change Parked Document	FBV2
73	Change Payment Advice	FBE2
74	Change Pricing Report	F/LB
75	Change Recurring Entry	FBD2
76	Change Report Settings for Transaction Figures	FDI2
77	Change Report: Settings	FGI2
78	Change Report: Settings	FKI2
79	Change Sample Document	FBM2
80	Change Vendor (Accounting Data)	FK02
81	Change Vendor (Accounting Data)	FK04
82	Change Vendor Line Items	FBL2

83	Check Extract – Creation	FCHX
84	Check if Documents can be Archived	FB99
85	Check Register	FCHN
86	Check Retrieval	FCHB
87	Check Tracing Initial Menu	FCHK
88	Clear Customer Down Payment	F-39
89	Clear Customer: Header Data	F-32
90	Clear GL Account: Header Data	F-03
91	Clear Vendor Down Payment	F-54
92	Clear Vendor: Header Data	F-44
93	Confirm Customer Individually (Accounting)	FD08
94	Confirm Customer List (Accounting)	FD09
95	Confirm Vendor Individually (Accounting)	FK08
96	Confirm Vendor List (Accounting)	FK09
97	Correspondence: Delete Requests	F.63
98	Correspondence: Maintain Requests	F.64
99	Correspondence: Print Interest Documents	F.62
100	Correspondence: Print Letters (Customer)	F.65
101	Correspondence: Print Letters (Vendor)	F.66
102	Correspondence: Print Requests	F.61
103	Create Bank	FI01
104	Create Check Information	FCH5
105	Create Customer (Accounting)	FD01
106	Create Payment Advice	FBE1
107	Create Payment Runs Automatically	F8BU
108	Create Planning Memo Record	FF63
109	Create Reference for Check	FCHU
110	Create Vendor (Accounting Area Data)	FK01
111	Credit Management – Mass Change	F.34
112	Credit Management – Mass Change	FD37
113	Credit Management – Master Data List	FDK43
114	Credit Management – Missing Data	F.32
115	Credit Management – Overview	F.31
116	Credit Master Sheet	F.35

117	Customer Account Analysis	FD11
118	Customer Account Balance	FD10
119	Customer Balance Confirmation: ABAP/4 Report	F.17
120	Customer Balance Display	FD10N
121	Customer Balance: Display with Work-list	FD10NA
122	Customer Changes (Accounting)	FD04
123	Customer Down Payment Request	F-37
124	Customer Interest on Arrears: Post (w/ Open Items)	F.2B
125	Customer Interest on Arrears: Post (w/o Open Items)	F.2A
126	Customer Interest on Arrears: Post (w/o postings)	F.2C
127	Customer Line Items	FBL5N
128	Customer Noted Item	F-49
129	Customer/Vendor Statistics	F.1A
130	Customers Drilldown Reports: Background Processing	FDIB
131	Customers: FI-SD Master Data Comparison	F.2D
132	Customers: Report Selection	F.99
133	Customers: Reset Credit Limit	F.28
134	Data Extract for FI Transfer	FC11
135	Delete A/R Summary	FCV2
136	Delete Cashing/Extract Data	FCHG
137	Delete Manual Checks	FCHF
138	Delete Payment Advice	FBE6
139	Delete Payment Run Check Information	FCHD
140	Delete Recurring Document	F.56
141	Delete Voided Checks	FCHE
142	Display Account Determination Configuration	FBBA
143	Display Bank Chains for House Banks	FIBHS
144	Display Bank Chains for Partners	FIBPS
145	Display Bank Changes	FI04
146	Display Bank	FI03
147	Display Check Information	FCH1
148	Display Customer (Accounting Data)	FD03

149	Display Customer Credit Management	FD33
150	Display Customer Line Items	FBL5
151	Display Document	FB03
152	Display Document/Payment Use	FB03Z
153	Display Dunning Procedure	FBMA
154	Display Electronic Bank Statement	FF.6
155	Display FI Amount Groups	F8+2
156	Display FI Main Role Definition	F8+0
157	Display GL Account Line Items	FBL3
158	Display House Banks/Bank Accounts	FI13
159	Display Intercompany Document	FBU3
160	Display of Payment Requests	F8BS
161	Display Parked Document	FBV3
162	Display Payment Advice	FBE3
163	Display Payment Document Checks	FCH2
164	Display Payment Program Configuration	FBZA
165	Display Payment Requests	F8BT
166	Display Payment Run	FBZ8
167	Display Pricing Report	F/LC
168	Display Recurring Entry Changes	FBD4
169	Display Recurring Entry	FBD3
170	Display Sample Document Changes	FBM4
171	Display Sample Document	FBM3
172	Display Text Determination Configuration	FBTA
173	Display Vendor (Accounting Data)	FK03
174	Display Vendor Line Items	FBL1
175	Display/Edit Payment Proposal	FBZ0
176	Document Archiving	F045
177	Document Changes of Parked Documents	FBV5
178	Document Changes	FB04
179	Down Payment Request	F-47
180	Download Documents	FBF4
181	Enter Accrual/Deferral Document	FBS1
182	Enter Bill of Exchange Payment Request	FBW1

183	Enter Customer Credit Memo	F-27
184	Enter Customer Invoice	F-22
185	Enter GL Account Posting	F-02
186	Enter Incoming Credit Memos	FB65
187	Enter Incoming Invoices	FB60
188	Enter Noted Item	FB31
189	Enter Outgoing Credit Memos	FB75
190	Enter Outgoing Invoices	FB70
191	Enter Payment Request	FBP1
192	Enter Recurring Entry	FBD1
193	Enter Sample Document	F-01
194	Enter Statistical Posting: Header Data	F-38
195	Enter Transfer Posting: Header Data	F-21
196	Enter Vendor Credit Memo	F-41
197	Enter Vendor Invoice	F-43
198	Exchange Rates Table Maintenance	F-62
199	F111 Customizing	F8BZ
200	Failed Customer Payments	FBZG
201	FI Account Assignment Model Management	FKMT
202	FI Display Structure	FINA
203	FI Easy Access – Banks	FBME
204	FI Easy Access – Customers	FDMN
205	FI Easy Access – Vendors	FKMN
206	FI Information System	F000
207	FI Initial Consolidation Menu	FCMN
208	FI Valuation Run	F107
209	Financial Statements Comparison	FC10
210	Financial Transactions	FBF2
211	Foreign Currency Valuation: Open Items	F.05
212	GL Account Assignment Manual	F.53
213	GL Account Balance Interest Calculation	F.52
214	GL Account Balances	F.08
215	GL Account Cashed Checks	FF.3
216	GL Account Interest Scale	FF_1

217	GL Account Line Items	FBL3N
218	GL Account List	F.09
219	GL Accounts Archiving	F042
220	GL Account Posting: Single Screen Transaction	FB50
221	GL Advance Report on Tax on Sales/Purchases with Jurisdiction	F.5I
222	GL Balance Carried Forward	F.07
223	GL Balance Sheet Adjustment Log	F.5F
224	GL Chart of Accounts	F.10
225	GL Compact Journal	F.02
226	GL Create Foreign Trade Report	F.04
227	GL Delete Sample Documents	F.57
228	GL Drilldown Reports: Background Processing	FGIB
229	GL General Ledger from Document File	F.11
230	GL GR/IR Clearing	F.19
231	GL Open Items	F.51
232	GL Post Balance Sheet Adjustment	F.5E
233	GL Profitability Segment Adjustment	F.50
234	GL Report Selection	F.97
235	GL Structured Account Balances	F.54
236	GL Update Balance Sheet Adjustment	F.5D
237	Generate Multicash Format	FEBC
238	Generate Payment Request from Advices	FF.D
239	Import Electronic Bank Statement	FF.5
240	Import Electronic Check Deposit List	FFB4
241	Import Forms from Client 000	FDIR
242	Import Lockbox File	FLB2
243	Import Reports from Client 000	FDIQ
244	Incoming Payments Fast Entry	F-26
245	Invoice/Credit Fast Entry	FB10
246	Maintain Bill of Exchange Liability	F.93
247	Manual Bank Statement	FF67
248	Manual Check Deposit Transaction	FF68
249	Mark Bank for Deletion	FI06

250	Mark Customer for Deletion (Accounting)	FD06
251	Mark Vendor for Deletion (Accounting)	FK06
252	Mass Reversal of Documents	F.80
253	Online Cashed Checks	FCHR
254	Open Item Balance Audit Trail: from Document File	F.58
255	Outstanding Bills of Exchange	FF-2
256	Parameters for Automatic Payment	F110
257	Parameters for Payment of Request	F111
258	Park Customer Credit Memo	F-67
259	Park Customer Invoice	F-64
260	Park Document	FBV1
261	Park Vendor Credit Memo	F-66
262	Park Vendor Invoice	F-63
263	Payment Advice Comparison	FF.7
264	Payment Advice Journal	FF-8
265	Payment Card Evaluations	FCCR
266	Payment Cards: Settlement	FCC1
267	Payment Request	F-59
268	Payment with Printout	F-18
269	Post Bill of Exchange Use	F-33
270	Post Collection	F-34
271	Post Customer Down Payment	F-29
272	Post Document	FB01
273	Post Electronic Bank Statement	FEBP
274	Post Electronic Check Deposit List	FFB5
275	Post Foreign Currency Valuation	F-05
276	Post Forfeiting	F-35
277	Post Held Document	FB11
278	Post Incoming Payments	F-06
279	Post Lockbox Data	FLBP
280	Post Outgoing Payments	F-07
281	Post Parked Document	FBV0
282	Post Payment Orders	FF.9
283	Post Tax Payable	FB41

284	Post Vendor Down Payment	F-48
285	Post with Clearing	F-04
286	Post with Reference Document	FBR1
287	Posting Period Table Maintenance	F-60
288	Preliminary Posting	F-65
289	Print Check For Payment Document	FBZ5
290	Print Payment Orders	FF.8
291	Realize Recurring Entry	FBD5
292	Reconciliation between Affiliated Companies	F.2E
293	Recurring Entries: ABAP/4 Report	F.14
294	Reject Parked Document	FBV6
295	Release for Payments	FB13
296	Renumber Checks	FCH4
297	Report Painter	FGRP
298	Report Painter: Change Form – Customer	FDI5
299	Report Painter: Change Form – GL	FGI5
300	Report Painter: Change Form – Vendor	FKI5
301	Report Writer Menu	FGRW
302	Reprint Check	FCH7
303	Request from Correspondence	FB12
304	Reset Cleared Items (Payment Cards)	FBRC
305	Reset Cleared Items	FBRA
306	Reset Cleared Items: Payment Requests	F8BW
307	Returned Bills of Exchange Payable	FBWD
308	Reversal of Bank-to-Bank Transfers	F8BV
309	Reverse Bill Liability	F-20
310	Reverse Check Payment	FCH8
311	Reverse Check/Bill of Exchange	F-25
312	Reverse Cross-Company Code Document	FBU8
313	Reverse Document	FB08
314	Reverse Posting for Accrued/Deferred Documents	F.81
315	Reverse Statistical Posting	F-19
316	SAP Office: Short Message – Create and Send	F00
317	Special Purpose Ledger Menu	FGM0

318	Vendor Account Balance	FK10
319	Vendor Balance Confirmation: ABAP/4 Report	F.18
320	Vendor Balance Display	FK10N
321	Vendor Cashed Checks	FF.4
322	Vendor Check/Bill of Exchange	FBW6
323	Vendor Down Payment Request	FBA6
324	Vendor Interest on Arrears: Post (w/ Open Items)	F.4B
325	Vendor Interest on Arrears: Post (w/o Open Items)	F.4A
326	Vendor Interest on Arrears: Post (w/o Postings)	F.4C
327	Vendor Line Items	FBL1N
328	Vendor Noted Item	F-57
329	Vendors Drilldown Reports: Background Processing	FKIB
330	Vendors: Calculate Interest on Arrears	F.47
331	Vendors: FI-MM Master Data Comparison	F.48
332	Vendors: Report Selection	F.98
333	Void Checks	FCH3
334	Void Issued Check	FCH9
335	Wire Authorization	FFW1

Material Management (MM)

Sl. No.	Are you looking for:	T-Code
1	ABC Analysis for Cycle Counting	MIBC
2	Allow Postings to Previous Period	MMRV
3	Analysis of Order Values	E81N
4	Archive/Delete Material	MM71
5	Archive Info Records	E17
6	Archive Purchase Requisitions	E97
7	Archive Purchasing Documents	E98
8	Archive Rebate Arrangements	EBR
9	Archived Purchase Requisitions	E5R
10	Archived Purchasing Documents	E82
11	Assign and Process Requisitions	E57

12	Assign Source to Purchase Requisition	E56
13	Assign User to User Group	EU0
14	Automatic Generation of POs	ME59
15	Buyer's Negotiation Sheet for Material	E1Y
16	Buyer's Negotiation Sheet for Vendor	E1X
17	Change Contract	E32K
18	Change Inventory Count	MI05
19	Change Material	MM02
20	Change Outline Agreement	E32
21	Change Physical Inventory Document	MI02
22	Change Purchase Order	E22N
23	Change Purchase Requisition	ME52N
24	Change Purchasing Info Record	E12
25	Change Reservation	MB22
26	Change Scheduling Agreement	E32L
27	Change Vendor (Purchasing)	MK02
28	Changes to Vendor Evaluation	E6A
29	Close Period	MMPV
30	Collective Release of Purchase Order	EW5
31	Conditions for Incoterms	EKI
32	Conditions for Invoicing Party	EKJ
33	Count/Difference	MI08
34	Create Conditions (Purchasing)	EK1
35	Create Contract	E31K
36	Create Material	MM01
37	Create Non-Stock Material	MMN1
38	Create Non-Valuated Material	MMU1
39	Create Operating Supplies	MMI1
40	Create Outline Agreement	E31
41	Create Physical Inventory Document	MI01
42	Create Purchase Order	E21N
43	Create Purchase Requisition	ME51N
44	Create Purchasing Info Record	E11
45	Create Quotation	E47

46	Create Request For Quotation	E41
47	Create Requirement Request	EW1
48	Create Reservation	MB21
49	Create Scheduling Agreement	E31L
50	Create Source List	E01
51	Create Vendor (Purchasing)	MK01
52	Currency Change: Contracts	EKRE
53	Delivery Addresses	EAN
54	Display Conditions (Purchasing)	EK3
55	Display Material	MM03
56	Display Material Archive	MM72
57	Display Material	IH09
58	Display Purchase Order	E23N
59	Display Purchase Requisition	ME53N
60	Display Purchasing Info Record	E13
61	Display Quotation	E48
62	Display Vendor Evaluation for Material	E6B
63	Display Vendor Evaluation	E62
64	Enter Inventory Count	MI04
65	Enter Storage Locations	MMSC
66	Evaluation Comparison	E64
67	Evaluation Lists	E65
68	Flag for deletion, immediately	MM06
69	Flag Purchasing Info Record for Deletion	E15
70	Goods Receipt – For PO Known	MB01
71	Goods Receipt – PO Unknown	MB0A
72	Goods Receipt Forecast	E2V
73	Info Records Per Material Group	E1W
74	Info Records Per Material	E1M
75	Info Records Per Vendor	E1L
76	List of Customer Rebate Arrangements	ER5
77	List of Vendor Rebate Arrangements	EB5
78	Maintain Outline Agreement Supplement	E34
79	Maintain Quota Arrangement	EQ1

80	Maintain Vendor Evaluation	E61
81	Market Price	EKH
82	Mass Change of Purchase Orders	EMAS
83	Material List	MM60
84	Message Output: Purchase Orders	E9F
85	Message Output: RFQs	E9A
86	Other Goods Receipts	MB1C
87	Physical Inventory Document Recount	MI11
88	PO Change	ME22
89	PO Create – Vendor Known	ME21
90	PO Create – Vendor Unknown	ME25
91	Price Change: Contract	EDL
92	Price Change: Scheduling Agreements	EKL
93	Price Comparison List	E49
94	Procurement Transaction	EW0
95	Purchase Order Price History	E1P
96	Purchase Order	EPO
97	Purchase Orders by Account Assignment	E2K
98	Purchase Orders by Material Group	E2C
99	Purchase Orders by Material	E2M
100	Purchase Orders by PO Number	E2N
101	Purchase Orders by Vendor	E2L
102	Purchase Orders for Project	E2J
103	Purchase Orders for Supplying Plant	E2W
104	Quotation Price History	E1E
105	Release Contract	E35K
106	Release Outline Agreement	E35
107	Release Purchase Order	E29N
108	Release Purchase Requisition	ME54
109	Release RFQ	E45
110	Release Scheduling Agreement	E35L
111	Reservations by Account Assignment	MB25
112	Reservations by Material	MB24
113	RFQs by Material Group	E4C

114	RFQs by Material	E4M
115	RFQs by Vendor	E4L
116	Source List for Material	E0M
117	Stock Overview	MMBE
118	Transfer Posting	MB1B
119	Vendors Without Evaluation	E6C
120	Web-based PO	EWP

Sales and Distribution (SD)

Sl. No.	Are you looking for:	T-Code
1	Access sequence	V/07
2	Assigning Sales Area to Sales Documents Type	OVAZ
3	Billing Due List	VF04
4	Billing Menu	VF00
5	Block Customer (Sales)	VD05
6	Blocked SD Documents	VKM1
7	Cancel Billing Document	VF11
8	Cancel Goods Issue	VL09
9	Change Billing Document	VF02
10	Change Billing Document	VF02
11	Change Condition	VK12
12	Change Contract	VA42
13	Change Customer	VD02
14	Change Customer (Sales)	VD02
15	Change Customer Price	V-51
16	Change Material Price	V-43
17	Change Price List	V-47
18	Change Sales Order	VA02
19	Change Shipment	VT02N
20	Create Billing Document	VF01
21	Create Business Partner	V+23
22	Create Condition	VK11
23	Create Consignee (Sales)	V-06

24	Create Contract	VA41
25	Create Customer	V-09
26	Create Customer	XD01
27	Create Customer (Sales)	VD01
28	Create Customer Hierarchy Nodes	V-12
29	Create Inquiry	VA11
30	Create Invoice Party (Sales)	V-04
31	Create One-Time Customer (Sales)	V-07
32	Create Ordering Party (Sales)	V-03
33	Create Outbound Delivery with reference to Sales Order	VL01
34	Create Payer (Centrally)	V-08
35	Create Payer (Sales)	V-05
36	Create Quotation	VA21
37	Create Rebate Agreement	VBO1
38	Create Sales Order	V-01
39	Create Sales Order	VA01
40	Create Scheduling Agreement	VA31
41	Customer Account Changes	VD04
42	Customer Hierarchy Maintenance	VDH1
43	Define delivery types	OVLK
44	Define Sales Documents Type (Header)	VOV8
45	Delivery Due List	VL04
46	Display Customer	VD03
47	Display Customer	XD03
48	Display Order	VA03
49	Flag for Deletion Customer	VD06
50	List of Blocked SD Documents	VKM1
51	List of Deliveries	VKM5
52	List of Outbound Deliveries for Goods Issue	VL06G
53	List of Outbound Deliveries for Picking	VL06P
54	List of Sales Documents	VKM3
55	List of Sales Orders	VA05
56	Maintain Pricing Procedure	V/08

57	Mark Customer For Deletion	VD06
58	Master data Menu	VS00
59	Material Determination	VD52
60	Modify Customer	XD02
61	Order Reasons	OVAU
62	Output for Shipments	VT70
63	Periodic Billing	V.07
64	Pricing Process Determination	V/06
65	Release Orders for Billing	V.23
66	Released SD Documents	VKM2
67	Sales Menu	VA00
68	Sales Support	VC00
69	Shipping Menu	VL00
70	Transportation	VT00

Production Planning (PP)

Sl. No.	Are you looking for:	T-Code
1	Change BOM	CS02
2	Change Order	CO02
3	Change Planned Order	MD12
4	Change Planning Calendar	MD26
5	Change Production Lot	MDL2
6	Change Standard Routing	CA02
7	Change Work Center	CR02
8	Collective Access of Planning Result	MD46
9	Collective Availability Check	MDVP
10	Collective Conversion of Planned Order	CO41
11	Convert Planned Order into PR	MDUM
12	Cost Center Assignment	CR06
13	Crate Standard Routing	CA01
14	Create Bill of Material (BOM)	CS01
15	Create Order for Project	CO10
16	Create Order for Sales Order	CO08

17	Create Order with Material	C001
18	Create Order without Material	C007
19	Create Planning Calendar	MD25
20	Create Planning Type	MC8A
21	Create Product Group	MC84
22	Create Production Lot	MDL1
23	Create Work Center	CR01
24	Delete Task List with Archiving	CA99
25	Delete Task List without Archiving	CA98
26	Display BOM	CS03
27	Display BOM Explosion Number	MDSA
28	Display Order	CO03
29	Display Planning Calendar	MD27
30	Display Production Lot	MDL3
31	Display Standard Routing	CA03
32	Display Work Center	CR03
33	Edit BOM Explosion Number	MDSP
34	Explode BOM by Date	OPPP
35	Factory Calendar	OP43
36	Individual Access of Planned Order	MD13
37	Interactive Single-item Planning	MD43
38	MRP List	MD05
39	MRP List Collective Display	MS06
40	MRP List Material	MS05
41	Multi-level BOM	CS11
42	Multi-level Project Planning	MD51
43	Multi-level, Make-to-order Planning	MD50
44	Order – Create With Material	CO01
45	Order Progress	CO46
46	Order Report	MD4C
47	Planning Result	MD45
48	Planning Run On Line	MS01
49	Print MRP List	MDLD
50	Print MRP List	MSLD

51	Replace Work Center	CR85
52	Shift Sequence	OP4A
53	Single Item – Multi-Level	MS02
54	Single Item – Sales Order	MS50
55	Single Item – Single Level	MS03
56	Single Item Planning, Project	MS51
57	Single-item, Multi-level Planning	MD02
58	Single-item, Single-level Planning	MD03
59	Stock/Requirement List Collective Display	MS07
60	Stock/Requirements List	MD04
61	Stock/Requirements List	MS04
62	Transfer Materials to Demand Management	MC90
63	Transfer to ABC	KSOP
64	Transfer to Cost Center	KSPP
65	Where used, Work Center	CA80
66	Work Center Hierarchy	CR08
67	Work Center List	CR05
68	Work Center Reporting	CA80

SAP Terminology

SAP Terminology

ABAP/4: A 4-GL language, Advanced Business Application Programming or ABAP/4, is the SAP programming language.

ABAP Editor: The program editor in SAP that helps you to create/test/change ABAP programs and the associated program/screen elements.

ABAP Query: A programming tool that enables you to create reports without any ABAP programming skill or knowledge. Based on the WYSWYG (What-You-See-is-What-You-Get) principle, ABAP Query enables you to select the fields from tables and arrange them in a report-layout. You may create simple reports (Basic List) or more advanced ones (Statistic or Ranked List).

ABC Classification: Helps in grouping your vendor or materials or inventory or any other object to classify into three categories, A, B, and C. A is the most important and C is the least important in the group. ABC classification enables you to have effective management and monitoring based on specific criteria.

AcceleratedSAP (ASAP): The SAP well renowned and path-breaking methodology to optimally implement SAP, both new as well as the upgrades, with a well-laid out Implementation Road Map.' ASAP comes bundled with 'Accelerators' that enable you to cut-down the implementation time substantially. It also comes delivered with tools such as 'Implementation Assistant,' 'Q and A Database,' etc., that aid in implementation.

Accelerator: Used in ASAP implementation methodology, 'Accelerators' are a collection of templates, 'how-to' guides, and examples to enable easier and faster project implementations.

Access Sequence: Used in GL, CO, SD, and other modules, Access Sequence relates to a set of steps, in a pre-defined order, accessing the Condition Tables searching for Condition Records for performing calculations for arriving at, for example, tax, discount, etc.

Account: A repository holding transaction figures within an accounting unit such as Company Code.

Account Allocation: Used in Asset Accounting (FI-AA), these reconciliation accounts help in posting the business transactions automatically to FI-GL.

Account Assignment: A specification that tells the system which account needs to be posted to during a business transaction.

Account Assignment Category: In MM, this is an identifier that specifies which account assignment details are required for an item (for example, cost center or account number). In CO, Account Assignment Categories determine the Settlement Receivers such as G/ L account, Cost Center, Internal Order, etc.

Account Assignment Group (of the Customer): The identifier in the Customer Master record of the Payer that groups certain Customers (Domestic Customers, Foreign Customers, etc.) for 'Account Assignment' purposes. For example, revenue from Domestic Customers would be posted to a Domestic Revenue GL Account, whereas revenue from foreign customers would be posted to a Foreign Revenue GL Account.

Account Assignment Group (of the Material): The identifier in a Material Master Record that groups certain Materials for 'Account Assignment' purposes.

Account-based Profitability Analysis: One of the two types (the other being Period-Based Profitability Analysis) of Profitability Analysis, which reconciles the cost and revenue data stored in accounts, between FI and CO.

Account Category Reference: A combination of Valuation Classes.

Account Determination: SAP's automatic system function to determine which accounts need posted/updated with the amounts during any posting transaction in the system. In CO, this relates to the determination of adjustment accounts for reconciliation postings between FI and CO, either manually or though automatic substitutions.

Account Determination Procedure: Assigned to a Billing Document Type, this procedure determines Revenue Account Assignment in Sales Documents.

Account Determination Type: A key that determines the Access Sequence and other conditions for Revenue Account Determination in the Sales Document.

Accounting Document: This is the document that records the value changes arising from accounting transaction postings. The accounting document contains one or more line items; you may have up to 999 line items in a single accounting document.

Account Group (FI): Specifies which fields are relevant to a master record and defines the Number Range from which numbers are selected for the master record. There are GL Account Groups, Vendor Account Groups, and Customer Account Groups, etc., that need to be defined in the system. An Account Group needs to be assigned to each of the master records.

Account ID: Refers to a unique, freely definable five-character code assigned to a Bank Account.

Account Key: A field that is assigned to Condition Types in the Pricing Procedure that enables the user to define GL Accounts such as revenue, discounts, or taxes.

Account Modification: This will allow the system to post to accounts that are different from the standard account assignment.

Account Modification Code: A code that is used to further subdivide a Transaction/Event Key/Process Key, which is assigned to a Movement Type.

Account Receivable Summary (A/R Summary): A collection of all credit-related information from the FI-AR that is used for credit checks during Sales Order Processing (SOP) in the SD. If you have a centralized FI system and a decentralized SD, then the A/R summary can be useful to reduce the number of times data is accessed from the databases.

Account Symbol: A key, in FI-GL, which groups accounts from different Charts of Accounts. Account Symbols are used in Account Determination in the Accrual Engine.

Account Type: Refers to an alphanumeric key that identifies the type of account such as D = Customer, K = Vendor, etc. This along with the account number helps you to identify a particular account.

Accounts Payable submodule (FI-AP): An integral part of the Purchasing system, this is used to record and administer the accounting data for all vendors.

Accounts Receivable submodule (FI-AR): An integral part of the Sales system, this is used in recording and administering the accounting for all the customers.

Accrual: The accrual concept helps to distribute expenses/revenues/profit/loss to the correct accounting periods based on the origin of the amounts.

Accrual Calculation: A method used in CO, to evenly spread out irregularly occurring costs by distributing them to correct periods. This helps to even out the irregular fluctuations in business expense occurrences.

Accrual Engine: A tool enabling calculation and posting of accrued costs automatically.

Accrual Order: An Internal Order in CO, used in monitoring the period-based accrual between the expenses posted in FI and accrual costs (such as bonus paid to employees) debited in CO.

Acquisition and Production Costs (APC): APC is the upper limit for valuation of an asset in the Balance Sheet. For all External Acquisitions, the APC is equal to all expenses of acquisition of the asset plus incidental expenses such as commissions and freight charges minus deductions to the purchase price such as rebates, discounts, etc. In the case of 'In-house Acquisitions,' the APC will be equal to all production costs and a portion of administrative expenses that can be associated with that asset.

Acquisition Year: The Fiscal Year in which the acquisition of the asset takes place.

Activity Type: The classifier in CO, used to classify the type of activity (such as the machine hours) performed in a Cost Center.

Activity Type Category: An indicator determining how an Activity Type is allocated (such as direct allocation, indirect activity allocation, etc.).

Activity Type Group: A grouping of similar Activity Types.

Activity Type Planning: A tool, in Cost Center Accounting, used to plan the various Activities (along with their price, their capacity, etc.) to be produced in a Cost Center.

Actual Costs: The costs that are actually incurred. In CO-PC, actual costs represent the total debits made to a cost object.

Actual Cost Entry: This refers to the transferring of primary costs from FI to CO. The transfer of primary costs occurs on a real-time basis via the primary cost element.

Additional Account Assignment: The extra items (such as payment terms, cost object, payment method, etc.) entered in a line item, in addition to the account number, amount, and posting key.

Additional Ledger: A ledger defined for evaluation/reporting purposes, this will contain values and quantities at a company or Company Code level.

Ad-hoc Estimate: A cost estimate (in Easy Cost Planning in CO-PC) that does not need an object to be created in the system.

Adjustment Method: Refers to adjusting individual line items on an account or the balance on the account for inflation.

Agreement: A Contract defined in the system, in SD, with a Customer.

Allocated Actual Costs: Relates to the credit of Cost Centers (and business processes) from activity allocations and/or orders from Goods Receipts (GR) and Settlements.

Allocation Category: An indicator, in Activity-based Costing (ABC), determining how activity quantities are planned/allocated. There are four allocation categories provided by SAP (manual entry-manual allocation, manual entry-no allocation, manual entry-indirect allocation, and indirect determination-indirect allocation).

Allocation Cost Element: A Cost Element used in Activity Allocation in CO.

Allocation Cycle: Consists of Header Data (valid for all Segments in a Cycle) and one or more Segments, with summarized rules and settings enabling allocation. The Segments within a cycle can be processed iteratively (one segment waits for the results of another) or non-iteratively (all the segments are processed independently) or cumulatively (to take care of variations in receiver Tracing Factors or sender amounts).

Alternate BOM: One of the Bills of Materials (BOM) in a BOM Group.

Archiving: This is the process of reading, removing, and saving data – which is no longer required in the system – to an Archive file. This helps in reducing the system load as the database is removed of unwanted data. Once the data is 'archived,' it can then be Marked for Deletion and then Deleted later on.

Area Menu: A grouping of Menus containing a set of functions for performing a particular task in a Company Code.

Assessment: A method of internal cost allocation from a sender cost center to receiver cost center/cost objects through an as Assessment Cost Element. The basis of such an assessment will be on user-defined keys such as Statistical Key Figures (SKF). It is possible to transfer a portion or the whole of the costs of the sender cost center to the receivers.

Asset Accounting (FI-AA): One of the submodules of Financial Accounting, FI-AA is actually a subledger used to take care of all business activities associated with Fixed Asset Accounting.

Asset Acquisition: Relates to acquiring Fixed Assets, through external means such as purchasing or through in-house production. It also deals with Subsequent Acquisitions (to an already capitalized asset) and Post Capitalization (in a period after actual acquisition).

Asset Class: A classification of fixed assets from a business and legal point of view. The asset class holds the control parameters and default values for depreciation calculation and other master data. Each asset master record should be assigned to one asset class. The most common asset classes include buildings, machinery, etc. Some of the Special Asset Classes are Low-Values Assets, Technical Assets, Assets under Construction (AuC), etc.

Asset Class Catalog: A list of all asset classes of an enterprise. The asset class catalog is valid at the Client level, though you will be able to maintain certain data (such as the Depreciation Key) at the Chart of Depreciation level.

Asset Catalog: A list of fixed assets according to branch-specific technical criteria.

Asset Component: This is nothing but a Sub-Asset forming a part of a Complex Asset. The asset components are, then, denoted by Asset Subnumbers of a Main Asset Number.

Asset Explorer: A versatile tool displaying all transactions of an asset in terms of its values; it displays both planned and posted values of the assets and their depreciation.

Asset History Sheet: A report displaying the history of an asset from the point of its initial capitalization or acquisition, displaying acquisitions, transfers, retirements, and accumulated depreciation.

Asset Portfolio: The total value of all the fixed assets used permanently in an enterprise. The value is shown as the balance sheet item.

Asset Subnumber: A unique number which, in combination with the Asset Main Number, identifies a Complex Asset. It is possible to use subnumbering for identifying the various components of a complex asset or subsequent acquisitions can be numbered as subnumbers. Each subnumber has its own asset master record.

Asset Transfer: Refers to the transfer of asset(s) from one Company Code to another of the same group company.

Asset Type: The classification of fixed assets in a company's balance sheet is known as the Asset Type, which is nothing but a definition of some of the features of an Asset Class. Some examples of asset types include movable assets, lands, buildings, low-value assets, etc.

Asset under Construction (AuC): AuC is a fixed asset that is being constructed or completed. These kinds of assets are shown as a separate balance sheet item and are typically managed using one of the 'special asset classes.' The investment on these assets can be managed in the form of internal orders or projects.

Asset Year-end Closing: This refers to the cut-off date after the end of a fiscal year. You will use the asset year-end closing programs that check postings of asset values to GL, depreciation postings, and adherence of rules for NBV (Net Book Value).

Assets Goods Receipt: The acquisition of new assets through the MM module, which is integrated with FI.

Automatic Postings: The postings, represented by separate line items, that are done automatically by the system during transactions such as tax (output/input), exchange rate differences, cash discounts, etc.

Availability Check: Whenever there is a goods movement in MM, the system runs an 'automatic stock check' that prevents the physical inventory balances of those stock categories from becoming negative. However, the same refers to a procedure in PP that will ensure that there are enough components available for planned/production orders.

Average Rate: This is the exchange rate used for settlement of foreign exchange transactions, and is the arithmetic mean between the bank buying rate and bank selling rate.

Backflush: Refers to non-manual but automatic posting of some components of the production order at the time of order completion confirmation.

Background Processing: The automatic execution of ABAP programs, with fixed settings, in the background. There will be no dialogue processing once the background job is scheduled.

Backorder: The Sales Order whose items cannot be confirmed due to non-availability or shortage of materials.

Balance: The difference between the debit and credit sides of an account or document. The balance can be a credit balance (when the credits are more than the debits) or debit balance (when debits are more than the credits). You will not be able to post an accounting document if the balance is not zero.

Balance Audit Trail: A record of all transactions posted to an account during a specified accounting period. From the trail, it will be possible to understand how the balance has changed over a period from the opening balance to the closing balance.

Balance Carry-forward: The accounting balances are carried forward from one year to another. All the balances on the asset side are carried forward to the respective accounts in the Balance Sheet, and the balance (profit or loss) of the Profit & Loss accounts will be carried forward to the Retained Earnings account(s) of the next year.

Balance Check: The system does a balance check of every accounting document before posting, to ensure that the credit side is equal to the debit side resulting in a zero balance. Otherwise, the system issues warning/error messages to correct the line items. The system will not post the document if the balance is non-zero.

Balance Confirmation: A method by which you want the customers or vendors to confirm the correctness of balance as per your book of accounts irrespective of the fact whether these balances are the same or different from their book of accounts.

Balance Notification: A method by which you notify your customer or vendor of the balances as per your books, and you expect a reply only when there is a discrepancy between your books and their books.

Balance Request: A request made to your customers or vendors asking for balance of accounts as per their book of accounts.

Balance Sheet Adjustment: This relates to the retrospective assignment of receivables/payables/taxes to Business Areas and Profit Centers when this assignment was not done earlier while posting the original documents. This is accomplished at a specified cut-off date during closing operations. This may also relate to the preparations such as (*a*) valuation and adjustment of AR/AP posted in foreign currencies, (*b*) AR/AP adjustment postings with a changed reconciliation account, (*c*) adjustment of customers (with credit balance) and vendors (with debit balance), and (*d*) break-down and adjustment posting of AR/AP according to the remaining terms before creating a balance sheet.

Balance Sheet Indicator: An indicator, in the GL accounts master record, to denote whether an account is managed as a balance sheet item or otherwise (P&L item).

Bank Buying Rate: A rate at which a bank buys foreign exchange (and securities, etc.).

Bank Chain: A chain specifying the banks through which the payments are made.

Bank Key: An identifier uniformly identifying the bank in the system, this may be same as the Bank Number.

Bank Master Data: The information – such as name of the bank, country related details, address, etc. – relating to a bank stored centrally in the system.

Bank Number: A number used to identify a bank in the system. This may be the same as that of the Bank Key.

Bank Selling Rate: A rate at which a bank sells foreign exchange (and securities, etc.).

Bank Statement Time Period: The frequency (period, key date, next due date, day of the week, etc.) in which a bank statement may be prepared.

Bank Transfer: Transfer of funds from one bank account to another.

BAPI Explorer: A tool, integrated in the programming environment, used in BAPI development. The tool enables to look at all the BAPIs available in the Business Object Repository. Use the Transaction Code BAPI to get into the explorer.

Base Condition Type: A key, in CO, differentiating the Direct Costs to which overhead such as material or labor costs – are applied.

Base Depreciation Area: The depreciation area from which the system takes the values for revaluation of an asset for inflation.

Base Object Costing: A tool – in COPC – enabling manual input of items, in the form of Unit Cost Estimates, for planning of prices. This may be used as the basis for planning cost estimates without quantity structure, CO production orders, etc.

Base Unit of Measure: A unit (of measure) in which the stock of a material is maintained.

Base Value: This is the value used as the basis for calculating depreciation in FI-AA.

Base Year: This is the fiscal year in which the data was first created for material valuation (FIFO/LIFO) in MM.

Baseline: In ASAP methodology, this is the base configuration agreed on for further development and configuration. This is also referred to as Baseline Configuration, which typically covers 80% of the scope.

Baseline Date for Payment: The date from which the Terms of Payment will apply. This date is used by the system in calculating the eligible cash discount and determining the due date for payment of an invoice.

Baseline Configuration: See Baseline.

Basic List: In CO, this refers to a list containing the information such as (a) number of objects processed in the processing step, (b) the criteria used to select the objects, and (c) status as to whether an object has been successfully processed or not. In ABAP, a 'basic list' refers to the List Level 0, where a program's output statements are written by default. In a drill-down reports, the List Level changes to the next increment when you move away from the basic list.

Bill of Exchange List: A journal listing all the bills of exchange received.

Bill of Exchange Payment Request: A request made to a customer to pay his debts by a bill of exchange. The system posts these requests as Noted Items. This kind of payment request is common in countries such as Spain, Italy, etc.

Bill of Exchange Receivable: A bill of exchange from the creditor's (drawer) view point.

Bill of Exchange Use: The practice of presenting a bill of exchange to a third party for getting payment by way of refinance. This presentation may be for collection or discounting, etc.

Bill of Lading: A documentary proof, issued by the sender of goods, accompanying the shipped goods containing the details of the shipped goods and its condition.

Bill of Material (BOM): A structured list of items or components required to make a product or an object. The components are called BOM Items.

Bill of Material (BOM) Category: SAP helps to maintain and manage BOMs for different objects. Some of the BOM Categories include: material BOM, equipment BOM, sales order BOM, etc. In order to provide product variants for production alternatives, the system provides Variant BOM and Multiple BOM.

Bill of Material (BOM) Component: Also known as a BOM Item, this refers to a part of a BOM.

Bill of Material (BOM) Item: Also known as a BOM Component, this is a part of a BOM. Many such items grouped together form the BOM.

Billing Block: The 'billing block' is used to prevent automatic release of billing documents from SD to FI. However, the blocked billing documents may be released manually.

Billing Category: This is the summary of 'billing document types' in SD. An example of a billing category is a Down Payment Request.

Billing Date: This relates to the date on which the billing is carried out, on the vendor side, and passed on to FI.

Billing Document: Refers to a general term used in SD to denote invoice, proforma invoice, credit/debit notes, etc. Each billing document is made up of a header and one or more line items.

Billing Engine: Refers to a tool in SAP that is used for facilitating the process of billing/invoicing. The engine is capable of producing invoices with items from different business transactions.

Billing Plan: In SD, a 'billing plan' refers to a schedule specifying when a specific amount or a percentage will be billed.

Billing Request: Refers to a document, in SD, mentioning the various items of 'billable expenses.' The billing request can be created for sales orders, customer requests, etc.

Billing Status: This is the 'document status,' in SD, as to whether a document has been fully billed or partially billed or relevant for billing.

Bill-to-Party: This refers to a company or a person who will be billed for a delivery. The bill-to-party need not be the same as that of the Payer or Sold-to-Party.

Block Indicator: In FI-AA, this refers to an indicator used to 'block' an asset from acquisition postings.

Blocked Stock: This refers to valuated stock owned by a company, which cannot be classified as 'unrestricted' and is not available for normal use. When making the 'availability check,' the system does not take this stock into account, but is regarded as 'not available.'

Blocking Reason: This refers to a key used in SD, for blocking the documents from further processing. There are different keys assigned with different reasons for blocking the delivery – such as credit limit, political reasons, etc., and blocking the billing – such as price missing, calculation missing, etc.

Blueprint Generator: In ASAP, the 'blueprint generator' generates a MS-Word document with inputs from the 'Q & A database' and 'CI templates.' The Business Blueprint consists of the scenarios and process arranged in a logical way to help in the implementation. This is considered the 'Bible' for the implementation.

Bonded Stock: This refers to the stock or merchandise stored in a Bonded Warehouse or admitted into a customs territory or area without paying any customs duty, on the condition that it would be used for exports or in production of goods for exports, and is not available for sales or use locally.

Book Depreciation: This refers to the valuation of fixed assets, for Balance Sheet purposes, based on certain laws relating to financial and accounting transactions. In SAP, the book depreciation is always denoted by Depreciation Area 01.

Book Inventory: The stock inventory, in the current period, as per the accounting books. It is necessary to correct the differences, if any, between the actual inventory and the book inventory, and is typically carried out at the year closing.

Boolean: Developed in the 19th Century by an English mathematician by name, George Boole, this is used to represent the logical combinatorial system of representing symbolic relationships using AND, OR, and NOT operators in computer operations. (Example: If A=X, then X is 'true' only when A is 'true'.)

Boolean Operator: The words AND, OR, and NOT are termed Boolean Operators. When they are combined in a logical statement, the result is 'true' only when all the individual arguments are 'true.' (Example: If a search query 'xANDy' is true only when both 'x' and 'y' are true.)

Branch Account: This refers to the account used to relate the head office with that of the branch offices of a customer or vendor. Each branch account is linked to a head office. When processing receivables or payables for the branch accounts, the transactions are posted to the Head Office Account. This is useful in cases of centralized procurements or centralized payments.

Breakpoint: Used in ABAP programming, 'breakpoints' help to interrupt a program at a particular point for analysis and debugging. The breakpoints may be Dynamic Breakpoints, Static Breakpoints, Event Breakpoints, Keyword Breakpoints, or Watchpoints.

Budgeted Balance Sheet: A balance sheet, on a key date, derived from the partial plans of sales plan, production schedule, investment plan, financial budget, etc.

Business Application Programming Interface (BAPI): A programming interface facilitating external access to data and processes in SAP. Defined in a repository called BOR (Business Object Repository), BAPIs offer an Object-Oriented view of business components in the SAP system, and are implemented and stored as RFC-enabled Function Modules in the Function Builder of the ABAP Workbench. A BAPI Explorer is used in managing the BAPIs.

Business Area: In FI, this internal organizational unit represents a separate operational responsibility. Separate business area financial statements (both Balance Sheet and P&L statement) can be created for internal reporting purposes.

Business Area Consolidation: This refers to the grouping based on consolidation Units, with each consolidation unit representing one Company Code and one Consolidated Business Area. This helps in bringing out consolidated financial statements for a 'business area' with the internal relationships between its consolidation units removed.

Business Blueprint: This refers to the second phase of the ASAP Roadmap. The deliverable of this phase results in the Business Blueprint Document detailing the business processes, scenarios, objects, etc., identified during the business requirement gathering workshops with the user community. (Refer to Blueprint Generator.) This 'Bible' helps you to define the 'Baseline Scope' and also the 'Project Schedule.'

Business Blueprint Document: This is the main deliverable of the second phase, Blueprint, in ASAP methodology of SAP implementation. (Refer to Business Blueprint.)

Business Configuration Set: Popularly known as a BC set, these templates contain the configuration settings for customizing SAP for an industry or a corporate group.

Business Explorer: A component of SAP's Business Information Warehouse, business explorer provides for flexible reporting and analysis tools for strategic analysis to support the decision-making process in enterprises.

Business Impact Map: A tool in ASAP, helping in prioritization of risk assessment that summarizes the perceived impacts of risks on the business at the division or unit level.

Business Intelligence Cockpit: A web-based control panel with the content from Business Intelligence (BI) for providing an overview of all relevant business data to the management, the same way one looks at a newspaper. For details, there are hyperlinks, drop-down boxes, and push-buttons. As 'i-views,' business intelligence cockpits are integrated with the Enterprise Portal.

Business Partner: This refers to a legal or natural person (or a group of natural or legal persons) having business interests. The concept of business partner does not refer to an organizational unit in SAP.

Business Process: In CO-ABC, a business process refers to a series of activities involving various departments and consuming costs from a number of cost centers.

Business Process Master List (BPML): In ASAP, this refers to an Excel Spreadsheet listing of SAP business processes/transactions corresponding to the project scope documented in the Business Blueprint. The BPML helps in configuring /testing the system in an iterative manner.

Business Process Owner: This refers to the person responsible for creating or generating the Business Blueprint for one or more business processes.

Business Process Procedure (BPP): A MS-Word template, used in ASAP, BPP defines the procedures which correspond to the transactions listed in the Business Process Master List. Done in the Realization Phase of the ASAP Roadmap, there will be one BPP for one transaction in the BPML.

Business Scenario: This refers to an application component (such as CRM) that uses certain functions of CO to analyze costs and revenues, and to determine the technical settings between the application and CO. (Example: CRM Sales.)

Business Scenario Questionnaire: Refers to the structured and open-ended questions in Q and A Database in ASAP, which enables requirement gathering on business processes or scenarios.

Business Segment: This refers to the clearly demarcated sub-activity of a Company relating to the production of a product/service.

Business Workplace: This refers to SAP's equivalent of a desktop which a user can use to process work items, manage and store documents, send and receive mails or messages, and distribute process information across his/her workgroup or among the entire company.

Business XML (bXML): This is the SAP version of the popular XML, used in the transmission of BAPIs with a BizTalk envelope and for the transmission of RFMs.

Calculation Base: This refers to a collection of Cost Elements to which costs will be applied. The customizing can be done to apply the costs either to a single cost element or a group of cost elements. The cost element(s) will be assigned to the calculation base.

Calculation Method: A part of the Depreciation Key, the calculation method is used in setting up the parameters for the program that calculates the depreciation. SAP comes delivered with a number of calculation methods such as Base Method, Period Control Method, Declining Balance Method, etc. Except the base method, all other calculation methods are Chart of Depreciation-dependent.

Calculation Procedure (for Tax on Sales/Purchases): This is a set of rules defining how to calculate tax on sales and purchases.

Calendar for Invoice Dates: In SD, this refers to a calendar based on which customers are billed on certain dates. During invoicing the system proposes these dates from this calendar, but the user can over-ride it.

Cancellation Document: In SD, a cancellation document can be generated to cancel a billing document. When such a document is created, the system copies the data from the billing document to this document and an offsetting entry is posted to FI to square the transaction.

Cancellation Procedure: A set of rules, in SD, used to determine the cancellation date.

Capacity: In CO, this represents the maximum possible output of a cost center and activity that is technically possible in a given time period. In PP, this refers to the maximum capacity of a work center.

Capacity Levelling: This relates to the exercise of streamlining the work load at various work centers by looking at the over-loads and under-loads.

Capacity Requirement: This is the required output capacity to fulfill the Work Orders (production or maintenance orders) and Planned Orders during a given timeframe.

Capacity Requirements Planning: A tool used, in PP, to determine the available and required capacities. This tool also helps in Capacity Levelling.

Capitalization: A procedure used in FI-AA to post the fixed asset values.

Capitalization Method: This is the method specifying the basis for capitalization. A typical basis is the APC (Acquisition and Production Costs) for all the newly acquired fixed assets.

Capitalization of AuC: This relates to the accounting procedure used in acquiring an in-house produced asset. The APC collected under AuC will be transferred to another asset, as an AuC is shown under a different balance sheet item. SAP allows transferring the entire costs (Summary Transfer), or it can be transferred on a line-item basis (Line Item Settlement).

Capitalized Costs: In CO-PC, this refers to the difference between the actual and calculated costs of an order, calculated using RA (Results Analysis). The system calculates the capitalized costs only when the actual costs exceed the calculated costs. Otherwise, the difference is shown as the 'realized loss.'

Capitalized Profit: In CO-PC, this is nothing but the difference between the revenue generatable inventory and the capitalized costs, and is arrived at using RA (Results Analysis).

CAPP Element: This is a method or formula or even a process used in PP to arrive at the Standard Values.

Cash Concentration: Refers to a process by which the balances of various bank accounts are transferred to a single header account (Target Account) without reducing the balance of any given account below a certain minimum. The closing balance at the target account is now available/used for various financial investments.

Cash Discount: A monetary reward for making payments within a certain period of time.

Cash Discount Base Amount: The portion of the invoiced amount, on which the system calculates the cash discount. This base can also be the entire invoice amount.

Cash Discount Terms: The terms under which a cash discount is offered. The Terms of Payment definition in SAP provides for three different cash discount terms. (Example: 5% cash discount for payment within 10 days, 3% for payment between 10 and 30 days, and due 'net' (no discount) between 30 and 45 days.)

Cash Journal: Showing the cash balance at any time (by adding the cash receipts and deducting the cash expenses, from the day's opening cash balance), the cash journal is a compact journal used to record the cash transactions in a double-entry format. Forming a basis for entries in GL, the cash journal is also called the 'Cash GL account.'

Cash Journal Document: This document contains the business transactions (of a Company Code) in a cash journal, showing the changes in values over a period of time.

Cash Journal Posting: The postings in a cash journal are made up of postings in the cash journal and transferring the cash journal postings to GL. When transferred to the GL, the system creates a follow-up accounting document.

Cash Management Position: Also known as Cash Position, this refers to the short-term activity in the bank accounts displaying cash management relevant FI postings to GL and memo records (such as payment advice notes) entered for planning purposes.

Cashed Checks: These are all the checks that have been paid by a bank. Banks generate data medium (DME file) that can be used to create postings in SAP.

CCMS: Computing Center Management System or CCMS helps in monitoring and administering SAP system landscapes through a set of tools. CCMS monitors various systems across the landscape, determines and displays statistics on system performance and manages the system by starting/stopping SAP instances, background processing, printing, configuration, database administration, etc.

Certificate of Origin: It is an official document declaring the name of the country where the imported goods have been manufactured.

Change and Transport Organizer: A tool in BC-CTS (Change and Transport System) for managing development projects in ABAP Workbench and in Customizing, and for preparing and managing transporting of objects across SAP systems.

Change Management: In ASAP, this refers to the way the project manages the changes in Scope, Time, Cost, and Resources. This may also refer, in general terms, to handling of SAP objects from one environment to another.

Change Manager: One of the user-roles defined in SAP Solution Manager's scenario, the person assigned with the role is responsible for accepting or rejecting a Change Request in change management.

Characteristic: In BW, this refers to one of the InfoObjects such as a Company Code, fiscal year, region, product, etc. The characteristics provide classification possibilities for the dataset, and the values are always some discreet names. In FI, this relates to the smallest unit in 'e-accounting': these characteristics enable valuation by user-defined categories. But it is mandatory that the standard characteristics such as fiscal year variant, currency type, accounting community, etc., are defined in variants along with the user-defined characteristics. In CO, a characteristic refers to a selection criterion such as cost center, cost element, activity type, etc. In CO-PA, this refers to the criteria used to analyze the sales/profit plan and the operating results. In EC-CS (consolidation), this refers to a classification (such as the consolidation unit, financial statement item, fiscal year, etc.) for structuring data.

Chart Engine: An interpreter in the Internet Graphics Server (IGS), this is used to generate business graphics and is compatible with Win32/UNIX /Linux environments. The chart engine is used only in the browser environment and is not compatible with the GUI (Graphical User Interface).

Chart of Accounts: This is a list of GL accounts used in one or more Company Codes for recording the accounting values. For each GL account, the Chart of Account contains the account number, account name, and other technical details. A Chart of Accounts must be assigned to each of the Company Codes and this chart is known as the Operative Chart of Accounts. The Company Code may also be assigned to a Country-specific Chart of Accounts if there is a legal requirement to that effect. Besides these two, there is another Chart of Accounts called the Group Chart of Accounts that is required for consolidation purposes.

Chart of Accounts Index: This is the index of all the charts of accounts that can be used in a Client.

Chart of Accounts List: A list of all charts of accounts that can be used in a Client.

Chart of Depreciation: A list of Depreciation Areas along with the rules for evaluation of fixed assets that is valid in a country or economic area. Each Company Code needs to be assigned to one chart of depreciation, and more than one Company Code can work with the same chart of depreciation.

Check Lot: The summarization of all incoming checks originating from a single source is called the 'check lot.' This may also refer to a collection of checks that need to be processed together. All the items of a 'check lot' will have the same 'currency key' and 'value lot' in the Payment Lot Header that prevents a different specification at the line item level.

Check Number Lot: The Number Range reserved for check number assignment is known as the check number lot.

Check Table: Also known as a Foreign-Key Table, this is nothing but a Table containing the Foreign Keys. If there are two tables, Customer Master (with Customer-id as the Primary Key) and Customer Transactions (with Customer-ID as the secondary or Foreign Key), when there is a customer transaction the 'customer master' table is checked to ensure that the customer (Customer-Id) exists in that table. So, the customer master table is called the Check Table for the foreign key (Customer-Id) in the 'customer transaction' table. SAP uses the contents of the check table to populate the F4 'drop-down' help.

Check/Bill of Exchange: A financial arrangement that helps the buyer to borrow money in the short term. The buyer uses a check for payment and requests the vendor to draw a bill of exchange on him, at the same time. The buyer then accepts the bill of exchange and discounts it with his bank thereby getting the required amount. On the due date of the bill of exchange, the bank presents the bill to the buyer who then retires it by making the payment to the bank.

Checkpoint: In ABAP, this refers to the Breakpoint. In Logistics, this relates to a physical location on the perimeter where all incoming or outgoing traffic (human as well as the transports) are checked in/out.

Classification of FS Items: This relates to a list financial statement items containing all the GL account master records and cost elements, ordered according to accounting principles.

Clean-out Order: In PP, this refers to the order, at the end of a production campaign, meant for preparing the line of production.

Clean-out Recipe: In PP, this refers to the recipe containing the labor/time/material/activity requirements to clean-out a vessel at the end of a production campaign.

Clearing: This refers to a process that results in one or more 'Open Items,' in FI, being termed paid or cleared or squared-off. (Example: An open sales invoice can be 'cleared' by an incoming payment of a matching amount.)

Clearing Account: This is a temporary account (also called Auxiliary Accounts), which is cleared from time to time. SAP uses these accounts when there is (1) a time-lag in accounting transactions as in the case of GR/IR clearing, (2) a distribution of tasks among various organizational units as in bank clearing, and (3) a need to clarify certain transactions but that will not happen immediately when a transaction is posted.

Clearing Document: This refers to a document generated automatically during clearing. The system, on Zero Clearing or when the Automatic Clearing Program is run, generates the document header automatically. The clearing document will not have line items, but there will be a note to indicate that this is a clearing document.

Clearing Procedure: There are two types of clearing procedures available in SAP: 'Account Clearing' and 'Posting with Clearing.' Account Clearing enables you to clear open items in one currency only, and is used in situations where there is no need for making additional postings to clear the items. In the case of open items in more than one currency, 'Posting with Clearing' helps to clear the open items as posting and clearing are possible in one step.

Clearing Transaction: This refers to the 'accounting transaction' triggering the clearing process of open items in FI. (Example: Incoming payments.)

Clearing Value: In MM, this relates to the sum of the amounts posted to the GR/IR Clearing Account when invoices are entered against a business transaction.

Client: This is the self-contained and top-most technical/commercial/organizational unit in SAP, with separate master data and its own set of tables.

Client Copy: The functionality in Basis administration that enables copying a Client (Source Client), with its entire customizing environment, to a Target Client, either in the same SAP system or different SAP system.

Client-Server Architecture: A system group comprised of Servers (at the back-end that typically store the information or data) and Clients (at the front-end which typically request service from the servers) connected in a network.

Client-specific Customizing: A task or transaction relating to a single self-contained unit is known as Client-specific customizing. The settings in Client-specific tables are valid only in the Client that is accessed during the log-on, and these settings do not affect other Clients on the system landscape.

Closing Date: This is the last date determining the period-end.

Closing Operations: This refers to the execution of a series of steps towards (1) day-end closing, (2) month-end closing, and (3) year-end closing.

Cluster Table: The data from several different tables can be stored together in a Table Cluster. Tables assigned to a Table Cluster are referred to as Cluster Tables. A Cluster Table should be used exclusively for storing internal control information (screen sequences, program parameters, temporary data, and continuous texts such as documentation). The records of all Cluster Tables with the same key are stored under one key in the assigned Table Cluster. The values of the key fields are stored in the corresponding key fields of the Table Cluster. Data of commercial relevance is usually stored in Transparent Tables. A Cluster Table, thus, exists only in the ABAP Dictionary and not in the database.

CO Interface: This program interfaces primarily with FI and also with various other application components such as SD, MM, PP, IM, etc., determining the programs that need to be accessed.

CO Production Order: An Internal Order representing a Production Order, in CO-PC, from the cost accounting view point.

Collaborative Business Map: Also known as a C-Map, this collaborative business map is a graphical depiction of inter and intra-company business processes, offering several views (business view, interaction view, etc.) about the business partners involved in the business process, the business benefits, etc.

Collection: Refers to the collection of FI-AR in general, but bill of exchange in particular, that is already due.

Collection Procedure: This refers to the procedure for automatic payment settlement by way of check, bank transfer, etc.

Collective Credit Memo: This is a credit memo but this single credit memo refers to a number of Purchase Orders.

Collective Document: Similar to a BOM, this collective document – in PP – contains a structure referencing a document info record containing both document and text items.

Collective Invoice: In SD, a collective invoice is nothing but a billing document for all the deliveries to a customer, created at the end of a specified period.

Collective Invoice Account: This refers to a special Contract Account in FI, where various line items belonging to different contract accounts are clubbed to apply the same Dunning/Payment Procedure for all the line items.

Collective Order: In PP, this refers to the linked Planned/Production Orders of several production levels.

Commitment: In FI, this refers to certain commitments/liabilities such as outstanding orders, open purchase orders, bill liability, etc. In CO, the commitment refers to the contractual or scheduled commitments – in CO production orders, internal orders, maintenance orders, production orders, sales orders, networks, cost centers, etc. – that have not yet been passed on to FI but will result in actual expenditure in the future.

Common Area: In an ABAP run-time environment, a common area is an Interface Work Area of a calling program and an external sub-routine.

Company: A Company – in SAP – refers to the smallest organizational unit for which individual financial statements can be drawn according to the legal/ commercial requirements. A company may contain more than one Company Code, with all these Company Codes using the same Operative Chart of Accounts and the same Fiscal Year Variant though they all can use different Currencies.

Company Code: This is the smallest organizational unit in FI with self-contained accounts enabling drawing up of financial statements as per the legal/ commercial requirements of the country where the Company Code is operating. Each Company Code is assigned to an Operative Chart of Accounts, and the same chart of accounts can be used by more than one Company Code. One or more Company Codes – with the same operational chart of accounts and the same Fiscal Year Variant – constitute a Company. Similar to the chart of accounts, a Company Code needs to be assigned to a Chart of Depreciation for enabling fixed assets accounting; more than one Company Code can work with a single chart of depreciation though one Company Code cannot work with more than one chart of depreciation.

Company ID: This is a user-definable unique 6-digit identifier, used in FI-LC (Legal Consolidation), for denoting a Company.

Company Pair: Representing a pair of Companies having some sender-receiver relationship, this concept is used in FI-LC.

Complex Asset: An asset (with an Asset Main Number) made up of several components, each represented by an Asset Subnumber, is termed a complex asset in FI-AA.

Computer Aided Test Tool (CATT): A tool in SAP for combining and automating business processes as repeatable test procedures to (*a*) process transactions/transaction chains, (*b*) check transaction results, (*c*) check system messages, and (*d*) generate data. CATT, a tool for transferring master data, is more suited for data transfer when setting up the system initially if the data load is small.

Concept Check Tool: One of the tools in ASAP, this helps in quality checks – during the first two phases of the implementation road map – on project preparation, configuration settings, and technical infrastructure, thereby alerting on potential configuration conflicts or performance issues well in advance.

Condition: In Logistics, a condition determines how the price – net or gross – will be calculated by the system.

Condition Basis: This is the condition type that forms the basis for calculation of taxes or discounts or surcharges.

Condition Category: This refers to a classification of conditions according to certain criteria that helps in certain analysis. (Example: discounts, packaging costs, surcharges, output taxes, delivery costs, etc.)

Condition Record: This contains specific output values – such as the product price or a special discount etc. – for a given input value (such as customer, product, etc.) and is valid for a specific period of time. (Example: A special discount for a particular customer for a specific period of time.)

Condition Table: This is a table containing price information, in SD, on a master data type, and Condition Records are created in the relevant Condition Table. This table determines the field combinations that a 'condition record' should be made up of.

Condition Type: In SD, SAP uses condition types to differentiate between the prices in the system as separate condition types are created for price, discount surcharge, etc. (Example: discount as a fixed percentage of the price of a product.) Each condition type will have its own Access Sequence, Condition Tables, and Condition Records. In CO, there are two condition types; namely, Base Condition Type and Overhead Condition Type. The overhead condition types define the percentage of overhead to be applied to the base condition type. The base condition type specifies the object (such as cost element) on which the overhead will be calculated.

Configurable Material: A configurable material is one which can have different variants, and can be represented by a Super BOM containing all components required for producing the variants of the material. It will also have a Super Task List for performing all the operations required for producing the variants. An example of a configurable material is a television that can have different screen sizes, cabinet colors, etc.

Configuration Assistant: The 'configuration assistant' is used in Smart Implementations for configuring Ready-to-Run R/3 (RRR) or mySAP.com packages. The assistant supports distribution of individual software components to different servers thereby simplifying the integration of the components on a system landscape.

Configuration Case: Used in ASAP, a 'configuration case' represents a business flow with the corresponding inputs, criteria, and conditions. The configuration cases are used to configure and fine tune configuration settings.

Configuration Cycle: ASAP comes with four pre-defined 'configuration cycles' aiming at development of configuration and test plans on a fast track. Each of these cycles represent a milestone so as to move to the next level of configuration, and there will always be an overlap from one cycle to another.

Confirmation: In LO (logistics), 'confirmation' refers to a part in order monitoring so as to distinguish between partial and final confirmations. A final confirmation, in SAP, determines at which work center the operation was carried out, who carried out the operation, what was the yield including the scrap quantity, etc.

Confirming Bank: Also known as the Advising Bank, this bank in the exporter's country will guarantee the payment of L/C (Letter of Credit) when the documents presented to the bank are correct and presented as detailed in the L/C.

Conhecimento: The name of a freight invoice in Brazil.

ConnTrans: A program, in mobile sales in SAP, allowing you to synchronize data between a mobile Client and its server.

Consignment: This is a type of business where the vendor (supplier) maintains his stock of materials at a customer's (buyer) site or warehouse, even though the ownership of the materials lies with the vendor. The buyer is billed only for the portion of the materials used by him and the vendor is notified periodically of the withdrawals from the stock. Such a stock is known as Consignment Stock, and the stocked material is known as the Consignment Material.

Consignment Order: This relates to the request from the ultimate purchaser to the consignment vendor (external supplier maintaining his stock with the purchaser/customer/company) to replenish the consignment stock.

Consolidated Balance Sheet: This contains all the translated balance sheets pertaining to the individual entities in the consolidation.

Consolidation: Also called Legal Consolidation (FI-LC), this refers to the grouping together of financial operating results, according to the Entity Theory of different companies within the corporate group to show the results as if from a single legal entity. This is achieved by (*a*) consolidation of investments, (*b*) elimination of payables and receivables, (*c*) elimination of intercompany profit or loss, (*d*) elimination of investment income, (*e*) elimination of revenues/expenses, and (*f*) possible re-classification.

Consumption Cost Element: The cost element corresponds to the inventory change account in the income statement.

Consumption-based Planning: Under MRP in PP, 'consumption-based planning' is divided into (*a*) re-order point planning, (*b*) forecast-based planning, and (*c*) rhythmic planning. This kind of planning takes into account the stock requirements as well as the past consumption values for the planning exercise.

Contextual Customizing: This refers to the settings used in several systems as, for example, in a Global ASAP implementation. With the Cross-Client System Viewer, the configuration settings across multiple systems can be viewed, compared, and changed. The setting up of a Currency Table is a classic example of contextual customizing.

Contract Account: Managed on an 'open-item basis' within contract accounts, receivable/payable, a contract account is one where the posting data for contracts or contract items are processed in such a way that the same collection or payment agreements apply to all such contracts or contract items.

Control Totals: This refers to the totals to check whether the amounts of posted documents were entered correctly. The system can be set up in such a way that the 'control totals' are updated when the posting is done in the system.

Controlling (CO): Focused on internal management for informed decision making, CO is nothing but managerial accounting. The CO module is, thus, primarily oriented towards managing and reporting cost/revenue. As with any other module, this module also has configuration set-up and application functionality. The module is oriented towards internal users, and helps management by providing reports on cost centers, profit centers, contribution margins and profitability, etc.

Controlling Area: A Controlling Area is the central organizational structure in Controlling (CO), and is used in cost accounting. The controlling area, as in the case of a Company Code, is a self-contained cost accounting entity for internal reporting purposes. The controlling area is assigned to the Company Code to ensure that the necessary transactions, posted in FI, are transferred to controlling for cost accounting processing. A Company Code needs to be attached to a controlling area (1:1 relationship); more than one Company Code can work with the same controlling area (1:n assignment). A Chart of Accounts can be assigned to more than one controlling area. And one or more controlling areas can defined under an Operating Concern. At the Client level, there can be one or more controlling areas.

Controlling Area Currency: This is the currency in which the cost accounting transactions are performed: it will be the same, by default, as the Company Code currency if there is a 1:1 relationship between Company Code and the Controlling Area. It can also be different, if the relationship is '1' controlling area: 'n' Company Codes (cross-Company Code controlling).

Corporate Finance Management (CFM): A component of FI, this is meant for analyzing and optimizing business processes in the Finance Area of a company. CFM helps in managing in-house cash, market/credit risk/portfolio analysis, etc.

Correspondence: This, in FI, refers to all the printed correspondence – such as dunning notices, payment notifications, order confirmations, etc. – of a company.

Cost Base: This, in CO-PC, refers to the quantity on which the costs of a product are based.

Cost Center: One of the cost objects in controlling, a 'cost center' represents the location for cost occurrence or collection. The cost centers can be defined based on 'functional requirements' or 'allocation criteria' or 'responsibility for internal management' or just as physical locations.

Cost Center Group: A collection of a number of cost centers, grouped according to certain criteria.

Cost Center Hierarchy: A hierarchical arrangement of cost centers as nodes based on certain criteria. There needs to be at least one such hierarchy in a controlling area known as a Standard Hierarchy. You may also have any number of Alternate Hierarchies.

Cost Component: This refers to a grouping of cost elements representing material costs, activity costs, etc., according to various requirements such as material valuation, profitability analysis, etc.

Cost Component Group: A condensed view of a group of cost components, in CO-PC, this definition of cost component group is done in customizing. This grouping is different from the cost component group used in Report Writer Reports – which is a copy of the Cost Component Structure, which can contain a maximum of 40 cost components.

Cost Component Split: Refers to the breakdown of costs into 'cost components' – materials, processes, and activity types – for providing cost information for accounting purposes. In SAP, there are two types of cost component splits; namely, primary cost component split and cost component split for COGM (Cost of Goods Manufactured). In CO-PC and CO-PA, the split may include material, internal activities, external activities, overhead, and others. In Overhead Cost Controlling (CO-OM), a split may comprise raw materials, labor, energy, etc.

Cost Component Split for COGM: This splits the cost of materials into various cost component items, and is used to create the Standard Price for a material. This split provides the necessary cost information to CO-PA with COGM or COGS (Cost of Goods Sold). Unlike Primary Cost Component Split, here the internal activities are shown as secondary cost elements.

Cost Component Structure: This structure, in CO-PC, groups the cost elements into various 'cost components' to show the activity price of an activity type, to arrive at the cost of a process and to calculate the planned cost of a product.

Cost Component View: This is nothing but how the 'material cost estimates' are structured according to the various requirements within the system. It is necessary to define, for each cost component, which portion of its costs is displayed in the cost component view. Some of the cost component views defined in the system include COGS, COGM, sales and administrative costs, physical inventory (commercial/tax), etc.

Cost Element: Comprised of primary and secondary cost elements, a cost element represents a cost carrier either from FI to CO (Primary Cost Element) within CO (Secondary Cost Element).

Cost Element Controlling: A component within CO, 'cost element accounting' represents collection and monitoring of costs in CO.

Cost Element Category: The categorization of cost elements, into material cost elements, settlement cost elements, etc., according to their use in CO.

Cost Element Group: The grouping of cost elements of the same type to help in reporting or processing more than one cost element in a single business transaction.

Cost Object: The objects in CO, identified/assigned with costs such as production orders, process orders, sales order items, product cost collectors, etc. The cost objects decide the nature of postings as real postings or statistical postings. The objects that are identified only with statistical postings are not termed cost objects (example: profit centers).

Cost Object Controlling: A component within CO-PC, 'cost object controlling' deals with assigning costs incurred in a company to various activity units of the company for comparing the actual against planned costs, actual, and target costs. This controlling component supplies cost data to FI, CO-PA, EC-PCA, actual costing/material costing, etc.

Cost of Sales Accounting: A kind of profit and loss statement, showing how the sales revenues match the costs or expenses, representing the economic outflow of various resources of the entity.

Cost Rollup: In CO-PC, this represents the process of allocating/rolling-up of the costs (in material costing) incurred at the lower level of production to the highest level. The costs are rolled-up by cost component. (Example: the direct labor costs in 'assembly' are rolled-up into the COGM as internal labor costs instead of material costs.)

Costed Multi-level BOM: Nothing but the itemization of a costed quantity structure, in CO-PC, 'costed multi-level BOM' is the hierarchical overview of all items of a costed material (BOM) according to the material's costed quantity and structure (Routing).

Costing Method: This refers to the method of creating a Cost Estimate in CO-PC. The cost estimate may be of Product Costing, Unit Costing, Multi-level Costing, or Easy Cost Planning. Normally, either Product Costing or Unit Costing is selected when a sales document is costed.

Costing Run: Refers to a process used in CO-PC for costing a number of materials at the same time. In the case of Product Cost Planning, the costing runs (identified by a user-defined name and date) are used to cost materials based on planning data. In contrast, the Actual Costing/Material Ledger costing runs (identified by a user-defined name and a period) relate to the costing of materials with the actual data.

Costing Sheet: Used in CO-OM-OPA (Overhead Orders) and CO-PC for calculating overhead, in CO-PA for calculating anticipated values and in CO-OM (Overhead Cost Controlling) for calculating resource prices, a 'costing sheet' helps to determine how the system calculates various costs. Typically a costing sheet consists of (*a*) base lines on which the overhead is calculated, (*b*) calculation lines containing the percentage rates to be applied to the base line(s), and (*c*) totals lines representing the sum of the base and the calculation lines.

Costing Variant: Refers to variant, in CO-PC, containing all the control parameters for costing such as how cost estimates are executed, how costing items are valuated, etc. In the case of, for example, Material Costing, the variant determines the purpose of the cost estimate, prices for valuating the quantity structure and overheads, applicable dates for actual cost estimates, how BOMs and routings are selected, etc.

Country Program: Refers to the program used to make country-specific customizing settings of objects and parameters in SAP. The program takes into account the legal/commercial requirements of the country in question.

Country Template: Relates to a series of customizing settings (with certain master data) supplied by SAP, along with the standard system, to take care of the legal/commercial requirements such as depreciation, charts of accounts, taxation, etc., of a particular county. The Country Installation Program is used to install the country templates.

Country Version: A 'country version' relates to the standard SAP functionalities localized for a specific country so as to cover that country's legal and (most) business requirements. A country version thus contains (1) Generic SAP functionalities, (2) Country-specific functions that are additional to the generic ones, and (3) a Country Template. As the standard system contains all the country versions (40 in all), any number of country versions can run, concurrently, from a single system.

Country-specific Standard Settings: These are all the SAP settings corresponding to the legal/business requirements of a specific country; SAP comes delivered with the settings relating to Germany as the standard country-specific settings. The Country Program is executed to activate and generate any other country-specific standard settings.

C-Project: A type of project in SAP Change Manager as a part of Solution Manager's Change Request Management scenario.

Credit Group: One of the control parameters in credit administration in SD, 'credit group' enables that all the business transactions assigned to a particular credit group are treated equally in a credit check routine.

Credit Memo: This refers to a transaction in FI that will bring down the account balance of AR. A credit memo, in SD, is created if the delivered goods turn out to be defective or when there is a mistake in pricing that has resulted in charging a higher price than what was actually agreed on. This credit memo document, then, will reduce the Bill-to-Party's liability to the vendor (seller).

Credit Memo Request: Before actually making out a credit memo for a customer, to compensate for higher-than-normal price charged or to pass-on a discount that was not put through when the sale was done, the system allows you to create a 'credit memo request.' Once this request is approved, then a credit memo is created. The use is known as Complaints Processing in SD.

Cross Application: Known as CA, 'cross-application' in SAP refers to an object accessing or 'talking' with many other data objects – tables or processes or entities – relating to more than one business component/application. (Example: workflow.)

Cross-Client: This relates to all the Clients. A setting made in one Client will affect all the Clients. (Example: Exchange rate table maintenance.) The Cross-Client Customizing enables logging-on to any of the Clients and making changes that will then be valid in all Clients. The tools such as Cross-System Viewer, Transfer Assistant, etc., are used in 'cross-Client customizing.'

Cross-Company Code Posting: A single transaction affecting more than Company Code is called 'cross-Company Code porting.' (Example: centralized payments for procurement.) The system creates a document for each of the companies involved in the cross-Company Code postings. A cross-Company Code Document Number is used to denote all the documents generated during a single cross-Company Code posting.

Cumulative Activity Price: An activity price that increases by successive additions or accumulation of costs is termed the 'cumulative activity price.'

Currency Type: This is nothing but the currency key to identify the role for a currency such as Local Currency, Group Currency, Hard Currency, Index Currency, and Global Company Currency. In addition to the local currency, it is possible to have two more currencies as the Parallel Currencies.

Customer: A Business Partner, in SD.

Customer Credit Memo: This will be the basis for processing a 'credit memo.'

Customer Enhancements: Also known as Customer Exits, these are all nothing but the User-Exits. These 'empty modification modules' help in creating additional or custom logic to meet the specific requirements of customers.

Customer exits are created using the Transaction Code SMOD, then selecting the required enhancement by using the Transaction Code CMOD. All these exits are safeguarded in future releases of the SAP software.

Customer Group: The grouping of customers for pricing or credit limits or for some statistical purposes. (Example: DEBI.)

Customizing: This is the overall implementation procedure for setting up SAP system(s) at a customer place, aiming to customize the standard SAP functionality to industry/customer specific business requirements, enhance the standard functionalities, and to complete the deployment of the SAP system in time on a cost-effective way. The Transaction Code SPRO leads to the initial Customizing Menu.

Customizing Cross-System Tools: See Cross-Client.

Customizing Data: Used in customizing, these are 'system settings' data stored in tables of delivery class C, G, and E. The 'customizing data' also relate to Project and IMG Documentation.

Customizing Object: This refers to a set of Customizing Tables/Views that are maintained or transported together. These objects are defined and managed in the Customizing Object Directory (Transaction Code SOBJ). They are classified as Standard Objects (views, Tables, etc.), Non-standard Objects (such as transactions, logical transport objects, etc.), and Other Objects. During customizing, typically one moves from the customizing initial screen (Transaction Code SPRO) to the customizing maintenance transaction to make new settings or change the existing settings.

Cut-Over: In ASAP, 'cut-over' relates to the transfer of data from the Quality (Assurance) System/Legacy System(s) to the Production System in SAP. A Cut-Over Plan details the activities to be carried out during this phase of the implementation.

Cycle: In CO, a 'cycle' represents the rules for cost allocation that are in-turn defined in Segments. Thus, one or more segments constitute a cycle. The rules (relating to the sender/receiver in the segments) are processed iteratively when a cycle is processed.

Cycle Type: This represents the use of a 'cycle' such as distribution, assessment, periodic reposting, indirect activity, allocation, etc.

Data Archiving: Data archiving relates to the removal of old data – not required anymore for the day-to-day operations – from the active database(s) and storing it in Archive files. This helps in reducing the load on the active system(s). If required, the archived data can still be retrieved and accessed.

Data Archiving Process: The Archiving Process include (*a*) reading the data to be removed and writing it to archive file(s), (*b*) storing the archive files in a file system or specialized storages, and (*c*) reading the archive files and 'Deleting' the data that have been 'Marked for Deletion.'

Data Browser: The data browser is used to display the table entries, table fields, and texts. The browser enables you to move from the table to the corresponding 'check tables.'

Data Extraction Tool: A tool that enables extraction of 'live' data from a SAP system, and helps in storing it in a text format.

Data Merge Tool: This tool enables you to merge the data extracts created by DART (Data Archiving Retention Tool).

Data Modeler: This enables creation of data models and mapping it to the ABAP Dictionary. All the data models created using 'data modeler' will conform to SERM (Structured Entity Relationship Model) in SAP.

Data Monitor: In FI-LC, the 'data monitor' helps to manage the transfer of individual financial statement data into the consolidation system.

Data Rebuild Tool: This tool helps in rebuilding the data extract done earlier using the 'data extraction tool.' This exercise may be required if there is a time lag between the initial data extraction and use, and there has been a configuration change in between. The tool uses the same data from the initial extract, but rebuilds it applying the new configuration parameters, if any.

Data Retention Tool: The tool, also called as DART (Data Archiving Retention Tool), helps in extracting and retaining data from SAP systems to meet the legal data retention requirements. Also helping in reporting, the tool extracts the data and stores the same in 'sequential' files. It also provides tools for viewing the retained data.

Data Transfer Workbench: This is the central tool in SAP for carrying out data transfer to the SAP system(s). Supporting various business objects (such as customer/vendor master data), it employs various methods/technologies such as Batch Data Input, Direct Input, BAPIs, etc. Besides this tool, SAP also provides another tool called the LSMW (Legacy system Migration Workbench).

Day-end Closing: The checking, at the end of the day, to ascertain whether all the business transactions have been processed correctly in the system.

Dead Stock: Representing the minimum stock level over a period of time, 'dead stock' is a key figure in Inventory Controlling for identifying materials with inefficient stock levels, for elimination of surplus stocks, etc. A higher dead stock suggests that the 'safety level' has been set too high.

Debit Memo: Exactly opposite to the 'credit memo,' a Debit Memo results in an increase in liability of the Bill-to-Party, to the vendor or his service agent. This may arise from a situation where a customer has been billed lower than what he should have been or has been provided with more discount than he was otherwise eligible.

Debit Memo Request: Used in Complaint Processing in SD, this is opposite but similar to the Credit Memo Request. The 'debit memo request' is a sales document such as a Standard Order. Once a debit memo request has been created and approved, the 'debit memo' can be processed in the system.

Debit Position: This refers to a receivable posting (A/R) in FI.

Deep Structure: A structure, in ABAP, containing at least one Deep Component.

Deep Table: An Internal Table, in ABAP, having one or more Deep Row Types.

Default Project: In SAP Customizing, a default project refers to the Project IMG which is set as the 'default' to have direct access, rather than accessing it through a 'Display List.'

Deficit Order: This relates to an order in CO-PC where the planned costs are more than the planned revenue. The system uses Results Analysis calculation to earmark some reserves for such orders.

Definitive Run: An update operation in FI aiming at adjusting GL or assets or materials for inflation. The update uses a Definitive Inflation Index.

Delete Program: This refers to the program used to delete the data from the database after archiving. The deletion is possible only when the record is 'marked for deletion.'

Deletion Flag: Also known as the Deletion Indicator, this is an identifier that, when set, enables the Delete Program to delete the data from the database.

Delivery Schedule Split: This relates to a function in SD triggering the creation of the Planning Delivery Schedule. A supplier splits the Forecast Schedule lines into Planning Delivery Schedule lines for use in planning and shipping.

Delta Balance Sheet Account: This refers to an FI account in CO-PC, to which the difference between the ending inventory valuation from periodic actual costing and cumulation is posted, with the offsetting entry posted to a re-valuation account.

Delta Customizing: This relates to the IMG activities that are required to be carried out – to make use of new functions in existing business applications – when there is a 'system or release upgrade.' All these IMG activities are collected in a Project View. The upgrade needs to be completed before attempting the delta customizing IMG activities.

Delta Posting: This relates to the posting to a delta balance sheet account. Refer to the Delta Balance Sheet Account.

Delta Version: In Activity-based Costing, a 'delta version' relates to an additional Statistical Version that is based on a Reference Version. A delta version enables additional allocations on selected transactions. However, as this is only of statistical significance, no process costs are updated in CO-PA, CO-PC, etc. The delta version itself can be a 'reference version' referencing another version.

Demand Planning: In APO (Advanced Planner and Optimizer), this refers to the component enabling forecasting of market demand for a company's products to produce a demand plan.

Dependency Planning: This is nothing but a type of manual planning in which the primary costs/revenues are calculated as the product of Activity quantity or as the quantity of Statistical Key Figure and a Factor defined by a user.

Dependent Depreciation Area: In FI-AA, this relates to the 'depreciation area' that adopts its values from another depreciation area in the charts of depreciation, with the 'take-over logic' defined there.

Dependent Order: An order – in SCM or APO or PP – that has a relationship or a pegging to another order that needs to be considered in a detailed scheduling.

Depreciation: This is the reduction in the book value of a fixed asset due to its use over a period of time. The depreciation can be calculated manually (Unplanned depreciation) or automatically (Planned and Special depreciations) in the SAP system.

Depreciation Area: This refers to an area indicating the valuation of a fixed asset. The depreciation areas can be Book Depreciation (01), Depreciation as per Income Tax Act (15), Cost Accounting Depreciation (20), etc. Along with these 'real' depreciation areas, SAP allows you to define 'Derived Depreciation Areas' where the values are derived (calculated) from two are more 'real' areas.

Depreciation Base: The asset value that is considered the base for calculating depreciation. The depreciation base may be the APC (Acquisition and Production Costs), Net Book Value (NBV), or the Replacement Value.

Depreciation below Zero: When depreciation is continued even after reaching a zero value of the asset, resulting in a Negative Book Value, this is known as 'depreciation below zero.' This is controlled by a key which indicates whether a particular asset continues to depreciate even after reaching a zero book value. The concept is useful for calculating the Inputted Costs on an asset, after the planned life of the asset.

Depreciation Forecast: This is the projected depreciation, calculated either manually or by the system, of assets during a fiscal year. All the transactions occurring in these assets result in an adjustment of the forecast already created.

Depreciation Key: The 'depreciation key,' used in calculation of depreciation values, contains all the control parameters including the depreciation methods, for each of the depreciation areas, for automatic calculation of depreciation and interest.

Depreciation Method: The method of depreciating an asset – Straight Line Depreciation, Sum-of-Year-Digits, Declining Balance, etc. – is known as the 'depreciation method.'

Depreciation Period: The periodicity with which depreciation is calculated is referred to as the 'depreciation period,' which normally corresponds to the Posting Periods in FI. SAP allows depreciating using Half-Periods as well.

Depreciation Trace: A system trace of different hierarchical steps in carrying out the depreciation. This is useful to pinpoint the errors occurring during a calculation.

Depreciation Type: The classification of depreciation based on certain criteria is known as the 'deprecation type.' SAP supports various depreciation types such as (a) Ordinary Depreciation, (b) Special Depreciation, (c) Unplanned Depreciation, and (d) Depreciation for Write-off Reserves.

Detail Management: A tool helping in the creation/editing of organizational units, and their assignments/relationships, in SAP.

Detailed Planning: Using exact data and time, a 'detailed planning' in CO-PP is based on 'routing' for short-term planning of individual capacities/people.

Determination Procedure: This refers to a structure, in SD's Condition Technique, outlining the order in which the system is expected to execute the Calculation/Processing Steps while determining the prices or discounts, etc.

Development List: In ASAP, this is a development list referring to an MS-Excel spreadsheet as a report from the Q & A Database, containing all the structure elements (such as reports, interfaces, data transfers, etc.) of the implementation scope corresponding to the BASIS area of SAP. The list, generated during the

Realization Phase, helps in managing the Functional and Technical Specification relating to all these elements, in a more structured way.

Development Review: This, in ASAP, helps to review the design and implementation of custom developments to ensure that they adhere to the established standards in design and development.

Diagram Explorer: Refers to a built-in tool of the 'Q & A Database' enabling you to view the contents (and also the assignments among the organizational units, input/output relationships, etc.) of the R/3 Reference Structure.

Direct Access: Refers to a method relating to the Read-Only access of the archived data.

Direct Capitalization: Refers to the acquisition of an asset where the costs are directly posted to the asset, instead of posting them to an AuC or order, etc.

Direct Input: One of the methods of data transfer, 'direct input' is an alternative to Batch Input. The direct input method results in faster data upload with the SAP function modules doing the consistency checks (instead of screens doing checks as in the 'batch input' method).

Direct Payer: The customer who is also the payer, in SD, is known as the 'direct payer.'

Direct Quote: A currency value expressed in terms of local currency per unit of a foreign currency is known as the direct quote or Direct Quotation or Price Notation. (Example: 1 USD (Foreign currency) = 41 INR (Local currency)).

Discounting: Refers to a practice of presenting 'bills of exchange' to a bank – before the due date – for receiving the payment for them. The bank deducts the discount (nothing but the interest for the period between the due date and bill present date) and a commission before making the payment to the presenter.

Distribution: A business transaction, in CO, referring to the allocation of Primary Costs.

Distribution Channel: Refers to a channel – such as retail, wholesale, direct sales, etc. – through which products/services sold reach the end customers. One or more distribution channels are assigned to a Sales Organization.

Distribution Rule: Forming a part of a Settlement Rule, this 'distribution rule' defines (*a*) settlement receiver, (*b*) settlement type – periodical or total, (*c*) settlement share (total or proportional), and (*d*) validity period for the distribution rule, for a settlement sender.

Division: Refers to an organizational unit, in SD, that is responsible for the sales/profits from a saleable material or service. For each division, you may define and maintain customer-specific parameters such as terms of payment, pricing, etc. The division may come under one or more Distribution Channels.

Document: A proof of a business transaction, a document in FI may be an original document – invoices, bank statements, etc., or a data-processing document

– accounting documents, sample documents, recurring entry documents, etc. A document – such as a sales document, billing document, shipping document, etc., – in SD relates to a printed record of a business transaction.

Document Date: Refers to a date on which the original document – such as the invoice in FI, shipping document in SD, etc. – is created.

Document Extract: In MM, this refers to a program that transfers the valuation information from documents in SAP to the tables for FIFO/LIFO valuation.

Document Flow: This represents the sequence of documents in a business transaction. (Example: A document flow in SD may represent Quotation > Sales Order > Delivery > Invoice.)

Document Header: The portion of a document which includes all the line items in a document is known as the 'document header.' (Example: Document Date, Document Type, Document Number, Company Code, etc.)

Document ID: Refers to a unique description assigned to an 'archived' document.

Document Number: A number identifying a document in a Company Code in a fiscal year is known as the 'document number.' SAP provides the capability to assign Internal or External Number Ranges to documents used in business transactions.

Document Principle: Refers to the basic principle in SAP transaction processing representing that postings are always stored in a document form.

Document Type: The 'document type' helps to classify a business/accounting transaction within the system, and is used to control the entire transaction determining the account types a particular document type can post to. For example, the accounting document type 'AB' allows you to post to all the accounts, whereas type 'DZ' allows you to post only to the customer payments. Every document type is assigned to a 'document number range.'

Down Payment: A portion of the full price paid at the time of purchase or delivery with the option to pay the balance later. The down payments are shown separately in the balance sheet. Down Payments Made are shown as part of fixed/ current assets, and Down Payments Received are shown as a part of Payables. In FI-AA, down payments relate to the payments made for an AuC.

Down Payment Request: Refers to a request made that a down payment be made at a certain point in time. Down payment requests – identified by a Special GL Indicator called 'F" – are Noted Items as they do not update any GL transaction figures, and are never shown in the financial statements. They are also termed Memo Entries as they serve to keep track of such obligations.

Due Date for Net Payment: This refers to the due date for payment with no discount being eligible on that transaction. This is the farthest date for payment in a Terms of Payment.

Dunning: This relates to the reminding of business partners about their payments that are due. The system 'duns' the Open Items from business partner accounts. Dunning is administered through a Dunning Program.

Dunning Amount: This corresponds to the total of all the due items outstanding to be dunned, for a Dunning Group.

Dunning Area: Refers to an organizational unit for which the 'dunning' is carried out. It is optional, and is required only if dunning is not done at the Company Code level. The dunning area can correspond to a Sales Division, Sales Organization, etc.

Dunning Block Indicator: An indicator, defined with a Dunning Block Reason, that helps to block certain accounts or line items from being dunned.

Dunning Key: Refers to a key that is used to identify the Dunning Level that needs to be used during a particular 'dunning run' for a particular account or item.

Dunning Level: This indicates how often dunning is carried out, for an account or an open item. Once dunned, the system automatically updates the dunning level information so that the correct level is selected when the dunning is done the next time.

Dunning Procedure: Refers to the specifications of how the customers/ vendors are dunned during a Dunning Run. The dunning process defines the Dunning Levels, controls the Dunning Intervals, determines the transactions to be dunned, determines the interest to be applied, etc.

Dunning Recipient: The business partner, who will receive the dunning notices, is known as the dunning recipient. This recipient need not be the customer.

Dynamic Credit Check: During the 'dynamic credit check,' the system will ignore all orders beyond the Credit Horizon Date. The dynamic credit check is split into two parts – Static Limit and Dynamic Limit – nothing but the Open Order Value. The sum total of Static and Dynamic limits should not exceed the Credit Limit established for the customer.

Early Watch Service: A remote diagnostic service provided by SAP to identify and resolve bottlenecks and issues in a new SAP implementation or in an existing production system.

Easy Cost Planning: Refers to a way of planning costs – based on Costing Models – quickly and easily for cost objects such as internal orders, WBS elements, internal service requests, etc.

EDI: EDI (Electronic Data Interchange) refers to the cross-company exchange of business transactions data, in a predefined electronic format, among domestic/international business partners having a number of hardware, software, and communication infrastructures.

EDI Inbound Processing: This relates to the processing of incoming EDI data into the SAP system. The incoming data is first converted to SAP's standard format IDoc (by an EDI sub-system) before transferring it into SAP. On transfer, SAP evaluates the incoming system and converts it into appropriate business transactions, for example, Purchase Orders.

EDI Outbound Processing: The business application transaction data, such as Purchase Order, is first converted into a SAP standard IDoc (Intermediate Document) by the EDI sub-system that transmits it to an external system in a standard EDI format.

EDIFACT: Refers to an international, branch-independent EDI standard known as Electronic Data Interchange for Administration, Commerce, and Trade.

Edited Table: A formatted display of fields in a table enabling clear table display for easy data entry and editing is known as an 'Edited Table' in the ABAP Dictionary.

EBPP: Electronic Bill Presentment and Payment (EBPP) refers to the conversion of bills of exchanges into an electronic format which then can be linked to (a payment service) a bank.

Elimination Entries: These – such as the elimination entries for payables and receivables, revenue and expenses, inventory profit and loss, etc. – together with other consolidation entries aid in transferring the individual summarized financial statements into 'consolidated financial statements,' in FI-LC.

Elimination Difference: The difference arising out of eliminating inter-company payables and receivables, revenues and expenses, etc., is known as the 'elimination difference' which can arise because of the exchange rate or other differences.

ELSTER: Refers to the electronic tax return, in Germany, and describes a procedure according to which companies in Germany must send their tax data to the tax offices.

End-to-End Scenario: In ASAP, this relates to a complete business flow cutting across various functional modules or components to complete the entire cycle of operation.

End-user Documentation: Refers to the company-specific documents prepared, in ASAP, for training the end-user community in the implemented SAP functionalities. These documents often serve as the 'reference' for the business procedures and the policies for the company people. The Business Process Procedure (BPP) document prepared earlier would be the ideal starting point for preparing the 'end-user documentation.'

Engineering Change Management (ECM): Refers to an application component in Logistics that allows objects to be changed with history or with certain conditions (parameters). SAP allows changing the object types – such as BOM, Task List, Documents, Materials, etc. – with a 'change number.'

Enterprise Controlling: An application component in SAP focused on EC-CS (Enterprise Controlling –Consolidation) and EC-PCA (Enterprise Controlling – Profit Center Accounting).

Enterprise Data Model: Refers to a semantic data model showing the entities and their relationships, in SAP.

Enterprise Information System (EIS): Refers to the information infrastructure of an ERP system.

Enterprise Intelligence (EI): This refers to, in CRM, the collection of AI (Artificial Intelligence) tools such as IIA (Intelligence Agent) and Knowledge Management Tools such as SDB (Solution Database). SAP's EI is very powerful in allowing the company to, dynamically gather, organize, and analyze comprehensive information for effective customer interactions.

Enterprise Model: Refers to the subset of the 'R/3 Reference Model' or 'Industry Model' for depicting the SAP functions required in a company.

Enterprise Organization: A logical representation of various organizational units – Company Code, Controlling Area, Cost Center, Cost Center Groups, Profit

Center, Profit Center Groups, HR Organizational Units, etc. – indicating their relationships.

Enterprise Portal: A portal application from SAP allowing a company to integrate applications, services, and information on a browser-based user interface is called the 'enterprise portal.'

Enterprise Structure: Refers to the hierarchical depiction of various organizational units defined for a company. This structure may be a Logical Structure – such as the plant, cost center, sales area, channel, purchasing organization, etc., or a Social Structure – such as departments, divisions, HR units, etc.

Environment Health and Safety (EHS): The application component within SAP to take care of health and safety at the workplace besides taking care of the environment is called EHS. The application addresses product safety, dangerous goods movement, waste management, occupational health hazards, etc.

EOG Order: In PP, this refers to an order created using extended order generation. To facilitate bottom-up propagation of characteristics of a product, the EOG order contains only one operation so as to split the product.

Equal Distribution: This refers to a situation in which, independent of the order quantities, the system distributes equally the available stock to all the orders.

Equipment BOM: This is nothing but the list describing the structure of equipment and the spares for maintaining that equipment.

Equivalence Numbers: The weighing factor, in CO-CCA, used to distribute the planned costs – that are not planned by activities – to the individual activities of a cost center.

Escape Sequence: Relates to the printer-specific operations/commands to control print operations.

Estimated Cost to Complete: Relates to the total costs expected for a project when it is completed based on costs that have already been incurred on that project and based on the information of Cost to Complete.

Euro Workbench: A tool enabling planning, monitoring, and executing Euro conversion related activities during the Dual Phase of the currency.

Eurojapan: Refers to the blended code pages, in ABAP, containing scripts of German, English, French, Italian, Danish, Dutch, Finnish, Norwegian, Portuguese, Spanish, Swedish, and Japanese.

Evaluation Criteria: In MM, this refers to the criteria used in evaluation of vendors. The evaluation criteria will be stored on an Evaluation Record containing header and line items.

Evaluation Group: This is one of the fields in an asset master record that can be used for classifying the fixed assets. The evaluation groups can be used in reporting as well as accessing individual assets belonging to an evaluation group.

Evaluation Structure: The structure on which the data analysis for LIS (Logistics Information System) is based on is known as the 'evaluation structure' and is made up of Characteristics (sales organization, purchasing organization, etc.) and Key Figures (invoice value, sales volume, etc.).

Exception Handling: Refers to a process that is triggered when there are errors in exception situations in IDoc processing, and these errors occur in the application or interface IDoc layer.

Exchange Rate: The rate at which one currency is exchanged for the other.

Exchange Rate Category: The key that identifies and stores exchange rates in the system is known as the exchange rate category; the category is used to store multiple rates for different purposes on the same date in the system.

Exchange Rate Difference: Refers to the difference in the valuation when a currency is translated using two different exchange rates.

Exchange Rate Type: Indicating the type of exchange rate in the system, this refers to buying rate, selling rate, average rate, etc.

Exchange Rate Variance: In PP, this refers to the variance occurring because of changes in the price of the objects due to the fluctuations in exchange rates.

Excise Document: The system document used in excise transactions in SAP. The excise document may be an excise invoice, sub-contracting challans, or ARE documents (ARE-1, 2, etc.).

Excise Invoice: An 'excise invoice refers' to business document that is issued when excisable goods are sold to a customer (or moved to another plant) from the manufacturing plant.

Execution Service: Refers to the process triggered by cost planning with Easy Cost Planning, in controlling in SAP. The service may trigger purchase requisitions, purchase orders, reservations, GI, etc.

Executive Menu: The compilation of various menus – mostly of non-customizing menus – under the EIS (Executive Information System).

Export Ledger: Refers to an additional ledger in the FI-SL (Special Purpose Ledger) when the data is to be sent from a local system to a central system. This export ledger stores all the data that have been sent to the central ledger; if data are to be sent more than once, only the incremental changes, over the last export, are sent to the central system.

Extendable IMG Activity: This is nothing but a customizing activity that includes a CMOD exit or any other user-exit.

Extendable Material: Refers to a material that has some data which are yet to be maintained by other user departments.

External Processing: Refers to the operations of one company performed at another company.

Extract: In FI-SL, this is nothing but the extracted data used for reporting.

Fact Sheet: In CRM, this refers to consolidated but concise information relating to a business partner. The information comes from a variety of sources such as master data, statistical information, reports, etc.

Fact Table: In BW, this refers to the central Table of an InfoCube Star Schema, containing all Key figures.

Factory Calendar: The 'factor calendar,' defined on the basis of a Public Calendar, contains sequentially numbered working days. The validity period of a factory calendar has to be within the validity period of the public calendar.

FERT Generator: Refers to the functional enhancement, in SD, of Variant Configuration enabling production of storable finished goods with their own master records from a Configurable Material instead of Material Variants.

Fictitious Cash flow: This refers to a part of a real transaction but there is no actual physical cash flow involved. Since it is not a physical flow, it is not included in any of the NPV (Net Present Value) calculations but needs to be included in any of the Gap analysis.

FIFO: Referring to First-In-First-out, this encompasses both the FIFO Withdrawal Method and the FIFO Valuation Procedure. The assumption here is that the first withdrawn material from the inventory was the one received first into the stock.

Final Backflush: In a Repetitive Manufacturing in PP, as a background job the system performs final confirmation with a 'final backflush,' where the BOM is exploded, goods movements are posted, planned orders are reduced, and finally the costs and statistics are updated.

Final Configuration: The result of an iterative configuration process, starting with the Baseline Configuration based on Business Blueprint and expanding through the configuration cycles to reach the final solution ready for delivery.

Final Cost Center: The bottom-most cost center that does not have any subordinate cost centers below it.

Final Costing: In CO-PC, this refers to the cost estimate of an activity-based on the actual costs incurred for that activity. Besides determining and monitoring the costs, final costing enables comparing Actual Costs with the Target Costs.

Final Preparation: Representing the Phase-4 of the ASAP Implementation Roadmap, 'final preparation' provides the structure and framework for complete Final Testing, User Training, and Cut-Over Preparation (data and system) for making the system 'live.'

Financial Document: Refers to a document used in Documentary Payments in Foreign Trade.

Financial Statement Imbalance: Refers to a situation where a transaction is posted to both the profit and loss account(s) and balance sheet accounts. SAP calculates the imbalance, in EC-CS, and posts the relevant adjustments automatically.

Financial Statement Version (FSV): This is the hierarchical arrangement of GL accounts based on certain (statutory) requirements. SAP comes delivered with country-specific versions that can be copied and modified.

Finish-Finish Relationship: In PS (Project Systems), this refers to a relationship where a new activity cannot start unless the predecessor one is finished.

Firm Zone: In MM Purchasing, this refers to the delivery schedule timeframe within which all the schedule lines are construed as binding and confirmed. If there is a firm zone of, say, 30 days, then all the schedule lines with the delivery dates not more than 30 calendar days from the current date are considered firm and the orders are known as Fully Binding Orders or Purchase Commitments.

First Consolidation: In FI-LC/EC-CS, this refers to the activity that brings in an organization for the first time into the consolidated financial statements as a subsidiary.

First Customer Shipment: Refers to the initial delivery of SAP software to a limited number of customers, to test and validate (not meant for any productive purpose) a technical upgrade of the software or the implementation itself.

First Productive Customer Program: Refers to a service program for customers who want to 'go-live' with the Controlled Availability (CA) release. The customers with the 'CA Release' need to get prior approval form SAP before 'going-live.'

First Teach: Refers to a course conducted for first-time SAP customers. This course material will undergo changes based on the feedback from the 'first teach' sessions.

Fiscal Year: This is nothing but the period – normally made up of 12 months – for which a company draws up their financial statements and values their inventory. The fiscal year can be a Calendar Year or a Non-Calendar Year. The fiscal year need not necessarily have 12 months (periods); in cases where the fiscal year is less than 12 periods, then it is known as a Shortened Fiscal Year.

Fiscal Year Variant: One of the important configuration elements in FI, a 'fiscal year variant' helps in defining the relationship between the calendar and fiscal years, specifying the number of Posting Periods and Special Periods required in a fiscal year. There can be a maximum of 12 posting periods and 4 special periods in a GL account; however, the special periods can go as high as 365 in the case of Special Purpose Ledgers. In EC-CS, when the consolidation elements use different fiscal year variants, it becomes important to convert these periods before transferring the financial data for consolidation.

FIX Value: This refers to the field value of a Business Configuration Set (BC Set) that is set as 'fixed' so that the value cannot be modified in the target system during customizing.

Fixed Asset Balance Sheet Account: As opposed to the Accumulated Depreciation Account where only the depreciation values are posted, 'fixed asset balance sheet accounts' are the GL accounts to which the Acquisition and Production Costs (APC) of fixed assets are posted.

Fixed Depreciation: This relates to the portion of the depreciation that is not affected by the use while calculating the depreciation. SAP enables you to configure an asset to be depreciated both as 'fixed' and 'variable.' The Multiple-Shift factor is applied on the variable portion to calculate depreciation that varies with use.

Fixed-Cost Variance: This is nothing but the difference between the planned and actually allocated fixed costs, and is calculated only in the case of Overhead Cost Controlling.

Flexible General Ledger: An enhancement to the normal GL accounting, 'flexible GL' incorporates SAP Dimensions (profit center, cost center, etc.) and also the Customer Dimensions (region, etc.). The flexible GL, requiring only a minor configuration as opposed to the Special Ledgers, enables year-end closing in both Period Accounting and Cost of Sales Accounting.

Flexible Upload: This is used in EC-CS to upload data from a front-end non-SAP system to an SAP system, for initial and additional financial data upload.

Flow Logic Editor: Offering some of the functionalities of ABAP Editor, this is used in Screen Painter for entering the 'screen flow logic.'

FM Area: One of the organizational units in SAP, Financial Management (FM) areas help in carrying out funds management.

Foreign Currency Valuation: Refers to the determination of the value of current assets/liabilities posted in a foreign currency, on a Key Date.

Form Painter: One of the ABAP tools. Form Painter helps in designing SAPscript Forms using either the Graphical Form Painter or the Alphanumeric Form Painter.

Format Tree: Refers to the DME file format defined by an external organization such as a bank.

Forward Scheduling: In PP, this refers to scheduling the operations of an order forward, starting from the planned date. The 'forward scheduling' helps in arriving at the scheduled start/end dates.

FPC: FPC refers to the First Productive Customer, who participates in CA (Controlled Availability) releases of SAP software.

Framework Order: Having an extended validity period instead of a fixed delivery date, this Purchase Order is used to procure external materials or resources, for accelerating the procurement process. The Order Type 'FO' is assigned to a framework order.

Free-of-Charge Delivery: In SD, this is a type of sales document used to deliver free samples to customers.

Front-end Statistics: In CCMS, this refers to workload statistics, containing the volume of data sent/received along with the front-end time, of individual presentation servers.

FS Chart of Accounts: The chart of accounts used in EC-CS to record values and value streams in group accounting to generate consolidated financial statements is known as the 'FS chart of accounts.'

Function Builder: The 'function builder' in ABAP, containing the Function Library, enables creation, testing, and documenting 'function modules.'

Functional Area: An organization structure based on Cost of Sales Accounting, the functional area helps in classifying the expenses of an organization by functions such as administration, sales and distribution, production, marketing, etc. In CO, all the cost objects need to be assigned to a functional area.

Functional Specification: In ASAP, the Q & A Database is used to collect the requirements, from a technical point of view, for enhancements, interfaces, reports, etc., and the document that documents these requirements is called the Functional Specification.

Functionality Releases: The upgrade version of the existing release of SAP software – usually to correct major software errors such as Prioity-1 problems – for introducing new or improved business process(es). All the functional releases are released as Hot Packages.

Future Standard Cost Estimate: Nothing but a 'material cost estimate' for the next period, the 'future standard cost estimate' helps in establishing the future standard price.

GL Account: Representing the account items in a Chart of Accounts, these accounts record the value movements in a Company Code. The transaction values are recorded per Posting Period in the GL accounts, the totals of which are used in reporting.

GL Account Document: An accounting document used to record the transactions in the General Ledger for a Company Code, this contains a minimum of two line items whose balance is always zero.

GL Account Master Record: Besides the account number, name of the account, etc., a 'GL master record' also contains control parameters on how data is entered into a GL account. The record also contains parameters controlling creation of the master records.

GL Increase Account: In SBO (SAP Business One), this account is an Offsetting Account used for recording negative differences arising out of inventory valuation.

GA Release: Referring to the General Availability (GA) Release, unlike a CA Release that cannot be used in a productive system without the prior approval of SAP AG, this can be used by customers even in 'live' systems without any restrictions. Support Packages are provided by SAP for the GA releases aiming to correct software errors.

Gain Posting: Refers to posting of gains, being the difference between the revenue realized during sale of an asset and its Net Book Value (NBV).

Gantt Chart: An outcome of PMBOK (PM Body of Knowledge), this refers to the graphical representation of schedule-related information, as bars with the activity or task name, task duration, etc., in 'project planning.'

General Cost Object: Refers to an independent cost object, in CO-PC, that can be used in a variety of operations such as planning and collection of costs.

General Download: Refers to the downloading of master data – exchange rates, versions, dimensions, FS chart of accounts, etc., – from a consolidation system to a front-end personal computer for data entry using MS-Access.

General Recipe: In PP-PI (Process Industries), this refers to a general description of a production process, outlining the products, components, resources, processes required, which is plant- and site-independent.

General Storage Area: In LE-WM (Warehouse Management), this area refers to a form of storage organization where only one Storage Bin is defined for each of the storage locations, and the Quants stored in this area are of mixed storage.

Generic Business Tools: These tools, in SAP, refer to the various functions used by the developers as well as end-users, to send e-mails, used to start, schedule, and stop certain operations, organize appointments, etc.

Geocoder: A tool available to convert an address into GEO-Coordinates – longitude and latitude of that location – is called as the Geocoder.

Global Company Currency: With SAP allowing the use of more than one currency in accounting, this 'global company currency' refers to the currency used for an internal Trading Partner.

Global Implementation Program: Referring to the overall activities, in ASAP, to be performed for implementing SAP for an entire corporate group, this implementation program is made up of Global Activities and Local Activities. The local units are defined and assigned to a global reference system based on the Global Template.

Global Ledger: In FI-SL (Special Purpose Ledger), this 'global ledger' contains data of Company Codes assigned to Companies. Because of this assignment, when an account is posted in the Company Code, it is posted to the local ledger of the Company Code and also in the global ledger.

Global Program Core Team: The team (comprised of employees of a management team, user departments, and IT departments) is free from other routine operations but engaged in the ASAP Global Implementation Program. This team will stay through the entire duration of the program from template design to development to rollout activities.

Global Reference System: The SAP system installed at the corporate headquarters of a company, containing global templates and shared data, serving as the common and reference source of configuration for rolling-out the implementation to other smaller downstream units is known as the global reference system.

Global Release: This refers to the global roll-out projects using the global reference system.

Global Rollback Process: A process by which the system settings/ configurations or the results of multiple local systems are rolled back into the global templates of a global reference system.

Global Rollout: This refers to a process by which the global template is installed in a local environment with modifications suited to the local situation, leading to a local production system.

Global Standards: The agreed-on criteria to be used in all the local SAP systems are known as the 'global standards.'

Global Template: A collection of global requirements – Models, IMG Projects, Customizing, Documentation, Data and Tests, System Topology and Transports, Customer Developments, etc. – for subsequent roll-out to the global subsidiaries during SAP implementation.

Global Template Version: Refers to a template version created by maintaining an existing template. The template version so created will be rolled-out globally.

Go-Live: A part of the final phase (5th) in the ASAP Roadmap where the SAP system is declared 'productive' or 'live' marking the end of the implementation and signalling that the system is now ready for commercial or business use.

Go-Live and Support: The 5th and final phase of the ASAP Roadmap signalling the move from pre-production to 'production' environment. The implementation team sets up a Help Desk to provide 'post-go-live support' for users and to optimize system performance.

Goods Clearing Account: In SBO (SAP Business One), this is an offsetting account used to park the open amounts arising from closure of purchase documents.

Goods Transit: Relating to the goods that have been shipped to the customer, these can be taken into account in the calculation of Results Analysis, which can be capitalized in the balance sheet.

Goods Movement: Refers to the logical or physical movement of materials resulting in changed stock levels for that material.

Goods Receipt (GR): Referring to the physical inward movement of materials / goods, the GR can be against a purchase order, can be with reference to a production order, or even without any reference at all.

Goods Receipt (GR)-based Invoice Verification: An invoice verification procedure enabling assignment of incoming invoices and deliveries to purchase order items is known as 'GR based invoice verification.' When defined for an order item, this enables entering an invoice with reference to a GR Document or Delivery Note Number for that item, at the time of GR. As a result, the system generates a separate invoice for each GR. The system further enables validating the price and invoice accuracy at the item level.

Goods Receipt (GR) Blocked Stock: Not to be confused with the General (non-GR specific) Blocked Stock, 'GR blocked' stock refers to the stock received from a vendor that has been conditionally accepted but not yet regarded as the part of the inventory.

Graphical Screen Painter: One of the two lay-out editors in Screen Painter, this graphical mode supports Drag and Drop functionality for faster developments. Refer to Form Painter also.

Group BOM: Created in the design phase before assigned to one or more plants for production, a group BOM is valid across the entire company and is not assigned to a specific plant.

Group Condition: In SD, this refers to a condition that can be used to determine the scale value of one or more items in a document where the system groups these items using the Condition Key for the appropriate Condition Record.

Group Costing: In CO-PC, this is nothing but the costing function calculating the value added for multiple profit centers across Company Codes, with the 'cost component split' generated for various partners such as plant, profit center, Company Code, business area, etc.

Group Currency: In FI-LC, this refers to the currency used in the consolidated financial statements. When individual entitities are consolidated, the individual financial statements in the Local/Transaction Currency are translated into the group currency.

Group Reference System: Refer to Global Reference System.

Group Template: Refer to Global Template.

Group Template IMG: Refers to a Project IMG, denoting the scope outlined in a Global Template used for local roll-outs.

Group Valuation: Referring to the valuation of fixed assets of subsidiaries for consolidation into total fixed assets for the entire group concerned, the 'group valuation' can be carried out separately in local currency as well as in the reporting currency for various depreciation areas.

Handheld Customizing: Refers to the customizing settings necessary for running SAP CRM handheld devices.

Hand-over Workshop: Refers to a two-day practical training at the customer site, this workshop aims at preparing the administrator for the Ready-to-Run R/3 (RRR) System to carry out the various tasks.

Hard Currency: Refers to the country-specific second currency used in accounting, when there is a high rate of inflation in a country.

Heap: This is the memory area reserved by the system to store the data generated during the run-time of a program.

Hierarchy: Consisting of nodes at various levels, a hierarchy helps to arrange the CO objects such as cost centers, orders, WBS, etc. All the nodes other than the end-nodes are used only for summarizing purposes.

Hierarchy Structure: In Customizing, hierarchy structure refers to a Table of Hypertext links that can be used for carrying out customizing or for accessing documentation.

House Bank: Refers to the designated bank through which the internal transactions of a Company Code are processed.

HR Master Data: Refers to the master data – personnel number, name, bank details, etc. – of employees that remain almost permanent in the system.

HTML Business Editor: A tool for editing HTML templates in 'SAP@Web Studio,' the editor helps in design, maintenance, and testing of HTML templates and flow files.

IC Elimination: Refers to the 'inter-company elimination,' in FI-LC, of payables/receivables, revenues/expenses, and profit/loss. Refer to Elimination Entries also.

ICMS: Referring to a percentage-included tax, this is a VAT levied at the circulation of goods and services in Brazil. ICMS is known as *Imposto sobre Circulação de Mercadorias e Serviços* in Portuguese.

ICO Number: This number is used to identify a company in countries such as Czech Republic and Slovak.

IDES: Internet Demo and Evaluation System, IDES contains several companies with sample business processes typical to the countries where these sample companies are situated. IDES is valuable for demos, training, and presentations.

IDoc: ALE (Application Link Enabling) uses IDocs – the Intermediate Document – as the standard interface for exchanging data between an R/3, R/2, or a non-SAP system. Typically, an IDoc is created when message types (the format for the data for a specific business process) and methods are distributed.

IDoc Interface: Refers to the Formats (IDoc Types) and Methods (port definitions) for EDI between SAP and partner systems (another R/3 or R/2 or non-SAP system).

IDoc Type: This is nothing but the format of an IDoc for transferring business related information as 'Logical Messages.' A 'single IDoc type' can transfer more than one kind of message.

IEPSL: A special type of tax, levied in Mexico, on goods such as tobacco products, alcoholic drinks, etc., this is typically calculated before charging VAT.

IMG Activity: The lowest node in an IMG Structure that is either an Executable Transaction for object maintenance or assignments with related documentation or an Organizational Activity used only for documentation.

IMG Info System: Helping in comparing (1) IMG activities between SAP Reference IMG and Project IMG, (2) IMG activities of Project IMG and its Views, and (3) repeatedly used IMG objects, the 'IMG Info System' is a tool for checking the scope of IMG activities in Customizing.

IMG Note: Refers to a document describing the customizing settings for an IMG Activity, with reasoning for such a customizing setting.

IMG Structure: Made up of Structure Nodes and IMG Activities, the IMG Structure is a hierarchical definition at the application level, and is a subset of the SAP Reference IMG.

IMG Structure Attribute: As a part of the IMG Structure, each of the IMG Activities has attributes such as Enhancement, Critical Function, Country Assignment, ASAP Roadmap Assignment, Business Application Component Assignment, etc.

Immediate Write-off: A method of depreciation in FI-AA, to write-off the entire value of Low Value Assets as depreciation (100% depreciation) in the year/ period of acquisition.

Implementation: Refers to the process of installing and configuring an SAP system at a customer location using any of the implementation methodologies such as ASAP. See also AcceleratedSAP and Solution Manager.

Implementation Assistant: An important tool in ASAP methodology, the 'implementation assistant' provides access to ASAP Roadmap, Question and Answer (Q&A) Database, Knowledge Corner, Concept Check Tool, and Business Process Procedures, for faster and effective SAP implementations.

Implementation Book: A tool for configuring the business applications in a SAP system, as required by the customer-Client, the 'implementation book' is structured in hypertext. For each of the applications, the book describes (1) the various steps involved in the implementation, (2) the SAP standard settings, and lists (3) the configuration activities that can be opened interactively.

Implementation Guide: Popularly called IMG, the 'implementation guide' outlines all the steps required to configure/customize the SAP application to meet the specific requirements of a customer. Arranged in a tree-like structure with the IMG activities at the bottom-most nodes, the guide is a hierarchal structure of different application components. The IMG comes with the SAP supplied standard or default settings along with the relevant documentation. The SAP Reference IMG is the starting point from which one can derive the Enterprise IMG and various Project IMGs.

Implementation Project: A project outlining and carrying out the various business, organizational, and technical tasks for enabling the required business processes or functions in SAP to become 'productive' on a declared date is called an 'implementation project.' There will be project team(s) comprised of the users/representatives from the customer, and from a SAP implementation partner(s) carrying out the project activities according to a plan and an ASAP Roadmap to achieve the phase-wise deliverables.

Implementation Strategy: SAP recommends three types of 'implementation strategy' for implementing SAP for a customer requirement: (1) Big-bang Approach where all the applications 'go-live' on a single date, (2) Phased Approach in which the required applications or business processes are covered initially, and the rest of the application components are implemented in a phased manner, and (3) Organization-wise Implementation covering departments, plants, etc.

Import Check: In BC-CTS (Correction and Transport System), the system carries out an 'import check' on the target system, during the export procedure, to determine whether all the objects of a transport request will be transported to the target system. In the case of any protected objects in the target system, the import will be blocked.

Import Queue: Refers to the all the transport requests, in BC-CTS, waiting to be transported.

Imputed Interest: In FI-AA, this refers to the 'opportunity cost' of capital tied-up in a fixed asset, which would otherwise have been economically deployed for earning some interest/revenue. SAP provides for taking into account this imputed interest for cost accounting purposes.

Inbound Delivery: The process starts with the vendor staging the goods at his/her shipping point and ends when the goods are received and GR is posted by the customer. The inbound delivery document is generated with reference to a Purchase Order/Shipping Notification/Customer Return. The term inbound delivery is often used, interchangeably, to represent the materials as well as the delivery documents.

Inbound Error: The error resulting from an incoming IDoc from an external system, when the incoming IDoc is processed further in a SAP system.

ICM: Incentive and Commission Management is the solution for processing and managing all kinds of variable remuneration for employees and partners.

INCLUDE: Refers to grouped fields, according to some criteria or characteristics, inserted into a table or structure, in ABAP.

INCLUDE Program: An ABAP program, within another ABAP program written using an INCLUDE statement. The INCLUDE program is not generated separately.

Incoming Invoice: Covering both the Invoices and Credit Memo in SAP, the incoming invoice is essentially a statement, from the invoicing party, with the details of the amount due from the previous purchase transactions.

Indirect Activity Allocation: A method of periodic allocation, 'indirect activity allocation' is useful when it is difficult to enter the activity consumed by the receiver. The total activity quantity is distributed from the sender to the receiver from the receiver's perspective.

Indirect Method: A way of calculating the Cash Flow, in FI-GL, where the items not related to the cash flow are subtracted from the Income Statement to arrive at the cash flow.

Indirect Quotation: Also known as Volume Notation, in an indirect quotation the currency value is expressed in terms of foreign currency per unit of local currency. Example: 1 EURO (Local Currency) = 1.0901 USD (Foreign Currency).

Individual Picking: In Logistics Execution (LE), 'individual picking' relates to picking an individual 'unit' of a material, and is the opposite of 'Complete Picking' which is nothing but picking from one Pick Area independent of picking units.

Individual Purchase Order: When a vendor finds that the goods ordered by a customer are not available with his/her location, they are ordered from one or more of his suppliers through individual purchase orders. The goods thus arrive at the vendor locations are managed as Sales Order Stock; the goods are delivered to the customer and invoiced.

Individual Value Adjustment: The devaluation of a customer's receivables, because of impossibility of collecting the overdue from the customer, is termed 'individual value adjustment.' This is nothing but writing-off of an overdue A/R.

Individual Model: In ASAP, this relates to the model configuration in the 'SAP Reference Model' to reflect a specific industry such as aviation.

Inflation Adjustment Account: A GL account used to post the adjustments in a transaction due to inflation, this account is usually posted on the balance sheet side with an offsetting posting on the profit and loss side. The adjustment results either in a gain or loss. Example: in the case of fixed assets, inflation adjustment will lead to either unrealized gain or loss.

Inflation Keys: These keys are defined in the customizing, and assigned to the relevant GL accounts which instruct the system on how to make the 'inflation adjustment.'

InfoCube: In a 'Business Information Warehouse,' an 'infocube' represents a self-contained dataset made up of relational tables created as per Star Schema. The dataset can be queried using 'BEx Query.'

Information Flow Model: Refers to the graphical representation of cross-application business activities in the system.

Infotype: Representing a group of data grouped together according to a specific subject matter, Infotypes are normally used in Personnel Management (PA) in HR. Identified by a 4-digit key, Infotypes are nothing but the exact replicas mirroring the logical set of data records.

Initial Cost Split: A 'cost component split' for raw materials, the 'initial cost split' contains separate cost components such as purchase price, freight charges, etc.

INN: A tax number issued to both the legal and non-legal persons, in Russia.

Input Quantity Variance: Caused by the difference between the actual and planned quantities of activities consumed, 'input quantity variance' is the difference between the actual and target costs.

Input Tax: A tax on purchases, 'input tax' is charged by the vendor while supplying the goods and services. The deductible portion of the input tax can be claimed from the respective tax authorities by submitting a claim.

Inspection Stock: In QM, this relates to a stock reserved for inspection, and is not released for regular use.

Installation Number: The 10-digit number printed on the 'Request Fax License Key' form, made available from SAP, when an Installation Package is delivered to a customer.

Insurance Type: In FI-AA, the insurance type is a setting used to control how an asset is insured, say, at the current market value or at its new value (as if purchased new).

Intercompany Billing: Refers to the process for invoicing the sales when the creation of a sales order and the delivery happens from organizations in two different Company Codes of the same enterprise. That is, the Company Code where the sale is created is different than that of the Company Code from which the delivery is done.

Intercompany Clearing Account: An account to clear reconciliation entries between CO and FI in the case of 'cross-Company Code allocations.'

Interest Base Amount: Refers to the total of all line items in a business transaction on which the interest is calculated by the system.

Interest Key: A key connected to the Interest Calculation Rule, the interest key controls how interest is calculated by the system.

Interest on Arrears: Refers to the interest paid to the creditors when the payable is not paid within the net due date.

Interim Account: In FI, this refers to a GL account where all the incoming payments are posted if there is a problem determining the correct contract account.

Intermediate Customer: Refers to the customer in between the final customer and the reseller/distributor in the DRM (Distributor – Reseller – Management) supply chain.

Internal Activity Allocation: Refers to allocating the valuated costs from sender cost centers to the receiver cost centers. The activity produced at the sender cost center is multiplied by the activity price, and the resulting cost is allocated to the receiver cost center by debiting the receiver and crediting the sender.

Internal Calculation Key: A part of the Depreciation Key, the 'internal calculation key' contains the parameters for controlling the depreciation calculation program.

Internal Order: An object, in CO, to monitor, collect, and settle costs (sometimes, revenues also) is called as 'internal order.' The internal orders can be (1) Overhead Orders, (2) Investment Orders, (3) Accrual Orders, and (4) Orders with Revenues.

Internal Trading Partner: The Company having a trading relationship with another Company in the same corporate group is called the 'internal trading partner.'

Intracompany Transfer: In FI-AA, this refers to the transfer of values from one asset to another necessitated by situations such as changed asset location, re-building of an asset, etc., leading to changes (say, in Asset Class) in an asset master record.

Inventory Adjustment Posting: Refers to the correction postings necessitated by the fact that there is a discrepancy between the actual and book inventory.

Inversion Posting: Refers to posting of the same values to the objects in CO, but with the inverted sign of '+' or '-'.

Invoice Deficit: In MM, this refers to the difference when the invoiced quantity is less than the GR quantity.

Invoice Split: Refers to the creation of multiple billing documents from a single reference document (such as a sales order). The Invoice Split Function, in MM, is used for this purpose.

Invoice Verification: Refers to a process in which the invoice from the vendor is entered into the system and compared with the purchase order and GR, checking from the angle of content, price, or quantity.

Invoice with PO Reference: Refers to the invoice entered into the SAP system, with reference to an existing PO in the local or back-end system.

Invoice without PO Reference: Refers to the invoice entered into the SAP system, without any reference to a PO in the system. This would be necessitated when there is an invoice in paper format, forcing someone to create the invoice manually in the system.

Journal: A listing of all transaction entries in a period is known as a journal in FI.

Journal Entry: Refers to a single line of entry in a journal.

Jurisdiction Code: A code denoting a 'tax jurisdiction' to where the goods and services are actually delivered. The jurisdiction code is used along with the tax code in calculating sales tax in cases where mutli-level taxation is in effect.

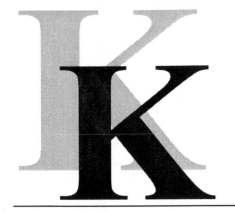

Kagami: Refers to the section in an invoice (both monthly and total) with the summary detailing the total amount billed, total amount paid, total amount due, amount carried forward, etc.

Kanban: An integrated JIT (Just-In-Time) production process, 'Kanban' refers to the replenishment or production of a material that will not be triggered until the production process actually requires the material. Kan meaning 'Card' and Ban denoting 'Signal,' Kanban translates into signalling the need for a material through a card. Workstations located along the production line will produce or deliver materials just needed, and this is done when they receive the 'Kan' along with an empty container; they then produce or deliver material or components just to fill up the containers so that there is no need for storage.

Kanban Card: An integral part of the Kanban production process, the Kanban Card is used to indicate the consumption of materials or components and also notify the required items which will then be produced or delivered by the workstations along the production line, eliminating the need for storage.

Kernel: Responsible for memory, process, and task management, this is the central part of an Operating System, and is loaded first when the system is started.

Key Figure: Refers to a quantifiable yardstick for measuring business or technical or personal performance. Example: Sales per employee, sales per division, actual costs in current fiscal year, etc. In BW, this just refers to a value or a quantity. Example: Sales revenue, fixed costs, etc.

Key Figure Category: In CO-OM-CCA, this refers to an indicator to determine whether the values for a SKF (Statistical Key Figure) need to be interpreted as a Fixed Value (Key Figure Category 1) that will remain the same across periods or as Totals (Key Figure Category 2) that will be valid only for that particular period.

Key Performance Indicator (KPI): Expressing abstract supply chain objectives in financial or physical units for effective comparison, KPI in the Supply Chain

Cockpit is used to evaluate the performance of the supply chain. In cross-application components, KPI indicates abstract company objectives in financial or physical units to evaluate the company's performance.

Knowledge Corner: One of the enabling tools in ASAP, the 'knowledge corner' contains a variety of documents (Links to SAP Online Documentation, MS-PowerPoint presentations, Made Easy Guidebooks, etc.) for facilitating various tasks during an SAP implementation especially in the initial phases of requirements gathering, blueprinting, and configuration.

Language Support Package: Refers to the package, in 'Online Correction Support,' used to import languages.

LaunchPad: This is nothing but the left-hand side frame of the web-browser, of the standard mySAP Workspace, used to launch an application or access information from a menu-tree.

Layout: In FI-GL, this refers to the definition of a screen layout with the various tabs used to process the master data relating to a GL master record.

Layout Editor: In ABAP, this refers either to the graphical or alphanumeric layout editor of the Screen Painter for designing screens.

Lead Currency: Stored in the transactions, the 'lead currency' is the main currency for transactions influencing the determination of fair value.

Lead Time: In PP, this is the difference between the order start time and order end time at the 'order level,' and is the difference between the start and end of an operation at the 'operation level.'

Lead Time Scheduling: A function in PP that is used in the calculation of production dates and creation of capacities in either of the two ways: Lead Time Scheduling using Routing and Lead Time Scheduling using Material Master.

Leading Company Code: When a number of Company Codes come together for forming an integrated company, one of the Company Codes is denoted as the 'leading Company Code' to handle all the communications with the tax authority. The leading Company Code will directly settle all the tax payables with the other Company Codes.

Lean WM: Lean Warehouse Management enables management of stock without storing it in bins. The Transfer Orders are used as the Pick Orders. As a result, the stock quantity is viewed in Inventory Management and not in Warehouse Management.

Leasing Type: In FI-AA, this indicator controls how a leased asset is managed (Operating or Capital Lease) for bookkeeping purposes.

License Key: Refers to the 24-character key supplied by SAP for installation of SAP. (In the case of Java-only installations of the SAP Web AS, the license key has more than 100 characters.)

Likelihood to Churn: In SAP CRM, this refers to the probability of a customer discontinuing business with a company.

Line Item: A part of an accounting document, a line item contains information such as account number, debit/credit indicator, amount, etc., relating to that particular item.

Line Item Display: For the accounts that are managed on an Open Item Basis, then it is possible to display the line item from one or more accounts. Mandatory for A/R and A/P, for GL accounts this needs to be maintained in the GL Master Record.

Lines Flip-Flop: One of the design elements for lines, this causes every alternate line to be displayed in color.

Link Table: In Archiving, this refers to an administration table where the reference between a business object and the corresponding archive document is created during a current operation.

Load Balancing: Refers to the distribution of server load among the various application servers. In SAP, this is achieved by the Message Server when users log into the system.

Loading Group: A key identifying the equipment required for loading, this could be a crane or forklift, etc.

Local Currency: This is nothing but the 'Company Code currency' (or Country Currency) that is used to maintain the local ledgers in FI. In FI-LC, if the local currency differs from the Group Currency, then it needs to be translated into the group currency.

Lock Entries: Comprised of the user, Client, time, table, etc., a lock entry can be displayed using the Transaction Code SM12.

Lockbox: Used mainly in the USA, this process is used to collect the checks, sent in by business partners, by a bank or lockbox provider so that the payee's account is credited immediately and the information is sent to the payee through file transfer.

Logical Database: Maintained through a Logical Database Builder, a 'logical database' is a run-time only object, where a special ABAP program provides other ABAP programs with data from the nodes of the hierarchical tree structure. Typically, a logical database is made up of a structure with nodes, a database program written in ABAP, and a Standard Selection Screen.

Logistics Payment Block: An indicator informing why an invoice document is blocked for payment. The payment block may be A (blocked due to reasons mentioned in the invoice), S (stochastic block), M (manual block at the header level), or W (blocked though invoice verification on the internet).

Logon Group: Referring to the grouping of instances in a SAP system, the groups are defined using the Transaction Code SMLG.

Long Text: Refers to a text in the software interface, with the length of the text being more than 45 characters.

Main Asset Number: Identified as the single unit for valuation, this refers to the unique number in FI-AA, representing a fixed asset in a Company Code.

Maintenance BOM: In PP, this is a list containing the structure of the technical object along with the spare parts assigned for a maintenance object.

Maintenance Order: In PM, this is a detailed planning aid, listing out the tasks to be performed on any of the order types such as Investment Order, Calibration Order, or Refurbishment Order.

Major Defect: Though not critical, a major defect is likely to result in a failure in performing a required function of a complex function or program.

Make-to-Order Production: Made up of both the Sales Order and Engineer-to-Order, 'make-to-order production' in CO-PC refers to the manufacture of a product for a specific customer.

Make-to-Stock Inventory: Refers to the products that were not produced against a specific Sales Order or Project.

Manual Cost Allocation: One of the methods of internal cost allocation in controlling, manual cost allocation is used to avoid making complex customizing settings for simple allocations. It is used to transfer the external data.

Manual MRP: In MM, 'manual MRP' refers to a process where the MRP controller creates the order proposals manually.

Mapping of SAP Services: Refers to assigning logical SAP services such as update, dialogue, batch, etc., to physical host machines.

Mark-for Store: In SD, this refers to a store that is the final recipient of the goods shipped.

Mass Change: Instead of changing one-by-one, this enables you to change the attributes of a number of objects (say, in the asset master) in one step.

Mass Document Change: A special report, in SD, enabling simultaneous changing of a large number of sales documents.

Master Data Management (MDM): A component in SAP, which in turn contains other components such as SAP BW (Business Information Warehouse), SAP XI (Exchange Infrastructure), SAP EP (Enterprise Portal), and SAP CI (Content Integrator).

Master Recipe: In PP-PI, this refers to the enterprise specific production process, in a process industry, which cannot be associated with any specific order. This is similar to Make-to-Stock Inventory.

Matchcode: Also known, now, as the Search Code, this is a key that enables you to find a particular record in a database. Example: Finding out the customer number by inputting information contained in that record. Press F4 while the cursor is on a field with a drop-down symbol to see the possible values.

Material BOM: Created with reference to a Material Master, a material BOM contains stock as well as non-stock items, document items, and text items.

Material Cost Estimate: A tool in CO-PC, this helps in calculating the COGS/COGM for providing a basis for material valuation with the standard costs. The material cost estimates can be created manually in Controlling (Cost Estimate without Quantity Structure) or can be created automatically in PP (Cost Estimate with Quantity Structure).

Material Credit Memo: Referring to the planned return of materials during a manufacturing process, material credit memos are represented as 'minus' items in a BOM.

Material Determination: Refers to finding out a material master by inputting a user-definable key instead of a material number during sales creation. Example: EAN (European Article Number), customer specific material number, etc.

Material Document: A document containing one or more items of material movements that can be printed as a GR/GI slip to accompany physical movement of goods.

Material Ledger: Forming the basis for Actual Costing, 'material ledger' is a tool in CO-PC used to valuate the material inventory in multiple currencies using different valuation approaches.

Material Number: A number uniquely identifying a material in SAP, it is necessary that all the materials in the system should have a material master defined.

Material Overhead Costs: Referring to costs that cannot be identified with individual materials, material overhead costs are some of the costs such as procurement costs, storage costs (when multiple materials are stored in a single storage area), etc.

Material Price Determination: A process for material valuation – in Co-PC – using the Material Ledger, material price determination (a) valuates the inventory in multiple currencies in different valuation areas, (b) makes new valuations in multiple currencies/multiple valuation areas, and (c) posts the differences arising from transactions to material stock accounts.

Material Stock: Managed at the plant or storage location level, 'material stock' is nothing but a part of the current assets of a company.

Material Substitution: The automatic substitution of one material with another during creation of a sales document is known as 'material substitution.'

Material Valuation: In MM, the 'material valuation' of a stock of material is based on the Valuation Price, Valuation Class, and Valuation Method (at a Standard or Moving Average Price).

Material Variant: Refers to the product variant of a configurable material.

MDoc: Refers to the objects (MIME - Multipurpose Internet Mail Extension - files, folders, document headers, document versions) that are stored in SAP Collaborative Room Document Management (SAP C-Room DM).

Menu Painter: A tool in ABAP that enables creation of a GUI (Graphical User Interface) consisting of title and status (Menu Bar with Menus, Standard Toolbar, Application Toolbar, and Functions with Function Key settings).

Mix Variance: In CO-PC, this refers to the variance resulting from the difference between the actual and planned product blends as a product can be manufactured using various manufacturing processes.

Mixed Costing: Refers to a costing methodology in which 'multiple cost estimates' are used to calculate the mixed price for a material that can be used to update the standard price.

Model Order: A template order, with default values, used to create orders in CO is known as the model order; a model order cannot be posted to.

Module Pool: Containing screens and dialogue modules, a 'module pool' is an ABAP program that can be run only through a Transaction Code.

Movement Type: An indicator for material movement such as GR, GI, etc., the 'movement types' enable the system to determine the pre-determined posting rules and account determination for correct financial and material accounting entries. Example: Movement type 101 is used in GR based on a purchase order, 201 GI to a cost center, etc.

MPX Interface: In PS, MPX interface is used for data exchange between PS and MS-Project.

MRP (Material Requirements planning): Aimed at guaranteeing material availability, MRP is the procedure that takes into account the dependent and independent requirements, during order creation proposal, for planning the future requirements for both internal and sales purposes.

MRP Area: 'MRP area' is an organizational unit, in PP, for which material requirements planning can be done independently. In APO, these MRP locations are transferred as 'locations.' There are three types of MRP areas; namely, (1) Plant MRP Area, (2) MRP Area for Storage Locations, and (3) MRP Area for Sub-contractors.

Multidimensional Product Cost Controlling: This is nothing but the cost accounting both at the product and responsibility area levels.

Multi-level BOM: A BOM consisting of assemblies (which in turn consist of components/assemblies) and components is known as a 'multi-level BOM.'

Multi-level BOM for Sales Order Item: This is made up of 'single-level Order BOMs' and 'single-level Material BOMs.'

Multiple Account Assignments: Refers to the assignment of multiple GL accounts to a single purchase order item, so that the costs can be apportioned based on quantity or amount.

Multiple BOM: This is nothing but a grouping of several BOMs describing more than one alternative combination of materials for producing a single product. During a planning run, it needs to be mentioned which one of the alternatives is to be selected by the system.

Multiple Work Center: In PP, this refers to several work centers in the production line, where the same work is done.

Multiple-shift Depreciation: Refers to the calculation of higher depreciation by applying the Multiple-shift Factor to the variable portion of the depreciation when an asset is subject to use in multiple shifts. The fixed portion will continue to depreciate normally.

mySAP Business Intelligence: A part of mySAP Business Suite, 'mySAP Business Intelligence' provides a comprehensive toolset for data warehousing, knowledge management, and data analysis delivered through an enterprise portal.

mySAP CRM: A part of mySAP Business Suite, 'mySAP Customer Relationship Management' is a comprehensive solution for managing customer relations through customer focused business areas, customer interaction channels (Interaction Center), etc.

mySAP Enterprise Portal: Refers to the portal solution from SAP that unifies all types of enterprise information, including business applications, databases, stored documents, and Internet information, for facilitating users' role-based access to and action on business-critical information within the extended enterprise.

mySAP Financials: A part of mySAP Business Suite, this helps companies improve their processing and interpretation of financial and business data, their handling of financial transactions, and communication with their shareholders. 'mySAP Financials' enables company-wide control and integration of financial and business information for strategic decision-making.

mySAP SCM: A part of mySAP Business Suite, mySAP Supply Chain Management enables companies to network their supply chains for greater business value. It integrates extended supply chains, allowing companies to participate in collaborative, self-organizing, and value-added trading communities transforming supply chain management from a linear, sequential process into a collaborative community that enables businesses to network, plan, execute, and coordinate with customers, suppliers, and partners throughout the entire life span of the product or service.

mySAP Workplace: A part of mySAP.com, this is a personalized Web Browser Enterprise Portal that is Role-based: the screen is tailored to the specific role of each user in a company. The Single Sign-On provides users with access to all the information, applications/services they need for their work. From mySAP Workplace, one can access (1) all mySAP Components, (2) Internet Application Components (IACs), (3) Self-Service scenarios, (4) Reports (such as SAP Business Information Warehouse reports), (5) SAP Knowledge Warehouse content, (6) Marketplaces, (7) any Internet and Intranet pages, and (8) Third-party Systems.

mySAP.com Components: Refers to the product that is part of mySAP.com. Accessible through mySAP Workplace this includes mySAP R/3, mySAP APO, mySAP Business Information Warehouse, etc.

mySAP.com Solution: Realized through mySAP.com Components, this a solution for business applications in the areas of Enterprise Portals, CRM, SCM, Electronic Marketplaces, Business Intelligence, Product Life cycle Management (PLM), SRM, Human Resources, Financials, and Mobile Business, as well as for industry-specific business applications.

Namespace: Beginning and ending with a delimiter '/' and consisting of up to a maximum of 10 characters, the 'namespace' in ABAP is an ID assigned exclusively by SAP allowing SAP customers/partners and SAP to develop SAP components using SAP applications without any naming conflicts that are otherwise common.

Native SQL: Refers to the database language allowing you to include database-specific statements in ABAP programs.

Negative Goodwill: A result of the consolidation of investments exercise, a 'negative goodwill' occurs when the purchase price of an acquired company is less than the fair value of its net assets. The negative goodwill is shown on the stakeholder's section of the balance sheet.

Negative Posting: Refers to a type of 'reversal posting' in FI that brings down the transaction figures in an account of GL/customer/vendor. During this, the transaction figures (following the reversal) receive the status they would have had without posting the reversed document and its reversal document.

Negative Stock: In MM, this refers to a situation in which there is some physical stock available but there has not been matching GR. As a result, if there is a GI then the stock becomes negative.

Net Actual Cost: Enabling you to arrive at the Total/Production Variances by comparing the net actual costs with that of the Target Costs, the net actual cost is nothing but the difference between the Actual Cost and the WIP (Work-In-Progress) + Scrap.

Net Book Value (NBV): In FI-AA, this is nothing but the net value of a fixed asset that is equal to its acquisition value or original value minus the depreciation.

Net Price: Refers to the price charged to a vendor after taking into account all the Discounts and Surcharges.

Net Target Cost: Represented by the Target Cost Version 0, 1, and 3 in the standard system, 'net target cost' is used to calculate the variance in Product Cost by Period (nothing but the Target Cost minus the WIP at Target Cost minus Scrap Variance) and by Order (equivalent to Target Cost minus Scrap Variance).

Net Value: In SD this refers to the Gross Value minus the Discounts plus the Surcharges.

Net Worth Tax: In FI-AA, this refers to the tax collected on a property that forms a part of a fixed asset.

Network: In PS, this refers to an object containing instructions on what tasks to be performed/executed, in what order and in what time.

New Visual Design: As opposed to the Classic Visual Design of SAP GUI appearing in the grey color, this 'new visual design' uses other colors in the GUI.

Non-Calendar Fiscal Year: Unlike a Calendar Fiscal Year that corresponds to the Calendar Year, a 'non-calendar fiscal year' can have any of the calendar months as the starting month for that fiscal year. Example: July to June.

Non-Conformity Costs: These are all the costs, in QM, associated with the defects. The costs may be associated with rework, scrap, repeat inspections, guarantees, etc.

Non-Critical Activity: In SAP Customizing, this refers to the attribute of an IMG activity, when non-completion of this step would not result in any negative consequence.

Non-Leading Ledger: In FI-GL, if there is Parallel Accounting, then one of the Parallel Ledgers need to be designated as the Leading Ledger. All other parallel ledgers, then, are known as 'non-leading ledgers.'

Non-Required Activity: In SAP Customizing, there are certain IMG tasks that are standard and do not need to be changed, normally, for customer-specific requirements, and these activities are known as 'non-required activities' and the system can be made to 'go-live' without customizing any of these activities.

Non-Standard Object: Refers to an object, in SAP Customizing, that has not been created using the Transaction Code SE54. All the 'non-standard objects' need to be maintained manually in the system.

Non-Stock Item: This refers to a material as one of the BOM components, but there is no stock for that material. Example: PR (Purchase Requisition).

Non-Valuated Stock: Refers to the stock maintained in a company, only on a 'quantity basis' without any valuation. To make use of such a stock, it is necessary that this is first transferred to 'Valuated Stock.'

Nota Fiscal: Refers to a legal document, in Brazil, accompanying goods delivery. This document is used both as an Invoice and Delivery Note. In its plural form this is known as 'Notas Fiscais.'

Note Assistant: Refers to the functionality that will enable you to load, apply, and implement 'SAP Notes' in a SAP system.

Note Log: Downloaded along with the 'SAP Note download,' this log will help in monitoring the various steps involved in implementing an SAP Note.

Note Type: SAP enables definition of various 'Note Types' according the content of these notes, in a project implementation. Some of note types are: Design, Minutes of Meeting, Issues, Project Standards, etc. A Notes Editor (MS-Word or SAPscript) is used to enter the information.

Noted Item: Refers to a special item in FI, which when posted does not affect the account balance. It is just a document used as a 'reminder.' Example: Down Payment Request.

Notification: A data record used to inform PM (Plant Maintenance), QM (Quality Maintenance), or CS (Customer Service) about some occurrence or event is known as the 'notification.' There are many Notification Categories such as Maintenance Notification, Service Notification, etc.

Novation: The transfer of some or all POs/Contracts from one vendor to another, necessitated due to buy-out or merger of companies.

Number Assignment: Refers to the assigning of numbers to various business objects (documents, organizational elements, etc.) in SAP. The number assignment can be Internal or External.

Number Format: Refers to the settings for displaying numbers in a report. The settings include Decimal Places (how many decimal places to be displayed) and Scaling Factor (display in hundreds, thousands, etc.).

Number Range: Refers to a range of numbers that can be assigned to similar business objects such as Master Records, Documents, and Materials, etc. Example: External Business Partners – Number Range 01 – Number Range Interval 100,000 – 199 999 – External Assignment.

Number Range Group: This refers to the combination of one or more Number Range Objects and one or more Number Range Intervals.

Number Range Interval: Refers to an interval of consecutive numbers (or alphanumeric characters) in a Number Range. There can be more than one 'number range interval' within a single number range.

Number Range Object: An object containing all the information that is required for assigning a 'number range' to a business object is known as the number range object. Belonging to one business object, a single number range object can have multiple Number Ranges.

Object Category: In Basis (CTS-Change and Transport System), the 'object category' refers to an area to which a maintenance and transport object is to be assigned. The categories may be: CUST (used for Client-specific customizing objects), SYST (system related customizing objects), CUSY (Client-independent customizing objects), and APPL (application objects).

Object Currency: The currency defined in the master record for a controlling object such as cost center, order, etc. While creating an object, the Controlling Area Currency is defaulted as the object currency but it can be changed.

Object Navigator: Displaying all the objects (relating to a particular Object Category) in a tree-like structure, the 'object navigator' is a tool used to process objects centrally.

Object Type: In CO, this refers to the type of account assignment object such as cost center, profitability segment, internal order, etc.

Off-Balance Sheet Transactions: These are all some of the transactions, such as Warranties, Guarantees, etc., that do not appear on the balance sheet but are shown separately as 'Notes' on the Balance Sheet.

Offsetting Entry: In a double-entry system of bookkeeping/accounting, this is the second entry offsetting the first entry so that the balance is always 'zero.'

One-System Landscape: Refers to a SAP system landscape with only one 'Production' system.

One-Time Account: Refers to an account in FI, which records the transactions relating to a group of customers/vendors with whom the company conducts the business once or very rarely. These accounts require a special master record, and some of the details such as address, bank, etc. are not updated in this master, but entered in the transaction document itself.

One-Time Customer/Vendor: Represented by a special master record for a collection of such customers/vendors, this customer/vendor is one with whom business is done very rarely or only once.

On-Order Stock: This is nothing but the sum of all Open Purchase Order quantities for a material.

Open Purchase Order (PO) Quantity: Refers to the PO quantity that has not yet been delivered. This becomes zero, when the PO quantity or more has been delivered. The open PO quantity is calculated by subtracting the Delivered Quantity from the Ordered Quantity.

Operating Concern: Having one or more Controlling Areas, an operating concern represents – in CO-PA – the sales market in a structured way by defining market segments as Profitability Segments, for analysing the profitability.

Operation: Referring to an activity in a work plan or work order, in logistics, an operation can be a production, inspection, etc.

Operation Scrap: Entered in the Routing or BOM, this refers to the material(s) processed in an operation that failed to meet the quality requirements.

Order Hierarchy: Refers to the summarization of order values, level-by-level with the levels being the Characteristics (controlling area, business area, etc.). A Total is calculated for each of the levels. The value totalled may include planned cost, actual cost, target cost, etc.

Order List: An overview of the status of a Sales Order, the 'order list' is useful with detailed information on the content, processing status of the order, delivery scheduling, etc.

Order Settlement: Referring to partial or complete crediting of an order, 'order settlement' results in debiting the accrued costs to one or more allocation receivers (such as cost center) in FI or CO.

Order Split: In PP, this refers to splitting of an original order (called as the Parent Order) into one or more orders (called Child Orders).

Order Type: Being Client-specific, the 'order type' contains all the information required to manage an order. The order type may include Production Order, Maintenance Order, Marketing Order, etc. A single order type can be used in multiple Controlling Areas of a single Client.

Orders with Revenue: Settled to Profitability Segments at the end of a period, these orders are used to replace the CO functions of SD sales orders if SD is not implemented in an organization, and to obtain revenue-to-cost information if billing is automated.

Ordering Costs: These are all the costs incurred on each of the PO or Production Orders, over and above the PO cost or 'cost of production,' regardless of the lot size of the order. The ordering costs are directly proportional to the number of orders placed.

Ordinary Depreciation: Accounting for the normal wear and tear of use, 'ordinary depreciation' is nothing but the Planned Depreciation that reduces the APC of a fixed asset over its normal Economic Life through a Depreciation Method.

Organization Model: Refers to the mapping of Logical Enterprise Structure of an organization structure to SAP Organization Elements.

Organizational Change Management (OCM): Refers to the systematic management changes in an organization with the implementation of SAP. In ASAP, an OCM plan is prepared to handle the changes, at every phase of the project, with recommendations for mitigating risks arising from the proposed changes.

Organizational Structure List (OSL): Consisting of all the organizational elements arising from the scope in a Q&A database, corresponding to SAP organizational units that need to be configured during the Realization Phase, OSL helps to define the structure and configuration of SAP organizational elements.

Original Document: A document in FI that will prove that a posting is correct.

Outbound Delivery: In Logistics, this is nothing but the operation that starts with Picking of goods and ending with Shipping. An 'outbound delivery document' is created during the process of (1) goods shipped to a customer, (2) goods returned to a vendor, and (3) Stock Transfer Orders. The entire operation results in a decrease in the stock quantity of that material or product.

Output Tax: An opposite of Input Tax, this is levied on the customers.

Overhead Cost Controlling: A part of the Controlling (CO) that is used to monitor overhead costs in an organization to provide strategic decisions to the enterprise to manage these costs.

Overhead Cost Order: One of the Internal Order types, this kind of order is used to monitor or collect overhead costs for a specific period, irrespective of the cost center structure or business processes of an organization, and settled at the period end to cost centers, WBS elements, profitability segments, or other internal orders.

Overhead Costing: The most common way of costing the cost objects in Cost Object Controlling, this type of costing first assigns all the Direct Costs (from Cost Element Controlling) to the relevant Cost Objects, then pro-rated overhead costs are applied to the objects in proportion to their direct costs.

Overhead Key: In CO-PC, this is used to calculate the percentage overhead rate for specific materials or orders.

Overhead Rate: Lump-sum or percentage or quantity-based, this is the rate at which overhead is allocated to the direct costs to be charged on the cost objects with the proportion of the overhead costs belonging to them.

Overhead Structure: Used in Cost Center Accounting to Accrual Costs, this structure defines how the overhead is calculated and posted. A typical structure consists of a (1) Base Row on which the overhead rate is applied, (2) Calculation Row contains the Overhead Rate that needs to be applied on the base row, and (3) Total Row is the sum of the base and overhead amounts.

P & L Statement Account Type: Refers to the key that is used to define the Retained Earnings account.

PA Transfer Structure: Use to settle orders to assign direct postings to Profitability Segments from FI/CO or allocated activities in CO, the 'PA transfer structure' is used to assigns costs/revenues from other applications. The costs/revenues are assigned to the Quantity and Value Fields in Profitability Analysis.

Package Builder: One of the Workbench tools in ABAP, the 'package builder' is used to define the hierarchy of packages, the interfaces for user packages, and create user access for use of services from other packages.

Packaging List: Not requiring a specific format, a 'packaging list' consists of goods and packaging.

Park: Refers to a function that enables 'parking' of an accounting document by saving the data in the database. A 'parked document' can later on be changed, deleted, saved, or posted.

Parked Invoice Document: The system uses the 'Park Incoming Invoice' function to 'park' a vendor's invoice in MM. The 'parking' becomes necessary when there is some information missing, or when the balance is not zero or when the invoice processing is done by several people. However, it is necessary that the information such as document number, vendor, invoicing party, and account assignment needs to be entered before parking an invoice.

Partial Clearing: Refers to the clearing in FI in which the Open Items are not cleared in full.

Partial Confirmation: In PP, this refers to the confirmation of an operation that is still being processed, and not yet completed.

Partial Delivery: Refers to the receipt of goods that is less than the ordered quantity.

Partial Settlement: This is the payment towards partial settlement of an outstanding invoice.

Partner Determination: The process of the system determining the 'partner' (Sold-to-Party, Ship-to-Party, Bill-to-Part, Payer, etc.) during the 'sales order' creation is known as the 'partner determination.'

Partner Function: In SD, this refers to the rights and responsibilities of each of the partners in a business transaction, and the function relates to the 'Sold-to-Party' and the 'Ship-to-Party.'

Payer: In SD, this refers to the person or entity paying the bill on behalf of the Bill-to-Party.

Payment Block Indicator: Entered in a customer/vendor master record or in the line item of a document, the 'payment block indicator' is a key used to block an account or a line item from being paid. The Payment Block Reasons are defined in the system and assigned to the payment block indicators.

Payment History Analysis: Refers to the history of customer payments. The analysis provides information on payment frequency, instances of customers missing the due date, cash discount offered to the customers, etc.

Payment Lot: Created either manually or automatically, the 'payment lot' refers to the grouping of payments, incoming/outgoing, that are combined for processing together.

Payment Medium Format: Refers to the format in which the payment information is created for processing by the banks. The formats include (1) International Formats such as MT100, IDoc, etc., (2) Document-based Formats such as Bank Transfer Forms, (3) Non Document-based Formats such as DME, EDI, etc., and (4) Countryspecific Formats such as ACH.

Payment Medium Workbench: Refers to the tool offered by SAP for creating 'payment medium files' based on customized settings and the generic file formats explained in Payment Medium Format above.

Payment Method: Refers to methods such as Check, Cash, or Bank Transfer specifying how the payment is made from/to the SAP system.

Payment Program: Refers to the program that controls the payment processing in SAP. The program results in Payment Documents and Payment Media, and enables posting of the payment transactions processed during the Payment Run.

Payment Tolerance: This refers to the Payment Rules for handling payment differences: what can be the maximum difference allowed between the invoice and actual payment made, how to account for the Residual Items, etc. This also takes are of the process to handle 'Payment Difference,' if any.

Payroll Account: The most important document on wages and salaries, the 'payroll account' is updated every time the payroll is run. The payroll account contains all the cumulated payroll information besides the personal information of all the personnel.

Pegged Order: This is used to determine that assemblies, planned or customer independent requirements, are not covered if delivery or production is delayed or incomplete.

Period Accounting: In contrast to the Cost of Sales Accounting, the 'period accounting' takes into account all the costs incurred in a particular timeframe irrespective of the fact of whether the matching revenue has been earned or not.

Period Closing Program: A program, in Logistics, used to ensure that data are properly updated in the correct period and, goods movements are posted properly in the respective period.

Period Control: A part of the Internal Calculation Key in FI-AA, the 'period control' enables determination of the start/end date of depreciation during asset acquisition or retirement. Allowing the defining of individual period controls for various transaction types such as acquisition, transfer, or retirement, SAP comes delivered with many default period controls such as Pro Rata Temporis, Pro Rata at Mid-period, First Year Convention, etc.

Period Indicator: In PP, this refers to the key specifying for which time duration the consumption/forecast values should remain in the system.

Period Lock: In the case of Internal Orders, this refers to the procedure that 'locks' the planned/actual transactions for a given combination of controlling area, fiscal year, and version.

Period-End Closing: Refers to the periodic transactions performed at the end of a period, after the Primary Cost postings have been made. In CO-CCA, this refers to the periodic transactions such as Assessment, Distribution, Periodic Transfer Postings, and Imputed Cost Calculation. In the case of Cost Object Controlling, period-end closing encompasses calculation of (1) Overheads, (2) WIP, (3) Variance, and (4) Settlement.

Periodic Allocation: Refers to how the costs collected on a cost center are periodically allocated to other cost objects based on a certain allocation basis.

Periodic Inventory: This is nothing but the period-end physical inventory of all the stocks of an organization.

Periodic Reposting: Aimed at correcting posting errors or discrepancies, 'periodic reposting' refers to an allocation method that uses Cycle and Segments to credit the allocation cost centers with the correct costs.

Personal Identification Number: This is nothing but the number used, in FI, to identify a natural person, in Korea. In SD, this may refer to the legitimate owner as the 'cardholder.'

Personal Ledger Account: Used in India, this refers to a bank account which collects all the excise duty payable from where the tax authorities deduct the appropriate excise duty for that organization.

Personnel Area: An organization element in HR, this is used in personnel administration, time management, and payroll accounting.

Phantom Assembly: A logical grouping of materials, this 'phantom assembly' is used to describe a number of components to manage them as whole, by placing the components in a Superior Assembly.

Phase: Represents a major milestone, ASAP contains five phases: Project Preparation, Business Blueprint, Realization, Final Preparation, Go-Live, and Support.

Picking: Refers to the process of grouping materials/products on the basis of sales orders, deliveries, etc., picking is carried out per the 'Transport Orders.'

Plan Version: In CO, this refers to a collection of functions. SAP enables planning in multiple versions, and the default version is '000' that is generated by the system when the Controlling Area is created for the first time. Only this version allows entering both planned and actual costs.

Planned Scrap: Resulting from the manufacturing of a product, the planned scrap may be Component-based or Operation-based. While the 'component-based scrap' is defined in the BOM, the 'operation-based scrap' is defined in the routing.

Planner Profile: A hierarchical definition of Planning Layouts and Planning Areas. One or more 'planning layouts' are used per 'planning area.'

Planning Layout: Refers to the structure of the data entry screen for planning, this 'planning layout' consists of a Header (Planning period, version, etc.), Lead Columns (Objects to be planned), and Value Column (the plan values).

Planning Period: Refers to the period for which a 'Cost Estimate' will be valid.

Planning Profile: In Controlling, this refers to a functionality used to group the control parameters for planning/budgeting operations.

Planning Run: Divided into main work steps such as (1) Lot Size calculation, (2) Net Requirement determination, (3) Procurement Element/Type determination, and (4) Scheduling, the planning run refers to the execution of Material Requirements Planning (MRP) for all the materials/assemblies.

Planning Variant: In Variant Configuration in Logistics, a 'planning version' refers to the variant for planning the components of a 'Configurable Material' that are critical or required frequently.

Planning Version: This is nothing but the planning data on 'SOP' (Sales and Operations Planning), stored in different versions. Though there are multiple versions in the system, in PP, version 'A00' is termed the Active Version, and all other versions are Inactive in the standard system.

Plant: A plant in SAP is an organization element where materials or goods/services are produced.

Plant-Specific Purchasing Organization: Refers to the 'purchasing organization' that is responsible for the procurement activities for a plant.

POH: 'Process on Help (POH)' is an event triggered by F1 for providing help information of an input field on the screen.

POS: POS or 'Point of Sale' is a Cash Point from which merchandise is sold to a customer.

Pool Table: This is one of the Tables in a Table Pool. Due to structure restrictions of Table Pool, the name of the Pool Table (also called as Pooled Table) cannot exceed 10 characters, and all the fields of this Table should have Character Data Type. It is also to be noted that the total length of all the Key Fields/Data Fields of a Pool Table cannot exceed the 'Varkey' or 'Vardata' field of the Table Pool.

Post Depreciation: The depreciation determined by the Depreciation Key or determined manually is posted in the system periodically. The Depreciation Posting Run, with all the necessary information for posting depreciation amounts to FI, creates a Batch Input Session that when processed creates the necessary postings.

Post to a Prior Period: When a transaction is entered with the posting date relating to a previous period, the system corrects the data for the current and previous periods.

Post-Capitalization: Refers to the correction of the value of assets in FI-AA, because the value of the asset was set too low previously as there was no capitalization in the past. The correction may also apply to the value of an asset that was considered an expense earlier.

Posting: As a document entry, posting in FI relates to updating of one or more transaction ledgers in the system with the data from the document entered.

Posting Block: Refers to a key that when entered prevents an account from further postings. The 'posting block' may be set Centrally affecting all the Company Codes or Locally at the Company Code level affecting only a specific Company Code.

Posting Key: A 2-digit numeric key determining how the line items in a document are posted by controlling the (1) posting side (credit or debit), (2) the account types to which a transaction can be posted, and the (3) screen layouts for data entry.

Posting Lock: In Contract Management, this refers to the locking of transactions due to business related reasons such as bankruptcy, death of the natural person, etc.

Posting Period: Derived from the 'Posting Date' of a document, the transaction figures are updated in the system, per 'posting period.' As a result, every transaction is associated with a posting period.

Posting Rule: In CO-PC, this refers to the rule determining which data from RA (Results Analysis) are transferred to FI-GL when the settlement takes place.

Posting Variant: Defined in customizing, a 'posting variant' is a system object which ensures that the asset revaluation, in FI-AA, is carried out at proper intervals.

Postponed Accounting System: Applicable only in Belgium, the Netherlands, and Luxembourg, this arises from a situation where the transactions between 'business partners' are exempt from tax yet need to be reported to the Tax Office. Under this system, the vendor shows a portion of the invoiced amount as both the Input Tax and Output Tax.

POV: Triggered by F4, a Process on Value (POV) request displays the Possible Entries of an input field of a screen.

Power User: Refers to one or more users, identified during the SAP implementation, having an in-depth knowledge of the business processes, and who are known as the Point of Reference for all other users.

Pre-Allocated Stock: By-passing the normal storage route, a 'pre-allocated stock' is one which when received at the warehouse is sent immediately to the goods issue area for transfer to the appropriate location.

Pre-Configured Client (PCC): Consisting of frequently used customizing settings for a country, this Client comes loaded with a country-specific chart of accounts, UOM (Units of Measure), etc., so that most of the basic processes in FI/CO, SD, and MM do not require any further customizing and are operational from the day the Client is set up.

Pre-Configured Material: Used as 'master data' in Quotations and Sales Orders, the 'pre-configured material' is a pre-set configuration of a product or material master item.

Pre-Configured System: A 'pre-configured SAP system' for a particular industry, this contains all the necessary structures, for that industry, with the default values and the corresponding knowledge for all these typical structures.

Preferred Storage Location: Refers to the first choice of a storage location, from which the materials are taken for fulfilling a delivery. Only when there are no materials at this preferred location, the system looks for other storage locations.

Preferred Vendors: Refers to the vendors proposed by the users, from an existing list, when the assigned/normal sources of supply failed to deliver the materials. The 'preferred vendors' need to go through the approval from the purchases before they become the 'supply sources.'

Preparation for Consolidation: In FI-LC, this refers to the preparations for enabling automatic transfer of data from application components such as FI, SD, MM, and EC-PCA, into the Consolidation System to maintain Additional Account Assignments such as Transaction Type, Trading Partner, Acquisition Year, etc.

PREPARE: Refers to the program, in SAP, that 'prepares' an existing system for an upgrade. Running in Sequential Phases, besides making Preparatory Checks automatically, this copies the Tools needed by the upgrade to the database, and also copies programs and data to the upgrade directory. Capable of resetting and repeating as often as required during the upgrade preparations, the tool helps to upgrade without pains.

Presentation Layer: Distributed across many Presentation Servers, the presentation layer (such as SAPGUI, Web Browser, etc.) is nothing but the software level of the SAP system displaying the User Interface, which processes the user instructions and passes them to the Application Layer.

Presentation Server: A single site server of an ABAP-based SAP system in which the Presentation Layer is realized either through the SAPGUI or the Web Browser.

Pretty Printer: Used to optimize the layout of an ABAP Program, this is one of the functions of the ABAP Editor.

Prevention Costs: These are all the costs associated with the preventive and corrective operations in QM.

Price Change Document: Refers to a GL document in MM, which records the changes in the valuation of the price of a material.

Price Control: Refers to the procedure of determining material valuation in MM, either at the Standard Price or the Moving Average Price.

Price Difference: In CO-PC, this is nothing but the difference between the Valuation Price and the price used for movement of a material with an external amount. When the Material Ledger is active, this price difference is collected to the Price Difference Accounts, irrespective of the Price Control Indicator in the material master for that material.

Price Difference Account: In CO, this refers to the account which records the difference in prices for a material managed on the Standard Price. The account is also used to record the difference between the PO Price and the Selling Price.

Price Group: Refers to the grouping of customers, such as retail customers, wholesale customers, etc., for the purpose of pricing.

Price Strategy: In CO-PC, this refers to the determination of how materials, production activities, external activities, etc., are valuated for a given costing type.

Price Table: In Controlling, this refers to a special 'Condition Table' used in resource planning.

Price Type: Refers to a key to identify a price in BW; the 'price types' such as Standard Price, Moving Average Price (also called as Periodic Unit Price), Tax Price, and Commercial Price are used in SAP.

Pricing Procedure: Refers to the process of defining Conditions (or Condition Records) and the (Access) Sequence in which the system will read these condition records for determining the price. SAP comes delivered with Material Price, Discount, Surcharge, etc. It is easier if the standard procedure is copied and changed for a specific requirement.

Price Reference Material: The Material Master record that is used by the system as a reference for determining the price is known as the 'price reference material.' When this reference is entered into a new material master, all those conditions applicable to the reference material will apply to this new material as well.

Pricing-Procedure Results Table: Refers to a table that stores the results from the Pricing Procedure. The system stores this information at each step of the processing and is used internally for transferring the relevant information to the document that is being created.

Primary Cost Component Split: In CO-PC, this refers to an alternative way of grouping COGM showing the Primary Costs for internal activities. In the case of Overhead Cost Controlling, the 'primary cost component split' shows how the price of an Activity Type is made.

Primary Cost Element: Corresponding to GL accounts in FI, 'primary cost elements' originate outside CO. This also refers to the Accrual Costs that are used for the CO purpose only.

Primary Product: In PP, this refers to the manufacturing of the primary product. Unlike the primary product, there will not be any independent order items created in the manufacturing of by-products and co-products.

Primary Table: In ABAP, this is nothing but the first table introduced in an aggregated object consisting of many tables, all of which are connected through the Foreign Key.

Print Output Program: Also known as Printer Writer, this program helps to maintain printer settings. The printer output program reads a Spool File from the Print Queue and sends it to the printer for printing.

Prior Vendor: A manufacturer of a product, the 'prior vendor,' is one step behind in a Supply Chain from a 'source' from which a material is supplied.

Pro Forma Invoice: A quotation, with the details of product description, quantity to be supplied, price, payment terms, selling terms, etc., from a buyer.

Pro Rata Temporis: In FI-AA, this is a Period Control used to calculate proportionate asset values by taking the 'first date' of the period as the starting date for depreciation calculation. In the case of retirements, full depreciation is calculated if the asset retirement falls in the first half-year; and no depreciation is calculated if the retirement is in the second half of the period.

Product Configuration: In SD, this refers to the compilation of a Product Variant from several variants, with the values assigned to the underlying characteristics of the underlying standard product.

Product Costs by Order: In CO-PC, this is nothing but the costs of Products by Orders (Production or Process Orders) as these orders are analyzed by period.

Product Costs by Period: Refers to the lot-based cost object controlling for periodic cost management at order/material levels.

Product Costs by Sales Order: Used in complex Make-to-Order situations, this refers to the costs of products by Sales Orders, where the planned/actual costs and revenues are calculated to a sales document item.

Product Cost Controlling: A component in CO, this is made up of (1) Product Cost Planning – with/without Quantity Structure, Simulation, and Reference Costing, (2) Cost Object Controlling – Product Cost by Period/Order/Sales Order, and Costs for Intangible Goods/Services, (3) Actual Costing/Material Ledger, and the (4) Product Cost Controlling Information System.

Product Cost Planning: Includes the tools for planning costs and setting prices for materials (Cost Estimate with/without Quantity Structure) and for other objects of cost accounting (Base Object Costing, Simulation Costing), which enables planning of costs before an order is commenced for manufacturing.

Product Costing: 'Product costing' calculates the COGM and the COGS per product unit. The products are priced automatically using the BOMs and Routings in PP.

Product Group: Refers to a collection of materials (or products) according to user-defined criteria. The group may contain products from other product groups (i.e., Multi-Level Product Group). In this case it is essential that the lower-most group contain materials.

Product Hierarchy: In CO-PC, a 'product hierarchy' is made up of: Plant > Product Group > Product > Order. The system uses the hierarchy to analyze the costs at each level. However, in Logistics the hierarchy refers to an alphanumeric string that groups materials according to certain characteristics and is used for pricing/evaluation.

Product Life Cycle Management (PLM): PLM in SAP refers to a suite of solutions for digitally managing a company's product information, throughout the life cycle of a product by (1) Life cycle Data Management, (2) Life cycle Collaboration, (3) Program and Project Management, and (4) EHS (Environment Health and Safety).

Product Structure: Refers to a list of objects in SAP – such as Material Document, BOM, or Change Number – that are functionally related.

Production Cost Collector: Created separately for each version of a product or material, the production cost collector is a cost object used to collect costs in

Repetitive Manufacturing/Kanban Production. The actual costs are collected from (1) Final or Reporting Point Backflush, (2) Internal Activity Allocation, (3) Overhead Calculation, etc., and settled to the inventory at the end of a period. At period-end closing, 'production cost collectors' perform (*a*) WIP Calculation, (*b*) Variance Calculation, and (*c*) Settlement.

Production Overhead: Refers to the costs incurred in a production process that cannot be assigned to particular cost objects.

Production System: Also known as the Delivery System in Global ASAP, this is nothing but the system containing the business processes of an enterprise that is used to record the 'live' or 'production' data. Direct access to the production system for making changes in customization is restricted, and is done through the CTS from the Quality Assurance System.

Production Variance: This is calculated as the difference between the Actual Costs and the Target Costs (the target costs are calculated on the basis of the actual lot size delivered to the stock), based on the Preliminary Cost Estimate for an order.

Profile Generator: This is used to generate Authorization Profiles for Role Maintenance.

Profit and Loss Adjustment: Done on a key date, the adjustment relates to some of the account assignment objects such as Business Area, Profit Center, Trading Partner Profit Center/Business Area, etc.

Profit Center Area: One of the structural elements in Profit Center Hierarchy, the Profit Center Area represents the lowest node in the structure to which Profit Centers can be assigned.

Profitability Analysis (CO-PA): Based on the Cost of Sales Accounting methodology, the 'profitability analysis' can be Costing Based or Account Based, in SAP.

Profitability Segment: Corresponding to an external Market Segment, this is an object in CO-PA to which costs and revenues are assigned. A part of the Operating Concern, the profitability segment is made up of Characteristics (system defined or user defined).

Program Type: In SAP there are several 'program types' such as Executable Program (ABAP Report), Include Program, Module Pool, Interface Pool, Class Pool, Function Group, etc.

Project: In CO, this refers to an object consisting of tasks within a specified Controlling Area, and is used to monitor schedule, resources, capacities, cost, revenues, and funds availability. In ASAP, this refers to the subset of Enterprise Model consisting of various implementation objects that are distributed into several Project Areas. (A Project Area is made up of implementation objects that are handled by a Project Team.)

Project Charter: One of the key deliverables of Phase-1 of ASAP, the 'project charter' is a document prepared by the project manager that contains a clear definition of the project, its scope, objectives, implementation time line/schedule, implementation strategies, resources, roles and responsibilities, etc. The charter prepared by the project manager forms the basis for further work on the project in terms of Project Planning and Control, and this needs to be ratified by the Project Sponsor or management. Each of the sub-projects within a major project needs to have separate project charters.

Project Documentation: Refers to the record of work on an implementation. In ASAP, this is made up of documentation of (*a*) Target structure/procedure based on Reference IMG, (*b*) System settings based on Customizing activities in the IMG, and (*c*) Day-to-day project administration and management such as the deliverables, minutes of meetings, status reports, etc.

Project Estimator: A tool in ASAP, the 'project estimator' is used to determine the first-cut information on the project scope, and time and cost relating to a proposed SAP implementation. Done very early, at the pre-sales phase, this tool contains several questions that when answered would provide the basic estimates.

Project IMG: Nothing but the subset of Enterprise/SAP Reference IMG, the 'project IMG' enables the implementing team to complete the customizing activities in a project in a structured way. The project IMG can be generated (a) manually from the SAP Reference IMG, (b) manually by selecting the Application Components, and (c) from the Q & A Database by assigning the various processes to the application components. Multiple Project Views can be defined for a project IMG to limit the customizing activities to different groups of the implementing team according to their responsibility area.

Project Object: Refers to Activities or Activity Elements or WBS (Work Breakdown Structure) Elements or Milestones in the SAP Project Systems (PS).

Project Plan: In ASAP, this refers to a plan made up of a Budget Plan, Resource Plan, and Work Plan.

Project Preparation: Refers to the first phase of ASAP, this involves definition of project goals/objectives, implementation scope, implementation strategy, project schedule, and implementation sequence. The project team is also set up during this phase.

Project Review: Focusing on monitoring project management in terms of deliverables and adherence to schedules, the 'project review' is recommended to be conducted at the end of each phase of the ASAP Roadmap. Aimed at identifying and resolving the issues for timely completion of project phases, the review is also expected to focus on Critical Success Factors.

Project Scope: Refers to the scope of the proposed implementation, this is the collection of structured items taken from SAP Reference IMG for meeting the exact functions of a specific enterprise. The scope is documented in the BPML (Business Process Master List) and transferred to IMG before the Project IMG is generated.

Project Standard: Aimed at removing unnecessary work, the 'project standard' refers to rules and procedures defined in ASAP for improving consistency and effective communication in a project. The standard needs to be developed for managing the scope, configuration, testing, issues, communication, and documentation.

Project Systems: A component of SAP, PS (Project Systems) enables planning, executing, and accounting projects as a part of the enterprise's business processes.

Project Type: Refers to a categorization of projects in PS, the 'project type' includes development projects, capital-intensive projects, customer projects, etc.

Proportional Consolidation: One of the methods of consolidation in FI-LC, 'proportional consolidation' relates to the investments of joint-venture companies.

Prototype: Used to check the results of specific business processes, within the context of Business Blueprint, configured in a SAP system before going ahead with the full configuration.

Public Holiday Calendar: A combination of Annual Calendar and Public Holidays in a year, the 'public holiday calendar' can be customized to show holidays for various countries in a year.

Purchase Order (PO): A request/instruction from a Purchasing Organization to an external vendor (or a plant within the company) to deliver a specified quantity of a material or to provide certain services at a certain point in time.

Purchase Order History: Refers to the deliveries affected or invoices received in respect to a PO item.

Purchase Requisition (PR): A request/instruction to Purchasing for procuring a certain quantity of a material/service at a certain point in time.

Purchasing Group: Being the primary channel for dealing with certain vendors, the 'purchasing group' is nothing but a buyer (or group of buyers) who is internally responsible for procuring certain materials.

Purchasing Info Record: Refers to the source of information for procuring certain materials from certain vendors.

Purchasing organization: One of the organizational structures in an enterprise, the 'purchasing organization' is entrusted with the procurement of materials and services from vendors form time to time. The purchasing organizations are assigned to the Company Code and plant(s). There are three scenarios for the purchasing organization structure: (1) Enterprise-wide: One purchasing organization fulfilling the requirements of all the Company Codes in a Client, (2) Company-Specific: One purchasing organization per Company Code, and (3) Plant-Specific: One purchasing organization per plant.

Putawy: This is nothing but the storage of goods in a Storage Area or Storage Bin, in SAP WM (Warehouse Management).

Quality Assurance System: Refers to a SAP system, into which the customizing parameters along with the tested and stable development objects are transported at periodic intervals, from the Development or Test System. Any transport to the 'production system' is routed through this system only.

Quality Costs: The costs associated with the planning/assuring a product/service quality and inspection activities are known as the 'quality costs.' The quality costs are classified into (1) Prevention Costs, (2) Appraisal Costs, and (3) Non-Conformity Costs.

Quant: Refers to the stock of a material in a Storage Bin. Created through warehouse movements, the quantity of a quant is increased when there is an addition to the stock.

Quantity Structure: Consisting of a BOM and Routing, the 'quantity structure' is the basis for calculating material cost estimates in CO-PC. In the case of Process Manufacturing, the Master Recipe is used in the place of a BOM, and in the case of Repetitive Manufacturing, a Rate Routing is used instead of routing.

Quantity Structure Determination: Refers to the process for determining a valid quantity structure for costing, this determination can be through the settings in the quantity structure control or through the default values in the material master.

Quantity Variance: In MM, this is the difference between the Planned (Budgeted or Target) Costs and the Actual Costs, arising from variations between the Planned and Actual Quantity of a material.

Query: Also known as ABAP Query or SAP Query, this relates to the creation of a report by users with no programming knowledge. These queries always relate to a Functional Area. To create a query the user needs to be assigned to a User Group, to which the functional area should be assigned. Refer also to ABAP Query.

Question and Answer Database: Popularly known as 'Q&A db,' this is one of the tools in ASAP that enables mapping of customer requirements to the various functionalities available in the SAP system during an implementation. The database consists of (1) SAP Reference Structure for defining the scope of the project by selecting, rearranging, and adding structure items, (2) Associated Items – such as questions, transactions, user roles, etc., that are assigned to the structure items – enabling you to draw the Business Blueprint, (3) Issue Management for collecting/managing project issues, and (4) Reporting Functions.

Quicksizer: One of the tools in ASAP, this helps in calculating the CPU, disk, and memory requirements based on the estimated number of users. Providing an idea of the 'system size' to run the estimated work load on the SAP system, this tool is invaluable for initial planning and budgeting in an implementation.

Quick Viewer: Another tool for defining reports, without any programming skills, the quick viewer enables creating WYSWYG (What-You-See- is-What-You-Get) reports by using the Drag and Drop functionality or through the functions in the Toolbars.

R/3 Implementation Tools: These are all the tools that enable SAP implementations and support. The tools include: SAP Reference Structure, IMG (Implementation Guide), Industry Models, Pre-Configured Clients, etc.

R/3 Repository: Referring to the central repository of ABAP/4 objects, the 'R/3 repository' contains objects such as Programs Objects, Function Group Objects, Business Engineering Objects, Dictionary Objects, etc.

R3up: Refers to the central coordination program used in SAP system upgrades. Once started, this program controls the upgrade in sequential phases through tools such as 'R3load,' 'tp,' and 'R3tran.' R3up uses RFC to communicate to the SAP system. The prerequisite to use R3up is that PREPARE modules should have been completed successfully. Refer to PREPARE also.

Rate Routing: This is the routing used in Repetitive Manufacturing for planning production quantities or volume. Refer to Routing also.

Rate-Based Planning: Refers to a part of the Capacity Planning, 'rate-based planning' makes use of Rate Routing.

Raw Material Cost Estimate: A cost estimate for raw material or a material component, the 'raw material cost estimate' uses the price data from the Purchasing Info Record or Purchase Order, to which the Delivery Costs (freight, etc.), Additive Costs, and Overhead Costs are all added to arrive at the cost estimate.

Ready-to-Run Implementation: This comprises a complete concept for administration of the mySAP.com Workplace, as well as Pre-Configured Interfaces for integrating component systems. The configuration of the system landscape is performed using the Workplace Configuration Assistant.

Realignment: In CO-PA, this refers to the retrospective changes to the master data, updating the Characteristics, in such a way that the values already posted are also changed.

Realization: Referring to the 3rd phase in the ASAP Roadmap in a SAP implementation, this phase enables implementation of the business processes/functions documented in the Business Blueprint, to set up the SAP system with the necessary customizing. During this phase, the implementing team also completes the User Manual and Training Material.

Rebate Settlement: In SD, this is nothing but the verification of all the volume rebate amounts relating to the business transactions within a validity period, for creation of the relevant Credit Memos.

Recipe: This is nothing but the instructions for a production process. There are two kinds of recipes: Manufacturing Recipes – Master and Control Recipes and Non-Manufacturing Recipes – Change-over, Set-up, and Clean Recipes.

Reconciliation Account: Represents a GL account used to post automatically whenever there is a transaction in a subledger account such as Customer, Vendor, Assets, etc. The 'reconciliation account' is set up in such a way that a group of GL accounts (i.e., accounts representing overseas vendors) posts to a single reconciliation account.

Reconciliation Ledger: Used to reconcile CO transaction data with the FI, this 'reconciliation ledger' displays only the summarized values. This is also useful in providing an overview of all costs incurred.

Reconciliation Posting: Refers to the generation of some adjustment items in FI, whenever there is a cross-company or cross-business area or cross-functional area posting in CO.

Recurring Entry Document: 'Recurring entry documents' are set up in FI to deal with the periodical postings of business transactions that happen regularly such as payment of insurance premiums, rent, etc. The mere creation of a recurring document will not update the accounting figures in the system. The system will create the accounting documents based on the recurring entry document. The templates for creating recurring entry documents are known as Recurring Entry Original Documents.

Reference and Simulation Costing: Used as the building block for other cost estimates, this is the tool for planning costs and setting prices in the form of Unit Cost Estimates.

Reference Currency: Refers to the currency used in the exchange rate calculation for a particular Currency Type.

Reference Document: This document is used as a reference while posting FI accounting documents. The 'reference document' may be an Accounting Document or a Sample Document. In SD, this denotes a document from which the data are copied to another document.

Reference Order: In CO, this refers to a postable order or non-postable order (also known as a Model Order) that can be copied while creating a new order.

Regenerative Planning: A planning run, in PP, where all the materials are included in the MRP run.

Region Code: Refers to the code used in SAP to denote a region both logically and geographically.

Register RG1: Used for excise purposes in India, this RG1 is used to record the movement of excisable finished goods from a factory to a store.

Register RG21A / 23C: Previously a statutory requirement, in India, to show the receipt of all excisable raw materials (RG21A) and capital goods (RG23C) separately, this is no longer the case. However, within SAP this distinction still remains.

Register RG23D: Used in India to record the goods issue / receipt as kept by the depots.

Regular Vendor: Not the opposite of one-time vendor, this refers to a vendor who supplies at the Client level (meeting the requirements of the entire corporate group).

Relationship: In PS, this refers to the start and end of activities in a Network. Used in Sequencing of activities, the relationship may be: SS (Start-to-Start), FS (Finish-to-Start), SF (Start-to-Finish), and FF (Finish-to-Finish).

Release: Referring to an activity in CO-PC, the release of a Standard Cost Estimate leads to writing the Material Cost Estimate into the material master, as the current Planned/Standard Price for that material. To be able to release a cost estimate, it is necessary that it is 'marked' before the release.

Release Note: Refers to the information about the changed or deleted or new functionality or structure changes since the last release of the (SAP) software. The release note may be a: (1) Functional Release Note (information on changed/deleted/new functions in IMG in an area), (2) Structure Release Note (information on changes to an existing structure in an area), or a (3) Composite Release Note (overview of all IMG structure changes in all application areas).

Release Procedure: Refers to the procedure followed in a company where the approved persons give the go-ahead for purchase of materials or services externally. The 'release procedure' is applicable to PR (Purchase Requisitions) and all external purchasing documents such as RFQ (Request for Quotation), PO (Purchase Orders), Scheduling Agreements, and Service Sheets. Release Strategies will be used for the release procedures.

Release Project: Refers to the list of customizing activities that need to be carried out because of a new release, and this may be Delta Customizing or Upgrade Customizing in SAP.

Release-Specific IMG: Refers to the Project View displaying all the IMG activities/documentation relating to a specific Release Note.

Relevancy to Costing: A tool in CO that is used in cost estimates with quantity structure to check (*a*) whether a BOM item is priced, (*b*) whether an operation in the Routing has been priced, or (*c*) what portion of Fixed/Variable Costs is used in the pricing.

Remaining Variance: This is nothing but the difference between the Target Cost and the costs that cannot be attributed to any single variance.

Remote Function Call (RFC): In ABAP, this refers to the 'calling' of a remote system using either a Function Module (in case the remote system is also a SAP system) or special programmed functions (in the case of non-SAP remote systems). The RFC may be (*a*) Synchronous, (*b*) Asynchronous, or (*c*) Transactional.

Remote Function Module: Nothing but an RFC-enabled Function Module such as BAPI.

Remote User: A user logging on to a SAP system by RFC from an external location.

RemoteCube: Refers to an 'Infocube' where the structure of the cube is defined in SAP BW, but the reporting data is read from an external source using a BAPI.

Reorder Point: In PP, this refers to the threshold value of the available stock (plant stock plus the fixed scheduled/receipt) below which procurement proposals may be created.

Repair Order: This refers to an order, in SD, for recording the business processes for handling the faulty goods sent in by customers for repairing.

Replacement Value: In FI-AA, this refers to the current valuation of an asset (that can be different from that of the APC) due to price changes (due to inflation or technological advancements).

Report Group: In CO, this refers to the collection of report(s) using Report Writer or Report Painter.

Report Painter: Helps in creating user-defined reports from the SAP supplied reports; the 'report painter' is a tool with which the reports can be created quickly, from various applications, by using the Graphical Report Structure.

Report Tree: Refers to the hierarchical arrangement of reports/pre-generated lists (both SAP supplied and user-defined) in the form of nodes attached to a tree.

Report Writer: Enabling you to report from multiple application areas, the 'report writer' is used to create specific and complex reports using functions such as Sets/Variables/Cells/Key Figures. Unlike Report Painter, this tool supports (a) multi-dimensional column structures, (b) user-defined inactive row/column combinations, and (c) using cells in column formulas.

Reporting Currency: Used in FI-LC for the consolidated financial statements, this is nothing but the Group Currency.

Reposting: In CO, this refers to the posting of Primary Costs under the original cost element (of the Sender).The 'reposting' may be a Periodic Reposting (on a real-time basis) or a Transactional Reposting (costs are initially collected in a Clearing Cost Center, then reposted at the end of a period).

Rescheduling: Refers to the automatic processing of backorders in SD. During this process, the system checks the availability again and creates new delivery date(s) if required.

Reserved Stock: This is nothing but all the stock that has been reserved for withdrawal from the stock.

Residual Item: Refers to the uncleared difference of amounts during 'clearing' of an Open Item in FI.

Resource-Use Variance: In CO, this refers to the difference between the Target Cost and the Actual Cost due to the use of a different input than the one originally planned to be used.

Results Analysis (RA): In CO-PC, RA refers to the periodic valuation of orders/projects so as to understand the relationship between the costs and the progress (towards completion) of an order.

Retail Ledger: Used in IS-Retail, this is used to collect data from FI, CO, HR, and MM as a part of the analytical application, Profit Center Analytics Retail.

Retirement: In FI-AA, this relates to the removal of an asset from an Asset Portfolio.

Returnable Packaging: Refers to packaging or transportation equipment that is supplied to a customer but needs to be returned to the supplier (vendor).

Revaluation: Helping to valuate the assets at their Replacement Values, in FI-AA, this refers to the adjustments made to an asset for compensating for inflation or for adopting market value principles.

Revaluation Area: Refers to the Depreciation Area for recording asset revaluations, in FI-AA. Revaluations need to be recorded separately (in a separate 'revaluation areas') so as to keep the revaluation separate from that of the APC.

Revenue Account Determination: In SD, this refers to the establishment of Revenue Accounts for posting prices/discounts/surcharges. SAP uses the Conditions to determine the correct revenue accounts during the transaction postings.

Reversal: In FI, this is nothing but the posting of an identical accounting document but on the opposite side of the account so as to offset the original transaction. A Reversal Document is created during a reversal.

Reverse Business Engineer: A tool in ASAP, this helps the customer who is running a SAP system to look back, from the data from the production environment, to analyze how the system is performing. This helps in identifying the potential for improvements in the business processes. This tool is used in the 3rd phase of the ValueSAP.

Rework: In CO-PC, this is taken as a variance as this relates to the costs involved in correcting the defects after a product has been manufactured.

Risk Category: In SD, this is used to group customers according to certain perceived credit risks associated with these customers.

Risk Matrix: In ASAP, this is used to plot the risks identified in a project, against the risk's influence on the project. The risks may be categorized as high, medium, or low and presented in the matrix.

Roadmap: In ASAP, this refers to the framework for implementation or upgrade or continuous improvement of SAP application deployment using well defined 'stage gates' or 'mile-stones' or 'phases' that are characterized by well defined deliverables and clear documentation aided by tools and techniques, accelerators, etc. The roadmap is made up of five phases: (1) Project Preparation, (2) Business Blueprint, (3) Realization, (4) Final Preparation, and (5) Go-Live and Support.

Rollout Roadmap: In ASAP, this refers to the modified or localized roadmap for setting up the SAP system locally, and may be linked to a central system (for master data, for example).

Routing: In PP, this refers to the sequence of operations in a production process. A Routing Group can be used to group routings with various lot sizes. Refer to Rate Routing also.

Run-time Analysis: This is used to measure the performance of programs, transactions, etc., to identify the bottlenecks in the programming statements in terms of unnecessary use of 'select' loops or function modules, database accesses, etc.

Run-time Error: Documented in the system as Short Dump, this results from a program with errors that cannot be handled during the program execution. When the 'short dump' is created, the system performs a Database Rollback as well.

Safety Stock: In PP/APO, this refers to the minimum stock that is always available to meet any unexpected high demand. Though not used in production (PP), this may be considered for production (in APO) should there be a delay expected in delivery.

Safety Time: In PP, this refers to the number of days the existing stock in the warehouse will meet the material requirements without any further material receipt.

Sales and Operations Planning (SOP): Supporting high-level and complex planning hierarchies, 'SOP' is a forecasting and planning tool used in setting targets for sales, production, and supply chains based on historical/current/estimated data. Capable of both the Top-Down and Bottom-Up planning, this can be used for both Standard SOP and Flexible SOP.

Sales Activity: Refers to recording of the activities (sales call/telephone call/ sales letter) involved in interacting with a customer or a prospective customer.

Sales Area: Refers to the combination of Sales Organization, Distribution Channel, and Division. The 'sales area' can be used for reporting purposes. A Sales Office is assigned to a 'sales area.'

Sales Deduction Account: Refers to an account to which the sales discount/ surcharges are posted.

Sales District: Refers to a geographical area (district or region) to which customers are assigned so as to generate certain sales statistics.

Sales Document: Consisting of a header and one or more document items, there are various types of sales documents such as Inquiry, Quotation, Sales Order, Outline Agreements (Contracts and Scheduling Agreements), and Complaints (Returns, Credit/Debit Memo Requests).

Sales Document Category: Made up of several Sales Document Types, 'sales document category' controls how the system proposes the right sales document.

(The sales document category 'Sales Order' includes Sales Document Types such as Standard Order (OR), Cash Sales (BV), Rush Order, (SO), etc.)

Sales Document Type: Refers to the control indicator for processing the sales documents defined in the system according to the type of a business transaction. Some of the pre-defined 'sales document types' include Inquiry (IN), Quotation (QT), and Sales Orders (OR).

Sales Group: Refers to an organizational group that is responsible for sales activities. The staff of a Sales Office may be formed into sales groups. Several Sales Persons can be assigned to a Sales Group.

Sales Office: Assigned to a Sales Area, this is nothing but the organizational unit in a geographical area of a Sales organization.

Sales Order: Received by the Sales Area that is responsible for fulfilling the order, a 'sales order' represents the request from a customer for delivery of goods/ services at a specified time at the specified price.

Sales Order Costing: The method of costing the items in a Sales Order is known as 'sales order costing' in CO-PC.

Sales Order Stock: Refers to the stock that is retained in the warehouse for fulfilling a specific sales order.

Sales Organization: This is nothing but the top-most organizational unit that is responsible for selling/distributing the products/services. One or more Distribution Channels are attached to a 'sales organization.'

Sales Plan: The starting point for demand management, a sales plan consists of specification of sales in terms of quantities to be sold in a future period.

Sales Unit: Refers to the unit of measure in which an item is sold. It is possible to define several sales units for a single material as the system is capable of referring to the base unit of measure.

Sample Account: Refers to a master record that enables defining default values for Company Code-specific data in GL account master records. To make use of sample accounts, it is necessary that Data Transfer Rules are defined properly to control how the values are transferred from the sample accounts.

Sample Document: One of the Reference Documents, the 'sample document' is used to create default entries while creating an accounting document. The figures in the sample document will not update account balances, but the accounting document created with reference to a sample document will update the transaction figures.

Sample Organizational Unit: Refers to the country-independent organizational units configured in the default SAP system, which can be used to create new units by copying it. Appropriate Country Templates needs to be applied to the copied units to localize them for the country in question. All the sample organizational units are numbered '0001' in the standard system.

Sandbox Client: A copy of the SAP Reference Client, the 'sandbox Client' is a Development Client used by the entire implementation team to experiment with the customizing and testing.

SAP Add-on Installation Tool: Refers to a tool for installing/upgrading 'add-ons' directly from the SAP system.

SAP Assistant: A PC tool used to access BAPI, RFC, or IDoc Meta data from outside the SAP system.

SAP Best Practice: Refers to a SAP product that is nothing but an industry-specific ASAP version and a Pre-Configured System that is ready to meet 80% of that industry's business requirements. Aimed at reducing implementation costs considerably, the 'SAP best practices' speed up the implementation.

SAP Business Connector: A middleware enabling bi-directional synchronous/ asynchronous communication between SAP and SAP/non-SAP applications, this makes all SAP functions that are available via BAPI/IDoc accessible to business partners over the Internet as an XML-based service.

SAP Business (Information) Warehouse: A core component of SAP NetWeaver, SAP BW provides data warehousing functions, with a business intelligence platform replete with a suite of business intelligence tools.

SAP Business Workflow: Aimed at cutting the lead time and cost of business processes to improve quality and efficiency, this workflow is nothing but an application component consisting of tools and technologies for automated control and editing of cross-application business processes.

SAP Collaborative Room: Provides users with a user-specific, context-sensitive and authorizations-based view of their projects. It integrates several communication services (such as poll, discussions, and conferencing tools), a document service, and system services (such as user management) with business services (such as shopping cart, contract, and decision support).

SAP Easy Access: This is the initial menu displayed by the system when a user logs on to an ABAP-driven SAP system. This may be an SAP Menu or a User Menu. Users can add their favourite Transactions to the SAP Easy Access Menu.

SAP Going-Live Check: A remote service, done pro-actively, by SAP to analyze the SAP system on the verge of 'going-live,' to determine the readiness for starting the production. The check consists of five Service Sessions: (1) Project Session – part of the project Preparation phase, the focus is on the planned implementation methodology, (2) Project Feasibility Session – done during the 2nd phase of the project implementation, the focus is to find out the feasibility of identified business process, and is done after the completion of the Business Blueprinting, (3) Analysis Session – focusing on hardware sizing this is typically done eight weeks before 'going-live,' (4) Optimization Session – focus is on optimizing the application components and business processes configured in the system, and (5) Verification

Session – done around four weeks before 'going-live' this is focused on system behavior, especially the system response time.

SAP GUI: Refers to the SAP system component on the Presentation Server, representing the SAP-specific GUI of the ABAP-based Application Server applications.

SAP Maps: A comprehensive approach for implementing SAP, this analytical tool in SAP is helpful in developing and implementing tailor-made SAP implementations by making use of (1) SAP Solution Maps, (2) SAP Business Technology Maps, and (3) SAP Service Maps.

SAP Query: Refer to ABAP Query/Query.

SAP Reference IMG: A complete implementation guide consisting of all the IMG activities arranged by application components.

SAP Smart Forms: A tool used to create forms in SAP; the 'smart forms' combine the print program component and the form component that were separate previously.

SAPNet: Also available to SAP partners/customers, this is the intranet portal of SAP that provides a role-based and personal interface using a Web browser as the GUI. Employees can personalize SAPNet to their individual needs and can use SAPNet as a personal inbox and central access point to Employee Self-Service and procurement.

SAPPHIRE: SAP conference that takes place several times a year, in various parts of the world where customers and partners share SAP success stories and discuss SAP developments or enhancements.

SAPscript: A text editor used in SAP for managing texts, besides creating SAP forms.

Schedule Line: Refers to the division of a sales item into various schedule lines according to quantity and delivery time.

Schedule Manager: Refers to a tool that is used to automate and simplify the definition, scheduling, and execution of tasks/operations that are all run periodically (such as period-end closing).

Scheduling: Referring to the calculation of 'start' and 'finish' dates of orders (or operations in an order), scheduling in PP is used in Material Requirements Planning, Capacity Planning, and Networks. The scheduling may be (*a*) Forward Scheduling, (*b*) Backward Scheduling, and (*c*) Current Date Scheduling.

Scheduling Agreement: In MM, this refers to the Outline Agreement for procuring materials at pre-determined dates over a certain period in the future.

Scheduling Type: In PM, this refers to an indicator controlling the calculation of a due date for maintenance. The standard SAP system comes delivered with 'scheduling types' such as New Start, Manual Call, Scheduled, etc.

Scope: In ASAP, this refers to the business process boundaries identified for the SAP implementation. Around 80% of the scope is covered during the Business Blueprint phase of the ASAP Roadmap.

Scrap: In QM, this refers to the non-conforming product that will not meet the quality requirements even after re-work, and it cannot be used for any other purpose. In MM, this refers just to the percentage of material that does not meet the quality standards.

Scrap Variance: This is nothing but the value of unplanned scrap occurring in the production process. The unplanned scrap is equal to the difference between the target scrap quantity and the actual scrap quantity.

Scrapping: Refers to a posting in MM that results from intentional/ unintentional destruction of material as the materials have deteriorated in quality or have become obsolete because of being in the storage for long.

Screen Painter: A tool for creating Dialogue Transaction Screens in ABAP, the 'screen painter' is made up of a Text Editor for defining the Flow Logic underlying the Form, and a Graphical Layout Editor for designing the Screen Layout. The 'layout editor' can be run in (*a*) Graphical Mode or (*b*) Alphanumeric Mode.

Screen Variant: This is nothing but an object determining the input fields that will be displayed on a data entry screen.

Secondary Cost Element: Used in CO, the 'secondary cost elements' help in allocating costs for internal activities. Unlike Primary Cost Elements, these secondary cost elements do not have corresponding GL accounts in FI.

Secondary Index: In addition to the Primary Index created on the Primary Key Fields of a Table, it is possible to create additional indexes for the same table, and these additional indexes are called the 'secondary index.'

Segment: In FI, this refers to the division (Business Segment or Geographical Segment) of a company for which Financial Statements can be created for external reporting. It is possible to derive the segment during transaction postings, as the segment is entered into the master record of a Profit Center. In CO-PA, this is nothing but the combination of Characteristics. See Cycle also.

Sender Cost Center: This is nothing but the Cost Center that provides Activities and/costs to other Cost Objects.

Sequence: In PP, this refers to the sequence of operations in a 'Routing.' The sequence may be Standard or Alternative or Parallel.

Service Part: This is a 'material' used in performing a repair in a service.

Service Report: Refers to the summarized findings from a SAP Service such as SAP Going-Live Check, SAP Early Watch Session, etc.

Service Session: Refers to one of the several remote analyses done through SAP the Service. For example: the SAP Go-Live Check has five 'service sessions,' with each of the sessions having specific objectives and detailed action lists to be performed. The service sessions are carried out using the computer-based Service Session Workbench that is an integral part of the SAP Solution Manager.

Session: In SAP, this refers to a connection between two logical units. When the connection is broken, the session 'expires.' SAP uses the Session Manager (a graphical navigation interface used to manage one or more SAP R/3 Systems and several Clients) to manage the sessions.

Set: In FI-SL, a 'set' refers to a specific or group of values assigned to a specific object. SAP's default sets include: Basic Sets, Key-Figure Sets, and Single/Multi-Dimension Sets.

Settlement: In CO, this refers to the partial/full allocation of costs from one cost object (Settlement Senders) to another (Settlement Receiver). Settlement Cost Elements are used in such settlements. All such settlements result in Settlement Documents.

Settlement Order: In PM, this is nothing but an order to which costs of a Maintenance Order can be settled.

Settlement Rule: Refers to the Distribution Rule that determines which portion of the Settlement Sender's cost is settled to the Settlement Receiver(s).

Settlement Type: SAP comes delivered with several settlement types, used in CO, such as PER (periodic settlement), FUL (full settlement), AUC (capitalization of AuC), PRE (preliminary settlement), and LIS (line item settlement for AuC).

Setup Order: Refers to a type of order that is in PP, which is used in the initial stages of production to set up and prepare the line for production. In the case of PP-PI, this is known as a Set-up Recipe.

Shipping Document: In LE, this refers to the document for a shipping transaction. There are several shipping documents – such as Delivery, Grouped Delivery, etc. – available in the standard system.

Shipping Notification: Containing the details such as anticipated delivery date, quantity, material details, etc., the 'shipping notification' is sent by the vendor to the recipient for imitating the details of the shipment. The notification can be by EDI or fax or any other media.

Ship-To Party: May not necessarily be the Sold-to-Party or Bill-to-Party, or even the Payer, the 'ship-to-party' is the one who will receive the shipment from the vendor.

Short Dump: An error message created and saved when a program execution is terminated due to a Run-time Error. Refer to Run-time Error also.

Shortened Fiscal Year: Used when there is change or shift from one Fiscal Year (i.e., Jan-Dec) to another (i.e., Jul-Jun), the 'shortened fiscal year' is set up in the system to cover the period from the end of the old fiscal year to the start of the new fiscal year (i.e., Jan-Jun).

Shutdown: In FI-AA, this refers to the temporary removal of a fixed asset from service, and is achieved by activating the indicator in the asset master record so that no depreciation is calculated by the system for this period.

Silk Road: In ABAP, this refers to one of the blended Code-pages containing Japanese, English, and Greek scripts.

Silo Stock: Refers to the stock containing one material or one batch of a material stored in a silo. The 'silo stock,' in PP, can be stored in different types of containers.

Simulation: In FI, this is a step used in 'creating' a transaction but before actually posting a document to ensure that the debits are equal to the credits. When simulated, the system brings up the data that helps in correcting the entries before actually posting the transaction. 'Simulation' does not update the database.

Simulation Costing: In CO, this is used to price the changed single/multi-level assemblies within a structure of a product to have an understanding of the cost implication of 'what if' there is a change in the assembly.

Simultaneous Costing: In CO-PC, this is nothing but the process of assigning the actual costs incurred, to date, of a cost object.

Single Material: In LE, this refers to the storage of a single material in a single bin location. Once defined as 'single storage,' the system will allow you to store only one bin quantity for that bin location.

Single Sign-On: Refers to a mechanism that obviates the need for signing-on to multiple systems; a 'single log-in' is sufficient to access any number of systems brought under this set-up for an authorized user.

Single-Level BOM: Refers to a 'BOM' made up of direct components of an 'assembly.' This can also contain an assembly as a component, but the assembly is not exploded any further.

Slow Moving Item: Refers to an inventory item that has not moved for a long time.

Smart Implementation: Referring to the comprehensive technical solution for implementing mySAP.com components easily and quickly, the 'smart implementation' has many advantages such as (1) Easy Configuration and Automatic Installation (using Configuration Assistant), (2) Pre-Configured Software components (Web server, ITS instances, etc.), (3) Easy Integration into a system landscape, (4) SAP Best Practices, etc.

SOAP: Simple Object Access Protocol.

Software Development Manager: Refers to a tool in SAP, for delivering non-SAP ABAP developments.

Sold-To-Party: Refers to the person or company placing an order for goods/services. Though this party can perform the functions of Bill-to-Party, Payer, etc., it is not necessary that the 'sold-to-party' should be the same as the Bill-to-Party, Payer, or Ship-to-Party.

Solution Review: In ASAP, this refers to the review of the application design and the business process parameters considered for implementation in a SAP system, and the review can be scheduled as early as the second Phase.

Source Document: In FI, this refers to the original document from which one or more accounting documents are generated. The system assigns a unique number to the 'source document,' which is saved in the corresponding accounting document(s) for easy tracing back and forth.

Source List: Refers to the list of sources for a material, with details such as when a source will be able to supply that material.

Special Asset for Gain/Loss Posting: Not an actual fixed asset, in FI-AA, this refers to an asset master record created with the sole purpose of collecting gains/ losses arising from asset retirements.

Special GL Account: Refers to a Reconciliation Account for recording special business transactions such as Guarantees, Down Payments, and Bill of Exchanges in the subledger, this special GL account should not be balanced with the A/R and A/P. An indicator, called the Special GL Indicator, is used by the SAP system to identify a special GL transaction.

Special Period: Refers to the last regular Posting Period that has been divided into one or more (not exceeding four) posting periods for enabling closing operations.

Special Purpose Ledger (FI-SL): A customer-defined ledger used for reporting purposes, the 'special purpose ledger' can be used either as a GL or as a Subledger with the necessary account assignments such as account, region, business area, etc.

Special Stock: In MM, this refers to some of the stock materials, such as Consignment Stock, that needs to be stocked separately because of reasons such as ownership, location, etc. MM uses Special Stock Indicators (E-Sales Order Stock, Q-Project Stock, W-Consignment Stock with Customer, etc.) to denote such stocks separately from other stocks.

Split Revaluation of Depreciation: Mandatory in some countries, this is necessary to adjust the revaluated depreciation for the inflation. The current month's revaluated depreciation is to be debited to the Depreciation Expense Account and credited to the Accumulated Depreciation Account. The revaluated accumulated depreciation so far needs to be treated separately: debited to the Inflation Gain/ Loss Account and credited to the Accumulated Depreciation Account.

Split Valuation: In MM, it is possible to valuate differently, the different stocks of a single material using 'split valuation.' This is required in case a portion of the stock is procured internally, and the rest is procured externally. SAP allows different 'account assignments' for these two different stocks, of the same material, and valuates them at different prices.

Splitscreen Editor: In ABAP, it is possible to display/edit two different programs, even if they belong to two different systems, side by side on the same screen using the 'split screen editor.'

Spool Request: In SAP, this refers to the document sent to the Printer or Archiving. The 'spool request' contains the data relating to the Print List of the current program.

Spread: Also known as the Exchange Rate Spread or Exchange Spread, this refers to the difference between the Spot Rate and the Buy/Offer Rate.

SSO Administration Wizard: A system tool in SAP that will enable configuration of log-on tickets for Single Sign-On (SSO).

Staging: In SAP BW, this is nothing but the process of preparing the data in a Data Warehouse.

Staging Area: In SD, this refers to an intermediate storage area in a warehouse, located near the doors. The 'staging area' is used for GR or GI before the goods are 'received' or 'issued.'

Standard BOM: Used internally for Plant Maintenance and Standard Networks, the components of a 'standard BOM' represent frequently occurring structures that are not object-dependent.

Standard Cost: Refers to a cost that will remain stable over a long period of time. Based on an activity unit, the 'standard cost' of a material can remain stable at least for a year.

Standard Cost Estimate: The most important pricing type in material pricing, in CO-PC, the 'standard cost estimate' is typically created for each of the materials at the beginning of a year (or season) and is expected to remain unchanged for that year/season. These estimates form the basis for Profit Planning/Product Costing with a focus on determining the variances.

Standard Hierarchy: In Cost Center Accounting, this refers to a tree-like structure consisting of all the Cost Centers of a Controlling Area. Assigned to the lowest nodes in the tree, the cost centers may be grouped into Cost Center Categories and represented in the hierarchy just above the end nodes. The name of the top-most node of the 'standard hierarchy' needs to be mentioned when the controlling area is defined. In the case of Activity-based Costing, the same structure holds well except that instead of the Cost Center, it is the Business Process that is assigned to the end nodes of the tree.

Standard Layout: In FI-SL, the 'standard layout' provides the default values (that can be changed) for the parameters for the reports. The layout parameters include row/column total parameters, row/column text parameters, general parameters such as page length/width, etc.

Standard Material Type: Defined in a standard SAP system, the 'standard material type' includes Raw Materials and Semi-Finished products.

Standard Price: In MM, this refers to the constant price of valuating a material irrespective of the goods movements and invoices.

Statistic: In ABAP, this refers to one of the three types of ABAP Query. Refer to ABAP Query/SAP Query/Query also.

Statistical Key Figure (SKF): Refers to the statistical values describing the cost objects (cost center, order, profit centers, etc.) in controlling. SKF is used as the basis for allocating costs, when it is difficult to apportion the common costs. A number of SKFs can be grouped into a Statistical Key Figure Group for processing these SKFs in a single step.

Statistical Order: Not an 'Order' in the strict sense, 'statistical orders' are used in controlling only for informational purposes as it is not possible to settle the costs of a statistical order.

Statistical Posting: Refers to the transactions (i.e., Down Payment Request) in Special GL Accounts with the offsetting entries posted automatically to a clearing account defined.

Steering Committee: In ASAP, this refers to the decision-making body that provides the direction during implementation.

Stock Determination: Using the Stock Determination Rule and the Stock Determination Group, the 'stock determination' is a process used to determine the stock from which a material is withdrawn (for stock removal or staging operations or order fulfilment).

Stock-in-Transfer: The material that has been taken out of the stock, but has not yet arrived at the point of receipt. The 'stock-in-transfer' material is considered part of the valuated stock but is not available for 'unrestricted use.' The essential difference between the Stock-in-Transfer and the Stock-in-Transit is that while the former denotes transfer postings (excluding movements arising from Stock Transfer Orders) within Inventory Management, the latter arises because of a Stock Transfer Order.

Stock-in-Transit: Refers to the material withdrawn from storage at the issuing plant based on a Stock Transport Order, but has not reached the receiving plant. This also forms a part of the valuated stock but is not available for 'unrestricted use.' The essential difference between the Stock-in-Transfer and Stock-in-Transit is that while the former denotes transfer postings (excluding movements arising from Stock Transfer Orders) within Inventory Management, the latter arises because of a Stock Transfer Order.

Storage Area: In LE, this refers to a logical or physical area based on the storage type.

Storage Bin: Often referred to as a Slot, this is the smallest storage space in a warehouse. The address of a 'storage bin' is determined based on Coordinates. Example: Coordinate 04-05-03 represents the bin at level 3, under stack 5 at row 4.

Storage Location: In LO, this represents an organization unit differentiating storage of various stocks of a material in a Plant. One or more 'storage locations' are assigned to a single plant.

Storage Type: In WM, this is nothing but the physical or logical division of a warehouse for carrying out certain functions. The 'storage type' may be a GR area, GI area, Picking area, and so on.

Straight-Line Depreciation: Refers to the method of depreciating a fixed asset, evenly throughout its economic life, so as to ensure that the Book Value of the asset becomes zero at the end of this period. Refer to Depreciation Method also.

Stress Test: In ASAP, this refers to testing the entire SAP environment that has just been deployed to test all the components to ensure that it performs to the pre-determined levels. Involving cooperation from Users, Basis/Application Consultants, the test aims at pushing the system to its peak capacity so as to make the system reliable and fast enough for the production use.

Structure Modeler: Using MS-Visio, it is possible to display the R/3 enterprise organizational structure in a graphical way using this modeler in ASAP.

Sub-Contracting: A form of outsourcing, 'sub-contracting' in MM refers to the processing of materials (supplied by a customer), by an external supplier.

Subledger Accounting: In FI, this refers to managing the accounts of vendors, customers, and assets at the subsidiary ledger level. SAP uses Reconciliation Accounts in GL while managing the subledgers.

Substitution: Refers to automatically substituting the values as they are entered into the SAP system, based on certain Boolean logic.

Supply Chain: Refers to the sequence of operations/centers through which the supplies move from one supplier to the ultimate customer or point of use.

Supply Chain Cockpit: One of the planning applications of the Advanced Planner and Optimizer (APO), the Supply Chain Cockpit (SCC) is a graphical instrument panel for modeling, navigating, and controlling the supply chain. It acts as a top planning layer through which the user can oversee other planning areas within an enterprise including demand, manufacturing, distribution, and transportation.

Support Package: Compiled periodically and made available at the SAP Market Place, the support package refers to the corrections for serious software errors in SAP software. SAP provides a tool called Support Package Manager for importing the support packages into the SAP system.

Support Release: Represents the SAP software release, together with all the SAP Support Packages until a certain point in time. SAP recommends using these 'support releases' as it may take a long time to import all the support packages from an earlier release.

SWIFT Code: Used for faster and automated bank payment settlements, this Society for Worldwide Inter-bank Financial Transactions (SWIFT) Code refers to the code assigned to individual banks.

System Administration Assistant: The SAP online tool for simple administration of SAP system(s).

Table Category: In ABAP, this refers to how a Table is implemented physically. The 'Table categories' include (1) Transparent Database Tables, (2) Pooled Table (Table data stored in Table Pool), and (3) Cluster Table (Table data stored in Table Cluster).

Table Cluster: This is nothing but the database Table containing the data from several logical Cluster Tables.

Table Pool: This is nothing but the database Table containing the data from several logical Pooled Tables.

Target Costs: In CO-PC this refers to the costs expected to be incurred when a certain quantity is produced. The target costs are used to find out the variances, to valuate WIP, and to valuate the unplanned scrap.

Target Quantity: In SD, this refers to the total quantity of a material a customer agrees to buy from a vendor.

Target = Actual Activity Allocation: An allocation technique in Controlling where actual quantities to be allocated are not entered directly but calculated by the system based on the planned activity input of the receivers.

Task: In the ASAP Roadmap, a 'task' is at the lowest level, containing instructions to be followed by a project team member. A number of tasks represent an Activity. A task can also denote an essential element in the Transport System. In this case a user can use a task to lock or unlock cross-Client objects for specific processing.

Tax Category: In SD, this refers to the 'categorization' used by the system to apply the 'country-specific taxation' during pricing.

Tax Code: Refers to the 2-digit code enabling the system to use certain specifications (such as Tax Rate, Tax Type – Input or Output Tax, Calculation Method – Percentage Included or Percentage Separate) for tax determination.

Tax Depreciation: In FI-AA, this is calculated to meet the special tax regulations, and is normally more than the Book Depreciation. The difference is shown as a special entry on the liability side of the balance sheet.

Tear Down: Refers to the process, in PP, where a work center is restored to its normal state after a production process.

Technical Review: In ASAP, this refers to an analysis of the technical implementation components and operational procedures such as security, back-up, performance management, printing, and desktop operations. Typically, it is performed during the Business Blueprint phase.

Technical Specification: In ASAP, this refers to the technical requirements for developing enhancement/interfaces/reports/conversions/forms, etc., for fulfilling the requirements outlined in a Functional Specification.

Test Case: A procedure to test an object in SAP, this is a description for either manual testing or automated testing using CATT. Refer to CATT also.

Test Catalog: Denotes one or more Test Cases in Hypertext format with some supplementary information or links to supplementary documents.

Test Plan: Represents a set of Test Cases used at a particular time for a particular purpose, and is based on one or more Test Catalogs.

Test Procedure: In ASAP, this refers to the procedure outlining how to set up, test, and evaluate a particular Test Case.

Test Workbench: A tool in SAP for managing the Test Cases in Test Catalogs.

Third-Party Order Processing: Refers to a type of external procurement in which a PO is issued to a vendor with the instruction to supply the ordered materials (or perform the services for) a third party.

Third-Party Purchase Order: Refers to a PO that is issued to a vendor with the instruction to supply the ordered materials to (or perform the services for) a third party.

TODO: A software Quality Assurance program that allows developers to find formal errors in their programs. It also provides an overview of the status of the checks they have carried out. The TODO, running regularly in the Consolidation System, monitors ABAP code, Usability, Messages, and IMG structures. Results from this check are then transported back to the Development Systems, and the monthly status reports in QM are based on these results. Use the Transaction Code TODO.

Total Variance: In CO-PC, this is nothing but the difference between the Target Costs calculated in the Standard Cost Estimate for a material and the Actual Costs. This can also be represented by the difference between the debit and credit for an order.

Tracing Factor: In CO, this is a 'user-defined key' for calculating cost/quantity assignments in periodic allocation.

Trading Partner: In FI-LC, this refers to a legally independent entity belonging to the same group of companies.

Transaction Code: Entered in the Command Field, in a SAP transaction screen, the 'transaction code' identifies a transaction in SAP. Made up of alphabets A to Z and numerals 0 to 9 a transaction code can contain a maximum of 20 characters including an underscore (_), with the stipulation that it should begin only with a letter. Use Transaction Code 93 to maintain/change/display transaction codes.

Transaction Figures: In FI, this refers to the sum of all postings made to an account, broken down into Posting Period-wise credits and debits.

Transaction Type: In FI-AA, this denotes various transactions such as acquisitions, retirements, transfers, etc. For example, the transaction type 100 is used for 'external acquisition,' 120 for 'goods receipt,' 150 for 'acquisition from affiliated company,' and so on. A 'transaction type' belongs to a Transaction Type Group.

Transparent Table: This is a database table defined in the ABAP Dictionary and created in the database.

Transport: In CTS (Change and Transport System), this refers to the movement of objects from one SAP system to the other. The components to be transported are listed in the Transport Request. Each transport undergoes a two-stage operation: (1) An Export process reads the objects or components to be transported from the Source System and stores them in a data file at the Operating System level, and (2) An Import process reads this information from the data file and writes it into the database of the Target System. Every 'transport process' is duly logged by the system for easy roll-backs.

Transport Management System: A part of CTS, this refers to a set of tools provided by SAP for organizing, performing, and monitoring Transports in the SAP system.

Transport Request: In CTS, this refers to a document for copying corrections between different system types. It records released corrections. When the transport request is released, the transport is performed.

Troubleshooting Roadmap: Refers to a guide for 'a quick diagnosis' of problems in the SAP System. It enables the administrator to localize the causes of standard problems and technical difficulties for taking appropriate action.

Unchecked Delivery: An 'unchecked delivery' can be converted to a delivery with a document status of 'checked,' which can be used for subsequent functions such as picking, packing, or posting goods issue.

Uniform Valuation: Refers to valuating all the stocks of a material with the same valuation criteria.

Unit Costing: In CO-PC, this refers to a method of pricing that does not use BOM or routings. It calculates planned costs for base planning objects. It also supports detailed cost planning for objects such as orders, projects, cost objects, and material cost estimates with quantity structure.

Unit of Measure (UOM): Denoting the size of a quantity of a material, the 'unit of measure' in SAP includes unit of issue, base unit of measure, unit of entry, etc.

Unloading Point: In SD, this refers to the goods receiving point at the Ship-to-Party's location.

Unplanned Depreciation: Refers to the (permanent) reduction in an asset's value, due to the occurrence of unexpected events (such as fire).

Use Variance: In CO, this denotes the difference between the planned and actual costs arising from higher use of inputs/time than what was planned originally.

Use Tax: In FI-AP, this refers to the one-time tax levied on the use of a personal property that is purchased in another state.

Useful Life: This is nothing but the economic life of an asset within the asset is depreciated fully. The 'useful life' – normally lower than that of the actual technical life – can be different in the individual depreciation areas.

Valuated Stock: Refers to the stock of a material owned by a firm that is part of its current assets. The valuated stock of a material at a plant is the sum of the unrestricted-use stock, the stock in quality inspection, and the stock-in-transfer.

Valuation Area: In MM, this is an organizational unit in Logistics, subdividing an enterprise for the purpose of uniform and complete valuation of material stocks.

Valuation Class: Assigning materials to a group of GL accounts, the 'valuation class' determines the GL accounts that are updated as a result of a valuation-relevant transaction or event such as a goods movement. The valuation class makes it possible to (1) post the stock values of materials of the same material type to different GL accounts, and (2) post the stock values of materials of different material types to the same GL account.

Valuation Method: In FI, this refers to the method of foreign currency valuation as a part of the closing process. In FI-AA, this refers to how an asset is valuated – through Depreciation Key, Useful Life, etc. – during its economic life.

Valuation Procedure: In MM, this refers to the option of valuating the materials according to different principles such as LIFO, FIFO, etc.

Valuation Strategy: In CO-PC, this refers to the strategy for the valuation of materials, internal activities, and external activities in pricing. It depends on the Costing Variant and the Valuation Variant.

Valuation Type: In FI-AA, this refers to the criteria of valuating an asset in a Depreciation Area. In addition to APC, the asset can be valuated using special valuation types such as Revaluation, Interest, Special Depreciation, Investment Support, etc.

Valuation Variant: The 'valuation variant' controls how the materials and activities in the cost estimate are valuated, in CO-PC. While a global valuation variant is valid for all plants, a local valuation variant is valid only for a specific plant. The valuation variant specifies the parameters such as (1) price in the material master (such as the standard price) or in the purchasing info record (such as the net order price) that is used to price a material in the BOM, (2) the planned or actual price that is used to valuate the internal activities, (3) the version in Cost Center Accounting that is used to valuate internal activities, (4) the costing sheet that is used to calculate overhead, and (5) whether, and to what extent, a BOM item or an operation in the routing is relevant to costing. In Cost Object Controlling, the 'valuation variant' is used for the valuation of work in process at Target Costs and for the valuation of Scrap Variances.

Value Filed: In Costing-based PA, 'value fields' represent the highest level of detail for analyzing quantities, revenues, sales deductions, and costs for Profitability Segments in profitability analysis or Contribution Margin Accounting.

ValueSAP: In ASAP, this is a strategic initiative geared toward optimizing the benefits of SAP software over the entire life cycle. 'ValueSAP' provides a combination of methods, tools, services, and programs that are used in a targeted manner in the phases 'Discovery and Evaluation,' 'Implementation,' and 'Continuous Business Improvement' to maximize the ROI (Return on Investment).

Variable Depreciation: In FI-AA, this refers to the calculation of depreciation proportional to the multiple-shift use of an asset. Refer to Multiple-shift Depreciation also.

Variance Category: In CO, this refers to the categorization of variances based on the nature of their cause. The variances on the Input side are categorized into scrap variance (CO-PC), resource use variance, input price/quantity variance, etc. On the Output side the 'variance category' includes output price/quantity variance, lot size variance, fixed cost variance (CO-PC), mixed price variance, and so on.

Variance Variant: This is nothing but the parameter determining the variance categories that are calculated in the system.

Variant BOM: A non-configurable BOM, 'variant BOM' is a combination of a number of BOMs describing one or more products that have a number of identical components. Refer to Bill of Material (BOM) Category also.

Variant Configuration: Refers to the description of complex products that are manufactured in many variants, for example, motor bikes. All variants are defined as one Variant Product, which has a Super BOM, containing all the components that can be used in the product, and a Super Task List, containing all the operations that can be used to manufacture the product. By assigning the 'variant product' to a class, the characteristics are assigned to the variant product. These characteristics are used to describe an individual variant. Object dependencies ensure that the correct components are selected from the Super BOM and the correct operations are selected from the Super Task List.

Vendor Account: A 'vendor account' contains transaction figures arising from business transactions and these value movements are recorded as periodic totals in the A/P subsidiary ledger. All the payables to the vendors are recorded simultaneously in a GL account by assigning a Reconciliation Account in the master record of the vendors.

Vendor Evaluation: In MM, this decision-making functionality helps in the selection/control of Sources of Supply. The system assigns a score to each of the main criteria (such as price, quantity, delivery, reliability, etc.) based on the weight given by the user for each of the criteria. The user will also decide the maximum attainable score against which the system generated score for a particular source or vendor is compared and evaluated.

Vendor Net Procedure: This procedure enables you to post materials to the inventory at invoice price less the cash discounts eligible.

Vendor Quotation: Refers to an offer from a vendor to a Purchasing Organization to supply materials or perform certain services as per certain agreed on terms and conditions.

Vendor-Managed Inventory: The vendor manages the materials of the customer-company's requirements, and is possible only when the vendor has access to customer's current stock and sales data, which may be made possible through EDI.

Version: In CO, this enables more than one planning (i.e., optimistic plan data, pessimistic plan data, etc.) for the same object for the same fiscal year. The 'version' is nothing but the collection of fiscal-year dependent indicators such as value date, methods of calculating actual activity prices, exchange rate type, copying allowed, etc.

View: Refers to the fields from one or more tables with a common interface. A view is created by business criteria, using the Transaction Code SE54 (the same as General Table Maintenance).

View Cluster: This is nothing but the collection of several Views.

Virtual Account Number: This is a dummy bank account number, in FI, issued by the House Bank to identify the payments from customers.

Virtual SAP System: Refers to a SAP system used as a placeholder for another SAP system that has not yet been configured.

Volume-based Rebate: In MM, this denotes the period-end cumulative discount granted by a vendor to a customer, and is based on the volume of transactions the vendor had with that customer during that period.

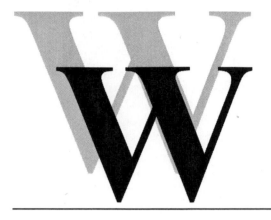

Walkthrough: In ASAP, this refers to the EPC (Event-driven Process Chain) where the user is 'walked-through' the entire process, step-by-step, stopping at every function, process, etc., to ensure that the user understands the process flow and the dependencies within EPC.

WBS Element: This is nothing but a task/partial task in the Work Breakdown Structure (WBS) in the hierarchical organization of a project.

Web Application Builder: This is a tool that enables development of web applications – both ITS (Internet Transaction Server) based and BSP (Business Server Pages) based from the ABAP/4 Workbench.

Web Reporting: This helps users to access the business information in a SAP system through a Web Browser. Made possible by a special WebRFC to access the data from the SAP system, 'web reporting' also has the flexibility of interactive reporting as the traditional ABAP/4 Reports.

WIP Calculation: In CO-PC, this refers to the period-end procedure for calculating the Work-In-Progress (WIP) for both Production Orders and Process Orders. Once settled, WIP postings will be generated in FI.

Withholding Tax: A kind of tax that is normally deducted (at the source) at the beginning of the value flow. The amount so deducted (withheld) is paid to the tax authority on behalf of the person who has been subjected to the tax. SAP supports both Classic Withholding Tax and Extended Withholding Tax. (The 'extended withholding tax' allows assigning of more than one 'withholding tax type' to a Business Partner, and is used in countries such as Argentina.)

Work Center: In LO, this refers to an organizational unit that defines where and when an operation needs to be performed. Each 'work center' has an Available Capacity. The work center can be a machine, people, assembly line, etc. The activities performed at the work center (or by the work center) are valuated by taking into account the activity price or charge rate. Several work centers with common characteristics are grouped to form Work Center Groups.

Work Center Hierarchy: A hierarchical arrangement of work centers at various levels; this is used in capacity planning to cumulate the available capacities or capacity requirements. It is also used to locate work centers.

Work Order: A generic term used to denote a task to be performed, the 'work order' may be a production order, process order, maintenance order, inspection order, etc.

Work Package: Refers to the collection of several groups of activities to complete a major portion of a phase in the ASAP Roadmap. More than one 'work package' constitutes a phase.

Work Plan: Refers to a subset of the Project Pan, a 'work plan' is made up of a detailed set of Phases, Work Packages, Activities, and Tasks from the ASAP Roadmap. Organized in a project management planning tool such as Microsoft Project, the work plan may result in a Gantt Chart to display timelines, dependencies, and resources.

Workbench Organizer: A part of the Change and Transport Organizer (CTO) within the CTS (Change and Transport System), the 'workbench organizer' is a tool to manage – both centralized and de-centralized – development projects in ABAP Workbench.

Workflow Builder: A modeling tool in SAP for defining a 'workflow.'

Work-list: In LO, this represents the grouping of documents requiring follow-up action. From the Work-list Overview, it is possible to perform the follow-up action either for a single document or multiple documents.

Work-list Monitor: A tool in Schedule Manager, this is used to monitor and manage the 'work-lists.'

WorkSpace: Refers to the right-hand side frame of the web browser in mySAP Workplace. Called also a Push Area, this browser frame is used for displaying the user-specific business applications.

WWI: Used in EHS (Environment Health and Safety), this is a modified version of MS-Word that is called from a SAP system to edit a document template.

XBRL: Based on XML, XBRL (eXtensible Business Reporting Language) can be used by enterprises to create, publish, analyze, and compare information, with special emphasis on financial statements.

XRFC: Previously known as RFC-XML, this is the XML format for transmitting the RFC (Remote Function Call).

XSF: This is nothing but the XML for SmartForms.

XXL: Known as eXtended eXport of Lists, XXL is a tool available in SAP for downloading list objects such as spreadsheets from SAP to a PC environment.

XXL List Viewer: This tool presents SAP R/3 data in MS-Excel, taking into account the information supplied by R/3 on the structure of the data. It makes available special functions in a separate menu and toolbar, and also limits Excel functions to guarantee the consistency of data supplied by R/3.

Year-end Closing: Refers to the closing of accounting, in FI, at the fiscal year's end to bring out the external statutory requirements such as Balance Sheet and Profit & Loss Statement.

Year-end Settlement: In CO, this refers to the settlement of Investment Orders that have not yet been closed. These orders are settled to AuC (Assets under Construction), at the end of the fiscal year.

Yield: In CO-PC, this denotes the production that is not categorized as Scrap. According to PP, this is nothing but the production that meets the quality standards.

Zero Clearing: In FI, this refers to the clearing of 'open items' in one or more accounts, which does not involve any clearing postings.

Zero Stock Check: Refers to a check/inventory procedure that checks, when a storage bin becomes empty after a goods movement, whether the storage bin is really empty. This is to ensure accuracy of stock figures, and the result is communicated to the system during the confirmation of the Transfer Order.

APPENDIX

ABOUT THE CD-ROM

- Included on the CD-ROM are figures from the text (most in color) and other files related to topics for SAP FI/CO.
- See the "README" files for any specific information/system requirements related to each file folder, but most files will run on Windows XP or higher.

INDEX

INDEX